# Buying Web Services: The Survival Guide to Outsourcing

JP Frenza

WILEY COMPUTER PUBLISHING

John Wiley & Sons, Inc.
New York • Chichester • Weinheim • Brisbane • Singapore • Toronto

Publisher: Robert Ipsen
Editor: Cary Sullivan
Managing Editor: Frank Grazioli
Electronic Products, Associate Editor: Mike Sosa
Text Design & Composition: Benchmark Productions, Inc.



This book is printed on acid-free paper. ♾


Published by John Wiley & Sons, Inc.

Published simultaneously in Canada.



***Library of Congress Cataloging-in-Publication Data:***

Frenza, J. P.
Buying Web services : the survival guide to outsourcing / J. P. Frenza.
p. cm.
"Wiley computer publishing.:
Includes index.
ISBN 0-471-31289-4 (pbk. : alk. paper)
1. Web site development--Contracting out. I. Title.
HD30.37.F&$ 1998
658'054678--dc21 98-33922
CIP

Printed in the United States of America.

10 9 8 7 6 5 4 3 2 1

# Contents

**Chapter 1 In or Out? An Outsourcing Overview** **1**

About This Chapter 1
About the Author 1
What Is Outsourcing? 4
The State of Outsourcing Web Services Today 5
In Favor of Outsourcing 7
Against Outsourcing 11
Outsourcing Scenarios 19
Understanding Your Company 28
Understanding the Web Development Process 30
The Process 31
The Players: Defining Roles 34
A Look at Different Web Teams 50
Summary 56
Checklist 56

**Chapter 2 Determining Your Goals, Developing a Concept, and Drafting a Request for Proposal** **57**

About This Chapter 57
About the Author 57
The Evaluation Process 59
Choose Your Own Criteria 59
Customize the Project Approach:
Designing for Your Company Expertise and Culture 64
Building Your Project Strategy 66
Business Goals 66
Site Goals 70
Marketing Goals 75
Create Your Own Readiness Plan 77
Making Your Project the One to Want 79
Summary 84
Checklist 85

**Chapter 3 Evaluating Proposals and Budgets** **87**

About This Chapter 87
About the Author 88
Choosing the Right Developer 89
How Important Is the Proposal? 92
What Should Be in the Proposal? 93
More About Costs 96
Looking Beyond the Proposal 98

Where Do You Find a Good Web Developer? 100
What Is the Worst Way to Find a Web Developer? 100
Summary 101
Checklist 102

**Chapter 4 Understanding Design 103**

About This Chapter 103
About the Author 103
What Is the Function of Design? 105
Design as a Multidisciplinary Approach 106
The Clash of Technology and Design 112
Good Design Can Help Businesses Transform 116
Web Designers Create New Corporate Identities 117
The Designer and Information Architecture 118
The Fundamental Steps of Design Activity 120
Supporting Documents for the Design Process 123
Summary 126
Checklist 126

**Chapter 5 Infrastructure and Site Hosting 129**

About This Chapter 129
About the Author 130
The Web Site Development Process: Technology Planning 131
Assessing Your Web Site Needs 136
Determining Your Web Site Needs 140
Hosting: The Long-Term Budget Implications 145
Choosing a Hosting Solution 150
Summary 160
Checklist 160

**Chapter 6 Covering Your Legal Bases 163**

About This Chapter 163
About the Author 163
Why Should I Read This Chapter? 165
Some Basic Internet Legal Issues 168
Web Site Ownership 178
Beyond Trademark and Copyright: Other Intellectual Property Rights 192
Legal Issues in the Operation of a Web Site 196
The Web Site Development and Hosting Agreement 199
Summary 207
Checklist 207

**Chapter 7 Managing a Long-Term Outsourced Web Project 209**

About This Chapter 209

About the Author 210
A Healthy Amount of Skepticism 211
Project Manager as Evangelist 212
Project Design: The Life Cycle 214
Semirepetitive Projects 221
New Project Components 222
Managing the Components 222
Selecting Your Site's Architecture 224
Managing Individual Projects 228
Closing the Loop 233
Summary 235
Checklist 235

**Chapter 8 When Things Go Wrong 237**
About This Chapter 237
About the Author 238
Confronting and Avoiding Development Problems 239
The Developer as Partner 239
Planning and Prioritizing 240
Getting Past the Bumps 242
Avoiding and Managing Design-Related Problems 245
Avoiding and Managing Technology Problems 248
Avoiding and Managing Usability Problems 251
Summary 254
Checklist 254

**Chapter 9 Working with Multiple Contractors 257**
About This Chapter 257
About the Author 257
Why Work with Multiple Subcontractors? 259
The Challenge of Working with Multiple Subcontractors 259
Hiring 261
Top-Ten Issues 262
How Two Companies Handle the Issues 264
Keeping the Project Moving 269
Summary 270
Checklist 270

**Chapter 10 Search Engines, Marketing, PR, and Advertising 273**
About This Chapter 273
About the Author 274
Search Engines 275
Marketing and Public Relations 279
Advertising 285

Directory Of Online Resources 293
Summary 295
Checklist 295

**Chapter 11 Going Forward: Next-Generation Sites and Building an E-Business 297**

About This Chapter 297
About the Author 298
Making Your Business an E-Business 300
Summary 327
Checklist 328

**Chapter 12 Web Resources 329**

About This Chapter 329
About the Author 330
Specialty Web Sites and Hotlists 331
Specialty Services for Web Site Owners Seeking Developers 332
Books 333
Periodicals: Magazines, Newspapers, and E-Zines 336
Daily Intelligence Sources 338
Trade Shows, Conferences, and Seminars 339
Industry Analysts 340
Trade Associations and User Groups 341
Regional User Groups 342
Discussions and Communities 343
Vendor Lists 343

**Chapter 13 The Web Roundtable 345**

June 5, 1998, New York City 345
Participants 347
Overview: Key Issues in Outsourcing 347
The Process of Web Development 353
Finding the Right Developer 356
But Do Clients First Need to Know What They Want? 361
Outsourcing: The Financial Relationship 364
Legal Issues 367

**Index 373**

# Foreword

# Learning from Web History

**Jakob Nielsen, Ph.D.**
*www.useit.com*

Jakob Nielsen, Ph.D., is a principal of the Nielsen Norman Group, a user experience consultancy. Until July 1998, he was a Sun Microsystems Distinguished Engineer and the company's Web usability guru. He has been usability lead for several design and redesign rounds of Sun's Web site and intranet (Sun Web), including the original SunWeb design in 1994. He is the author of the well-read, biweekly Alertbox column on Web usability with a readership of 4 million page views per year. Dr. Nielsen coined the term "discount usability engineering" and has invented several usability techniques for fast and cheap improvements of user interfaces. He is the author of the best-selling books *Multimedia and Hypertext: The Internet and Beyond* (AP Professional, 1995), *Usability Engineering* (paperback edition published by AP Professional, 1994), and co-editor, with Robert Mack, of the definitive work *Usability Inspection Methods* (John Wiley & Sons, 1996). *The New York Times* called him the guru of Web page usability, Ziff-Davis Network called him "the smartest person on the Web," and *WebWeek* dubbed him "among the Web's most recognized human-interface experts." His next book, *Designing Excellent Web Sites: Secrets of an Information Architect*, will be published in January 1999.

There are three common scenarios in Web outsourcing:

Client is clueless: needs a truck but asks for a bus. Consultant says "Yes, Sir/Madam" and builds a bus as ordered.

Client is clueless: needs a truck but asks for a bus. Consultant carefully explains why it would be better to build a truck.

Client is clueless: asks the consultant to build something that moves. Consultant analyzes the client's needs carefully and builds a truck.

Of these three options, I much prefer scenario 2. At first, scenario 3 might seem more promising, since an experienced consultant knows much more about the Web than someone who is managing his or her first Web project. However, I strongly advise against abandoning responsibility: The Web will be the most important business tool of the twenty-first century and all companies need to build up internal expertise in Web strategy in order to control their own destinies. Outsourcing is an opportunity to get advice from more experienced Internet experts, but no one can tell you how to run your business. Good consultants will tell you when you are on the wrong track, so you need to be receptive enough to avoid scenario 1, but the ultimate decision is your own responsibility.

Of course, there is a fourth possibility: The consultant is clueless and insists on building useless sites filled with animations and slow downloads. Since the Web expands so rapidly, new people enter the field of outsourcing all the time and they all need to make their own mistakes on their first projects. Anytime you hire a new art director with a background in print design, it's here-we-go-again time with overly graphics-intensive pages. However, people who are good at what they do quickly pick up the special characteristics of the Web, so cluelessness is rare in the ranks of experienced Web consultants.

There is no shame in being clueless with respect to the Web, since everybody is clueless the first time they run a Web project. The Web is a new medium and requires a new approach, but those who do not know history are doomed to repeat it—experience shows that almost all companies make the same mistakes on their first Web projects. If you get good advice, however, you can do better as long as you are willing to modify your initial ideas.

In five years of lecturing about Web design at events in thirteen countries on four continents, I have met Web staff from hundreds of companies and government departments who have all made the same mistakes in their projects. Worse, I made every single one of these mistakes myself in my first Web projects. I finally came to realize that the reason for the many mistakes is not that I am stupid, or that every single company is run by stupid executives. The true reason is that the Web intrinsically leads you down the wrong path if you approach it without knowing its special characteristics. It's a new medium with new rules. The natural way people run Web projects based on their non-Web experience leads to fundamental mistakes at all levels:

**Business model:** usually based on a small number of big transactions with large overhead even though Web technology is better suited for many small transactions with low overhead. It is also common to treat the Web as a marcom brochure and not as a fundamental shift that will change the way we conduct business in the network economy.

**Budgeting:** viewed as a one-time expense without acknowledging the need for maintenance and continuous renewal.

**Project management:** managing a Web project as if it were a traditional corporate project. This leads to an internally focused design with an inconsistent user interface. Instead, a Web site should be managed as a single customer-relationship project.

**Information architecture:** structuring the site to mirror the way in which the company is structured. Instead, the site should be structured to mirror the users' task and their view of the information space.

**Page design:** creating pages that look gorgeous on the art director's high-end color monitor and evoke positive feelings when demoed inside the company. Instead, design for an optimal user experience under realistic circumstances, even if your demos will be less "cool." (This means: Make pages download fast at 28.8kbps modem speeds.)

**Content authoring:** writing in the same linear style that you have always used. Instead, force yourself to write in a new style that is optimized for online readers who frequently scan text and who need very short pages with secondary information relegated to supporting pages.

**Linking strategy:** treating your own site as the only one that matters, without proper links to other sites and without well-designed entry points for others to link to. Unbundled content and services are often superior to closed sites, and it is a poor idea to ban external links in an attempt to imprison the user on your own site (Get over it. The users own the mouse and control the navigation, so they are not going to stay on your site anyway if they don't get good service).

**Server capacity:** forgetting the exponential growth rates and spiky access patterns that characterize the Web. Insufficient spare capacity and lack of tracking traffic growth result in overloaded servers that turn away customers.

On all these levels, any company's first Web project is doomed to failure. All are destined to repeat history and make all the same mistakes as everyone else; unless, of course, they learn from those who have been in the trenches for some time and have seen these problems again and again. Avoiding these many traps is the ultimate reason to get outside help.

# Acknowledgments

The most important acknowledgment that I would like to make is in the recognition that when it comes to the Web development business, technology and complexity are by necessity forcing a greater sense of cooperation and fairness in today's workplace.

While my sense is that this is not the case for the majority of small Web sites (where salaries and budgets remain remarkably low when compared to expectations), it is certainly true when it comes to medium-sized and large Web sites, and that, at least, is an encouraging start.

It is no secret that the Web is becoming increasingly mission critical. It is also no secret that large-scale Web development is not easy—the process is difficult; the technology, at times, unreliable; and the experience sometimes draining.

More often than not, the eye-catching Web sites presented in this book—the product of positive relationships between Web developers and their clients—were created because both parties recognized that they were engaged in some sort of real partnership. In this light, the Web developer exists not as an outsourcer to be exploited at the lowest possible cost, but rather as a partner (you will hear that word consistently throughout this book) with whom to grow in a mutually beneficial way; in short, the old concept that has its roots in the tradition of the labor movement: "An honest day's pay for an honest day's work." Unlike the manufacturing sector, where outsourcing tends to be seen as a way to cut wages, slash jobs, and reduce overall expenses, in this burgeoning new industry we call Web development, outsourcing is an opportunity to establish partnerships, accomplish more, and grow business in a productive manner.

Okay, that's probably enough of the political stuff. Here's the other well-deserved acknowledgments.

As an example of the power of outsourcing, I offer this book, which was, of course, outsourced to a group of experts to whom I owe my greatest acknowledgment.

All of the contributors to this book, whose names and bios accompany the chapters they contributed, are already probably overworked and trying to keep their company ahead of the curve that moves so quickly in the Web development industry. Yet, each took the time to get involved in this project so that we could collectively learn from their experiences. I owe each of these co-authors and colleagues special thanks for truly proving that "those who can't, do indeed outsource."

I would also like to thank the extraordinary team of people at the Earth Pledge Foundation, the organization that I have been a part of for the last several years. In particular, I would like to thank Theodore W. Kheel, for not only founding Earth Pledge but also for spending more than half a century working to improve the standing of labor in a wide range of industries. Extra special acknowledgment also goes to Leslie Hoffman, our executive director, as well as my confidant and friend. Very special thanks as always goes out to Kristen Kiger, who at first responded to this project with, "What! You mean you are going to do another book?" which quickly transitioned into "Hey, there's something to this outsourcing stuff," when the book was finally complete.

Much thanks also goes to Cary Sullivan, Christina Berry, and the team at Wiley Computer Books for their help throughout the development of this book.

Finally, I would like to thank all of the companies, organizations, and individuals who spend their hours hacking away at the sites that make the Web a truly valuable and dynamic medium.

**JP Frenza**

*jpfrenza@earthpledge.org*

New York City

# Introduction

**J.P. Frenza**

*jpfrenza@earthpledge.org*

## This Book Is Your Guide

This book is your survival guide to creating a Web site. It is the definitive guide that will help you find the right developer and help you work with that developer to produce a top-notch Web site on time and within budget as you increase your company's presence on the Internet, protecting and growing your business along the way.

You'll learn all of the steps involved in creating a Web site. Your company can use this book to take full advantage of all the Web has to offer while avoiding the common pitfalls associated with the Web development process.

From determining whether or not your company should build its site in-house or work with an outside contractor, developing a concept, evaluating proposals, understanding design, site hosting, handling legal contracts, and managing a large Web project to anticipating what might go wrong, working with multiple subcontractors, marketing your site, managing future technology, and researching more information on site development, this book will help you save time and money.

This book was not written by consultants offering information on what the Web development process *should* be. It was written by experts in the Web development industry who have taken the time to document what Web development really *is* and how you can navigate the complicated process of developing a site.

As the chapters of this book unfold, you'll find out how Web professionals, who have produced successful Web projects in their own unique ways, deliver demonstrable benefits to their clients. Each of these experts will help you gain insight into the nuts and bolts of building a Web site—what to do and, just as important, what not to do.

When you are reading the chapter on, for example, understanding design or hosting a Web site, you are reading a chapter written by a developer who has several years of experience in designing and hosting Web sites for companies just like yours. And when you are reading about covering your Web site's legal bases, you are not reading the words of a Web commentator; you are reading advice from one of the most accomplished attorneys in the new-media industry.

## Who This Book Is For

This book is for interested parties from every small, medium-size, or large business who understands the importance of the Web to their business and who need to build a Web sites or improve existing ones to help their companies grow and their businesses operate more efficiently and effectively.

This is not a technical book, but it provides advice on how technical staff can contribute their experiences to a company's Web site.

This is not a marketing book, but it speaks to the marketing department as it attempts to use the powerful media of the Web to its maximum marketing potential.

This is not a sales book, but it speaks to every sales person who wants to use the Web to increase company sales.

This is not a management book, but it speaks to every manager who wants to manage the Web development process to its maximum gain.

In short, this book is about the process of establishing an effective presence on the most powerful communications medium of this century: the Web.

## Why This Book Is Important for You

For business, the Web is a process. The Web is not about hiring someone to do work; it is about finding a partner to help your company grow its business. If you operate a small business and can barely afford to allocate $10,000 to establish a Web site, this book is about finding a company that will work as your partner as you establish your business and grow your company. You might have to make some sacrifices and contributions to your developer along the way, and your developer might have to make some sacrifices and contributions to you as well. View your developer as a partner and frame the spirit of your working relationship along those lines. Partnerships can evolve to the mutual benefit of each company.

If yours is a large business, your Web developer should be the expert partner who will encourage your company to try new and more ambitious goals on the Web. Chances are that you will succeed and your partnership will push your business forward in ways that you never expected.

This book is about the process of Web development and is written from the perspective of one important standard: If you choose to work with an outside developer to build your Web site and your site succeeds beyond your company's wildest dreams, would your company make Web development a department at your firm?

Unlike other types of services your company purchases, the Web developer is not on the periphery of your business. Your Web developer has the potential to *shape* your business.

This book will help you prepare for that eventuality.

### What Is in the Book

This book is organized according to the general flow of building a Web site. It begins by helping you determine whether or not your company should outsource its Web site and proceeds through the process to the end of development, when you start to market your site and begin to consider your site's next generation as you move forward.

You can read this book through from beginning to end, gaining a step-by-step look at the process of building a Web site as you go. Or you can read only those chapters that are relevant to you.

For example, if you've already made the decision to work with a certain Web developer (or that decision has already been made by someone else at your company), you might want to review Chapter 6, "Covering Your Legal Bases," and spend some time with Chapter 8, "When Things Go Wrong," so that you can anticipate and prepare for potential challenges along the way. Similarly, if your company is about to make a decision on where to host your site, you might want to read through Chapter 5, "Site Hosting."

In short, you can use this book to understand the complete process of building a Web site, or you can use it to review only those topics that are immediately relevant to your company.

Each chapter begins with a short introduction that describes the topics covered as well as a brief biography of that chapter's author and his or her credentials. Where appropriate, interviews with additional experts in the field are presented as a way to supplement the information contained in the chapter.

Each chapter concludes with a checklist—a brief summary of things to do that you may want to share with your colleagues as you develop your Web site. Each checklist highlights the information presented in the chapter and gives you a good starting point for discussion with your staff and your Web developer.

### A Chapter-by-Chapter Look at Buying Web Services

Here's a chapter-by-chapter look at what's inside this book:

**Chapter 1: In or Out? An Outsourcing Overview.** This chapter presents the pros and cons of outsourcing, helps you determine whether or not your company should outsource its site, and presents an introduction to the Web development process from design and content to programming and marketing your site.

**Chapter 2: Determining Your Goals, Developing Your Concept, and Drafting a Request for Proposal.** This chapter presents insight into everything that you need to do before you get started, including how to figure out what your company should be trying to accomplish on the Web, define your goals, and draft a request for proposal that will effectively communicate your needs to a Web developer.

**Chapter 3: Evaluating Proposals and Budgets.** This chapter helps take the guesswork out of choosing from among a stack of proposals, budgets, and potential Web developers. You'll gain insight into what qualifies as a good project proposal and budget and what warning signs to watch for when choosing one firm over another.

**Chapter 4: Understanding Design.** No question about it—design will be one of the most important aspects of your site. It might also be one of the hardest to understand and manage. This chapter takes you through an understanding of the design process so that you can work effectively with your Web developer to produce a look and feel for your site that meets your goals, challenges your developer, and works for your customers.

**Chapter 5: Infrastructure and Site Hosting.** The Web is a technological medium; the company with the best infrastructure wins. Understanding the infrasructure of the Web and your site hosting options will help you make the right decisions as you attempt to grow your site from a marketing presence to a complete electronic business.

**Chapter 6: Covering Your Legal Bases.** Perhaps the single most important issue regarding your Web site will be in regard to the law. This chapter surveys all of the areas in which your company could incur legal responsibility and discusses what they mean for your Web site and your business. Also included is a sample legal contract that you can use when hiring the developer of your choice.

**Chapter 7: Managing a Long-Term Outsourced Web Project.** Once work on your site begins, you will no doubt face several organizational and managerial challenges: how to keep track of all of the information you want to put on your site and how you can implement new features and technologies. This chapter presents the issues and strategies involved in managing the production and maintenance of a large-scale Web project.

**Chapter 8: When Things Go Wrong.** Why wait until things go wrong to think about the possibility? This chapter is a dose of preventive medicine. It surveys the common areas of Web development in which errors, miscommunications, and entanglements are likely to occur and discusses the warning signs and strategies you can use to address potential problems and pitfalls.

**Chapter 9: Working with Multiple Contractors.** Many companies find themselves working with multiple subcontracts when building their sites. For example, a company hires a design firm to design the site, a networking and installation company to set up a Web server, and a Web developer who specializes in Java or Active Server Pages to handle programming for the site. Working with multiple subcontractors raises several issues, and they are examined here.

**Chapter 10: Search Engines, Marketing, PR, and Advertising.** Once you've built a Web site, you face your biggest challenge: attracting an audience. This chapter gives you a basic understanding of search engines, teaches you how to register your site so that people can find it, and provides you with a site marketing plan of attack.

**Chapter 11: Going Forward: Next-Generation Sites and Building an E-Business.** Building a Web site is an ongoing process. This chapter provides observations on how to further integrate a Web site into your business—a concept that IBM appropriately calls "e-business." You'll also gain insight into growing your site, as well as how to evaluate and incorporate new technologies along the way.

**Chapter 12: Web Resources.** Now that you've made the partial plunge, you want to keep abreast of the latest news in the Web industry. This chapter provides you with a list of what to read and where to go to find everything you need to know about the Web industry.

**Chapter 13: The Web Roundtable.** This chapter is a transcript from a discussion in which several Web developers and Web clients talk about the development process: what works, what doesn't, and where the industry is headed.

### Ready or Not, the Web Will Change Your Business

The U.S. Commerce Department reported that by the end of 1997, 100 million people were logging on to the Net. That makes the Internet the fastest-growing mass medium in this century. According to the Commerce Department study, radio needed 38 years to reach an audience of 50 million, while television took just 13 years to reach the same size audience. The Net hit the 50-million mark in just four years.

What do all these numbers mean for your business? The answer is, "Plenty."

Numbers (and hype) aside, we're now on the verge of a significant economic transformation—one that is radically changing how businesses relate to their customers and how they interact with one another ( "business to business"). The Web is fundamentally altering the sales, distribution, and manufacturing processes. New businesses are being created, and established businesses are being significantly reinvented.

Consider the following points:

1. The very sales-intensive process of purchasing an automobile has moved to the Web with astonishing results. According to an article in *The New York Times*, "One in five auto purchases is made by buyers

who consult the Internet or a traditional car buying service ... About a third of those who consult the Internet or a buying service actually buy cars through them, while many of the other buyers use the process they obtain to wrangle better bargains." As a result of Web services, such as Auto-by-Tel, experts predict that up to half the nation's auto dealers will disappear within five years. That's a 50 percent decrease in an entire industry's retail business channel!

2. Hilton Hotels are currently taking $1 million worth of room reservations per month through the company's Web site, *Internet World* magazine reports. Although that revenue represents a drop in the bucket compared with Hilton's $1.7 billion in total revenue, company officials report that the Web "is cheaper to operate than an 800 number" and that four out of every 10 people who have called Hilton's 800 number now turn to the Hilton Web site.
3. Egghead Software, once the nation's largest retailer of computer software, has closed all the doors of its physical operation (80 stores) and now sells software products exclusively on the Web. According to a report in *Computerworld*, presented by staff writer Sharon Machlis, "Egghead's Internet revenue rose to $11.8 million in the quarter ended December 27, 1997, up from $9.3 million a year earlier. And the average value of an Internet transaction at www.egghead.com rose from $121 in the first quarter to $300 late last year." Machlis concludes, "The firm predicted revenue of $500 million in three years as electronic commerce grows."
4. Cyberian Outpost has no physical retail presence, but that doesn't stop its Web site from moving an average of $4 million worth of computer products per month.
5. Dell Computer has built a $1 billion business selling computers over the Net. According to financial documents released by the company, www.dell.com "now is generating sales of more than $3 million per day. This is equivalent to an annual run rate of approximately $1 billion."
6. Stock photo agency PhotoDisc launched its Web site in June 1995. The Web commerce portion of its site went live in October of the same year with secure credit card transactions. How is the site doing? In six months, of a reported $20 million in sales, $2.4 million were generated from the company's Web site. Furthermore, according to a PhotoDisc spokesperson, revenue generated over the Web was over $500,000 in the month of June 1997, a growth rate of approximately 21 percent over the previous 12 months. What company wouldn't consider a 21 percent increase in sales something to celebrate?

7. DigitalThink, a company begun in March 1996, now offers more than 35 Web-based training courses designed for programmers, developers, systems administrators, and end users. The company reports that it has more than 16,500 registered users in the Americas, Europe, Asia, Australia, Africa, and Russia as well as a roster of corporate clients that includes Texas Instruments, Adobe Systems, Lucent Technologies, Johnson & Johnson, and Eastman Kodak.
8. Yahoo, the venerable Web-based search engine reported net revenue totaling more than $25 million for the fourth quarter of 1997, a 181 percent increase from the fourth quarter one year earlier. The company, which makes its money primarily on advertising, grew to an average of 65 million page views per day—not bad for a company that has become the de facto starting point for most novice Web users by offering the simple benefit of searching and categorizing information on the Web.
9. Apple Computer has succeeded in Web commerce. At the end of 1997, the company decided to sell custom-built computers through its Web site to meet the needs of its higher-end, more specialized customers. As a result, the Apple Store (www.apple.com/store) received over 4.4 million hits and booked over $500,000 of orders during its first 12 hours of operation.
10. Financial services powerhouse Charles Schwab has led its industry's charge on to the Net. The company announced that, thanks to the Web, its customers can now research investment ideas and select stocks that were previously available only to professional investors and customers of traditional brokerage firms. The company is currently on a campaign to educate its customers about its efforts to continue to expand the possibility of online investing by hosting a series of seminars at its 270 branch offices nationwide. Customers can expect that what Schwab has done for investing, it will continue to do with its online presence at www.schwab.com.

One common complaint heard about the potential for Web-based commerce is that online success is for big business only. The investment and expertise required to succeed on the Web require far greater resources than most businesses can afford.

That's not the case for Billy Bags, a furniture designer and manufacturer of audio and video equipment stands.

High-end audio and home theater is a world in which aficionados spend anywhere from $10,000 to $100,000 for custom systems to reproduce the experience of live music and movies in the confines of a living room, listening room, den, or study. Billy Bags is known for making furniture for those expensive systems.

Traditionally, Billy Bags' product line is sold through distributors, who then sell it directly to high-end audio and video stores. The company is a small business, especially compared with the Dell Computers of the world. Its products are carefully designed and then made by hand. But its aspirations on the Web are large. "I am using the Web to increase the global image of my small business," says Bags. "Mid- to high-end audio and video is a global business. I am using my Web site to attract new dealers interested in selling my products. I am also using the Web to enable the end consumer to drive product sales. People who are looking for the perfect furniture rack to house their stereo search for it on the Web. They then go into the local audio or video store and ask the dealer if they carry my product. When that happens, it gives people an incentive to contact me and set up a relationship selling my product."

Billy Bags does sell directly to consumers, but only if there is no dealer in the customer's area (the customer still pays retail, however). According to Bags, the Web is already having an impact on his small business at www.billybags.com. "For example, several times people have visited my Web site and made the decision that they wanted to buy my product. They call a nearby dealer and order it over the phone and have it shipped to them, or they stop in the store to pick it up. The Web has really helped distribution for a small company such as mine, and these sales have had a major impact."

**Are You Ready?**

For business, the Web is not the future. The Web is here and now. Web sites are no longer *part* of a company's business but quickly becoming integral to a company's *entire* business.

Gone are the days when a company used its Web site solely as an adjunct to its marketing efforts—a sort of electronic marketing brochure with pages to be clicked through rather than turned. Today, the Web, for many companies, is becoming the business—a way of revolutionizing the sales, customer service, distribution, and manufacturing processes. When businesses start to shut down their distribution systems and instead opt to reach their customers virtually, we will know that the Web has truly arrived.

As more companies attempt to take advantage of the opportunities that the Web offers, they will need help as they quickly realize they cannot tackle nor tame the Web alone. Small, medium-size, and even large businesses need help as they try to conceive, design, produce, host, and maintain their Internet presence. The more commerce potential that technology makes possible, the more help companies need in implementing that technology on their Web site.

The Web development process is not a simple one. Web development is fraught with complicated technology and difficult sales and marketing decisions. For companies that do not understand the Web development process, the learning curve can be difficult and the results can be catastrophic. Consider the following real-world examples:

1. One small business established a Web site to better communicate with its specialized customer base. The company set up a server and had that server located at a Web developer. Unfortunately, the developer went out of business. It took two months before the company could gain access and control of its Web and mail server. By the time the company could re-establish its Web presence, it had already received several angry phone calls from its customers asking why repeated emails to the company went unanswered. Unfortunately, the company also lost some of its important accounts.
2. One midsized business hired a Web developer to design and produce its Web site. The developer was a small graphic design studio that had a project manager, a senior designer, and two graphic designers. The developer subcontracted all of its programming work to a freelance programmer. The relationship between the developer and the programmer was never solidified with the proper legal documents. Months after the job was finished and the site went live, the midsized business received a cease-and-desist notice directly from the programmer, who claimed that the custom CGIs he wrote for the Web site were his property; he sought additional compensation, claiming he originally licensed his work to the Web developer for a period of only one year. The midsized business faced an unexpected bill and the Web developer found its reputation with one of its major clients in serious jeopardy.
3. One large business paid a Web developer more than $200,000 for its extensive Web site, which featured an innovative product catalog and commerce center. Management at the company changed hands, and the incoming staff responsible for the Web site brought in another Web developer to manage the site. In retaliation, the firm that created the product catalog and commerce center stripped the function off the company site, demanding it be paid a fee to part with its proprietary technology. A costly and complicated legal battle ensued.

If you look at all of the people who are succeeding on the Web—from Dell Computer down to the small business of Billy Bags—each has been a success because it had good people involved in the process and good relationships with Web developers (whether the site was developed in-house or outsourced).

chapter

# 1

# In or Out? An Outsourcing Overview

### About This Chapter

The decision to develop a Web site in-house or to work with an outside Web developer is a significant one requiring careful participation and review from many departments and individuals at a company.

This chapter provides an overview on outsourcing Web services as it takes a look at the state of outsourcing today; examines arguments for and against Web outsourcing; presents outsourcing scenarios for small, medium-sized, and large businesses; and offers insight into helping you determine whether your company is the type of organization that can outsource effectively.

Finally, a review of the Web development process as well as key members of a Web team and a snapshot of some of the Web teams from highly respected Web development firms provides you with a sound basis for moving forward as you work with a subcontractor to shape your Internet presence.

### About the Author

J. P. Frenza worked in publishing and the pharmaceutical industry prior to joining United Digital Artists, a new-media talent agency, where he served as vice president of marketing and business development. He is the co-author of the critically-acclaimed *Web & New Media Pricing Guide* as well as *Smart Card Technologies and the Internet*. He has consulted with a number of high-technology clients, including Apple Computer, IBM, and Microsoft Corporation. He currently serves as director of Earth Pledge Foundation's Web group, Sustainable Media, a full-service new-media agency that creates and manages educational seminars, hands-on workshops, Web site development, marketing assistance, and special projects for the nonprofit and corporate community.

**Early this year the management of Ryder TRS, Inc. announced plans to outsource the company's entire information systems operations.**

**According to a cover story in the February issue of *Computerworld,* which defines itself as "the newsweekly for information technology leaders," Ryder, the nation's second largest consumer truck rental firm, has contracted with Cambridge Technology Partners and the Perot Systems Corporation to outsource "everything and anything to do with information systems—including its chief information officer."**

If a company can outsource an entire MIS department and its staff right along with it, it seems only logical that the same company can just as easily outsource all of its Web development needs.

However, outsourcing computer management and information systems is one thing. Outsourcing Web site development is an entirely different matter. The nature of designing, building, and maintaining an effective Internet presence requires a unique and ongoing relationship, with deep commitments from both the company and its chosen Web developer.

Hiring an outsourcer to install a network involves some planning, but for the most part it is a discernible physical task with a clear start and completion date. Outsourcing companywide computer repair services or help desk support is a specific fee-for-service contract that is fairly objective and not unlike the same type of agreement that a company might have for its photocopier repair.

This type of relationship can be broken down into easily manageable steps: First, the computer crashed; second, an employee called the outsourcer to indicate that a repair was needed; finally, the service agent fixed the machine. Evaluating the quality of the outsource contract involves reviewing how long it took to repair the computer and the total cost of the repair. An ambitious client might even investigate employee satisfaction with the repair and the additional service offered by the vendor.

The Web doesn't work that way. As more and more companies recognize the importance of conducting business via the Internet, the types of relationships and the terms of those relationships become more complicated. Performance becomes harder to manage. Questions such as these arise: How does the company determine whether or not its Web presence is cost-effective, given the infancy of the Internet? How can a company fairly evaluate the success of its Web development outsourcer when standards for evaluating success of the medium have yet to be determined?

Some business analysts have argued that Web site development must show a clear and decisive return on investment (ROI) in order to justify continued spending and commitment. Even this normally tried-and-true approach fails to yield conclusive results. For example, how does one factor in the cost of establishing a brand in cyberspace? More important, how does one factor in the cost of not establishing a brand in cyberspace? Is there a benefit to having potential customers wade through an interactive database of a manufacturer's products and parts, even though they do not have the option of purchasing online? What is the value of learning about the Web as a medium so that when the opportunity presents itself, a company can be poised to take advantage of the power of networking with its customers?

This is not to say that a company should not or cannot outsource its Web site development with the same degree of bottom-line concerns as it outsources other aspects of its business. The fact that outsourcing the Web offers its own unique challenges presents an all the more important reason to look at a fair definition of what it means to outsource, review the state of outsourcing today, and evaluate the reasons in favor of and against outsourcing in a generic sense —not as is generally presented in the computer trades, but rather outsourcing specifically related to Web development services.

## What Is Outsourcing?

Perhaps it could be said that, to borrow and modify from Mark Twain, work consists of whatever a body is obliged to do, and that outsourcing consists of whatever a body can pay someone else to do.

For the purposes of presenting a definition that forms the basis of the discussion throughout this book, outsourcing refers to the process via which one company purchases goods and/or services (in the case of the Web, mostly services) from an individual or business. It seems pretty straightforward: Company A hires Company B to design, program, and host its Web site.

Interestingly, *Webster's New World Dictionary* (Third College) defines outsourcing with a slightly more political tinge, suggesting it is "the practice of purchasing parts or finished goods from domestic non-union shops or from foreign companies."

What about purchasing services? And what, then, does it mean to subcontract? A literal, dictionary definition suggests that a subcontract represents "a secondary contract undertaking some or all of the obligations of a primary or previous contract" and that a subcontractor is "a person or company that assumes by secondary contract some or all of the obligations of an original subcontractor."

For our purposes (and also because our industry chooses to do so), we use the two terms—outsourcing and subcontracting—interchangeably, despite the fact that we now recognize that there is a technical difference between the two.

When it comes to the Web, it is understood that a company can *outsource* its site to a Web developer. That Web developer may perform all of the work at its studio or it may, as is common, *subcontract* parts of the site to firms or individuals that specialize in certain tasks (such as Java, design, connecting Web front ends to legacy databases, etc.).

## The State of Outsourcing Web Services Today

Because Web developers include not only businesses devoted exclusively to Web development, but also thousands of small and medium-sized businesses operating behind the scenes in a wide range of fields, it is very difficult to get a grasp on the size of the Web development industry and the number of small, midsize, and large firms outsourcing their Web development efforts.

Geri Spieler, a research analyst at The Gartner Group, estimates that by the year 2002 electronic marketplace managers will spend as much as $5 billion to $6 billion on out-of-office expenditures related to their Internet needs. Spieler points out, however, that the figure could be much higher if a company's accounting system allocates Internet-related expenses in other categories or does not report such expenditures at all.

Anecdotal evidence presented in *WebWeek*'s *Second Annual Survey*, conducted in October 1997 and reported on by Elizabeth Gardner, revealed that the publication, which has since changed its name to *Internet World*, "had no trouble locating dozens of design firms with at least one Fortune 1000 client on their rosters." The fact that the survey included 91 respondents, up from 39 in its 1996 survey, seems to suggest that a healthy amount of Web services outsourcing is taking place.

Some of the best evidence comes from Managing Web Developers, an Interactive Technology Strategies report published by Forrester, the well-known and highly respected market research firm based in Cambridge, Massachusetts.

The Forrester report, conducted in September 1997, interviewed 50 new-media managers at Fortune 1000 companies regarding their use of Web development firms. Among the many of Forrester's findings:

- ***Business is outsourcing its Web development needs.***
  Roughly two thirds of those firms surveyed "currently employ two or more outside Web developers," a healthy increase from the 1996 report, which found only one third of the firms surveyed used outside contractors to meet their Web development needs.

- ***Companies prioritize their outsourcing needs.***
  According to Forrester, "coding and scripting and site design are the most outsourced tasks" in Web site development. Those two functions are followed, in order, by content creation, content management, systems management, and strategic planning for the Web.

- ***Companies choose outsourcing for specific reasons.***
  Not surprisingly, Forrester found that the number-one reason for outsourcing site development was a lack of internal staff. Other reasons cited were (in order): no technical resources, lack of expertise, and the fact that outsourcing was easier. Interestingly, the least important reason companies cited was the fact that outsourcing was more cost efficient. This supports the claim earlier in this chapter that the justification for outsourcing Web development services is something other than cost, traditionally one of the most important factors considered when outsourcing other types of information services. The "talent, not cost" sentiment was echoed by one executive producer at a large entertainment company who observed, "When we subcontract, it is not about saving a few bucks. If we could find the right people, we'd hire them in a second."

- ***The future points to more outsourcing.***
  Outsourcing will not only continue to be the buzzword of the next few years, but Web developers can expect work to remain plentiful. The

Forrester survey found that "fifty-five percent of the average Internet budget is allotted to outsourcing" and that "over the next year, 86% of new-media managers plan to either increase or sustain the current level of outsource spending."

## In Favor of Outsourcing

For many businesses, outsourcing represents a cost-effective method for ensuring that a company's Web development efforts do not distract valuable resources from the corporate mission—the "we make widgets, not Web sites" argument.

Before you make the decision to actually outsource your Web site, key departments in your company—marketing, sales, operations, customer service, MIS, and management—should examine the outsourcing benefits presented in this section.

If there is widespread recognition and agreement that your company will benefit from outsourcing Web development services, you will have engaged in an important consensus-making process that will go a long way toward encouraging teamwork and laying the framework for a successful relationship with the Web developer your company decides to hire.

If no consensus exists (and in some cases, the process divides rather than unites the various departments), it is clearly better to find this out at the beginning of the project. In some cases, the company may find that it has no choice but to put the brakes on the outsourcing process. In other situations in which the company does indeed go forward without consensus, it is better to have all of the "turf wars" exposed prior to starting the project and risking a negative and costly Web site development experience. In a perfect world, it would be best if the company could resolve departmental conflicts prior to working with an outside developer. In many instances, conflicts simmer below the surface and various groups maintain agendas that remain hidden. For example, an MIS group may want to delay cooperating with an outside Web developer but may indicate that its delay is based on more pragmatic concerns—for example, that Web development falls after nine other priorities. In any case, exposing potential turf battles and interdepartmental conflicts early on creates the opportunity for a company to overcome such hurdles by setting approved companywide priorities. If the process is an open one from the beginning, there's less chance that hidden agendas can stay hidden.

**The Cost Factor.** For many companies, the most important consideration in outsourcing the company Web site is cost. Relying on an outside firm enables your company to accomplish more work without necessarily hiring (read that paying) for the staff to carry the work out.

Determining and comparing the costs of developing your site in-house versus working with an outside Web developer is a fairly simple process. First, define the specifications regarding your site. How many sections will it contain? How many pages will each section house? What are the technology requirements necessary to make your site work? For more information on developing your concept, setting goals and drafting a request for proposal, see Chapter 3.

After you have a rough project specification, go through the exercise of estimating what it would cost to build the Web site in-house. Do you currently have all of the staff that you will need? Or will you have to hire one or two additional staff members in order to build the Web site according to specification? In this case, you will want to prepare a detailed budget for your Web site. In doing so, be sure to include additional hardware and software that you will need to purchase, the cost of hosting your site, etc. If you have people in-house, be careful to assess whether you will have to pay those people overtime for work they spend beyond a normal work shift. If the people work in other departments find out whether or not your department will be charged for recruiting their services. Finally, be sure to add the cost of overhead for additional staff members—health care benefits, vacation time, profit sharing, desks, phone charges, computers, etc.

Reviewing all of the true costs you are likely to incur will give you a clear picture as to what developing your Web site in-house will cost. That, of course, assumes that your company has the expertise to produce your Web site in-house. If you don't, be sure to add a hefty amount to the budget for training.

Compare your internal costs to several bids submitted by Web site developers. If you estimated honestly, your answer should be obvious.

Cost should not be the only basis for choosing not to outsource Web site development. If you find that outsourcing your Web site only costs 10 to

20% more than developing it with internal staff, you will most likely find that the other benefits of outsourcing more than make up for going it alone—something you might not find out until you find yourself struggling to get your JavaScripts to work on more than one browser at two o'clock in the morning.

Cost should not be the overriding justification to outsource, or not outsource, your Web site development needs. A great many businesses do not choose to outsource because of cost but rather because of need. The need to grow their business and take full advantage of the newly developing online world. Companies that make their decisions solely on the basis of price are likely to find that they will incur the ultimate cost: the cost of lost opportunity. By not working with the best and the brightest Web developers, a company might never develop its Web site enough to take full advantage of the opportunities the Web offers. And that cost alone can have the biggest impact on your bottom line.

**Knowledge and Expertise.** A significant factor in the decision to outsource Web site development revolves around whether a company possesses the in-house knowledge and expertise required to establish an effective Internet presence.

A good Web developer specializes in figuring out what works on the Web and, more important, what does not work—both in terms of technical capability and measuring effectiveness.

Small businesses may lack the time needed to fully understand the best option for presenting their business on the Web. Medium-sized and large businesses might have the luxury of freeing up a limited amount of resources to tackle a Web project, but they still might lack the knowledge to implement all of the minute technical details of a Web project. If you don't have a Web expert in your company (and you can't afford to bring one on staff), an important benefit of outsourcing is that you'll gain a Web developer who has the knowledge and expertise to build a more effective site than you could have produced otherwise.

**Growth.** Outsourcing your Web site is a great way to dedicate and focus attention on your company's core business. An outsourcing arrangement not only frees up your time and energy, but it also keeps your company growing and preparing for the future.

A number of larger companies outsource the task of designing and producing the company's second-generation Web site while the company's own MIS group puts the finishing touches on its first-generation site. That way, the company can test and implement new systems and technologies via an outsourcing strategy without adversely impacting day-to-day operations. Using a Web developer to build a future site in parallel is an effective method of sustaining growth and progress.

**Speed.** Today's companies understand that competing in the marketplace requires designing products and developing solutions at breakneck speed. If managed properly, the use of outside Web developers can enable your business to focus on targeted goals and achieve their implementation at a much quicker pace. Web developers can be given financial incentives to deliver their services at a faster rate. Furthermore, because Web developers can specialize in certain aspects of site development, their expertise is likely to add a level of efficiency that your company could not achieve.

**Specialization.** Not all Web developers are created equal. Each developer has a distinct approach to the Web that can serve its clients best interests. For example, T3 Media is a company that specializes in the development of dynamic Web sites delivered with Microsoft Windows NT Server and Microsoft SQL Database. The company has other areas in which it excels, but its database solutions form the basis of its excellent reputation. Through specialization, T3 Media has achieved a level of excellence that a small, medium-sized, or large business might take years to match. Other firms might specialize in helping their clients establish brand identity on the Web; still others may concentrate on integrating front-end Web solutions with legacy databases. Some might specialize in creating highly targeted banner ads, and another developer might have a focus that includes Java development or implementing a specific electronic commerce solution.

Outsourcing is a way to leverage the specialized experience of the Web developer for your company.

**Technology Relief.** If your company creates health insurance plans, your business focuses on the design and delivery of the best (and hopefully the most affordable) health care packages. Keeping on top of legislative changes affecting the delivery of health care can be a daunting task. Try doing all of that and keeping on top of the latest and greatest Web technologies, too. For that matter, try just keeping the most recent version of Netscape Navigator or Microsoft Internet Explorer maintained and running on your computer desktop.

Technology comprises the entire sum and focus of your Web developer's life (assuming that time in between programming actually leaves time for a life to begin with). Outsourcing offers you the tremendous advantage of having a specialist tame technology for you. A successful Web outsourcing relationship is one in which your Web developer synthesizes all of the technological change sweeping the industry and presents it to you so that you can make effective decisions regarding the future development of your business. You know you are experiencing the true benefits of outsourcing when you move from the Internet to an intranet to an extranet, all the while delivering better products and services to your customers at a better price—and all based on the advice of your outsourcing partner.

### Against Outsourcing

There's no question that this book is in favor of outsourcing Web development services. This pro-outsourcing position, of course, assumes a willing and capable company and a competent and professional Web developer. In addition, this book assumes that the company making a decision to outsource its Web development services understands the process of building a Web site and is prepared to make the commitment necessary to ensure the project's success.

Yet outsourcing is not necessarily a de facto decision that companies need to feel compelled to make—despite what they read in the computer trades. Outsourcing Web sites has its definite downsides.

Our goal in this section is to present the arguments *against* outsourcing Web development services. The hope is that a company in the process of deciding whether or not it should outsource its Web services will review these arguments carefully, analyze how they may or may not be relevant to a particular situation, and proceed in the outsourcing process, knowledgeable about the potential pitfalls that the process might bring along the way. These arguments are not presented to deter a company from outsourcing its Web site development, but rather to use these issues as red flags to look out for along the way. Many of the issues discussed in this section reappear in the various topics covered throughout this book.

The first set of arguments is applicable to your company's internal operations, while the second set identifies the risks of outsourcing from the perspective of working with a Web developer.

**Internal Outsourcing Risks.** Outsourcing is not a "no-brainer" decision. In fact, for a number of very serious reasons, outsourcing can be disruptive for your company. These reasons include are described in the following sections.

**Company Culture**

One of the most significant barriers to the effective outsourcing of services has to do with a company's corporate culture—the largely unwritten rules of operations that play a powerful role in determining how a company conducts its business.

Some companies are simply not prepared to outsource their Web development services. Many do not understand that designing, producing, and maintaining a Web site requires involvement and support from multiple groups within the company: marketing, sales, customer service, management, and MIS. For a Web site to be successful, each of these departments (and still others) must contribute to or at least be aware of the company's Web site development. Coordinating day-to-day operations is a time-consuming task. Add to that the requisite coordination and management tasks—first among departments, then with an outside Web site contractor—and it becomes a task that many firms find they cannot manage. As an outsourced project continues, the delay in providing the contractor with input and approvals will delay the project, reduce the chance of its success, and potentially have a negative impact on the budget.

These risks are further complicated by the fact that, as should become obvious as this book unfolds, building and maintaining Web sites is a very labor-intensive, nonscientific task that has a tendency to evolve rather than be completed in a finite, predictable manner. A company might start to build a Web site only to see its needs and the capability of technology change to the point in which the Web site needs to be entirely redeveloped. Many companies without experience in outsourcing are likely to be uncomfortable with, or at least surprised by, what is essentially the nonfinality of a Web site. "We're used to product cycles," said a manager at a manufacturing firm. "Three months of design, two months of specifications, followed by having a vendor build our product. It is a specific product cycle. With the Web there's this constant. The product is never 'finished.' We were unprepared for that."

In addition to being unprepared for the continuous engagement that building a successful Web site requires, many a company fails to recognize that it is indeed not the "outsourcing type." Companies that are traditionally secretive and those that choose to run their business too "close to the vest" might have difficulty trusting Web developers to apply their expertise to the firm's Web presence. Inevitably, it is difficult for a company that has never outsourced any aspect of its business—from product design to development, marketing, and sales—to make the leap to trusting an outside vendor to determine the best way to present the company on what could potentially end up as the company's largest sales, marketing, and distribution channel. Companies of this nature tend to trust less and control more—something that makes a Web developer's tough job that much more difficult.

**Brand**

A high-level executive at one of the major credit card companies observed that "we aren't opposed to outsourcing, we just don't let the database leave the building." The executive was referring to the fact that a great many businesses cannot outsource because, rightly or wrongly, they need to control their product brands or proprietary information.

Playboy, one of the most instantly recognizable brands found anywhere in the world, hesitates to outsource the development of its products because, in essence, the value of the company is entirely in the company's name brand—the bold type found on magazines on newsstands all over the world.

If your company is overly protective of its brand, or of proprietary information that it is reluctant to share with outside contractors, the type of open relationship required to make outsourcing successful might be more difficult. You still might make the decision to outsource, but the entire process will most likely be dictated by your primary concern: protecting brand. This means that everything—from the selection of the Web developer to produce your site to the site's security and marketing efforts—will have to be scrutinized carefully throughout the Web site development process.

**Politics and People**

Ask yourself honestly: Is your company a political land mine? If your group needs to accomplish a goal, do you get positive assistance and feedback from other groups in the company? Or do you invariably face an uphill power struggle to implement your initiatives? Does marketing cooperate with sales and customer service and MIS? Or is each group entrenched in territorial battles that are bound to make the process of building a Web site rife with politics and disruptive agendas?

These are tough questions that need honest answers if the process of building a Web site is to meet the needs of every group in the company. Many Web developers have horror stories to tell about working with a company's marketing department only to find the firm's legal department would not approve one sentence on the company's Web site and would not cooperate in the process of changing the wording. In some companies, it is axiomatic that the bigger the Web site's ambition, the bigger the turf battle. Of course, the bigger the turf battle, the more convoluted the Web site coordination, and that usually translates very quickly into project delays and higher costs.

Behind the politics, however, another important issue concerns the role of people in their companies—their job satisfaction and career development. This is particularly true of an MIS group. It's no mystery that the Web is the hottest project that an MIS group can undertake. Figuring out a Web site certainly far exceeds network maintenance and management when it comes to intrigue. MIS teams read the computer trades. They know that for their skills to continuously develop, they need to gain understanding and experience in implementing Web-based solutions. A company that makes a decision to outsource Web development potentially takes one of the "neatest" jobs away from a staff that spends its days performing the sometimes less appreciated tasks of, for example, network maintenance. "We work twelve hours a day doing grunt work and they hire a bunch of hip consultants to play with our Web site," says one disgruntled MIS worker. "I'm out of here." All of the trade magazines suggest that good MIS professionals are very difficult to find. Your decision to outsource a Web site just might put your company in the hunt for those scarce workers as your MIS staff leaves to go work on more exciting projects at, ironically, a Web development shop.

This is not to say that the MIS group should necessarily be the team that produces your company's Web site. In fact, many MIS departments have turned down the option based on their focus and as a result of their long "to do" lists. However, it does make sense to involve the MIS team in the process and make sure that the project has their buy-in, approval, and cooperation. You might also find out that the MIS group can contribute parts of the Web site development, thereby reducing the costs of using an outside contractor.

**Cost** And what of reducing the costs of using an outside contractor?

It might be theoretically true that outsourcing reduces costs, but several business studies indicate that the results are inconclusive at best. The Web development industry is young, and whether it makes sense to go it alone or contract with a partner remains to be seen.

Cost is also difficult to measure. For example, if a company decided to produce its Web site in-house, it might find that because it lacks the personnel to undertake a large-scale Web effort, it will scale back and produce a more limited Web product. Does it necessarily follow that, because the company worked with a qualified Web developer and as a result established more ambitious goals and therefore spent more money, it would have been less costly to develop the site in-house? If the company outsources its Web site and loses several valuable employees in the process, is it fair to say that outsourcing is more cost-effective in the long run?

This raises a key point in the outsourcing debate. Outsource because of expertise. Outsource because it will make your business better. But don't count on being able to actually prove that outsourcing was conclusively less expensive. If your company can present an objective analysis proving that outsourcing is less expensive, you will be well ahead of the game. Many firms, however, find that outsourcing is actually more expensive, but they find it is worth it, given what their Web site can do to enhance their strategic advantage. It seems that on the Web, as with most everything, you always get what you pay for.

**The Web Developer.** Not only does outsourcing carry with it internal risks for your company, but there are external risks as well—risks that specifically relate to working with an outside Web developer. These risks include those discussed below.

**Competence** With investments from venture capitalists, mergers and acquisitions, and an influx of cash from advertising agencies scrambling to connect with key technology skills, you would expect the Web industry to have reached a certain level of operational maturity. However, company after company that hires Web developers complains about a lack of business professionalism and an inability to deliver on long-term, technology-intensive projects. As one executive at a major entertainment company pointed out, "Our Web developer was fired for having the manners of children and the ability of infants."

This is not to say that there are not very capable Web development firms throughout the country. In fact, in New York City alone, at least a dozen Web developers have already delivered on multiple large-scale projects within budget and on time. The same holds true for San Francisco, Chicago, Boston, Los Angeles, and other hot beds of Web development.

But for every Web site success, there are companies that have hired Web developers and had disappointing results. The ultimate competence of a Web developer—the ability to deliver solid designs, cutting-edge technology, and a host of solutions—is a key issue in determining whether or not your company should outsource its Web development.

**The Trap**

Working with a contractor to build your company's Web site involves making a major commitment to that contractor. Your contractor's success will, in the end, be your success. If your contractor fails, your project could fail. A number of incidents have occurred involving very big (and prestigious) companies hiring a Web developer, only to have that developer hold the company's Web site hostage over a disagreement on funding or other contractual issues. If your caterer has a dispute over the bill, you might not have breakfast ready for an important meeting, but if your Web developers have a dispute with you, they could be in control of your Web server and all of its contents—in short, a major part of your business could be held hostage.

As soon as you decide to outsource your Web site, your company becomes vulnerable. Outsourcing has its risks. The fact that Web developers sometimes go out of business makes this issue particularly important. More than one Web developer has gone "belly up" and had its doors padlocked by its creditors while clients peeked through the locked windows, staring helplessly at their unattended servers.

Unfortunately, no sure-fire advice can ever guarantee that your company will avoid these potential outsourcing downsides. In a general sense, one of the best ways to avoid being trapped is to educate yourself (and your company) about the Web development process, the subject of this entire book. If you work with a reputable Web developer and pay a fair price for the services you purchase, chances are better that you can avoid problems with the outsourcing process. Of course, protecting your site and your business is ultimately a legal issue, one that is covered in greater detail in Chapter 7.

**Accountability**

One of the most important reasons to keep a project in-house, assuming that your company has the expertise, is final accountability. If employees at your company cannot deliver on a project, your firm has clear and immediate leverage. You might not want to use that leverage, and it might remain unstated, but the fact is that employees who cannot deliver on a project (assuming no extraneous factors are at play) realize that their relationship with the company is limited. In short, they can be fired. In addition, employees at a company know that if they succeed (and most employees want to do a good job and succeed as professionals in their chosen field), they will face rewards: a raise in pay, additional benefits, promotions, and so forth. The point is that the company has leverage over its employees, and employees know that.

Your company has less leverage with a subcontractor than it does with an in-house employee. The subcontractor might have multiple clients, of which you are only one, who warrant their attention and service. Also, the more pressure you put on your Web developers to perform "the impossible," the greater the chance the Web developer will decide to focus on profitable relationships and possibly drop you as a client. That scenario might seem strange, but in an industry in which large-scale, profitable projects abound, more and more Web developers are focusing their business on firms with which they feel comfortable working. Web developers, it seems, can afford to be choosy. This is the same lesson that anyone who has ever contracted to remodel their kitchen has faced: be kind to your contractor. Your old kitchen has been demolished, there's plenty of work to do before you can use the stove again, and the contractor has a stable of clients who will be happy to have his attention focused on their project instead of yours.

In order to protect yourself against these circumstances, you will need to be on the lookout for potential warning signs that your project might be "going wrong." The signs and strategies to manage them are discussed in greater detail in Chapter 9. Of course, issues of performance and parting ways should be covered in your legal agreement with your developer. We cover both in Chapter 7.

When it comes to the Web, accountability can be a very delicate matter. In addition, if you think it is easy to move your Web site and start over, think twice. First, starting over is not a simple task; second, it is not an inexpensive one.

## Outsourcing Scenarios

So how does a very simple Web site shake out when it comes to considerations of cost? This section takes a look at three simple Web sites and compares the costs of producing each in-house against hiring a subcontractor to produce the site. The numbers presented here are not meant to be absolutely conclusive. In any Web project, it is necessary to develop a comprehensive statement of goals and a carefully drafted request for proposal (RFP) and then have that proposal bid on by multiple Web development firms. The purpose of these brief snapshots is to identify a basic snapshot of outsourcing costs for small, medium-sized, and large Web sites. Here we distinguish among the possible sizes of Web sites, not by the size of a business, but instead by the functions and capabilities of the site itself. A large company—a Fortune 100 firm, for example—might not have the need for a large Web site, while a small business might. It follows, therefore, that on the Internet, the size of a company might not be the sole determinant in the size of the company's Web site.

We make some very simple assumptions that indicate the rationale behind the numbers. The circumstances at your company might differ dramatically, and in order to get a more accurate analysis, you may want to plug your own numbers into this basic format.

The numbers and estimates in this section were polled informally from several companies that hire Web developers and consultants, as well as several Web developers, all of whom were happy to contribute to the process but preferred not to be identified due to the sensitive nature of how much they pay or charge for their services.

**Small Business Web Site.** This case site (see Table 1.1) is a very simple Web site that has the goal of establishing a marketing, public relations, and media kit for a small business customer. The site includes the following information: about the company, the product line (10 product snapshots and specifications), contact information, a database of dealers who sell the product, news and announcements from the company, and warranty and repair information.

For the small business, the company saves money by outsourcing the development of its Web site and, as a result of the Web developer's expertise and specialization, ends up with a more sophisticated Web site that includes the ability to search a database of distributors of the company's products.

**Medium-Sized Web Site.** In this case (see Table 1.2), the company that is evaluating whether or not to outsource its Web site development has no expertise in-house and would have to create a Web development division

**Table 1.1** In or Out? A Look at Outsourcing a Small Web Site

| Web Function | In | Out |
|---|---|---|
| **Item**<br>Site concept<br>**Description**<br>Structure, architecture, navigation | **Explanation**<br>Prepared by marketing manager, sales manager, operations manager at several staff meetings<br>**Salary: Cost to Company**<br>$100 per hour<br>**Assumption:**<br>Number of people: 3<br>Number of hours: 40 | **Explanation**<br>Twenty hours of work prepared by a project manager at Web developer; another 10 hours of client liaison and approval<br>**Salary: Cost to Company**<br>$50 per hour<br>**Assumption**<br>Number of people: 1<br>Number of hours: 30 |
| | **Subtotal** **$4,000** | **Subtotal** **$1,500** |
| **Item**<br>Site design<br>**Description**<br>Concept to color comp | **Explanation**<br>Marketing staff designer makes $1,000 per week; it takes the designer two weeks.<br>**Salary: Cost to Company**<br>$1,000 per week<br>**Assumption**<br>Number of people: 1<br>Number of weeks: 2 | **Explanation**<br>Two days from a senior designer and five days from a junior designer.<br>**Salary: Cost to Company**<br>Senior: $50 per hour,<br>Junior: $25 per hour<br>**Assumption**<br>Number of people: 2<br>Number of hours: 48 |
| | **Subtotal** **$2,000** | **Subtotal** **$1,800** |
| **Item**<br>Editorial<br>**Description**<br>Write all copy for the Web site | **Explanation**<br>Sales manager, marketing manager, operations manager work on the Web site's copy; three people spend 20 hours each.<br>**Salary: Cost to Company**<br>$100 per hour<br>**Assumption**<br>Number of people: 3<br>Number of hours: 60 | **Explanation**<br>Web developer pays a free-lance writer with whom the company has an affiliation.<br>**Salary: Cost to Company**<br>$50 per hour<br>**Assumption**<br>Number of people: 1<br>Number of hours: 40 |
| | **Subtotal** **$6,000** | **Subtotal** **$2,000** |
| **Item**<br>Production<br>**Description**<br>Conversion of designs to HTML, indexing pages, etc. | **Explanation**<br>The company does not know how to produce Web pages. It has two options:<br><br>A. Hire a Web specialist for approximately $38,000 (including benefits, vacation, overhead, etc.)<br><br>B. Train the designer to produce the final HTML pages.<br>**Salary: Cost to Company**<br>Cost A: $3,166 per month<br>**Assumption**<br>Number of people: 1<br>Number of hours: 1 month (the company adds $250 worth of software) OR | **Explanation**<br>The Web developer uses a junior production editor who completes the pages in three weeks.<br>**Salary: Cost to Company**<br>$40 per hour<br>**Assumption**<br>Number of people: 1<br>Number of hours: 120 |

*(Continues)*

**Table 1.1** In or Out? A Look at Outsourcing a Small Web Site *(Continued)*

| Web Function | In | Out |
|---|---|---|
| | **Salary: Cost to Company**<br>Cost B: $1,000 per week<br>**Assumption**<br>Number of people: 1<br>Number of hours: 4 weeks (the company adds $250 worth of software, two HTML classes, and several books to its cost) | |
| | **Subtotal** $3,416–$5,000 | **Subtotal** $48,000 |
| **Item**<br>Programming<br>**Description**<br>Coding for the database | **Explanation**<br>The company does not have a programmer and the staff struggles to build the retail database; the section of the Web site is dropped<br>**Salary: Cost to Company**<br>$0 per hour<br>**Assumption**<br>Number of people: 0<br>Number of hours: 0 | **Explanation**<br>The developer uses a high-end production person who has training in building simple databases<br>**Salary: Cost to Company**<br>$50 per hour<br>**Assumption**<br>Number of people: 1<br>Number of hours: 2 weeks |
| | **Subtotal** $0 | **Subtotal** $2,000 |
| **Item**<br>Site hosting | **Cost to Company**<br>Register URL: $100<br>Host at ISP: $600 ($50 per month * 12) | **Cost to Company**<br>Register URL: $100<br>Host at ISP: $600 ($50 per month * 12) |
| | **Subtotal** $700 | **Subtotal** $700 |
| | **Total** $16,116 | **Total** $14,800 |

in order to build the site. For the purposes of our discussion, we assume that the company has an MIS group and that the Web development group would function under the MIS group's review as an independent unit.

Also for the purposes of our discussion, we assume that the company will include the following options on its Web site:

- Basic information about the company, such as history, background, key personnel, press releases, etc.
- A special section for investors, including the annual report presented online.
- A large product catalog, updated yearly, that includes 500 products and all of the various product specifications. The company does not sell directly to the public; therefore, the Web site will direct interested consumers to the nearest retail showroom where customers can consult with a specialist from whom they can purchase the product. This

portion of the Web site also includes a section that allows customers to request a catalog.

- A large-parts catalog for all of the products that the company has manufactured over the years. The company can sell these products directly to consumers; therefore, this section of the Web site includes a secure order form via which customers can place orders for parts, with an option for overnight shipping. The company will ship parts via an extensive shipping department located at its warehouse.
- The site will also feature a multimedia-rich section in which visitors can take a look at presentations that display the company's products being used in homes and businesses across the country.

The company predicts that it will most likely take six to nine months to implement the site correctly, and the company has made the decision that at project completion, the staff will start to plan the second generation of the site, which will include many new products and developments that the company plans to roll out as part of its expansion.

**Large Web Site.** Let's run the numbers for a large Web site (Table 1.3)—for example, a site for a magazine or information service to meet the specific needs of a group of trade professionals.

The magazine wants to update content on a daily basis and intends to generate enough advertising revenue from the site to cover operating costs and produce a substantial income. For example, the magazine budgets its operational costs at close to $1 million per year and expects to generate several million dollars in advertising sales.

Here we can see that in the case of this magazine, the numbers point to a cost-effective advantage in terms of keeping the Web site in-house.

This scenario indicates that the larger the Web site, the closer the numbers come to being in favor of keeping the Web site in-house. This is largely because when the Web developer has to maintain a large staff dedicated to one particular project, it loses its advantage of being able to leverage employees across multiple projects.

**Table 1.2** In or Out? A Look at Outsourcing a Medium-Sized Web Site

| Web Function | In | Out |
|---|---|---|
| **Item**<br>Site concept<br>**Description**<br>Structure, architecture, navigation | **Explanation**<br>The company will place the responsibility of this aspect of the site in the hands of the director of sales and marketing, who makes an annual salary of $80,000 and will dedicate one-half of her time to the project each year<br>**Salary: Cost to Company**<br>$40,000<br>**Assumption**<br>Number of people: 1<br>Number of hours: 1/2 year | **Explanation**<br>To manage this aspect of the site, the Web developer will assign an executive producer who makes $70,000 per year and can produce four sites per year; the executive producer will rely on a producer who makes $50,000 per year and can produce two sites in one year<br>**Salary: Cost to Company**<br>Executive producer: $17,500,<br>Producer: $25,000<br>**Assumption**<br>Number of people: 2<br>Number of hours:<br>Executive producer: 3 months<br>Producer: 6 months |
| | **Subtotal $40,000** | **Subtotal $1,800** |
| **Item**<br>Site design<br>**Description**<br>Concept to color comp | **Explanation**<br>The company will hire a full-time Web designer at the cost of $50,000 to work on the project<br>**Salary: Cost to Company**<br>$50,000<br>**Assumption**<br>Number of people: 1<br>Number of hours: 1 year | **Explanation**<br>The company pays $50,000 to its designer, who can create an average of six Web sites per year<br>**Salary: Cost to Company**<br>$8,300<br>**Assumption**<br>Number of people: 1<br>Number of hours: 2 months |
| | **Subtotal $50,000** | **Subtotal $8,300** |
| **Item**<br>Editorial<br>**Description**<br>Writing all copy for Web site | **Explanation**<br>The company will hire full-time the freelance copywriter with whom they've been working; one-half of his time will be allocated to the Web site<br>**Salary: Cost to Company**<br>$25,000<br>**Assumption**<br>Number of people: 1<br>Number of hours: 1/2 year | **Explanation**<br>The company has several writers on staff; each makes $40,000 per year and serves in a variety of capacities, including business development, writing, and on occasion, project management. Allocation: half-time<br>**Salary: Cost to Company**<br>$20,000<br>**Assumption**<br>Number of people: 1<br>Number of hours: 1/2 year |
| | **Subtotal $25,000** | **Subtotal $20,000** |
| **Item**<br>Production<br>**Description**<br>Conversion of designs to HTML, indexing pages, etc. | **Explanation**<br>The company will hire a full-time production staff member at a cost of $32,000<br>**Salary: Cost to Company**<br>$32,000 per year<br>**Assumption**<br>Number of people: 1<br>Number of hours: 1 year | **Explanation**<br>The company will allocate two production people at a salary of $30,000; each will allocate one-third of his time<br>**Salary: Cost to Company**<br>$10,000 per year<br>**Assumption**<br>Number of people: 2<br>Number of hours: 1 year |
| | **Subtotal $32,000** | **Subtotal $20,000** |

**Table 1.2** *Continued*

| Web Function | In | Out |
|---|---|---|
| **Item**<br>Programming<br>**Description**<br>Coding for the database | **Explanation**<br>The company will have to hire a full-time programmer who will program the database of products, implement the commerce part of the site, and tend to the server for an annual salary of $80,000; a consultant will assist the programmer on a fee-for-service budget of $10,000 per year<br>**Salary: Cost to Company**<br>Programmer: $80,000 per year<br>Consultant: $10,000 per year<br>**Assumption**<br>Number of people: 2<br>Number of hours: 1 year | **Explanation**<br>The developer pays its programmer $70,000 per year; the programmer will focus half of his time on the project and can handle two to four clients per year (this might not be the same person, but the allocation of programming costs will be the same)<br>**Salary: Cost to Company**<br>$35,000 per year<br>**Assumption**<br>Number of people: 1<br>Number of hours: 1/2 year |
| | **Subtotal** **$90,000** | **Subtotal** **$35,000** |
| **Item**<br>Site hosting | **Cost to Company**<br>T1: $12,000 ($1,000 per month)<br>Server hardware and software: $7,500<br>Installation: $2,500 | **Cost to Company**<br>$1,000 per month includes connection, hardware, and software |
| | **Subtotal** **$22,000** | **Subtotal** **$12,000** |
| **Subtotal** | **$259,000** | **$145,000** |
| **Overhead** | **$25,000** | **$25,000** |
| **Profit** | **$0** | **$85,000** |
| **Total** | **$284,000** | **$255,000** |

The numbers presented here are based on a limited circumstance; they can't be extrapolated accurately to every circumstance. If your company is building a large Web site, it would be a good idea for you to run the numbers and get an actual comparison based on your specific circumstances. Remember: The larger the Web site, the greater variance in circumstances and the greater swings in terms of cost.

Use the process with which these numbers were calculated to determine the fiscal analysis for your own company's Web site project. If the numbers shake out in favor of using an outsourcer, you're on your way. If the numbers are close, you might want to consider some of the other factors in favor of outsourcing presented in this chapter as part of your decision-making analysis.

**Table 1.3** In or Out? A Look at Outsourcing a Large Web Site

| Web Function | In | Out |
|---|---|---|
| **Item**<br>Site concept<br>**Description**<br>Structure, architecture, navigation | **Explanation**<br>The site will have an executive producer, a producer, and a project manager on a full-time basis<br>**Salary: Cost to Company**<br>Executive producer: $80,000 per year<br>Producer: $60,000 per year<br>Project manager: $40,000 per year<br>**Assumption**<br>Number of people: 3<br>Number of hours: 1 year | **Explanation**<br>The Web developer will have an executive producer who can handle two projects per year, an account representative who can handle four accounts per year, a senior producer who can handle two clients per year, and a full-time project manager<br>**Salary: Cost to Company**<br>Executive producer: $40,000 per 1/2 year<br>Account rep: $30,000/1/4 year<br>Senior producer: $30,000 per 1/2 year<br>Project manager: $40,000 per year<br>**Assumption**<br>Number of people: 4<br>Number of hours:<br>Executive producer: 1/2 year<br>Account pep: 1/4 year<br>Senior producer: 1/2 year<br>Project manager: 1 year |
| | **Subtotal** $180,000 | **Subtotal** $140,000 |
| **Item**<br>Site design<br>**Description**<br>Concept to color comp | **Explanation**<br>The company has a full-time creative director and a full-time designer<br>**Salary: Cost to Company**<br>Creative director: $75,000 per year<br>Full-time designer: $50,000 per year<br>**Assumption**<br>Number of people: 2<br>Number of hours: 1 year | **Explanation**<br>Creative director can oversee two projects per year ($40,000) and two designers half time ($30,000)<br>**Salary: Cost to Company**<br>Creative director: $40,000 per year<br>Designers: $30,000 per year<br>**Assumption**<br>Number of people: 3<br>Number of hours: 1/2 year |
| | **Subtotal** $125,000 | **Subtotal** $100,000 |
| **Item**<br>Editorial<br>**Description**<br>Writing all copy for Web site | **Explanation**<br>Senior editor at half time, borrowed from the magazine, and two staff writers<br>**Salary: Cost to Company**<br>Senior editor: $40,000 per 1/2 year<br>Staff writers: $40,000 each per year<br>**Assumption**<br>Number of people: 3<br>Number of hours:<br>Senior editor: 1/2 year<br>Staff writers: 1 year each | **Explanation**<br>Editor, two staff writers<br>**Salary: Cost to Company**<br>Editor: $60,000 per year<br>Staff writers: $40,000 each per year<br>**Assumption**<br>Number of people: 3<br>Number of hours:<br>Senior Editor: 1 year<br>Staff writers: 1 year each |
| | **Subtotal** $120,000 | **Subtotal** $140,000 |
| **Item**<br>Production<br>**Description**<br>Conversion of designs to HTML, indexing pages, etc. | **Explanation**<br>Maintaining the production work in-house will require two production staff members<br>**Salary: Cost to Company**<br>$35,000 each per year | **Explanation**<br>One full-time production staff member at $35,000 per year and one production staff member who can work on this project as well as make a contribution to other Web sites |

**Table 1.3** *Continued*

| Web Function | In | Out |
|---|---|---|
| | **Assumption**<br>Number of people: 2<br>Number of hours: 1 year each | **Salary: Cost to Company**<br>Full-time production staff: $35,000 per year<br>Part-time production staff: $20,000 per year<br>**Assumption**<br>Number of people: 2<br>Number of hours: 1 year |
| | **Subtotal** $70,000 | **Subtotal** $55,000 |
| **Item**<br>Programming<br>**Description**<br>Coding for the database | **Explanation**<br>One programmer<br>**Salary: Cost to Company**<br>Programmer: $75,000 per year<br>**Assumption**<br>Number of people: 1<br>Number of hours: 1 year | **Explanation**<br>One programmer who can work on two projects per year and a junior programmer who can work on two projects per year<br>**Salary: Cost to Company**<br>Programmer: $40,000 per 1/2 year<br>Junior programmer: $25,000 per 1/2 year<br>**Assumption**<br>Number of people: 2<br>Number of hours: 1/2 year |
| | **Subtotal** $75,000 | **Subtotal** $65,000 |
| **Item**<br>Site hosting<br>**Description** | **Explanation**<br>Requires a server administrator, a full-time staff member providing technical support<br><br>T1: $12,000 ($1,000 per month)<br>Server hardware and software: $7,500<br>Installation: $2,500<br>Server admin: $50,000 per year | **Explanation**<br>Company maintains a server administration group that handles multiple Web sites for a variety of clients<br>**Salary: Cost to Company**<br>$4,000 per month(includes connection, hardware and software, and server admin). |
| | **Subtotal** $72,000 | **Subtotal** $48,000 |
| **Item**<br>Sales | **Explanation**<br>Two full-time sales reps responsible for selling advertising space, sponsorships, and custom marketing programs<br>**Salary: Cost to Company**<br>$50,000 each per year<br>**Assumption**<br>Number of people: 2<br>Number of hours: 1 year | **Explanation**<br>This function will not be outsourced; therefore, company incurs the same cost<br>**Salary: Cost to Company:**<br>$50,000 each per year<br>**Assumption**<br>Number of people: 2<br>Number of hours: 1 year |
| | **Subtotal** $100,000 | **Subtotal** $100,000 |
| **Subtotal** | $742,000 | $648,000 |
| **Overhead** | $222,600 | $194,400 (30% of the budget); note that the company has allocated this amount to this client as a means of covering overhead expenses |
| **Profit** | $0 | +$194,400 |
| **Total** | $964,600 | +$1,036,400 |

## Understanding Your Company

Of all the decisions your company can make about outsourcing, the most important is whether you are equipped to handle outsourcing your Web site. Determining whether or not your company is organizationally equipped to outsource its Web site will give you some early answers that will save you time, effort, and energy later. As you begin to address your outsourcing needs, consider the following issues:

- **Are you the outsourcing "type"?** Are you a do-it-yourself control freak? When you considered redesigning your kitchen, did you order a stack of books from www.amazon.com and start hanging out at the Home Depot? Or did you call a kitchen designer and have them provide you with designs and an estimate? More important, when the job began, did you find yourself peering over the carpenter's shoulder? Make a list of all of the projects currently under development in your company. How many are on hold because you haven't had the time to conduct the research, write the job specification, and start the process yourself? How many did you turn over to someone else to tackle?

  If you are not the kind of person who delegates tasks easily, you are probably not the outsourcing type. Carefully examine your personal and professional tendencies to establish whether or not you should outsource your company's Web site. At the very least, if you take a hard (and honest) look at yourself, you'll be able to communicate your style to the Web developer that you hire. Different Web developers have different approaches to client relationships. Some seek to immediately establish a partnership with their clients and actively encourage them to be a member of the team. Other developers look for clients that tend to take a more "hands-off" approach. Neither approach is incorrect as long as the developer and the client are comfortable with the relationship. In either case, it is best to know your tendencies and be up-front with a subcontractor about them.

- **How's your outsourcing track record?** Has your company outsourced projects in the past? Is it currently outsourcing some aspect of its business? Take a careful look at past or current projects. Were these projects successful? If so, which department contributed to their success? Does your company have a history of unsuccessful outsourcing relationships? If so, why? It might be painful (or painfully obvious!) which department in your company has played the biggest role in making your outsourcing effort less than successful, but that's something that you should know up front. What were the other factors that contributed to the negative results? More important, are the departments or factors that prevented successful outsourcing relevant to your company's Web site development? In other words, if the marketing group is the reason your last five outsourcing efforts resulted in cost overruns, people leaving the company and a lawsuit from the subcontractor, and the marketing department is a key group for the Web site's success, then you know you're going to face some problems. You might want to scale back your expectations and produce your site in-house. Or perhaps you want to involve higher management in the process as you voice your concerns. Better to clear the air before the project starts than spend nine months waiting for design approvals, as happened in one case we know of.

It's a good idea to review the numbers on previous outsourced projects. Were projects delivered on time and on budget? Were they delivered on time but over budget? Or were they delinquent in both? As a general rule, a Web site requires far more cooperative work across a wider group of departments than do most outsourcing projects. Therefore, a poor outsourcing track record will only get much worse when it comes to creating a successful Web site.

- **What's the procedure?** Barriers to effective outsourcing are not usually as obvious as a single, easily identifiable barrier such as the marketing group or the MIS department. Often, the real barrier to outsourcing is whether your company is structured to work with outsourcers in an efficient, systematic manner. Does your company have a method, process, or procedure in place to make work among employees go smoothly? How about with outsiders? Are there established procedures in place to manage the approval and revisions processes? Web site development is an inexact science and an ongoing process. The more methods your company has set up to manage the process, the smoother the results will be.

For example, let's say your Web developer creates a working prototype of a database that will contain all of the products manufactured by your company. Do you have a procedure in place for working with your developer to test and review the prototype? Do you have a procedure in place for everyone in your company (or the appropriate department) to contribute to that discussion? Do you have a place where comments and feedback are collected so you can create a reference for your site's development, thereby making it possible for you to document, review, and evaluate the decisions that were made along the way?

- **How do you share?** It is not enough to develop procedures that work within your department. If you are considering outsourcing your Web site, you need to ask yourself how well various departments cooperate with each other.
  Your Web site will most likely involve at least the marketing team, the MIS department, the legal department, the sales force, and customer service. How do these groups normally work together? Does your company tend to suffer from department "territory-ialisis"? Many Web site developers complain that they ramp up to work with a client, only to have that client's Web site put on hold because the client's legal department doesn't have access to the Internet and can't check the site for trademark compliance.

  If your interdepartmental track record is weak or nonexistent, you could be headed for trouble. If the various groups in your company can't cooperate, chances are you'll run into problems trying to produce a Web site. There are many examples of interdepartmental conflicts so intense that it actually led to several departments developing their own version of the company Web site in competition with one another! It is hard enough to create a single attractive and compelling Web presence, let alone three or four sites.

## Understanding the Web Development Process

Once you have made the decision to outsource your Web site, you will want to spend some time gaining a basic understanding of the Web development process. Understanding this process will help you develop an insight into the kinds of issues for which you will be responsible and accountable as you start to shape your company's Web presence.

### The Process

The following sections provide a simple bird's-eye view of the basic Web development process. They address Web development, independent of outsourcing. In your situation, you may have one person on the team from your company and another person on the staff of the firm to which you have chosen to outsource your Web project. As you review this process, keep two points in mind. First, this process describes the general development of a Web site. The goals, functions, and various technologies that you attempt to implement on your site will more than likely change during development. Still, for our purposes—and for the purpose of laying the foundation for this book—this overview is helpful. Second, this process is not an entirely linear one. For example, this outline describes the programmer getting involved much later in the process than would actually occur. Ideally, the programmer would be directly involved in the determination of the site concept, goals, and functions.

**Developing the Concept.** During the development phase of the project, the client company and its outsourcer determine the goals of the site. For example, our goal is to reduce customer service expenses by creating a Web site that will deliver important information to our customers as they need it.

**Functions.** After goals are determined, the Web team translates the goals into specific site functions. Given the example of the customer service goal, this is translated into the following: In order to fulfill our goal, we will have the site perform the following functions: (1) We will provide our entire product manual on our Web site; (2) we will make our technical support database available to our customers; (3) we will make our latest technical notes available to our customers; (4) we will enable our customers to communicate with us and each other to discuss the issues involved with using our products most effectively; and (5) we will make available to our customers information on product upgrades, plug-ins, and the like.

**Who?** Who should be involved in the concept phase: the project manager of the site, the designer, the programmer, the editorial person and other key people interested in contributing to the development of the site, as well as the outsourcer.

**Technology Assessment.** After the goals and functions are set, the technical experts seek to determine the appropriate platform and technologies necessary to fulfill them. During this stage of the site development, the company drafts a technical specifications document that indicates the technology options and the benefits and disadvantages of each. This effort should be overseen by the MIS group at the company, with input and oversight from the company's executive management. Smart companies will make sure that this development doesn't occur in isolation and will have active participation from the project manager, the editorial group, and even the site designer. Why? The project manager needs to fully understand the basis for the technical decisions in order to better manage the project. The person responsible for the editorial aspect of the site will need to know how the technology functions so that he or she can provide information and instruction in the most effective manner possible. And the designer must understand how the technology operates so that he or she can best design the end-user experience.

**Site Architecture.** After the technology assessment, the project manager works in tandem with the designer, the editorial contributor, and the programmers to create, review, and approve the Web site architecture. During this process, decisions are made on how many main sections the site will contain, what they will be named, and how they will be structured.

**Design.** During the design, the look and feel of the site is created by a team that might include a creative director, a designer, and a team of graphic artists (which could include an illustrator or photographer if the creative direction calls for it).

**Editorial.** During this process, the structure of the site is translated into user-friendly language that will guide the Web surfer through the site. Editorial copy for every page on the site is written, edited, and proofread. One of the most overlooked aspects of Web site development is often the site's instructional copy. For example, a company might be sure to include a summary of the company's history or the new fall catalog line, but many Web sites will neglect to include a paragraph introducing the company's products and a few sentences that explain each of the types of products made by the company. A good example of instructional copy is, "Click here to browse our award-winning line of high-end stereo amplifiers." If you visit a Web site where the text is well written but the instructions are poorly constructed, there's a good chance that the site was based on a well-produced printed brochure written by an editorial professional, while an inexperienced programmer did little to adjust copy for an online environment.

**Production.** The production process involves preparing the graphics for viewing on the Web—a process generally recognized as *indexing*—and coding the final text with HTML. Production also includes the development of specialty multimedia aspects of a site such as animation, sound, or video and basic "soft" programming such as CGI scripting.

**Programming.** While all of the previously mentioned steps are in development, the programmer is working to implement the various technologies outlined earlier in the process. Programmers, or technical staff, are generally starting to split into two categories: *infrastructure specialists* and *delivery specialists.* Infrastructure specialists focus on the server side of the technology equation. They manage the connectivity aspects of the site as well as the server itself, including security, Web server software, backup and administration, and the like. Delivery specialists focus on making the site work. This might include writing custom Java applets or programming a database. Many individuals can master both types of technical work. You might find a programmer who can build, connect, and set up your server *and* install and program your SQL database, but recent trends in the industry suggest these types of experts are being swamped with so much information and so many technical options that some degree of specialization is necessary.

**Testing.** Web sites require testing, and lots of it. Some Web developers have suggested that as much as one third of a Web site's development cycle should be allocated to testing to ensure that the site works well on a wide variety of computer platforms and browsers. One thing is certain when it comes to testing: the more ambitious the site, both in function and technology, the greater the necessity to test, test, and test again.

**Marketing.** What good is a great product if no one knows about it? By the same token, what good is a Web site if no one visits it? The marketing phase of site development includes everything from properly registering the site with search engines to conducting a public relations campaign and advertising the site both in print and online.

**Maintenance, Management, and Ongoing Development.** After the site is completed, many Web developers say the real work begins. Not only does the site need to be maintained, but it must also be updated to include new content, new features and options, and new reasons to keep people coming back. New technologies should be integrated continually, whether they enhance the server, optimize database performance or just plain dazzle your intended audience. A solid site should be reinvented every six months to keep from projecting a stale, passé image.

### The Players: Defining Roles

The Web development process and the players involved vary greatly, depending on the scope of the site. For example, sites with specific marketing goals that don't involve commerce or other major evolving technologies will not involve sophisticated programming and intensive testing and debugging. Some team members come and go; however, the majority of Web site development efforts include basic team members such as designers, production artists, editorial experts, producers, and programmers. This section features two interviews from each of the major types of Web team member. The more you know about what each contributes to a Web project and the issues they face as professionals, the more insight you will have when it comes to buying Web services.

## Interview:
*The Designer*

**Lee Goodman**
*goodman@the-factory.com*

*Lee Goodman has worked in print design for Milton Glaser and Rolling Stone magazine. A designer by trade, he has worked as a creative director at Adam Curry's company THINK and as group creative director at Poppe Tyson. He is currently creative director of his own shop, The Factory.*

**Q: Suppose I run a business and I'm new to the Web development process. Can you explain the difference between a creative director, an art director, and a graphic designer?**

A: Sure. The creative directors are at the top. They coordinate with an account manager to develop a core strategy for your Web site project. The creative director will help you take your marketing goals and translate them into a strategy that can be understood by your customers.

The art directors execute the strategy. They will generate ideas that grow out of the strategy and develop rough concepts that will form the basis of the final Web site design.

**Q: Any thoughts on how that is done?**

A: Well, it varies depending on the type of art director. Some art directors are very hands-on. They will sit down and create some general page concepts in Quark or Photoshop. Others will pull together ideas and turn to a graphic designer and say, "Here are some images, colors, and general concepts that I think manifest the creative strategy. Create some designs that reflect this feel."

**Q: So the graphic designer...**

A: Well, they are the ones that work the typography. The good designers will go off on their own and come up with variations on the creative theme.

**Q: So in your mind, the designer should know HTML and such?**

A: I think a good designer should know HTML simply so that they have an understanding as to how their design would be built. The analogy to print here is a good one. You wouldn't expect a designer to run down to the print shop and fill cans of ink and start the press, but they have to know enough to know about issues such as trapping. The more the designer understands how a page is produced, the more successful the design will be.

**Q: Any final thoughts?**

A: If you are the client, the entire design chain is about developing and extending a strategy that makes sense. The creative director will develop your strategy, and every person that follows in the creative process should give that strategy greater definition.

**Michelle Szabo**
*michelle@3dimentia.com*

*Michelle Szabo is the co-author of the Web & New Media Pricing Guide, the first book on the market to open up the discussion about fair standards for pricing Web development services. She is the creative director of her own firm, New Media Designs, and a regular columnist for MacWeek magazine.*

**Q: Lee Goodman was talking about the creative process and the difference between the creative director, art director, and graphic designer. His insight was making reference to advertising companies and larger design firms. What role does a designer play on Web sites that fall into the small to medium-sized range?**

A: I think the designer is the person who works very closely with the client and the programmer to ensure that the Web site is pleasing to look at, easy to navigate, and functional for the end user. The designer really has to be the advocate for the end user.

**Q: So you believe in the concept of "designer as project manager"?**

A: Absolutely. Think about the fact that the designer must balance not only the needs of the client with the budget and time constraints, but also the limitations of the Web, its users, and the programming parameters. If that isn't project management...

**Q: So a client who works with you or other more specialized design firms can expect to work with the designer as the primary contact?**

A: It surely works out that way. Design is really about the communication process, and the designer has to safeguard their client's communication. I also find that the designer's role in working with clients has grown substantially to include that of educator. Because clients know it is the designer's role to make the Web site function in a visual sense, you find yourself on the phone a lot of the time answering a client's general questions about marketing, positioning, and the Web itself. As the medium grows, clients reach to the designer as a primary source of information on how to deal with it. A client can and should expect education to be a design service, and the designer must deliver on that service.

## Interview:
*The Production Artist*

**Lise Despres**
*ldespres@connix.com*

*Lise Despres is a designer in the Road Runner Group, a division of Time Warner.*

**Q: Can you define that all-elusive person: the production artist?**

A: Well, job descriptions vary from place to place. I would say that a production person is responsible for HTML and graphics. The production person would not have to worry about design, they would be more concerned with applying templates created by a designer.

**Q: What additional skills do you think a production artist should possess?**

A: I expect the production artist to be able to create animated GIFs and to create any of the other pieces that a Web site needs, such as AVIs, images, and so forth.

**Q: And when it comes to what we will loosely call the soft-core programming skills?**

A: I wouldn't expect a production person to have too much programming knowledge. This, of course, may show my bias, since I come at Web site development strictly from a design paradigm. But at Time Warner, we are increasingly seeing a need for a production person who can handle CGI scripts, JavaScripts, and so on.

**Kris Kiger**

*kkiger@earthpledge.org*

*Kris Kiger is an illustrator and creative director at Earth Pledge Foundation. She has designed both print and Web projects for a number of clients, including Microsoft Corporation, The Soros Foundation's Open Society Institute, Metropolis magazine, The Feminist Press, Aetna Health Care, and Joe Breeze Bicycles, among others.*

**Q: In traditional print design, there's a fairly clear distinction between the graphic artist and the production person. Do you find this is the same for Web site development?**

A: I think it depends on the size of the company that you are working for and the size of the client that you are working with. Larger Web developers tend to have a distinct design staff and a separate production staff. At the smaller shops, designers are, by necessity, forced to delve into hands-on production work.

**Q: As a classically trained designer, does it bother you to focus on the production aspect?**

A: No. To have the knowledge of how pages are produced is beneficial. Even though the technology changes very quickly, the more understanding you have about the process, the more ambitious your designs can be.

It also helps to know what you can't do—what the technological limitations are today. Some of the limitations of today will disappear tomorrow and create the potential for greater design flexibility. The closer you are to understanding those changes, the more you are able to incorporate them into your work.

**Q: As someone who does creative development and design as well as oversees the production process, what would you describe as the optimal Web production skill set?**

A: Above all else, I think a meticulous, organized, and patient manner—something that is often overlooked in favor of knowing the latest and greatest programs—is critical. In addition, the ability to think clearly and follow through are undervalued skills that are very important when it comes to the production aspect of a large Web project.

New software continues to be developed specifically for Web site production. Work-arounds using software initially intended primarily for print production give way to tools that offer a one-step solution. Less and less, the production person really has to know "what is going on under the hood."

**Q: Can you give me some examples?**

A: Claris Home Page and Go Live Cyber Studio made HTML easier through its graphical interface. Dreamweaver is tackling the very complex issues of creating DHTML pages. Fireworks is on its way to replacing the generation of vector-based graphics in Illustrator, preparing additional effects in Photoshop and indexing in them in Debabelizer. In one fell swoop, Macromedia's Fireworks has the potential to replace three different programs and a three-step process. Although I will always love Adobe and Equilibrium!

That said, a true production person has to be proactive in evolving their skills and embracing new technology as it becomes feasible.

**Q: So what does that mean for the production person of the future?**

A: Depending on where production people find themselves, they will have a range of options. In the larger Web shops, there might be enough large-scale production work that they will be called upon to crank out massive amounts of work of the same type.

In smaller Web shops, depending on their individual aptitude and client needs, they could, with training and direction, start to assume functions normally reserved for designers, or they could move toward the programming side of Web site development as they grow their skill set to include tasks such as more intricate JavaScripts, CGIs, database connectivity, and off-the-shelf commerce solutions.

## Interview:
*Editorial*

**Mat Zucker**

*www.matzucker.com*

*Mat Zucker is the creative director/copy at Manhattan Marketing Ensemble, an advertising and communications firm. He has written for and created several major commercial Web sites, including sites for Nabisco, Gorton's, and Ragú. He was formerly a copywriter at Foote, Cone & Belding.*

**Q: What is the state of the state when it comes to editorial in the Web world?**

A: For the most part, online editorial as it stands today is the poor cousin to traditional media. It lacks the professionalism and experience in the far more evolved print and broadcast media. Media companies, however, are becoming more sophisticated in the face of larger audiences online, so this will indeed change. As editors learn to successfully navigate the environment of new media, online magazines will give way to more compelling and interactive forms that actually leverage technology and meet the interests of emerging audiences.

**Q: So let's take a look at the role of the editorial assistant in this new and improved world.**

A: In traditional print media, the entry-level editorial assistant is one of the most overworked, underpaid positions in mass media. Online, the demands escalate, but so do the possibilities. Editorial staff find ways to deliver information in an environment that is far more responsive than today's publications. From managing threaded discussions, establishing live chats, and offering multidimensional (not to mention multimedia) support to any published piece, the new responsibilities for editorial staff are more complex, more demanding, and more creative than ever before.

Once online, editorial staff not only learn about writing but about interactive communication and technology in an environment that changes overnight. Not only is tomorrow's online editorial staff more skilled, they have more job opportunities ahead of them. In theory, if not in practice, online editorial staff don't have to follow the traditional track towards editor but could also seek opportunities in the producing or managing of sites and information services.

**Q: What does the online writer do that is unique?**

A: While commercial and journalistic editorial is very distinct in traditional media, on the Web the environment allows writers to be just writers. In traditional media, there were writers or journalists for publications and copywriters for advertising. Online, these jobs blend into one either can fulfill.

**Q: And, as you put it, what's a hard day in the life of an editor and the editorial staff like?**

A: While the editor begs for budget, assigns stories, edits bad grammar, and grapples with overdue invoices, the editorial staff scrambles to meet deadlines, respond to emails and an art department that created a cool graphic that has nothing to do with the op-ed piece going up later in the evening. Good online editorial staff will seek ways of leveraging the technology to support any word, sound, or effort achieved by its site. Whether it is simply furnishing a good hyperlink to elsewhere on the Web from a key word or loading a savvy midi file, there's plenty to do and just a few hours to do it. The good news, of course, is that one can change anything online at any time. Goodbye sense of completion.

**Q: Any final cautions?**

A: The Web allows the possibility of smaller sites to survive, but the smaller scale of these operations will place additional demands on staff, lacking much of a support infrastructure. People will have to do more, and there will be fewer of them available to do it.

**Deanna Vincent**

*Deanna@aol.com*

*Deanna Vincent is the VP/general manager of the Better Health Network, iVillage. Previously, she was the managing editor at New York CitySearch and an editor at Home Office Computing magazine.*

**Q: Mat Zucker talked a lot about traditional writing and what editorial staff members do on a Web site. Do you have any thoughts to add on the function of an editor? Does every site need one?**

A: Oh, yes, of course, and they should be well paid, too!

In general, it is the job of the editor to be critical—of the subject matter and of the writing itself. It's a "poking holes" job. It's an editor's responsibility to make sure all premises are substantiated, that the writing is clear enough to leave no questions in the reader's mind.

**Q: Larger sites that require more and frequently updated content tend to have an editor-in-chief. What does the editor-in-chief contribute?**

A: An editor-in-chief keeps an eye on the mix of articles and content for the site, sets the editorial tone of voice, manages the entire creative staff, approves all content ideas, oversees design and production, is usually the outside spokesperson for the site content, and often sets up partnerships with outside entities. The editor-in-chief also has input into the site's public relations and marketing (such as press releases and marketing campaigns).

## Interview:
*Producer and Project Management*

**Holly Coleman**
*www.organic.com*

*Holly Coleman is a producer at Organic, one of the oldest and best-known Web development shops in San Francisco's famed Multimedia Gulch.*

**Q: At Organic, a producer has a wide range of duties. What would be a typical job description for a producer?**

A: First, mentor the production coordinators by teaching them budgeting skills and scheduling skills as well as assisting in the problem-solving process.

Second, prepare and maintain production schedules and budgets, including tracking the status of all team members and working with Organic's client services group to constantly maintain client expectations.

Third, coordinate project specifications such as budgets, time frames, technology development, and our company's quality assurance plan.

Fourth, develop and maintain the client's budget. This includes updating all of the team members on the status of the budget at appropriate times during the project.

Finally, a great deal of coordination among the various aspects of site development.

**Q: Can you define the coordination aspect in more detail?**

A: Sure. There's a great deal of coordination with the site architect to coordinate the production and process involved in developing a Web site. A producer also has to have a great deal of coordination with the creative services group for identifying and reserving the resources necessary to produce the project. The producer also creates, distributes, and maintains a list of deliverables from the client to the team and from the team to the client. Coordination also includes internal and external site reviews, tracking internal and external approvals, and final sign-off on the project.

**Q: So what are the most important skills that a successful producer should have?**

A: Basically, the ability to see the big picture and not get lost in the details, and the ability to guide a project and make decisions on what is best based on the desired final outcome.

**Paul Marcum**

*pmarcum@modemmedia.com*

*Paul Marcum is a senior producer at Modem Media, a major East Coast Web site development and marketing firm with offices in Connecticut and New York City. Modem Media clients include AT&T, Delta, JC Penney, Lucent, Citibank, and Compaq Computer, among others.*

**Q: For the benefit of a client that might be seeking to better understand the roles of a senior producer, associate producer, and producer working on their Web site, can you explain the difference?**

A: Sure. Let's start with the associate producer. An associate producer works with the production coordinator to address the issue of resource allocation across the creative and production teams.

An associate producer should have the knowledge necessary to make a Web site work, although that knowledge varies. The associate producer works in conjunction with the producer or senior producer but generally has no client contact. Primary responsibilities include scheduling the creative, technical, and production resources on a Web project. The associate producer should also focus on the site's functionality and, although they don't have key client contact, associate producers generally take the lead on making the project happen once the project is sold.

**Q: And the producer?**

A: The producer generally has a great deal of client contact and translates the client's needs to the director of production and or the senior producer.

**Q: And the senior producer?**

A: At Modem, a senior producer is an individual who has a great deal of experience producing Web sites, knows several of the aspects necessary to develop a site, and has key project management responsibilities. The senior producer will run the production process and manage the client relationship.

**Q: How does that translate on a daily basis?**

A: On a daily basis, a senior producer leads the production process and can also spend a fair amount of time on the company's operations. Overall, though, the senior producer leads the production process and manages the production staff on a project.

**Q: How technical is a senior producer?**

A: Well, at Modem the producers do not necessarily have the most technical knowledge. We have a rather robust technical group. Our producers know technology but are more involved in scheduling, budgeting, allocating resources, and translating the vision of the site from the creative to the technical.

## Interview: *Programmer*

**Andrew Wint**
*wint@d-m-d.com*

*Andy Wint is a partner in Digital Media Designs, a Silicon Alley start-up focusing on unique Web solutions for a wide range of clients, including Debeers Jewelry, The Emek Group, The Financial Times, Con Edison, Live On-Line, and the Intel Music Festival, among others.*

**Q: How do you define the role of the Web programmer?**

A: Quite simply, the Web programmer makes a site work. People no longer want to use the Web to look at pictures and read text. They want interactivity. They want to see their bank account online, conduct transactions, and interact. The programmer's role is to make that happen.

**Q: If you could define a core set of skills that a good Web programmer should have, what would they be?**

A: Certainly, a programmer should be well versed in CGI and Perl, although in the case of CGI, it's becoming a bit passé.

I also believe that a good Web programmer should have a working knowledge of Unix and NT, and a solid knowledge of linking databases to Web sites is critical.

Knowledge of JavaScript is also important, as is Lingo if your site is going to feature Shockwave. And then there's Java.

**Q: How much knowledge of Java should a good programmer have?**

A: Basic. A good Web programmer should know how to compile the language and make edits. But if you are interested in developing a full-scale Java applet, the Web programmer might find that they need a Java specialist.

**Q: What about HTML?**

A: HTML is a no-brainer. I never consider it because it is so simple and it is a given.

**Q: What's the worst part about being a programmer?**

A: Without question, making Web sites work in every direction—across platforms, across different browsers, and, of course backwards for older machines and browsers.

The backend side of Web development is also becoming much harder. That is the area where programmers will be the most challenged in the future.

**Nicolas Cianca**
*ncianca@lightbulb.com*

*Nicolas Cianca is the owner of the Silicon-Alley-based Lightbulb Factory Inc., a developer of databases and Web sites with clients in finance, banking, entertainment, retail, defense, space, and government.*

**Q: What is the role of a programmer on a Web site?**

A: Certainly less than in the past. Various technologies have made it much easier for skilled Web developers that are not programmers in a traditional sense to create interactive Web sites that are fairly complex.

**Q: For example?**

A: Take a programming tool like Tango (made by the Everyware Development Corporation). Three years ago, to create an interactive database, you had to write your code in C. Tango greatly simplifies a very complex process and makes it possible for nonprogrammers to do things normally done by programmers. Other tools such as Microsoft InterDev have the potential to make nonprogrammers [into] programmers when it comes to the Web. Even basic programs such as Claris Home Page are now integrating a variety of CGI functions into the application, with simple and successful results.

**Q: Where does that leave the Web programmer?**

A: I think you will see more and more programmers involved in the creation of the tools themselves, or taking the software tools and creating mini-applications that people will download, swap the content and other graphics, and use on their site. Microsoft's ActiveX is an example of a technology that has enabled developers to create precanned components that people can use in various capacities on their Web site.

Programmers won't go entirely away, though. There are some very complicated intranet projects that need trained programmers to make them work. Also, the further integration of databases to the Web and things like hard-core uses of Java require experienced programmers to make them work.

**Q: What skills should programmers have?**

A: A Web programmer, which is a different person than a traditional programmer, should have knowledge of Java and JavaScript and be able to implement sophisticated solutions on the server side. We've all seen what Java can do, and now Java is moving to the back end, which is really the domain of the traditional programmer.

It's also important to be able to integrate databases. The number-one requirement in most businesses is maintaining data. Normally you do that in a database, and normally the person who makes that happen is a programmer.

**Q: What can be outsourced?**

A: The decision to host a Web site in or out of house need not be a total one. Some companies choose to identify their strengths and seek an outside Web developer to help them fill in the gap by providing functions and skills that they do not have the capacity to deliver.

Subcontracting certain skills may make sense for many companies and it may, if properly managed, result in reduced Web site development expenses.

Key areas that a company may feel inclined to outsource include the following:

- **Connectivity, server maintenance, and site hosting.** Many companies do not have in place the high-speed communications lines, such as a T1, that are necessary in order to deliver optimum Web site performance. If high-speed lines are in place, the company may have reserved available bandwidth to meet its other telecommunications needs. In addition, maintaining a Web server requires a unique skill that in-house MIS staff may not be prepared to administer or may not have the time to manage given its current workload. If that's the case, hosting the site out of house could make solid business sense. The benefits of server hosting and maintenance could also extend to outsourcing your site's security needs. Again, managing Web site security requires a specific expertise and one that your technical staff may not have the knowledge or capacity to deliver.

- **Programming.** Programming is one of the most significant aspects of site development that, due to its unique nature, is often subcontracted to outside vendors. Programming for the Web often requires the use of knowledge and skills that change quickly—HTML to CGI to JavaScript to Java to ActiveX. Many companies cannot afford the luxury of waiting for their staff to get up to speed on a particular technology, only to have it replaced by an entirely new skill requirement. A survey from Forrester Research found that outsourcing programming was the number-one aspect of outsourced Web site development as a means to help companies take advantage of new technologies as they become available. In the words of one corporate MIS manager who did not want to be identified, "We outsource programming so that our developer is on the bleeding edge of this technology...not us."

- **Site development.** In the Forrester Research survey, site design was tied for first place among Web site functions outsourced. Companies feel confident in outsourcing concept development, site architecture, design, and content because they may not have staff to handle such tasks or they do not have the expertise required to do so. For example, the company may have a great designer in house who is fully capable of producing outstanding marketing materials, but it is a big leap to indexing graphics and preparing designs for a Web site that the designer may not have the time to make. "Been there, done that," said one Web master at an insurance company. "Don't quote me by name, but feel free to make the point that some great print designers just do not have the aptitude to create for the Web."

  In the case of concept development and site architecture, companies may feel inclined to seek an outside opinion as a means of achieving better results. "We obviously know that our Web site should have our company catalog," said the Web master at a large retail firm. "We're not that stupid. But we looked to an outside Web developer for help because we wanted someone outside our company to take a fresh look at who we are and what we should do on the Web."

- **Site maintenance and management.** Many companies are ill prepared for the ongoing work involved in maintaining a successful Web presence. Those companies that marvel at their accomplishment of producing their first Web site wane when they quickly realize the time, effort, and capital investment required to maintain their sites.

  One well-known financial institution found that the burden of updating press releases and updating staff promotions and deletions in its Web-based company directory was enough to send the company looking for an outside firm to manage its Web site, even though it had produced the site entirely in-house. Many Web developers themselves struggle with helping their clients keep their sites updated. They can teach the client to update the sites themselves, but that is something clients may not have the staff to do. Or the developer can handle the maintenance and updating in-house. The problem is that maintenance can be a low-margin business and not worth the effort for many development firms that need to thrive on high-margin initial site development costs. The most likely scenarios for the future include higher fees for site maintenance, packaged deals in which the developer bundles site maintenance and updating with a suite of other services, or the development of new Web development firms specializing in keeping sites fresh and working with clients to make changes.

## Interview:
*Outsourcing*

**Geri Spieler, Research Analyst at Gartner Group**
*geri.spieler@gartner.com*

*Geri Spieler is a research analyst in the Electronic Commerce and Extranet Applications Service at Gartner Group. Her research focus is on electronic catalog applications and e-bill presentment in addition to electronic data interchange, World Wide Web/intranet services, and overall electronic commerce strategies. Prior to joining Gartner Group in 1996, she was the senior editor of Electronic Commerce News.*

**Q: Any overall thoughts on outsourcing when it comes to the Web?**

A: At Gartner, we definitely see outsourcing Web services as a growing trend. Companies want to avoid the overhead of doing their Web development in-house.

Whether they run small or large businesses, people are starting to clearly see they can't do everything in-house.

**Q: Do you have any numbers on how much outsourcing is taking place?**

A: Well, it is difficult to tell. Our assumption is that, for 1997, electronic marketplace managers outsourced 7% of a $2 billion to $3 billion marketplace. We see that percentage growing to 24% of a $5 billion to $6 billion market. That includes sales, marketing, service, bidding, sourcing, and value-added Internet services—anything contracted out of the office related to Internet needs.

**Q: What does Gartner see as the main reason to outsource?**

A: Obviously, many businesses do not have a large infrastructure for IT services. They look at the real numbers, see how much money it costs to hire Web people, factor in benefits, and make the decision to hire that function out.

There's also the concern that the Web is a 24 × 7 responsibility. When you consider that and you look at the numbers as to what it takes to have the work done on the outside, outsourcing looks favorable. Of course, no two businesses are the same, but that is the general trend we are seeing.

**Q: What are some of the factors you see that companies are finding important to consider?**

A: We are seeing that large businesses believe outsourcing their Web site makes sense. Medium-sized and small companies are also coming to the same conclusion.

For the business, you have to look at your infrastructure and ask yourself: What business are you in? If you have a one-person IT department, you need to ask yourself honestly whether or not that person can develop and maintain a site. Do you have the capacity to handle all of the functions that it takes to make a Web site happen? My guess is, probably not.

So the smart companies start to look at the process of building a site and evaluate what they can do and what they can't do. They think about design and the prospect of hiring a design firm. They look at the cost to host the site and the cost to have an outsider host the site. They think about the cost to have someone maintain the site in-house versus the cost to have someone maintain the site out of house. They evaluate each piece in the process and make a decision based on the numbers.

**Q: As each component of Web development is addressed, what do you think a company should be thinking about in its evaluation?**

A: No question—who is responsible! This is not a technology decision; this is a business decision. Technology people will evaluate each step in the process as if it is a technology decision. But it is not. It is really a decision about the future business direction of a company. We feel that it is a business decision implemented by technology. Everyone should have something to say, everyone should have something to add, but there is a bottom-line decision to be made, and it should be made by the business for the business. Above all else, the Web is a business issue, not a technology issue, although the technology aspect is very, very important.

**Q: You have had some research analysis on the cost of outsourcing a large-scale site. Can you share some of that data?**

A: Sure. We estimate that a fully transaction-enabled Web site, which gives the end user the ability to make a purchase and have that purchase delivered in an automated process, will cost a large business a million to a million and a half dollars. That includes large-scale transaction software, a large-scale database of products, catalog fulfillment, etc. I can also say we believe that our estimate is a conservative one.

**Q: Any final key issues a company should consider?**

A: First, decide what you are going to build and buy the tools and the technology to make it happen. In doing so, look at vendors that have solutions that are a success on the Web already.

Second, carefully analyze the build versus buy. Off-the-shelf technology can be much more effective.

Third, figure out what you are going to do, what you are going to outsource, and where the line is drawn.

The scariest thing about outsourcing a Web site is where we are in the development of this industry. There's a lack of stability and history. For awhile everything will continue to be experimental. People want the best solution, but we don't know what the best solution is just yet.

All that said, Gartner is high on outsourcing Web services.

**Vlad Edelman**
*vedelman@cbs.com*

*Vlad Edelman is a senior producer at CBS New Media. He runs the CBS mini-Web site unit, which builds Web sites for CBS's flagship shows such as Brooklyn South, CBS News, David Letterman, Chicago Hope, and others.*

**Q: What's your position on outsourcing Web services from the perspective of a company that has a huge presence on the Net?**

A: I tend not to have a blanket position in favor of or against outsourcing. I believe in outsourcing only when there is an overriding reason.

**Q: Such as?**

A: Well, if we do not have enough people in-house to accomplish a certain task. Our people may be busy, we may have multiple, simultaneous deadlines, or we may need to move quickly on a project.

I also believe in outsourcing when it is less expensive to use an outside developer than it is to add staff or tap existing staff from other departments within CBS.

There are, quite frankly, times when outside people are quicker and better at specific tasks we need to complete.

**Q: For example?**

A: Well, the creation of Java applets for one thing, and also specific Shockwave projects.

Overall, our biggest outsourcing need is programming. One thing we have learned is that all programming is definitely not the same.

**Q: What do you mean by that?**

A: There is a varying quality of programming skills among Web developers. If an outside Web developer steps into a situation regarding a database, for example, they might not necessarily be familiar with all of the intricacies involved in working with our specific technology, and within our specific agenda. That lack of familiarity can make our costs soar.

**Q: How do you guard against that?**

A: For the most part, we only outsource specific tasks that have defined specifications for those companies that understand the technology and have a history of implementing specifically what we need. That way, we only get what we want and not more than we need.

## A Look at Different Web Teams

Each developer has a unique approach to the development process. This section takes a look at five successful individual Web developers and outlines the type of approach each takes in structuring its Web team.

## Organic

*www.organic.com*

Organic was one of the first large-scale Web development shops in San Francisco. The company now also has offices in New York City. Organic is known for its quality designs and technical expertise.

A typical team at Organic, according to Cimeron Dunlap, the firm's director of marketing communications, includes the following team members. The division of labor ensures that an expert is tackling each aspect of Web development for a client.

**Account manager:** Responsible for client contact, making sure that the client objective is reflected in the final Web site, and translating the business objective into a final solution.

**Producer:** Pulls together the assets—photographs, logos, illustrations, video, editorial—needed for the Web site and sets the budgets and the project schedule. The producer is the person responsible for making sure the Web site works on all platforms, and he keeps the account manager briefed on a daily basis as to the site's progress.

**Strategic planner:** Communicates directly with the client and has a deep understanding of the Web, the objective, and the audience for the project. Researches audience demographics and is responsible for setting the overall strategy for the Web site and the site's blueprint.

**Creative lead:** Responsible for the site's information architecture. Oversees the creation of assets as needed. Includes working with illustrators, designers, and user interface specialists at the company to create a successful, user-friendly product.

**Lead software engineer:** Responsible for engineering specific technology solutions such as electronic commerce, backend system development, addressing legacy integration, and database development on projects where it is appropriate.

**Hosting engineer:** Addresses server needs and technology infrastructure. Organic estimates that 20% of the Web sites they develop require hosting at Organic. In fact, Organic was the first company to offer extensive site-hosting capabilities.

### Studio Archetype

*www.studioarchetype.com*

With Organic, Vivid Studios, and CKS, Studio Archetype leads the elite West Coast Web development community. Eric Wilson, the firm's senior vice president, defines the company as a creative integration firm. "We don't look at ourselves as a company that creates ads or does systems integration. We solve problems for our clients from a user-centered perspective, whether the end product is interactive, print, or packaging. The company is quickly emerging as one of the premium Web developers in the country with clients such as IBM and Nintendo," according to Wilson.

A project team at Studio Archetype is co-led by a creative integrator and a creative director. The company doesn't believe in account executives, and thus the creative integrator works with the client as well as leads the strategy for a given project and handles project management as well. The creative director leads the various teams at Studio Archetype, which can include one or all of the following, depending on the demands of the project:

**Content developer/Content strategist**, which is supported by writers and editorial staff as needed, is responsible for all of the editorial for a particular Web site.

**The design group**, which includes information design, print design, human interaction design, interaction, and visual design capabilities. This group also includes the company's user research group, which is dedicated to studying how people interact with design and print and interactive technology.

**Web development group**, which includes technology development specifically for the Web as well as various programmers.

**Project management** for print and interactive projects.

If the Studio Archetype process seems intricate, it is. But then again, not just any company can work with Nintendo to design everything from product packaging all the way to the Web.

**FMA**

*www.fmaonline.com*

FMA is a high-end digital media production company that includes among its clients the Ad Club of New York, Apple Computer, and IBM.

"We're definitely a boutique. We focus on implementing specific technologies, and we believe that smaller teams for what we do are definitely better," says Rich Shupe, a partner in the company. "We try not to have one person responsible for too many things. We focus on quality. For example, if we bring in an editor, they are not writing copy as well. Our experience is that you can't write and edit. You need the best possible person to focus on taking care of one specific task."

The company focuses on a three-person team, which it believes is more efficient in producing a Web project. The team is then overseen by a project producer who handles client relations, project management, budgets, deadlines, and so on. The three-person teams includes:

**Graphic designer or artist** who creates assets.

**HTML coder or a programmer** if the project calls for it.

**Media specialist** to tackle video or audio functions.

**Rare Medium**

*www.raremedium.com*

Rare Medium has established a huge presence in the New York City Web development community with its award-winning Web site for Betty Crocker. According to Devon Brady, the company's director of marketing, Rare Medium is a full-service interactive agency offering integrated solutions to a client's digital communication needs. Rare Medium has offices in New York, Los Angeles, San Francisco, and Detroit.

A typical Rare team includes:

**Account manager:** The primary client contact who oversees all production, deadlines, and budget.

**Executive producer:** Oversees the production of site projects and works with the line producer to tie together the creative and marketing goals of the client to the final product development outcome.

**Marketing specialist:** Works with the client's existing marketing or public relations group to extend the company's strategies to the Web. Serves as a complement to the client's real-world marketing strategies. Also conducts focus groups, researches, and develops Web marketing and promotion strategies.

**Technical lead:** Handles in-house technical development, including database development. Also tackles a client's simple technology challenges such as browser usage, download speeds, quality assurance, testing, and browser compatibility. Oversees the client's backend site needs.

**Creative director:** An artist, illustrator, or other print and interactive specialist who develops the design, look, and feel for a particular project.

### Hewson Group

*www.hewsongroup.com*

The Hewson Group is a business-to-business communication firm that works with professional services firms, law firms, financial service institutions, and other Fortune 1000 companies. The company develops comprehensive communication programs, visual identities, annual reports, marketing brochures, recruiting brochures, and advanced electronic media on CD-ROM and the Web. Due to the prestigious nature of many of the Group's clients, the emphasis is on applying fundamental principles of business-to-business communication to the evolving medium of the Web.

The company team is very client-communication focused and is led by the firm's founder, Jane Hewson, who is responsible for setting each project's strategic and creative direction. Her 20-person staff of creative and production artists has been working with high-end corporate clients for more than 18 years.

Next in line is the company's director of new media, Philippe Stessel, a veteran of several well-known new-media developers, including the Voyager Company. As director of New Media, Stessel oversees every Web site's marketing and technology development as well as directing the production process, project development, and client management. "Our absolute focus is on client satisfaction and service at the highest level," he says.

Stessel works with one of the company's several project directors, each of whom are responsible for managing client relations, ensuring that the clients needs are met at every step in the Web development process. The project director is also the key liaison between the creative and production personnel and the client.

In addition to a project director, each client is assigned an art director who works with Hewson and Stessel to realize the visual concept and establish an information architecture that reflects the Hewson Group's knowledge of each client's marketing needs.

A graphic designer works with the art director to translate the visual concept into Web designs that safeguard each client's communication projects. Various production staff are responsible for maintaining the integrity and functionality of the final Web site and work closely with the programming and technical staff to make sure that the technology works.

## Summary

This chapter provided an overview to outsourcing and the Web development process. At this point, you should have insight into the pros and cons of working with an outsourcer, and you should also be able to develop a budget that should shed some light on whether or not outsourcing your Web site is cost-effective. Now that you have been able to determine whether or not your company is the outsourcing type and you have a real-world understanding of how developers approach Web projects, you are ready to proceed with the next step outlined in Chapter 2: Determining Your Goals, Developing Your Concept, and Drafting a Request for Proposal (RFP).

### Checklist

- ☐ Review the arguments in favor of outsourcing that are relevant to your company. Are there other pro-outsourcing arguments relevant to your company that you believe should be considered?
- ☐ Review the arguments against outsourcing that are relevant to your company. Are there other arguments against outsourcing relevant to your company that you believe should be considered?
- ☐ Prepare a budget for your Web site. Compare that budget to several bids from outside Web developers.
- ☐ Evaluate your company's outsourcing ability. Prepare a summary of past projects and review each in greater detail to determine the success of the project.
- ☐ Familiarize yourself with the Web development process and get to know each of the key team members.
- ☐ Assess what part of your site your company can contribute to in-house. Determine what your companies strengths and weaknesses are.

chapter

2

# Determining Your Goals, Developing a Concept, and Drafting a Request for Proposal

**Sarah Cooper**
**vivid studios**
*scoop@vivid.com*

### About This Chapter

This chapter takes you step by step through the important initial phases of determining your project goals and creating an effective Request for Proposal (RFP). You'll also learn how to maximize your company's expertise in a way that will enable you to work effectively with your Web developer, create a project scope that will highlight the capabilities of your company and your project team, define the evaluation process that best suits the strengths and culture of your company, create an effective RFP, and set up your project for success from day one.

### About the Author

Sarah Cooper is the director of business development at vivid studios, a leading Internet architect based in San Francisco's famed Multimedia Gulch. Sarah's responsibilities include overseeing vivid's team of executive producers and account managers, as well as the development of what vivid calls "new processes and metrics in the areas of sales and project priorities, profitability, client management, employee training, and management effectiveness."

## The Evaluation Process

**Your mission is to choose the best agency for your project, position your project for success, and prepare your company and stakeholders—all while doing as little work as possible. This should be the approach you take throughout the evaluation process. The two main reasons to begin this way are both rooted in project quality, as opposed to laziness.**

First, sticking to what you know will ensure that you bring only the strengths and expertise of your company to the project. You'll avoid the wasted time and frustration of trying to guess at building the project definition in areas in which you have no history. For example, if you're not experienced with the methods and timetables of a Web development project, you do not need to specify project milestones. You can simply define your business objectives, some key required features, a preferred launch date, and request that your agency set appropriate milestone dates within its proposal. Similarly, if you are not an Information Designer, you should not attempt to lay out page contents and site navigation. A much more valuable task would be to include the types and samples of information that must be represented in the site and ask the agency to outline its information process.

Second, allowing the agency to do more ensures that your project requirements are well-defined. This will motivate a high-quality agency response and make your decision process a straightforward, disciplined one that will lead to an innovative and well-planned project. Experienced Internet agencies will appreciate a clear communication of your goals. They'll be motivated by a Request for Proposal (RFP) that contains realistic business targets that reflect an experienced stakeholder team as opposed to an RFP that attempts to specify outcomes that aren't feasible or simply reflect a lack of experience.

In the following sections, you'll see how to create a project definition based on your own expertise and the strengths of your organization.

### Choose Your Own Criteria

This section outlines several approaches you can use to evaluate and choose your project agency. Keep in mind there is no set rule book for the process and you should feel free to mix and match criteria to create the best process for your decision criteria and company culture. Be careful not to require an absurd obstacle course of RFIs, meetings, design treatments, creative and technical briefs, whitepapers, proposals, and formal presentations—this sometimes suggests there is internal confusion about the decision criteria. (Also remember it is not fair to request that an agency demonstrate so many capabilities that it practically delivers a complete Web site, or at least final plans for implementing a complete site, to you during the evaluation process.) Determine whether your company will respond best to a thorough proposal or a well-rehearsed presentation. Asking an agency to provide both for a project that is less than $500K is inappropriate and inconsiderate of its resources. If you will require a formal presentation to a variety of stakeholders, simplify the proposal structure and specify exactly what you need. If your company will need to review complete proposals (including a project strategy, creative brief, architectural schematic, ecommerce options, case studies, project activities, deliverables, schedule, and budget), requiring a formal presentation that needs separate materials, planning, and rehearsal is a bit over the top. If you want to complement the complete proposal with a follow-on meeting, specify that the purpose of the meeting is to discuss project approach and proposal, and not to receive a formal agency pitch.

The following section summarizes several different approaches you can use as your process for agency evaluation.

**Request for Information (RFI).** This process enables you to hire an agency to serve as an overall strategy and development partner in the long term, as opposed to delivering a specific project. It allows you to assess its capabilities and cultural fit in advance of having to define a specific project scope in detail. Once you have selected an agency, it will assist you in defining the project approach, budget and schedule, as well as implement a series of strategic projects. The RFI approach allows for the least amount of definition on your part, although you may need to spend time coaching each agency on its presentation since you will not be issuing a documented RFP.

Here are the steps involved in using an RFI approach:

1. ***Phone call***

   This is your "heads-up" flag to tell the agency that an RFI will be arriving within a few days. In this conversation, you'll want to explain why you have chosen an RFI approach, give some background on your company and business objectives, and lay out the timetable of your evaluation process.

2. ***RFI***
   The request for information will ask questions about the agency's process and development philosophy, capabilities, and portfolio, without providing specific project details. In most cases, the RFI responses will be submitted and reviewed by your team before the Discovery Meetings take place. Your agency list may be narrowed down based on responses.

3. ***Discovery Meeting***
   Several of your team members meet with key talent from the agency to discuss your company and current broad objectives. You can also request that the agency provides a company backgrounder, case studies of relevant projects, and an overview of its development process.

4. ***Define a short list of three agencies***
   Communicate your decision to each agency with a phone call. It helps to be as specific as possible on your assessment of their strengths and weaknesses within the perspective of your company's needs. For the agencies on your "short list," identify your goals for the next presentation, outline the individual interests of stakeholders who will attend, and provide as much coaching as possible to motivate the best presentation from each agency.

5. ***Agency formal presentation***
   Presentation to your management with a specific agenda defined with the agency in advance.

**Venture Launch.** This scenario is for the new company or new division launching a Web-based business. You are looking for a long-term partner who has a disciplined development process and record of ontime launches. You want a company you can count on to help with the myriad of variables surrounding your launch, such as your promotional plan, recruiting targets, content partnerships, and hosting relationships. You should aim to hire an agency that has expertise in online business strategy. It should offer feedback or formal consulting on your revenue model, partnership strategy, content fees, subscription model, and advertising partners. Finally, you need an agency that can provide in-depth research, analysis, innovation, and a release plan that will be appropriate for your target audience and business goals.

Here are the steps involved in the venture launch:

1. ***Phone call***
   This is your "heads-up" flag to tell the agency that an RFP will be arriving within a few days. This helps the agency's planning immensely and ensures that your document is delivered to a captive audience, already invested in your project.

2. ***Issue RFP or explanatory document***
   You can choose to issue a formal RFP or simply provide documentation of your business goals, product strategy, audience profile, and target launch schedule. If you choose not to create an RFP, you are challenging your agencies to assess your needs and "propose" what they will include in the proposal. This is fine, provided you are in agreement with your stakeholders on this approach and prepared to provide a great deal of feedback on interim recommendations made by the agency and engage in exploratory dialogues with the agency contacts. You cannot expect the agencies to put a great deal of time into their proposals if they do not receive specific feedback on their suggestions. If there is general agreement on feature set, release plan, budget, and schedule early on, you can then both decide that you are sufficiently aligned and the agency can commit to build a proposal around the agreed upon scope and schedule.

**No Request for Proposal (No-RFP).** The no-RFP approach can be a lifesaver for new companies. It allows them to engage in explorations and make a variety of judgments on each agency prior to receiving the proposal. These judgments could include whether the agency seems to understand their business, has proposed innovative features, speaks of a disciplined development process, and has provided appropriate education on the budget and schedule. Of all the possible approaches, this one allows you to engage in a deep working relationship with the agencies and motivates a final decision informed by working style, cultural fit, and general commitment to your business.

Here are the steps involved in the No Request for Proposal approach:

1. ***Phone call***
   Contact each agency to verify that your document was received and begin discussions on the project. Set the date for the Discovery Meeting and agree on who will attend, the meeting, objectives, and the agenda. The agency may ask you to complete a questionnaire that provides further details and helps it prepare for the meeting.

2. ***Discovery Meeting***
   This is the same format as with the other approaches; however, if you haven't issued an RFP, you should provide the agencies with enough time to research your market and brainstorm potential features they will want to discuss in the meeting.

3. ***Feature set draft and approval***
   Following the Discovery Meeting, the agency will finalize its proposal feature set and provide it to you for approval. The purpose of this step is to agree on a scope. The scope provides the foundation of the agency's plan, schedule, and budget.

4. ***Budget and schedule estimate***
   Prior to beginning the proposal, you will need to come to a general agreement with your agency on a budget and schedule. This avoids an agency making a large investment in a proposal that may pertain to a budget or launch time that you cannot accept. If you have not issued an RFP and have not designed the feature set yourself, you must come to an agreement on scope prior to finalizing a proposal format and due date.

5. ***Formal proposal***
   This document can take a variety of forms. You can either specify exactly what you would like covered or you can allow each agency to recommend a proposal structure and contents based on the areas already discussed. Be sure that you have clearly identified the proposal contents that are absolutely necessary for your decision and that you provide the agency with sufficient time to create a proposal. A complete proposal takes one to three weeks, depending on what has taken place between you and the agency. For example, if all of the meetings and agreements just discussed have taken place, you can request a proposal in one week. The entire process may take three to four weeks.

**Single Request for Proposal (RFP).** This process pertains to a single-release project with a feature set, budget estimate, and schedule target defined by you. You must issue an RFP for this approach, but you can refine your scope and budget following agency meetings and subsequent internal dialogues.

Here are the steps involved in the Single Request for Proposal phase:

1. ***Phone call***
   Since you are choosing an agency for only one project and not a lengthy, highly invested relationship, you may want to proceed the RFP with a "heads-up" phone call to assist the agency in planning. You simply want to communicate that the RFP is coming, the business objectives of the project, a little about your company, and the response timetable so that the agency can begin reserving time with individuals who will form the response.
2. ***Issue an RFP***
3. ***Discovery Meeting***
   This is your opportunity to meet the team and provide extensive detail on the project.
4. ***Budget and schedule estimate***
   Upon receiving this estimate from the agency, you'll need to either agree with it entirely or explain the variation to which you can commit. This assurance will be necessary prior to the agency committing to build a complete proposal for you.
5. ***Formal proposal***

### Customize the Project Approach: Designing for Your Company Expertise and Culture

Your next task is to decide how to customize your project for the strengths of your particular organization and the personalities and history of its unique culture. Not only is this is a luxury, it's a requirement for success.

Billions of projects have caused unnecessary frustration and taken more time and money than they should have because the client has come to the table with a secondary agenda, usually to hide some organizational weakness or lack of expertise on the part of a team member. This is common and understandable from a political standpoint; however, it greatly weakens Web initiatives and is unnecessary in an industry in which the speed of innovation means that most team members will be required to work in new arenas. Since you are the client and you're the one hiring the Internet agency, you must be very clear on your current Web knowledge, the internal resources you can and cannot depend on, and your assessment of the organization's capabilities in supporting this project. These elements are a reality of each and every project, and spelling them out up front will allow you to specifically ask your agency to accommodate them.

If specific team members or stakeholders will need help understanding Internet strategies or the basic process of Web development, ask your agency candidates for suggestions on the best books that serve as primers. Ask them if they have whitepapers that provide an introduction to specific internet topics and how they have helped new teams with past projects. Indicate that you would like some level of education to be included, either in the Discovery Meeting or as part of a formal presentation. For example, at vivid, we provide prospective clients with a variety of materials to educate them on Internet technology and design issues. These include primers on the development process, whitepapers on interaction design and usability testing, and even a glossary on commonly used terms in the Web industry.

You should also review the background, expertise level, and particular needs of each of your team members and be candid with your candidate agencies. Providing them with this information will assist the agencies in choosing the right style and level of education to use with you and help them find the right approach for the entire project. Don't hesitate to spell out where they will need to take special care in assisting you to educate a sponsor or address the concerns of a technical member.

In addition to positioning the requirements of each team member, you'll want to share insights into your company's cultural approach to large projects. When you meet with each agency, describe elements of past successful projects and lay the groundwork for criteria of the current project management process. This can include daily status reports, lots of visual examples, or the ability to present to large groups of stakeholders at regular project milestones. Also outline common elements of unsuccessful projects; you will certainly have examples of other vendors who were a poor fit, did not respond appropriately to cultural signals, or perhaps did not ask insistently enough for information that was required for the project to move forward. Sharing these stories, whether they are a specific list of dos and don'ts or informal insights shared in your meetings, will not only lead your agency to appropriately customize their project approach, their responses will also provide you with another angle from which to judge your candidates.

### Building Your Project Strategy

This section describes each major area that you will need to explore as part of your project preparation.

The purpose of this initial exploration is to determine which areas you will define and which areas you will have an agency address for you. At vivid, we frequently see projects falter or lose valuable opportunities for innovation because clients feel an obligation to figure it all out themselves. Clients sometimes assume they must be experts in defining all elements of their online product or service, including building a revenue model, structuring the right partnerships, creating the right brand strategy, identifying the best features, and even specifying browser requirements. Although these are all important, no one company culture is likely to possess world-class capability in all of these areas. Even if the expertise exists in a large organization, it is unlikely to be included in or available to a single project team. Overwhelmed by this reality, project sponsors frequently focus on what they can get their arms around, like budget and key features, and ignore important success criteria like revenue model and site traffic requirements.

Your objective in this exploration is to define those areas to which you can apply company expertise and identify areas for which you will hire agency talent. This section lists the key areas for exploration: business goals, site goals, and marketing goals. To help you assess how you can outsource some of your own strategy and planning, each section also details how you can assess an agency's capabilities to perform and what process and deliverables should result.

### Business Goals

This section defines your product or service plan and your revenue goals. So many poorly planned business objectives find their way to

Internet agencies that a well-defined business goal, articulated in terms of near-term metrics and long-term vision, will add extraordinary credibility to your RFP. This does not mean you need to include a lengthy business plan or inappropriate insight into your business challenges; however, you will greatly benefit by signing up your agency to contribute to specific business milestones. Since Internet agencies exist in a low-margin space, they are particularly interested in your ability to identify a high-profit space and your strategy for owning a specific market. A clean articulation of your business model will earn their respect and commitment.

**Product or Service Plan.** Clearly and simply identify the key attributes and competitive advantage of your offering. Include an explanation of current industry drivers and trends and explain how your initiative pertains. This will educate your agency on how your innovation is on-trend, how it anticipates or responds to competitive pressures, and how it will be received by existing customers and press. Identify your main competitors and provide your opinion of their Web presence and the site experience or online product they provide. You may choose to convey some of this information in verbal conversations rather than documenting your competitive assessments; however, do be sure to share this with your candidate agencies. A good firm will immediately check the sites of your competitors and begin to assess your opportunity.

**Can Your Agency Deliver?** The product plan is one of the few areas your company will need to completely define internally. You can request feedback and recommendations to be provided by the agency within the proposal, as Internet firms will have additional wisdom to share on elements of successful online product and services models.

**Meta-Goal.** A meta-goal is your one-sentence site objective. Every Web site initiative can be summarized in a meta-goal, whether it's an intranet for employee updates, a prototype for an online product, or even a simple site redesign or update. Here are some examples:

"Deliver a relationship-based Web environment in which ACME clients can customize the way they manage their investments and accounts, and stay current on relevant news and data in a secure, integrated manner."

"Establish a place where customers feel comfortable, in control, and secure to manage their personal banking finances."

"Create the lifestyle site for amateur and semi-pro musicians that will so completely meet their personal and professional needs associated with music that it will merit their site visits three times a week."

**Can Your Agency Deliver?** The meta-goal is the second area your company will need to define internally. Doing so will ensure that all project stakeholders share the same high-level vision of the site objectives.

**Revenue Model.** Although it is still rare for clients to share their revenue model, doing so will ensure that your agency provides a relevant site strategy and commits to your defined business goals. It will also make your RFP stand out among a sea of Web initiatives lacking rational business revenue structures. Your revenue model can communicate your vision and commitment, as well as provide inspiration to the agency that becomes excited about your business.

It has become clear that this missing definition of financial targets for Web initiatives is due to a general lack of solid data on operational costs and revenue opportunities on the Web. At this early stage of online businesses, clients initiating profit-oriented Web projects frequently engage in a strange posturing of revenue hopes and dreams expressed in terms of vague profit expectations, rather than annual and quarterly revenue targets and operational costs. Your Internet agency should be your partner in business success and market innovation on the Web.

You can define a very simple revenue model and request feedback from the agency. You may decide that the proposal itself should include feedback on this model and initial recommendations on revenue opportunities. If you choose to provide a simple first-guess revenue target, you should specify your complete project budget, with an estimate on expenditures over the first 18 months of the project to encompass the first launch and subsequent updates. There is no need to delineate separate costs such as hardware and software infrastructure, site maintenance, training, and content acquisition; you can ask your agency to provide this detail with the actual project. However, your detail on the high-level investment and profit expectations will greatly inform the strategy the agency creates to serve your business goals.

Additionally, you can require a detailed financial model as a project deliverable, and specify that the proposal itself include a description of the research methodology, research and analysis activities, and the financial modeling deliverables that will occur within the project. The revenue model will be your road map to measuring site success and future investment capability. Success is accomplished by creating a model that is driven by measurable business targets such as site traffic, subscription rates, commerce revenue, content fees, and advertising rates. These target metrics will allow quarterly assessment of the current site functionality and new release plan.

You may define the complete business plan and financial forecast prior to approaching an Internet agency or simply delineate a set of operational and profitability targets and challenge your agency to provide a customized revenue model research and deliverable as part of the project. The approach you choose in structuring your RFP will depend on the core competencies you identify within your company's capability.

**Can Your Agency Deliver?** To assess your candidates' ability to define or augment your revenue model, ask for examples from their portfolio of past strategic financial modeling for other initiatives. You may be fortunate to find a firm with experience in a similar space or industry to yours, but this will be rare and could indicate a conflict of interest. Ask the firm to define the structure of the final deliverable and list the activities and roles that will be applied in creating it.

**Audience Profile.** Specify your user characteristics in terms of standard demographics (age, sex, education, and geography, if appropriate), as well as browser access requirements. Include the types of activities each profile will do on the site and the behavioral styles that will motivate their emotional needs as well as their feature requirements.

**Can Your Agency Deliver?** You can supply your assumptions about user requirements and request that your agency extend this into a set of detailed user profiles. Agencies that excel at frontend experience design may even provide user scenarios that describe a set of activities and brand experiences the user will have on your site.

**Site Traffic Projections.** Identify how many times per week or month your most loyal 25 percent of site visitors will return. Based on your revenue requirements, you should provide an early estimate on your expected levels of traffic for each audience segment. Assessing traffic for your top two to three profiles is sufficient. This will inform the agency of your content strategy and your publishing workflow and engine functionality.

**Can Your Agency Deliver?** Request that your agency provide qualitative feedback on these expectations within its proposal; however, appropriate research to build a solid revenue model and traffic projections should be considered part of the project.

**Success Metrics.** This is your opportunity to pin down your sponsor and project stakeholders and get them to commit to requirements for the Web initiative. Define the metrics you will use each quarter to assess the success of your Web site. You'll want to include both quantitative metrics such as commerce revenue, new customers, and site traffic, as well as qualitative metrics such as press coverage, users profiles, design awards, and internal support throughout your organization.

**Can Your Agency Deliver?** You can request that the agency recommend some success metrics within its proposal, although it will not be able to completely define them until the project is under way and it has a better understanding of your business.

## Site Goals

This section gets down to the brass tacks of the actual site experience. Be disciplined about documenting and communicating those goals that already exist, either from strategic site research and planning, or from strongly held, nonquantitative beliefs that reflect cultural expectations. You will be able to require your agency to provide more research and recommendations on any of the following areas that you are unable to fully define.

**Branding and Site Experience.** This is your opportunity to describe the brand experience. First, inspire yourself by starting with the audience characteristics. List adjectives to describe how the users wish to see themselves. These adjectives will point to a site experience that suggests or reinforces a desirable self-image. Second, move into adjectives that the users would apply to describe the brand. Use specific positive adjectives as well as negatives, as demonstrated here for a financial services site.

- Current
- Savvy
- Well-read
- Well-informed
- Well-connected
- Access to the most accurate information
- Uses information to immediate benefit
- Elite

The brand attributes that will apply to the site experience might be:

- Exclusive
- Sophisticated
- Witty
- Strong
- Confident
- Bold
- Maverick

You can also provide a great deal of insight to your agency by sharing your opinion of other sites and brands. Many clients hesitate to do this because they worry that a site they find visually appealing may have terrible information design. They suspect that the agencies will engage in condescending eye-rolling, while asking each other, "Can you believe they like that site?" Rest assured, this does not happen. Agencies know that different sites have different strengths, and the right agency partner will be mature enough to delve into the specific features you find appealing.

You can identify any attributes you want to highlight as long as you can be specific. For example, you might include several sites that have memorable and impressive visuals (like O'Neil surf wear). You might want to identify a site that has applied superb interaction design to create a very intuitive configuration and purchasing process (like Apple), or another site that successfully engages its audience around a particular lifestyle (like ESPN SportsZone). Additionally, any opinions you can share on other brand positioning efforts will help your agency. For example, you might say, "We want to be the Porshe of bicycling" or "the Waterford crystal of writing instruments."

**Can Your Agency Deliver?** Ask the agency to share its initial insights into your brand attributes within the proposal.

**Key Features and Functionality.** This is the basic list of features and general functionality areas your organization has already identified as requirements for your business objectives. You should be able to list basic functionalities you know the site will require, such as a database, ecommerce, or remote publishing. You need not guess at the effectiveness of chat (for example) toward your customer support goals; your RFP can require the agency to recommend features and functionalities that serve your business requirements. To complement your short list of "must have" features, you may want to educate the agencies by providing an extensive list of preliminary features that should be considered possibilities. Rather than a long list of features that reflect brainstorming and informal dialogues, provide the agency with a well-structured set of elements that are required to achieve a phased set of business goals.

**Can Your Agency Deliver?** Depending on how specific you have chosen to be in your RFP, you can ask the agency to provide a recommended feature and functionality set as a precursor to the proposal.

**Content Requirements and Partnerships.** This section lists the main content areas, the source of each area of content, the workflow required for publishing, and the frequency expectations for updates and maintenance. If you haven't applied considerable strategy and research to your content sources and partnerships, you can require this expertise from your agency and request this as a major project deliverable. However, this is too significant an area to request as part of the proposal. You should ask that the agency detail within the proposal its process, deliverables, applied expertise, and portfolio experience that will build the content strategy and system.

If you do have a complete content strategy and are setting up your partnerships, you will benefit by including the publishing workflow, the publishing and document management engine, and the update strategy in your project scope.

**Can Your Agency Deliver?** Although you should not ask your agency to create a content strategy for you as part of the proposal, you can request an outline of the process it will use to build this plan during the project. Additionally, you can request that the proposal contain feedback on your current list of content partnerships.

**Market Data.** Your site is the way customers interact with you online. Consider what sort of information you would like to gather. Although your agency will be able to update you on the latest trends in tracking customer activity and current commentary on customer backlash, privacy issues, and true effectiveness of tracking engines, you should not let yourself be distracted by these variables. At this point, you want to take a broad look at all opportunities you have to track customer activities and site frequency. You may want to consider:

- Tracking which pages are the most frequently visited
- Determining which pages customers spend most of their time at
- Which page is the most frequent point of exit
- What sequence of interactions results in the highest commerce activity
- Navigation paths of new arrivals versus loyal subscribers

This is your opportunity to carefully define the market research you will accomplish on your site. A tight set of requirements up front will reduce the time you spend doing an internal assessment of required market research data during the project.

**Can Your Agency Deliver?** You can request that the agency provide a high-level listing of market data that can be tracked on the site. This list can be similar to the preceding sample with some additional detail.

**Site Constraints.** This brief section simply lists platform, operating system, and browser constraints that you want to set as criteria for your site. Here you will also define your performance requirements, such as the amount of time you feel it is acceptable for your site to download, and so on. Site constraints are enormously helpful to your Web developer because they set the criteria that dictates your entire Web development process, from the visual design to the use of multimedia and other Web technologies.

**Can Your Agency Deliver?** You can request that your agency recommend the appropriate site constraints. It can easily provide some early guesses within the proposal, provided you have shared sufficient profile information on your target audience and their demographics.

**Hosting.** This section outlines your requirements for hosting and maintenance of the site following the initial launch. Even if you plan to host the site internally, explain this expectation and the infrastructure and roles that will be applied to this function within your RFP. This will provide helpful context to the agency about your internal resources and how it should expect to work with you as the project timeline approaches launch. To specify your hosting requirements for a scenario in which the site will be hosted by an external company, identify your expected volume of traffic, what systems you plan to collocate and any historical hosting needs that will indicate the complexity of the system. For example, you may need access to a system administrator or database administrator who is available to reboot your server 24 hours a day, 7 days a week. Although many Web agencies are offering hosting services, if their primary business is Web development, they will fall short of investing in the proper infrastructure and bandwidth to keep your site up and running, stable, fast, and scalable for future growth. You should either expect to host the site internally or, assisted by your agency, work directly with a large hosting firm. You may want to have your agency host the site during its soft-launch phase as the integration with the hosting firm is finalized, but this should be considered a well-planned, temporary option.

**Can Your Agency Deliver?** If you have provided sufficient detail on your hosting requirements, you can ask that the agency describe in its proposal what type of hosting scenario it would recommend. A full hosting plan and introductions to appropriate hosting companies, however, should only be required within the project.

**Maintenance.** Carefully consider the type and frequency of site updates you'll require. In order to help your agency assess whether you need a full team updating the site weekly or simply one BuildMaster one day a week, you'll need to describe your maintenance scenarios. Identify the areas of the site or main sections of content that will need to be updated, describe the type of content (articles, graphic images, video, etc.) and the frequency of updates you expect. Indicate how the content will be supplied by your company and the turnaround time required between your content delivery to the agency and updated site posting.

**Can Your Agency Deliver?** If you have provided sufficient detail on your maintenance needs, you can require the agency to provide a budget, resource plan, and general maintenance approach within its proposal.

### Marketing Goals

Insight you can provide on your marketing strategy will greatly increase the agency's ability to make your Web site a strategic asset. You will want to provide as much detail as possible on the position of your target audience profile within the entire market. This will help the agency establish an online brand that effectively positions you against your competitors. Understanding your promotional plan and the partnerships you are targeting will assist the agency in making appropriate decisions on the various elements of functionality within the overall release plan.

**Market Segmentation.** This section overviews the major segments of your market and underscores the audience the site is targeted to attract. This does not need to be an exhaustive market study, but it should delineate the various market segments. You may choose to draw distinctions based on usage patterns, demographics of age, sex, or income, proclivity to buying online, or even levels of experience in your particular space (for example, your market segments could be as descriptive as an experienced golfer or a new homeowner). This will further increase your Web agency's understanding of the audience profile and assist it in accurately assessing the competitive offerings in your space. It will also help your project team to appropriately prioritize feature sets and recommend suitable functionality trade-offs.

**Can Your Agency Deliver?** This area will need to be defined by you and your organization, although you can request feedback from your agency during the Discovery Meeting or subsequent conversations.

**Promotional Plan.** Since your agency will be invested in the ultimate success of the site with its intended audience, it needs to understand how its work fits into your larger business plan. As with other areas, you can fully define this internally and include the details in your RFP, or you can explicitly ask that a media promotional plan be part of the project deliverable. Be aware, however, that sophisticated media planning is best done by firms that have specialized in this area for many years. Although some Internet agencies see this as a revenue opportunity, few have sufficient experience with all other media planning to create a well-integrated plan that will be capitalize on your Internet investment. If your agency candidates have media planning divisions, you can include this in your RFP; otherwise, you'll want to complement the agency's site strategy with the work of a separate media planning firm. You may wish to stack the deck in your favor and request a media planning quote from an established firm against which to assess the media quotes submitted by the Internet agencies. Regardless of the source, you can request that the proposals include some initial recommendations on media planning relative to your overall strategy.

If you plan to provide the media plan, include the following quantitative and qualitative details in your RFP. Your dialogues with each agency will greatly increase understanding of your overall business and the agency's role in its success.

Quantitative:

**Media promotional plan.** Provide ballpark estimates of your planned investment in each media area (print advertising, online banners, and so on) and the timeline of your placement.

**Advertising agency.** Identify your current agency or the timeline in which you expect to hire an agency, any commentary you can provide on the type of agency you need, and the services you expect to provide that provide context to your overall media plan.

Qualitative:

**Source for first-time site visitors.** List promotions you expect to drive new visitors to your site, identifying which you think will be responsible for the greatest number of new users.

**Motivation for repeat visits.** List the motivations that will bring a first-time visitor back to your site.

**Loyal visitor.** List the reasons that loyal users will return to the site repeatedly.

**Key Partnerships.** Building on the list of content partners you have identified earlier, consider other partners and sponsors who will contribute to the credibility and success of your site. This is your opportunity to explore possible sponsors for online events, partners who will broker personalities for chat sessions and forum management, suppliers of product you will sell online, the fulfillment house for order management, and suppliers of key applets such as a retirement planner, mortgage calculator, travel itinerary calendar, or golf score archive.

**Can Your Agency Deliver?** You can include a partnership strategy and costing model as a requirement of the project and request that the agency outline its approach and deliverables for this strategy within the proposal.

### Create Your Own Readiness Plan

This checklist will assist you in completing and publishing your preparation for the agency evaluation process.

- Operational preparation

☐ Budget draft approved

☐ Site management plan

☐ Asset acquisition

- ☐ Content partnerships
- ☐ Internal site sponsors
- ☐ Organizational capability and hiring timeline
- ☐ Roles and expertise
- ☐ Technical infrastructure
- ☐ Content workflow
- ☐ Launch timeline
- ☐ Marketing and promotional strategy

- Project readiness checklist

- ☐ Budget and timeline milestones (launch date, major releases)
- ☐ Sponsor and sign-off roles defined
- ☐ Stakeholder education and management plan
- ☐ Agency expertise requirements defined
- ☐ Project plan approved
- ☐ Agency evaluation schedule and process defined

**Building Basic Knowledge and Skills.** Just as you carefully educate, choose, and prepare your Internet agency for a successful project and relationship, consider how you can do the same for your internal project members. As you envision the perfect project and team structure, assess how you can excite your own organization to confidently contribute to an innovative Web initiative. Fortunately, since Web knowledge and skills are becoming requirements for professional success, your colleagues will probably welcome your opportune use of the company's Web initiative to educate the organization. At vivid, we've had the luxury of working with quite a few clients who augment their project teams with outside consultants, special education initiatives, and research projects. This not only conveys the importance they place on this initiative and motivates our continued investment, it increases project momentum and innovation. This section describes some ways you can prepare your company for success.

**Web Development Process.** In addition to asking your agency to overview its development process and requesting recommendations on helpful books, periodicals, and educational Web sites, you can also ask what the agency (or other agencies outside the evaluation process) would charge to create a one- to four-session curriculum for you. Rather than determining the curriculum yourself, you can explain the Web initiative and the background of each stakeholder before requesting a curriculum, schedule, and cost from the agency. Alternatively, instead of providing general education for your stakeholders, you may want to hire a temporary mentor or coach. Consider approaching a senior player in the Internet world and asking him or her to provide consultation while you plan your project, evaluate the agencies, and position your stakeholders. Conference participants, Internet authors, and individuals from reputable agencies who may not be able to bid on the entire project due to bandwidth or scheduling constraints may be suitable consultants.

Retain a consultant from an experienced organizational development firm to assist you in aligning the divisions and management levels within your organization. Assistance available in this arena includes defining roles for stakeholders, facilitating meetings to establish business goals, and building an organization-wide communication strategy to involve your company in this and future Web initiatives.

**Vertical Expertise.** In addition to hiring a top Web development agency, you may want to augment your team with outside expertise specific to your vertical industry. For example, if you are in the airline industry, your developer might have an expertise with the Web. However, a consultant with a great deal of expertise in the "vertical" of the airline industry can be very useful in ensuring that you are bringing best practices associated with your internal structure as well as external partnerships.

## Making Your Project the One to Want

There are common elements of high-quality prospects and well-designed RFPs that communicate the right combination of excitement and credibility. These RFPs go straight to the top of the priority pile. They come off the fax machine and go right into the agency's strategy session, during which the agency management begins to assess how they can win the project and begin helping to build your business. These top-priority opportunities get the most creative investment, the most diligent engineering design, the most effective market research, and the most carefully thought-out business strategy. This section explains not only how you can garner this type of attention, but also lists some mistakes you'll want to avoid to ensure that your company is always considered a hot prospect.

**How to Make Yourself a Hot Prospect.** Although different agencies value different client characteristics, there are key elements you can provide in your RFP and good client behaviors you can exhibit in meetings and conversations.

**Clearly share the business vision.** Emphasize the business bottom line behind the specific criteria you've identified for your project success. Service agencies live to support others, so the easier you make their process of understanding your goals, the more momentum they'll be able to effectively direct to your project. Agencies don't want to invest in a hazy project, because if the criteria for your final decision is unclear, then it's highly probable that they will have to waste a lot of time guessing. Spell out your requirements and watch the agencies knock themselves out.

**Explain why your business or the service provided by the site is an innovation.** Even if your site is simply a service provided for a group internal to the company, explaining why it will be an exciting solution for this captive audience will convince the agencies that they want to be part of this initiative. If you're creating an entirely new business, explain how it will revolutionize a marketplace and how important your agency choice is to the success of the entire business model.

**Drop names and numbers to communicate the long-term success of your company.** Mention specific sales numbers that represent your leadership in the industry, venture capital funding secured, key management talent and their histories, influential board members, and anything else that will position your company as exciting and interesting.

**Enthusiastically describe how invested you and your company are in this initiative.** Agencies will sense that you will invest the same energy in your promotions, your product plan, your partnerships, and all other areas of your project. When the agencies are assessing prospects, they'll spend the time on a project that has the greatest investment in the business. This is the project that yields the highest probability of being a future portfolio star for the agency. Naturally, this client will also be more responsive, fun, and creative.

**Candidly explain your weaknesses.** Clearly share the areas in which you or your organization will need extra support. You may need more budget detail to educate your stakeholders, stunning visual treatments to sell management, research on commerce packages, or guidance on structuring the project phases. The talented agency will respond to your needs and take the extra steps.

**Clearly define and explain the decision criteria.** This may be a difficult task, but identifying your top criteria for choosing an Internet agency should be a requirement. These decision factors can be ten must-haves that are weighted equally, three key criteria in order of importance, or whatever you feel best fits your decision-making process. Examples of decision criteria are on-time delivery records, design innovations, the creation of scalable system architecture, branding excellence, a development methodology, and exemplary industry knowledge.

**Specifically identify your budget range.** If you have no idea what a reasonable budget is for your initiative, ask each agency to have a phone conversation with you to provide you with some rational options before you finalize your RFP. Providing a draft feature list to the agencies will ensure you get the most accurate budget help possible.

**Clearly explain the process timeline.** Allow at least two weeks for the proposal process, make your decision in one week, and allow more than one week between the project award and the project start date. Set these dates in stone, communicate them clearly, and stick with them.

**Have fun.** Your style and demeanor during the proposal process communicates what you'll be like to work with. Everyone would rather work with a fun client.

**How Companies Land on the Gray List.** Internet agencies don't keep and compare black lists, but they do have a sort of gray list. This is the informal mental listing of companies that have proven themselves to be undesirable prospects. You would be surprised to overhear some of the names that fit in this category. The following list describes some of the behaviors and tactics that will land a company on the gray list and ways to handle yourself if you find these constraints affecting the evaluation process.

**They don't provide a budget range.** By refusing to be specific in terms of budget criteria, a client essentially positions him or herself as an irrational planner. The client is asking the agencies to guess at the business cash flow. The cost of an ecommerce site can vary widely from $100,000 to $1.5 million. Don't waste the agency's time in a guessing game. You may also risk insulting the agency by implying that its budgeting lacks integrity—you're communicating the assumption that the agency will "scope up" to meet your highest budget range.

**They won't list all the agencies they're considering.** When companies insist that they can't share the names of the other firms they're considering, they essentially give themselves more work to identify the strengths and weaknesses of each firm. If they shared the names of all candidate agencies, the agency firms can then provide more accuracy in positioning their strengths within the overall industry. Sharing the competitive landscape will in no way weaken the responses you receive. It will, however, motivate competition and educate the agencies on the types of firms you are considering.

**They change the scope of the project during the proposal process.** Changing the project scope will waste the time of each agency by forcing it to create an entirely new bid. If you find that your scope is changing, make your agency choice based on your original scope and the unchanged selection criteria. Once you've announced your decision to the chosen agency, tell it that your scope has changed and you need it to submit and detail the changes involved in creating a new bid. Because you have already accepted the first bid, the agency's changes will be presented with integrity. The agency will also be much more willing to provide an additional assessment when it knows it is investing in a relationship with a current client.

**They ask for a navigation flowchart as part of the proposal.** Information design is part of the project and must be done through a detailed analysis of your audience, site messages, and business goals. Only an agency that doesn't have expertise in information design would attempt to guess at what form a flowchart would take within the proposal.

**They require a proposal in a short turnaround time.** Agencies that take pride in their work are very uncomfortable providing a proposal that, due to time constraints, lacks in-depth thought, accuracy, and planning. If you have no choice on the timeline, ask the agency what it can do well in that time period and alter your requirements to fit its strengths.

**They ask the agency to make their presentation to a large group of stakeholders, including individuals who haven't read the proposal and aren't invested in the project.** Unfortunately, this type of broad, group decision-making means that the room will invariably include people who will see their involvement as a waste of time and communicate a frosty reception to the agencies that have slaved over their presentation. One way to prepare a group of decision makers that have limited time to review a lengthy proposal is to prepare a two-page summary that you can hand out 15 minutes before the presentation; you can also prepare the group by verbally summarizing key proposal elements.

**They are unresponsive.** This communicates that the evaluation process is not a priority and may lead the agency to believe the decision has already been made. It also suggests that the agency will need to compensate for an absentee client who is divorced from and uninvested in the final project.

**They make their decision in one day.** Most companies couldn't possibly read and evaluate proposals and assess even two candidate agencies in one day. This quick turnaround communicates that the evaluation process is merely a formality and a decision was made long before proposals were submitted. (If you really are wildly efficient and capable of making your decision in one day, explain this to the agencies so they understand that you value the work they are investing in your project.)

**They take over two weeks to make their decision.** This indicates that the company is really not ready to begin the project and probably rushed the proposal schedule. Unfortunately, in addition to sending the signal that they're disorganized, it also means that the project will lose momentum and excitement within the agencies. When the company does finally make its decision, its main agency contacts will have been focusing on other opportunities. (Note that the agency will be working to determine the right project resources while the decision is made, so that a team can be ready to begin as soon as possible. If a final decision takes too long, the agency will give up trying to retain these people for the project and the resources will become assigned to other areas.) If you know that you will have a lengthy decision cycle due to internal constraints beyond your control, communicate this clearly to your candidate agencies. Tell them what the specific timeframe is between the proposal due date and decision date, what is occurring in that timeframe, the required start date, and what role, if any, they should have.

**They expect to start the project less than one week after the decision award.** Although it's understandable that once a decision is made, a company will want to start the project as soon as possible, expecting a candidate agency to have a full team on deck prior to being awarded the project is unreasonable. This also implies that the agency should resource your project with whoever happens to be available, rather than choosing talent with skills and working style that best fit the project. Ask each agency how long it needs between the decision date and the project kick-off. You will only weaken your project by requiring the agency to cobble together a team in an unreasonable timeframe.

### Summary

This chapter focused on helping you to figure out what you want to do on the Web by planning an approach that works for the specific culture of your organization. You also saw first-hand how to build your project strategy, including setting your business and marketing goals, and developing a readiness plan that will help your company prepare for its Web development experience. Now that you know what you want to do and what type of contribution your company can make to the process, you are ready to begin to review proposals, budgets, and make the final decision on which developer to work with. We offer insight into that process in the next chapter.

## Checklist

- ☐ Select your evaluation process: Request for Information, Venture Launch, or Single Project Request for Proposal.
- ☐ Review the process of customizing your evaluation process to fit your particular corporate culture.
- ☐ Review and identify your organization's business goals.
- ☐ Review and identify your organization's site goals.
- ☐ Review and identify your organization's marketing goals.
- ☐ Create your own readiness plan, including developing an operational preparation plan and a project readiness checklist.
- ☐ Review your company's knowledge base. Do you know enough about the Web development process to work with your developer?
- ☐ Name three reasons why a busy developer should consider working on your project.
- ☐ Have you identified a budget range? Be prepared to share this information with prospective developers.
- ☐ Are you the kind of company that is going to land on the "gray list?" Review the Web don'ts before you make your final decision to contact Web developers.

chapter

# 3

# Evaluating Proposals and Budgets

**Aliza Sherman**
**President, Cybergrrl, Inc.**
*Aliza@cgim.com*

## About This Chapter

This chapter offers insight into a nearly impossible task: choosing the right Web developer for your project. Not only do your developers need to know intimately rather complex technology, but they must also know your business, be pleasant to work with, and have pricing structures that you and your budget can live with.

Although there is no guarantee that the final decision you make will indeed be the most appropriate one, there are some things that you can do to maximize your chances of finding the perfect client/developer match. First, you can analyze your potential developer's business model and position in the industry to determine whether or not it is consistent with that of your company. You can also figure out if the developer's focus on a given type of technology is the right mix for you and your business. There are also some warning signs that you can look for in the proposals and the budgets that the developer submits as part of the pitch for your business. What you should look out for, the do's and don'ts of finding a Web developer, are all found in this chapter.

## About the Author

Aliza Sherman is the author of the best-selling book *Cybergrrl: A Women's Guide to the World Wide Web* (Ballantine, 1997). Sherman is the president of Cybergrrl, Inc., a media and entertainment company specializing in content and resources for women online. *Newsweek* magazine called her one of the top 50 people who matter most on the Net.

## Choosing the Right Developer

**Before we go into the specifics of what makes a good proposal and offer general guidelines for choosing your Web developer, let's look at the most important question to ask during the selection process: What makes a good Web developer?**

In the early days of the Web, sites were simple HTML constructions. Often called "brochureware," the sites weren't dynamic and were essentially just electronic versions of printed marketing pieces.

These sites were created by small teams that only carried out very basic tasks: design, HTML production, and a working knowledge of File Transfer Protocol (FTP) to upload a site. Most of these teams' skills were learned on the job during late-night phone calls to Internet service providers.

Today, Web sites can be far more complex, demanding not only superior design and production but also an understanding of new, more sophisticated technologies, systems and infrastructure, online marketing and advertising, and even editorial development. Some Web development projects also require more than a passing knowledge of specific industries, such as entertainment, travel, and banking.

Chances are you are looking for a developer that can deliver on more than one of those fronts. Given the importance of your Web site to your company and the fact that you will probably spend a great deal of money on it, you will most likely expect your Web developer to be a financially solvent, stable company with a professional decorum or an independent consultant with an established track record of satisfied clients. You want some assurance that the company or individual you hire will be in business two years down the road to help you and grow with your site as your needs change. For independent contractors, this could mean having a collection of associated freelancers; however, you want to make sure that the team has worked together on projects before and that roles are firmly established. The team must have demonstrated expertise in meeting project deadlines and delivering a strong final product on time and within budget.

In short, the person or team you want to program your all-important e-commerce system should have a track record and good references. You want to be able to look at their portfolio and feel comfortable with your choice.

Today, the Web industry is undergoing a period of consolidation, transformation, and sometimes confusion. One developer gets bought up by or merges with another developer. Employees are constantly jumping from one company to another in the hopes of a big payoff, and even the technology is changing rapidly and continuously.

Just as ad agencies focus on different types of advertising and public relations firms specialize in clients such as pharmaceutical companies or packaged goods manufacturers, Web developers are beginning to specialize as well. These include Web shops that focus on e-commerce, database-delivered Web sites, or experts in certain types of programming, such as Java applications, online video and audio, and more.

The advantage of traditional, experienced Web developers is that they represent the core skills of Web development and are responsible for pushing the technology to create the most innovative sites on the Web today. As these developers deliver their services to large-scale corporate clients, their companies will grow and their clients will reap enormous benefits in the form of state-of-the-art Web sites.

In addition to traditional Web developers, traditional design firms have entered the Web development realm. Design firms have their definite strengths—largely design—but they can be weak on delivering the complex technology needed for larger, more dynamic Web sites that require intensive back-end server knowledge and e-commerce or intranet development . Lacking such expertise in house, these companies tend to partner with programmers or smaller companies that can offer these services.

Ad agencies have made quick moves to deliver Web development services. Agencies' strengths in Web development are their creative and design staffs, an understanding of the nature of their clients' business, and knowledge of marketing and advertising. What ad agencies initially lacked in terms of technical expertise, they are quickly making up for by acquiring, investing in, or partnering with Web developers or building in-house staff.

For many clients, however, agencies have their weaknesses. Technology-intensive Web sites are likely to pose problems for many traditional ad agencies, and, if a company were to need technology integration—such as the building of an intranet or e-commerce system—ad agencies are usually less qualified for the job, given that their expertise lies in brand development.

Recently, and as a result of the Web's increasingly complex technology needs, a new type of developer is emerging: the systems integrator. Companies known for installing large networks, servers, and computer systems are now offering Web development services as part of their suite of customer services. And for good reason. As the Web requires more intense integration with a company's internal computing systems, who better to provide those services than the people who design, install, and implement those services? The same is starting to hold true for Internet service providers, which, after years of maintaining Internet connections and servers for business, are now offering design and site development. Chances are good that these types of companies offer an expertise that rivals the most technically sophisticated Web developers, but they may be lacking in design, online marketing, or brand-building skills.

An interesting development is the trend toward industry-knowledgeable Web developers who specialize in building Web sites for vertical markets such as the travel, automotive, or the financial services industries. These developers have a great understanding of a particular business, along with a very solid understanding of how technology can work in a particular sector. On the negative site, their prices tend to be higher because of their specialization and because, by their nature, they will have fewer clients. (You can't really work with Ford *and* GM without some level of a conflict of interest.)

Last, but not least, are new-media marketing companies that are governed by their philosophy and individual expertise. For example, Cybergrrl, Inc., has, from the very beginning, focused its business on providing Web development and marketing consultation services to companies interested in reaching women online. These types of companies can offer great advantages in that they understand the Web as a medium, the technology, and Web development—a good fit for many companies. The one caveat regarding Web developers is that their focus tends to be very specific. These aren't the kinds of companies that meet and greet a client, then add staff to deliver any old product. They tend to work with a limited number of long-term client relationships, rather than haphazardly building up a stable of clients, so if you do not fit their mission, chances are they won't want to work with you.

**Which Type of Developer Is Appropriate?** The answer depends on your goals. You can't realistically expect one developer to be an expert at creating custom software, great design, outstanding programming, total system integration, superb business consulting, legacy system integration, and e-commerce solutions as well as specialize in your industry.

Every choice you make will likely be a trade-off. The best strategy is to determine what your real needs are and look for a developer that has demonstrated experience in meeting those needs, at the same time giving you the confidence that they can rise to the occasion and build with you over the long term.

For example, say you set out three criteria for your Web developer:

1. Must have a proven ability to implement e-commerce solutions
2. Must demonstrate the ability to deliver eye-catching design
3. Must have in-depth knowledge of high-end kitchen appliances such as commercial grade stoves and refrigerators

If a developer were to meet the first two criteria and give you the confidence that it could work with you to learn the third, why wouldn't you choose that developer? The little secret of this industry is that the majority of the best sites on the Web were built by developers who understood the technology, were capable of the design, and were hungry and energetic enough to learn the rest.

### How Important Is the Proposal?

A proposal is often your first impression of a Web development agency, and first impressions last. Presentation isn't everything, but it's certainly indicative of the way an agency works. A clean, clear proposal, in both content and appearance, is a good sign.

Much of Web development requires the ability to synthesize information and present it in a visually pleasing and easily accessible manner, so a proposal is the first part of the Web development process and should be scrutinized as you would the final product.

The proposal should be in direct response to your careful, detailed request for proposal (RFP) or an initial informational meeting. A thoughtful agency will call you to follow up on key areas of your RFP or project that may not be clear. Your job in the selection process is to provide the agency with as much non-proprietary information as possible so it is able to truly address your needs.

### What Should Be in the Proposal?

No two proposals are alike, but each should include at least the following elements so you can evaluate them on relatively equal terms.

**The Objective.** Usually placed at the beginning of the proposal, this brief paragraph or statement should tell you immediately that the developer understands the goals for your Web site, that they've done their homework on your company and industry, and that they are prepared to help you achieve your goals.

Here is an example of an objective statement:

> *The goals of the Allure magazine Web site are to increase subscriptions to the magazine and inform women 18–34 about beauty trends. Currently, there is a lack of quality, content-rich Web sites for women regarding specific beauty information, particularly from experts. The Allure Web site can fill this gap and set itself apart from the sites of other national women's magazines.*

First, this objective presents a clear statement of the goals of the Web site. Next, it has a statement about competitors on the Web, showing that the company did some research. Last, there is a statement about the Web site standing out, which sounds great, but the rest of the proposal must demonstrate exactly how the differentiation will be achieved.

**Web Site Components.** The breakdown of the components or elements of the Web site should clearly support the goals stated in the objective. Most elementary Web site proposals will include construction of the "Who We Are" information such as company history and philosophy, staff bios, press releases, information about products and services, and contact information.

What you are looking for is the innovation that the Web development agency brings to the table. What unique ideas and perspective do they give you about ways to achieve your Web site goals?

"If a client states clearly what they are looking for, a good proposal will still offer suggestions and alternatives," says Michael Diamant, president of T3 Media, a Web development agency that made a name for itself building sites for Broadway shows. "Even though they may not be relevant, they still show that the agency is taking the time to think about your project and is trying to improve it or lend their expertise to it." Diamant also believes that clients should be willing to sign non-disclosure agreements (NDAs). "If you want an agency to offer some of their intellectual capital in a proposal, then the client should be willing to protect that capital."

In assessing an agency, you're looking for a few good ideas that show the agency is both thinking creatively and focused on making your Web site a success. The components must be clearly defined, in a language free from jargon (or at least filled with layman's explanations), and you must be able to see, without any technical knowledge of your own, how their recommendations will directly help achieve the goals of your Web site.

Here is an example of a description of a component to a Web site:

> *Item #4: Threaded Messaging Board*
>
> *The Allure site should provide a Web-based forum for subscribers to discuss beauty with experts and with one another. The most common Web-based forum for discussion is a Threaded Messaging Board, where visitors can "leave behind" messages, respond to other messages, and basically carry on an ongoing dialogue about the topic at hand: Beauty.*
>
> *By building community features, such as a Threaded Messaging Board, into the Web site, Allure will become a destination on the Web for young women looking for beauty advice as well as looking to make friends in a comfortable environment. By making the forum only available to subscribers, there is instant incentive for a young woman who visits the site to subscribe to the magazine to become a part of this exclusive community, thus helping to achieve the main goal of the site.*

**Cost Breakdown.** The cost breakdown for a Web site is often the most confusing part of the proposal, mainly because the industry has had pioneers creating their own rules for pricing out a job. Then, as traditional ad agencies and marketing firms began to enter the new media world, they brought with them their own pricing systems.

The most important thing to look for in a cost analysis for a Web site is a clear breakdown of elements and services followed by a price. An agency can't always give you their formula for pricing each component, but you can safely assume it is some combination of the following:

1. Hourly rates of the team members whose skills are required for the project multiplied by an estimation of the number of hours a project will require
2. A markup to cover company overhead
3. Possibly the licensing of a proprietary software solution (this should be stated)
4. Possibly an extra few hundred or thousand dollars for good measure

Does the last one shock you or scare you? If you represent a very large corporation with seemingly deep pockets, you might get a slightly more inflated price than if you represent a nonprofit organization. Often, a company estimates costs using a grid containing a range that they could charge for the job, and they use instinct and experience to guess how much the client will bear. Also, the working process during Web site development may take longer than expected (and it usually does), and agencies have learned to under create a buffer to offset those unexpected extra hours. As uneasy as it might make you feel, this is a common practice in any service industry that estimates hours for a project.

Asking for the inside formula breakdown of costs is an exercise in futility. No agency will divulge their internal pricing system, but they should present you with the most detailed breakdown possible. Keep in mind that some of the justification for prices is based on the agency's reputation, expertise, and the intellectual capital that has enabled them to produce sites that stand out.

In order to have a successful working relationship with your developer, a certain amount of respect and trust is needed. If you don't have that, move on to another agency. If you find that no agency will break down a project or price it in the way you want, you might be better off hiring an independent consultant for the project. Keep in mind, however, an independent consultant may not have the resources that an agency does. Bottom line: You must trust your contractor, whether an agency or an independent Web developer, in order to build a successful site and working relationship.

### More About Costs

There are a few more things you need to consider regarding development costs for your site.

**The Phase Approach.** A nice touch in a proposal cost breakdown section is a phase approach. A sign that an agency is interested in building a long-term relationship with your company is when they recommend several alternatives for your Web site, then offer up several phases of production.

For example, in Phase I you might have a single Web page with 10 frequently asked questions (FAQs) that address some of the immediate information needs of the visitor to your site, with an email link for the visitor to ask any question not answered in the FAQs.

Phase II might be to add a form for visitors to fill out that can capture and store demographic data about them based on their answers. In addition, Phase II could include a function that automatically emails a visitor's questions to the appropriate person within your company.

Phase III might include adding a searchable database of questions and answers based on new questions submitted by visitors and answered by your staff. Now the visitor can search by keyword and find all of the FAQs addressing their needs.

The phase approach says, "We want to work with you, and we respect the fact that your budget this quarter is small. We will provide you with the information to go back to your company and prepare an expanded budget for the next quarter and for the following year. We see our relationship as a lasting one."

**Hidden Costs.** Beware of hidden costs in a proposal. At some point, you are going to have to sign a contract for the job described in the proposal. Before you do, don't be afraid to ask whether there are any costs not mentioned in the proposal.

The developer's answer should be that there are no hidden costs, but they may point to a contingency clause on their cost breakdown. "Any company which does not ask for some sort of contingency or right to revise the budget after a pre-production phase of research is a problem," says Diamant regarding aspects of the proposal that might require a needs assessment period and further research.

Unless the agency is privy to every aspect of the project from your point of view—how your company works, how your data is stored and delivered, and so on—chances are that their proposal may need additional refinement. Get the agency to state to you whether you are talking hundreds, thousands, or hundreds of thousands of dollars, and you need to be firm about where your budget ends. Some agencies address this issue by including a planning phase to their payment schedule to meet with the necessary departments within your company to hash out technical and detailed issues before submitting the final cost for certain components.

A good agency will be honest with you if they cannot complete the project within the budget before starting the job. In that case, they will either walk away from the business (if they don't want to risk losing money on the job) or they will make it clear to you that they'll provide the service, take a loss, and trust that a long-term relationship with your company will make up for it in the future.

**What's in a Budget?** Table 3.1 is a summary of costs that illustrates what a typical Web development budget might include. Note that the budget presents these elements in a very general way. Chances are good that most developers will be reluctant to break costs and assumptions down to a very detailed level.

**What's in a Proposal?** The following list illustrates the types of sections that you are likely to see, or should expect, in the proposal prepared by your Web developer. Every proposal is unique, but there are some basic elements that you, as a client, should expect. Developers who do not include the elements marked with an asterisk are likely to be less experienced firms that may have the understanding of the technology but an unproved track record in delivering product and services to clients. The list includes a complex set of the elements that should be included in a proposal and asterisks marking the bare minimum items:

**Table 3.1** Summary of Costs

| | |
|---|---|
| Basic site design, navigation, and architecture | $20,000 |
| (Includes HTML programming and original art) | |
| Pages/areas included: | |
| Homepage | |
| About the magazine | |
| Masthead | |
| Table of contents page | |
| Subscription information | |
| Main components: | |
| Threaded message board | $11,700 |
| Searchable FAQ | $4,000 |
| Subscription form | $5,600 |
| Secure server for credit card ordering | $6,700 |
| **Total site creation cost for *Allure* Web site** | **$48,000** |

Title Page

Table of contents

Summary and objective*

Define project by components or elements*

Description of Web development agency and bios of development team

Press clippings

List of clients and references

List of deliverables (subject to change after planning meetings)*

Top-level timeline (subject to change after planning meetings)

Rough flowchart of site based on information you have provided

Competitive analysis of market

Budget of costs*

If the proposal doesn't have enough background information about the agency and team members, request the agency's media kit.

### Looking Beyond the Proposal

Is there a way to select a Web development agency that looks beyond the proposal? Many clues to the agency are hidden in the proposal, as mentioned in this chapter. Here's some additional elements to look for or pay careful attention to during the selection of your Web developer:

1. Statements that show the agency has done their research about your company and industry
2. Aspects of the proposal that suggest a long-term strategy as opposed to a "one-shot deal"
3. A solid client list and willingness to immediately provide you with references
4. A good reputation in the industry, a track record, and a strong team
5. Clear language that presents the proposal with enthusiasm

In addition to these ideas, Tery Spataro, CEO and chief artifex of Stir in New York City, lists the following as important information to gather about your potential Web development agency:

**Their location.** Where are their offices in the city? What do they look like?

**Years in business.** Are they a new company without a track record?

**Size of agency.** Are you a Fortune 100 company? You need an agency with a staff that can fulfill your needs.

**Other value.** Does the agency specialize in e-commerce, banner advertising, traditional advertising, online marketing?

**Pricing.** Have they stayed within your budget (which you should have defined in your RFP)?

**Signs of a Bad Proposal.** The following list outlines some warning signs of a bad proposal:

1. The proposal doesn't respond directly to your RFP or fit your needs as you have stated them.
2. The proposal is unprofessional—there are typos in the text or coffee stains on the pages.
3. Another company's name appears on one or several of the pages (a sure sign of boilerplate-itis, which indicates laziness, lack of understanding of your project, lack of care, or all of the above).

4. A list of features for your Web site without explanation, particularly ones that don't seem to suit your audience or your needs—the ultimate triumph of technology over purpose.
5. One lump sum cost without any breakdown.
6. Techno-jargon that you don't understand, such as "a BBS system utilizing perl programming to facilitate user interaction." One of the biggest tasks of the Web developer is to teach you about technology and your site. You may have to pay for it, but make sure it is part of the process. Developers that use too much jargon or are condescending will rarely give you what is in your best interest.

### Where Do You Find a Good Web Developer?

According to Spataro, one of the best places to check is with professional organizations. For example, New York City has the New York New Media Association (NYNMA). A wealth of resources on the Web development industry is provided in Chapter 12, "Web Resources."

Spataro also suggests going to Internet trade shows such as SIGGRAPH or the conferences put on by research firms such as Jupiter Communications. "Read the reviews (of Web sites) in the trades: *Adweek, AdAge, Internet World, TechWeb* (online), *Communication Arts,* and *ID Design.*" Finally, if you are surfing the Web and you find a site that you think is done well—good graphics, easy to navigate, appropriate use of technology—look for a producer credit or call the company directly.

According to Diamant, "Every city has a number of leading agencies, all of which have a specific focus. It is not hard to find out who the top 15 to 20 firms are, both locally and nationally. Request their media kits. Talk to a salesperson. Look at their company site. You may want to try to solicit proposals from a few with a range of focuses that all fall within the boundaries of your needs. Learn about the industry."

### What Is the Worst Way to Find a Web Developer?

Avoid using family members or friends of friends, unless they work for an established agency and aren't the final decision maker within the agency. Friendships have been lost due to overpromising and underdelivering, not to mention underqualification.

Avoid information overload. One client interviewed eight firms for a small Web site project, thinking that they'd learn more about the industry and the Web by meeting with more agencies. In reality, one good agency could teach you more than eight mediocre agencies. Also, meeting with that many agencies makes it harder to remember who said what, which makes it harder to make a final decision. You will also have more proposals to read and compare, which can be a daunting task. If you are overseeing a large Web project, meeting with eight firms isn't as uncommon, as long as you set up a clear list of qualifying questions to ask each agency and a criteria checklist that you use during the screening process.

Avoid flash and hype. Your Web site is an ongoing means of digital communication, not a special event. Look for substance as well as style from your agency. Bigger is not always better; glitzier is not always more effective.

Leverage your existing relationships. Does your company have a graphic design firm? A computer services vendor? Have those companies continually delivered high-quality services to you over a long period of time? Chances are good that if your design firm really understands your business and has delivered good services, they would be a logical first place to start your quest for a Web site. If you have a relationship with them built on trust, you can count on them to guide you through the process.

## Summary

Evaluating a proposal and budget for your future Web site requires part critical reading, part intuition, and a lot of learning on your part as the process progresses. Think of your Web development agency as a partner. They stand to gain as much as you do if you're satisfied with their work and your Web site is a great success. You are truly in the driver's seat when selecting an agency. Keep in mind that you have a lot to offer them, such as repeat business, referrals to your colleagues, and recognition for their work within your industry. After you've made the final choice, the biggest task you will have to tackle with your Web developer concerns the conceptual development and design of your site. We address those key elements of the Web development process in the next chapter, "Understanding Design."

## Checklist

- ☐ What type of developer is pitching your company? Ask or identify their business model.
- ☐ Review the pros and cons of working with that type of developer. For example, is it a developer that specializes in technology when you, in fact, really prioritize design and creativity?
- ☐ Proposal check: Does it respond to your RFP or is it completely different?
- ☐ Objective review: Is the objective clear? Does it match your goal?
- ☐ Web site components review: Check the proposal to identify what components will be delivered on your site. Are you happy with them? Do they meet your requirements? Do you understand them?
- ☐ Does the developer present a timeline for delivering various elements of the project? If not, why not?
- ☐ Budget check: Does the price seem logical and based on the reasoning presented in the proposal or is it just a number on a page with no rationale?
- ☐ Phase check: Is the implementation of your site broken down into phases? If so, are you comfortable with those phases? Or are they too slow? Too fast?
- ☐ Review the list of key elements that should be in every proposal. Are they in yours?
- ☐ Company review: Share the proposals that you received with key members of your team. Have a meeting to discuss feedback and input.
- ☐ Gut check: It sounds cliché, but is there anything in your mind that makes you nervous about the developer you are considering? Apply the same standards to selecting your developer that you would toward hiring a new employee, because that is exactly what you are doing—with the exception that with the developer, you are actually hiring several people to add to your team

# chapter 4

# Understanding Design

**Peter Seidler**
**Razorfish**
*seidler@razorfish.com*

## About This Chapter

Similar to great art, everyone has strong opinions as to what constitutes good design. This chapter won't make you a design connoisseur any more than an art history class will make you a qualified art critic. Our purpose is to define the function of good design, review some highly successful designs, and, more important, gain insight into the challenges and factors of creating those designs from the perspective of one of the leading design pioneers in the Web development industry.

This chapter looks at the fundamental steps of design activity—from defining need, the research process, incubation and immersion, to preliminary design, detailed design production planning, and production. Last, we present a look at the types of documents that designers use to assist them in the creative process, such as creative briefs, design strategies, and navigation architecture documents.

## About the Author

Peter Seidler is the chief creative officer of Razorfish, a leading New York City Web development firm. He was named chief creative officer after the company merged with Avalanche, the pioneering Silicon Alley Web shop Seidler founded in 1994. Seidler's forward-thinking design and technology vision have provided the creative direction for such clients as The Warner Music Group, Guardian Insurance, Sotheby's International Realty, and the famed Carnegie Hall. Prior to joining Razorfish, Seidler developed successful interactive communications projects for such corporate clients as Bankers Trust, *Cosmopolitan* magazine, Elektra Entertainment, KPMG, Con Edison, FAO Schwarz, NBC, Price Waterhouse, and Viacom.

Seidler is widely recognized as an expert on design and technology and is a frequent contributor at design conferences and Internet industry events and serves as an adjunct professor at New York University's well-known Interactive Telecommunications Program (ITP). His work has been featured in *Creative Web Design* (Michael Baumbardt, Springer-Verlag, 1998) and *Creative Killer Web Sites* (David Siegel, Hayden Books, 1997); he serves as judge of prestigious advertising awards such as Communication Arts, The Clios, and The One Club. An active member of the New York New Media Association and the Association of Graphic Designers, Seidler holds a BA in philosophy from New York University and an MFA in conceptual art from the California Institute of the Arts. He completed postgraduate work at the Whitney Museum's Independent Study Program, and his conceptual art projects are in the collections of Peter Norton, Walt Disney, Bonnie Raitt, and the Museum of Modern Art.

The design work highlighted in this chapter was created at Avalanche and, as a result of its merger with Razorfish, is credited to that company.

## What Is the Function of Design?

**As the Internet becomes an increasingly integral part of doing business and as Web sites become truly mission critical, companies must place greater importance on the quality of interactivity they offer to all the people with whom they do business.**

We've all visited Web sites looking for information about a product, only to find our efforts thwarted by a confusing site structure and graphics that were unclear or misleading. We might leave that site and never return. If our customers or potential customers visit our site and find the same problems, they will likewise leave, and we will lose business. Investment in all the technology in the world will have no value if our customers do not find the interface intuitive to use.

Design is responsible for creating an environment that makes the Web a truly interactive experience. On the Web, this discipline is referred to as visual user interface design. Design has taken on a new importance in the business world with the emergence of the Web, where good design requires the following:

- Establishing a brand identity that is an identifiable, unique, and consistent Internet presence for the company, one that extends the company's visual identity from the real world or helps shape a new brand identity if the business objective calls for it.
- Creating a context—a visual look and feel—that is both attractive and functional.
- Integrating content and technology so that the technology can perform complex tasks without making those tasks seem difficult to the end user.
- Conforming to the technical specifications that have been established for the project. For example, if the target audience for a site is high-end corporate users who'll access the site over high-speed networks, the design should take full advantage of the large bandwidth and offer a rich experience for those high-end users. On the other hand, if the project specifications indicate that the target audience is home computer users who'll connect to the Internet with a modem, the designer must accommodate these users. The design must be delivered on time

and on budget, and its value should be measurable according to the goals established at the onset of the project.

Of all the aspects of Web site production, design is the one that most people feel is least intimidating. Programming can be difficult and is reserved for specialists; most clients don't look over the shoulder of programmers while they are working in C or Java and tell them to "adjust the code over there or drop that command line here." Likewise, when it comes to editorial content, clients are reluctant to micromanage. True, clients review the site and make suggestions, but they're not likely to get directly involved in the process.

When it comes to design, clients hesitate less to get involved. Many clients feel their color preferences are as valid as the color palette that a designer spent weeks researching and testing. In addition, powerful design tools are widely available. Now, almost everyone can purchase a few fonts, a page layout program, and a graphical HTML editor, and within a few hours, create a "passable" design. But what is passably attractive and what is professional are different things.

Good design is critical to the success of a Web site, and a successful Web site is critical to the success of many enterprises. Some of today's most successful businesses—BMW, Cuisinart, Mont Blanc, Knoll, and U.S. Robotics—place a strong emphasis on product and marketing design.

### Design as a Multidisciplinary Approach

Interface design for the Web does not exist in a vacuum. Graphic design, navigation, and technical support are some of the factions to be considered when designing an interface. For example, a great graphic design and intuitive navigation solution are irrelevant if the site's technical architecture doesn't support it.

When considering Web design, it's important to be prepared to work with several departments at a company, because representatives from information technology (IT), marketing, business development, sales, and customer service will often each have their own needs. That multidepartmental approach requires a design that works for each of a company's departments.

Following are two examples of Web sites produced by Razorfish that successfully represent the interests across a wide range of functions at a company.

**Example One: The Guardian Insurance Company** (www.guardianbenefits.com). Over a period of two years, Razorfish worked closely with The Guardian to launch a new online brand identity, streamline business-to-business communications, and extend the company's business to the Internet.

Razorfish has conducted extensive research and analysis resulting in a series of "white papers" supporting a two-year plan for a phased rollout of Guardian's online initiatives. The use of white papers in the creative development process is a common practice. White papers by definition provide information for an objective framework from which one can measure a product or service's appropriateness to online strategy needs.

In working with large, well-established clients like The Guardian, Razorfish consults various corporate divisions and considers multiple projects as facets of the overall Internet strategy. Working to bridge marketing and information technology departments ensures that the same standards apply to all projects. The online enrollment interface presented in Figure 4.1, for example, provides a branding message that's consistent with information resource areas available to the general public and familiar to plan administrators.

Information that resides in a mainframe and is traditionally accessible only through proprietary computing environments must now be easily accessible to novice Web users and needs to meet the requirements of the multitiered access model of the Web (see Figure 4.2). While communicating consistent messages, the interface designer now takes into account the technology requirements of existing complex systems and the issue of multiple audiences accessing different levels of information.

**Example Two: Sotheby's International Realty** (www.sothebysrealty.com). This site is part of Razorfish's effort to improve Sotheby's International Realty communications both internally and externally. Our online initiative for Sotheby's includes the development of flexible site architecture, interface design, database entry tools, database integration, and marketing and promotion strategies.

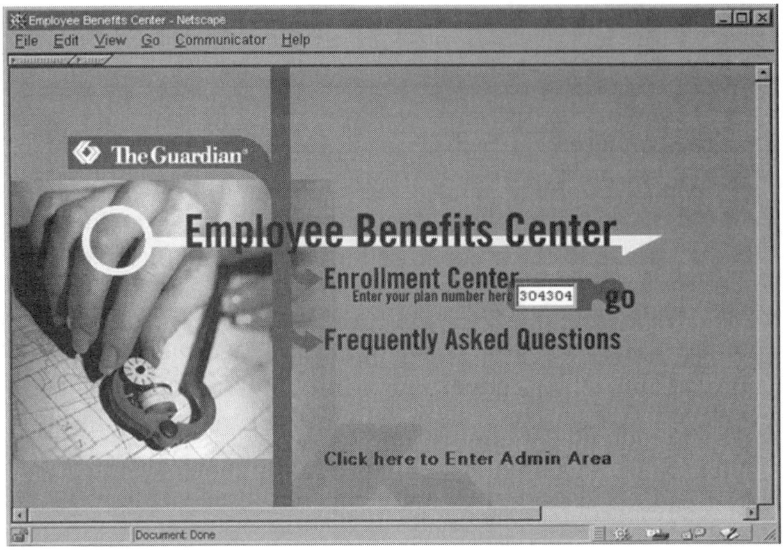


**Figure 4.1** Branding the Employee Benefits Center for The Guardian's Web site. Visitors access their benefits by entering their plan number and selecting "Go."

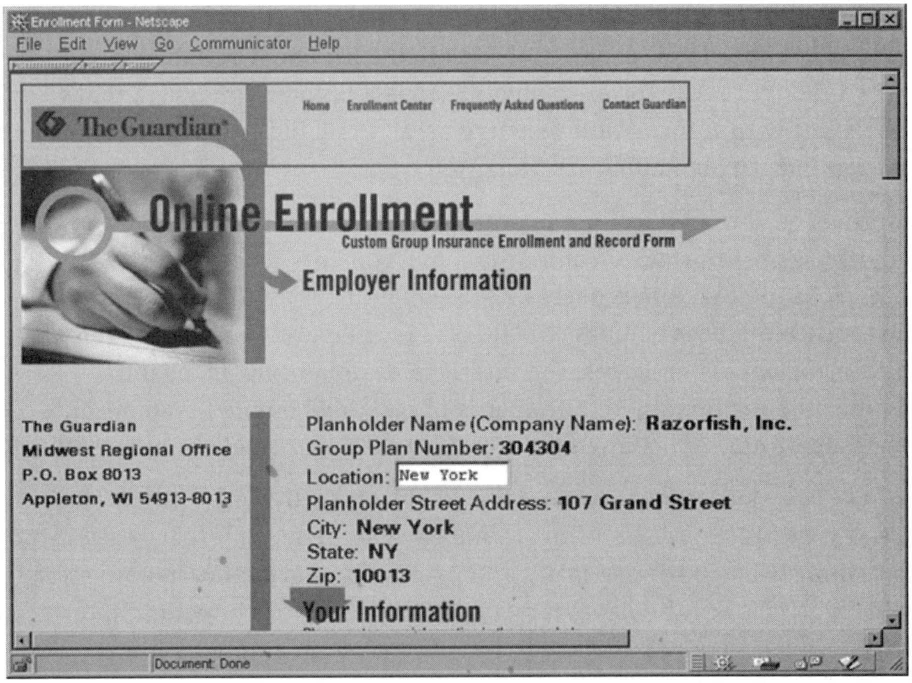


**Figure 4.2** A carefully designed graphical interface provides user-friendly access to complex databases of information.

This site meets several business requirements. The examples shown in Figures 4.3 through 4.6 express a consistent brand identity. We achieved this effect by working closely with the marketing group at Sotheby's and with their IT department. Razorfish implemented an Oracle database with Java administration tools and middleware that produced pages consistent with the look of the overall site. In this case, *middleware* refers to products that consist of various kinds of software that allow content from a relational database to be assembled and sent to a Web page. The database design had to serve the needs of the sit, while integrating perfectly with Sotheby's finance department. This required carefully considered server software decisions, which in turn were a factor in what users would see on screen. We needed to ensure that the input tools that we created would allow data to be entered through the Web and be merged with existing company information in existing formats. The corporate data management tools also needed to be able to access the information over their already established local network.

The business development departments at Sotheby's were interested in the qualified sales leads that the site could generate. This determined the prominence of a call to action that appears on pages that feature specific properties. The call to action refers to the fact that each property on the Sotheby's Realty site has a prominent link enabling an interested customer to send a query directly to one of the many Sotheby's representatives. The email is routed directly to the affiliate who represents that property. The specific data requested by the direct marketing group determined what information we asked of the site participant. Using their expert knowledge of their audience, we determined where the visitor surveys would appear and what screen changes would occur based on visitor responses.

The input of all the Sotheby's project team members at Razorfish affected the qualities of the interface. The solutions manager who developed the business strategy developed priorities for the interface. These included an emphasis on call to action throughout the site and consistent messaging to brokers within an intranet area. The design group explored various visual design directions. After research and experimentation, they developed a visual system that controlled the look and placement of graphic elements such as logos, photographic treatments, text layouts, and screen compositions to achieve the right balance of elements that satisfied Sotheby's needs (see Figure 4.7).

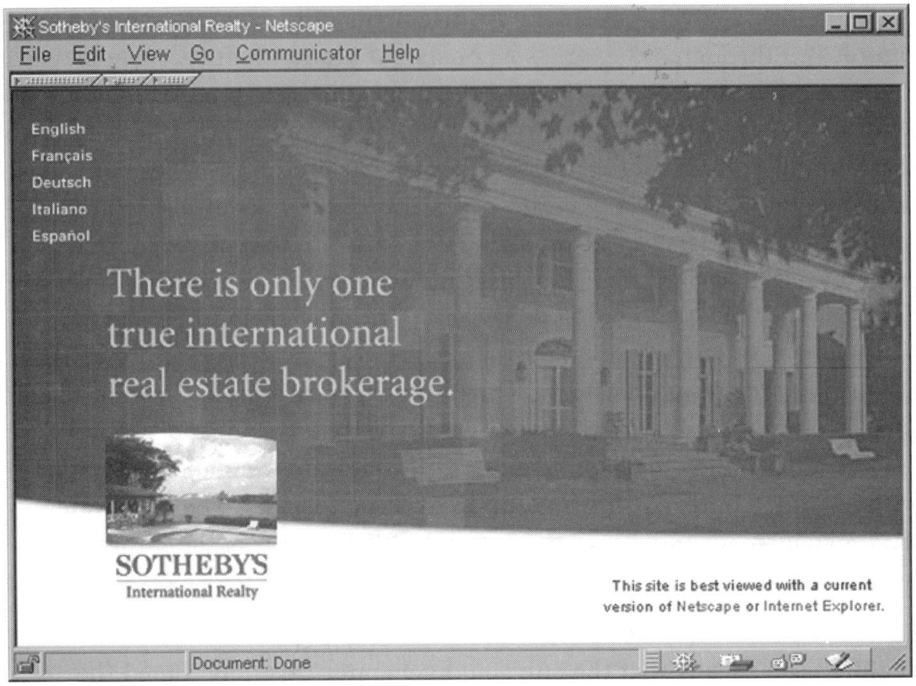


**Figure 4.3** The home page for Sotheby's International Realty clearly establishes the company's brand to potential clients. ©1997 Sotheby's International Realty, Inc.

**Figure 4.4** The site for Sotheby's extends the developed brand even as the number of user options increases. ©1997 Sotheby's International Realty, Inc.

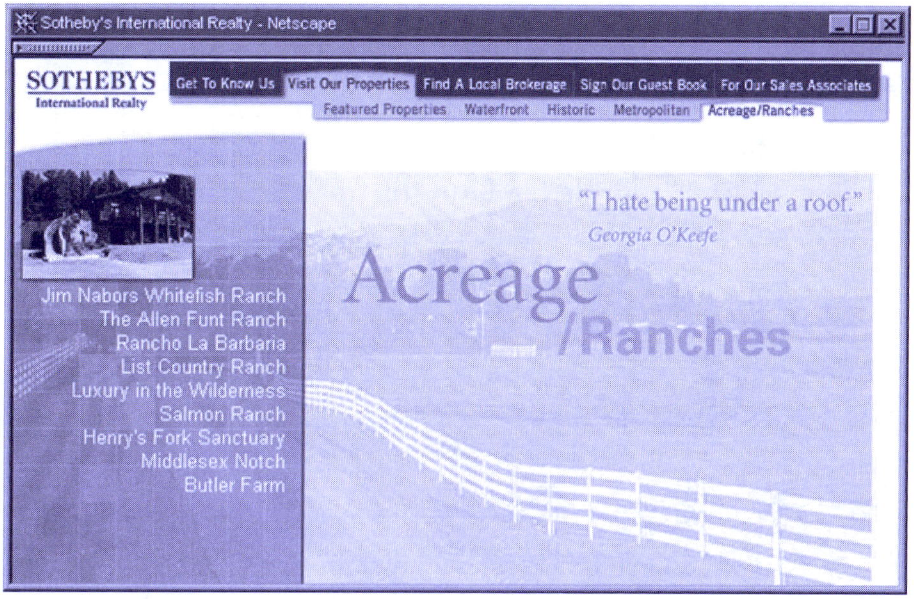


**Figure 4.5** As visitors move into areas of the site that present specific real estate properties, the Razorfish design retains the look and feel of Sotheby's branding. ©1997 Sotheby's International Realty, Inc.

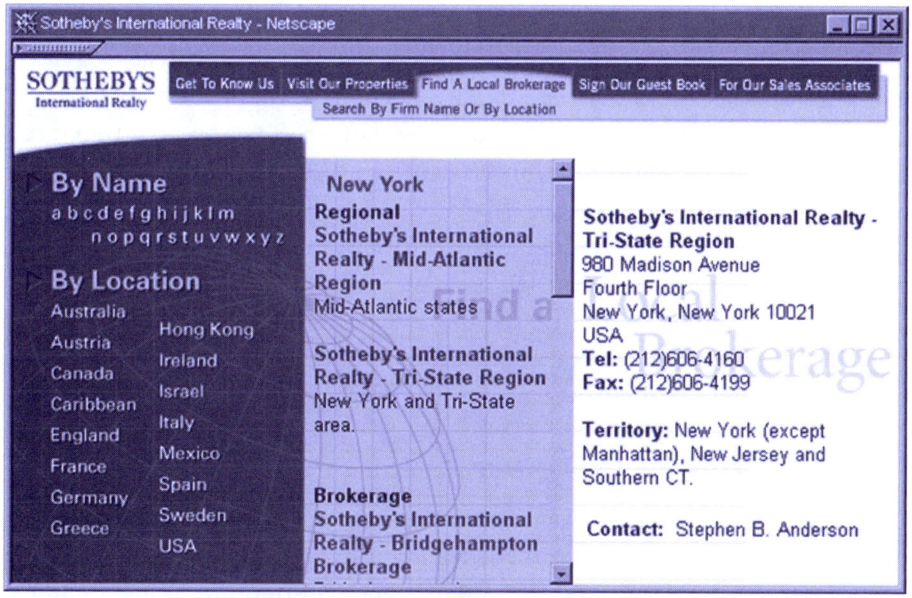


**Figure 4.6** The site's brand extends to the user at all levels of the site, providing access to a wide range of data, such as specific contact information. ©1997 Sotheby's International Realty, Inc.

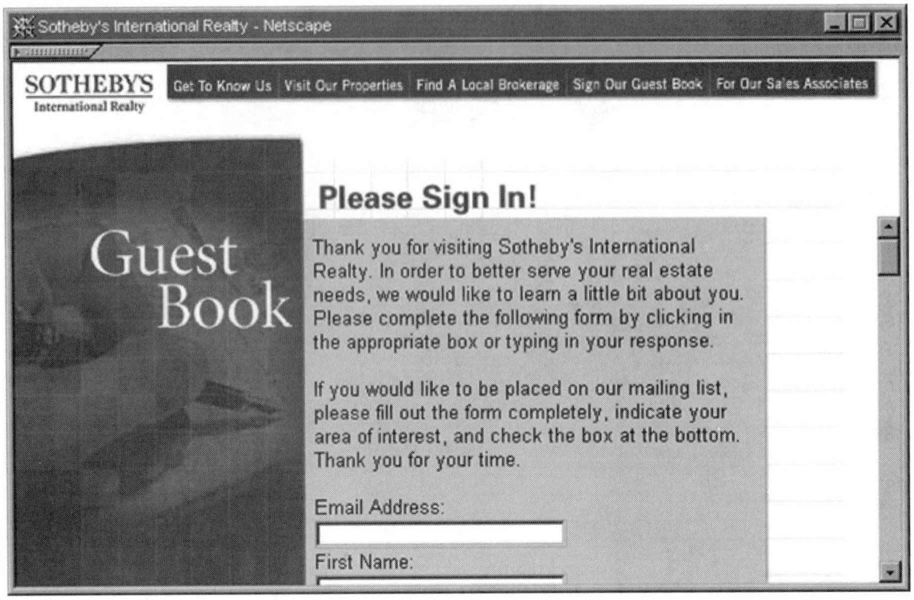


**Figure 4.7** Graphic design choices included consistent placement of the company's brand identity (the logo in the upper-left corner) and clear and consistent site navigation tools (presented in the menu bar at the top of the page). ©1997 Sotheby's International Realty, Inc.

The Web development group determined browser standards and developed a JavaScript menu that helped define the user experience—that is, the information design and implementation we felt was critical in determining what the Web site users' experience is like when they visit the site. In short, we considered what the Web surfer sees and how they are directed through the information presented on the site. Programmers worked with the team to ensure that the pages could be produced by the database and that the technical architecture supported design requirements. This became necessary given that, with this site, many of the pages are assembled on the fly using information pulled from different sources. One of the stages of development consists of mapping out how the information is pulled together in the HTML environment.

### The Clash of Technology and Design

One of the most important issues in interface design is the creative process and how to reconcile the often-competing interests of technology and design. Technology requires consistency and building reusable lines of code. Ideally, technology is developed to work the same way each time—that is, it is important that the code follows specific rules and flawlessly executes the user's commands. Bugs in the code need to be found and removed. Technology favors stability above all, and once a technology solution is selected and built, stability takes precedence over change.

In contrast, visual user interface design demands continual reinvention, and often its requirements for success are fueled by change. Multiple cultural streams—the simultaneous and overlapping layers of constantly changing cultural signifiers that form the cultural matrix—are unpredictable and can sometimes seem irrational and feed visual user interface design: There is enormous pressure to push the envelope and create designs that show bold new directions. Although technology and design are equally creative activities, the differences in methodologies necessary to produce outstanding work are sometimes in conflict. On a positive note, these differences can lead to creative clashes that generate breakthrough ideas.

**Example: Warner Music Group: Ear1** (www.ear1.com). The Ear1 Web site, which Razorfish developed for the Warner Music Group, illustrates how reconciling the competing requirements of technology and design can result in a unique new-media solution (see Figure 4.8).

Combining the vast musical resources of Warner Music Group's record labels, Warner Bros./Reprise, Elektra, Atlantic, and their affiliates, Ear1 is one of the largest artist-driven Web sites. Razorfish developed the Ear1 site structure to leverage and house the continuous flow of dynamic content. This content is automatically displayed when the user calls up a Web page. Thus, the system allows for continuous input of new content that is immediately and dynamically available to users who visit the site. Leveraging a relational database, Warner Music Group and Razorfish incorporated many layers of functionality that allow for easy access to the site's vast artist and music resources. Relational databases offer infinite flexibility because the information is not housed in a static, rigidly structured manner. A relational database is a collection of tables of data, with the data stored in specific tables. Tables have columns, rows, and names. The programmer of the database can allow for the tables of data to be related to one another. For example, the command "Show me all of the rock guitar players" would query a database of musicians. In a relational

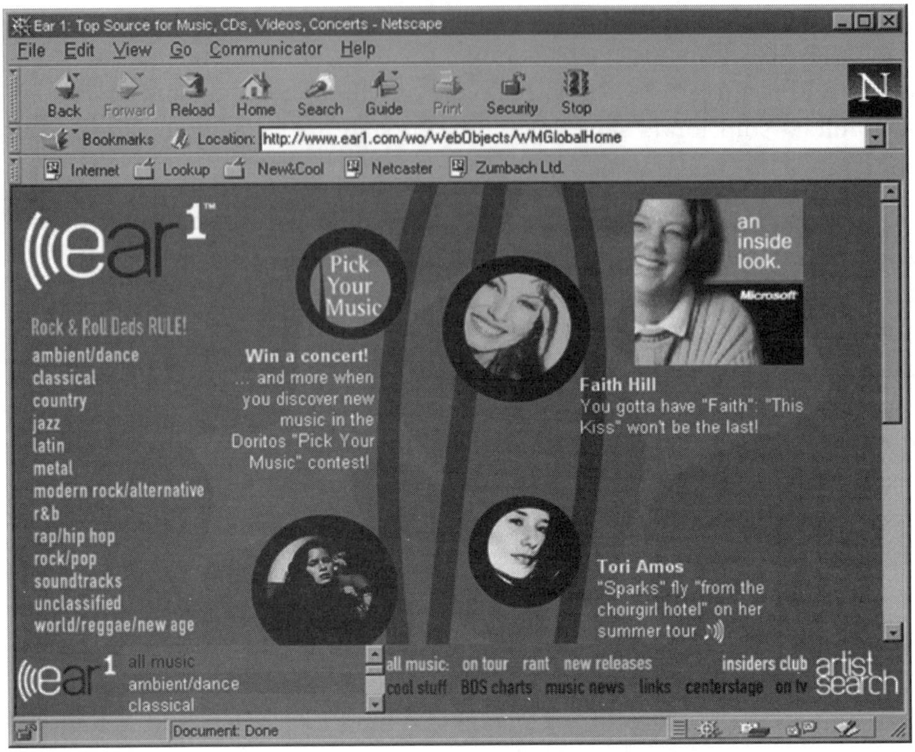


**Figure 4.8** The design challenge of the Ear1 Web site was to balance a wide range of information with a progressive-looking site that would entice music lovers. ©1998 Warner Music Group.

database, we could add to our query and ask, "Show me all of the rock guitar players who also have made records with Muddy Waters."

The relational database structure supporting the site provides a dynamic publishing system that serves up media objects in a grid that functions with unchanging precision. In contrast, the interface offers the visual pleasure of curves and evokes an atmosphere conducive to musical exploration (see Figure 4.9). The editorial tools used to input content run scripts to reliably update content while throughout the site there are changing abstractions of sound waves for different areas. In addition, a new font was designed for the site. Fonts are full of associations and references, and we wanted to have the Ear1 brand identified as a unique presence.

Leveraging a relational database, Warner Music Group and Razorfish incorporated many layers of functionality that make it easy for users to move through and organize the site's vast artist and music resources.

**Figure 4.9** A solid design can add an upbeat energy that shields the end user from the enormously complex technology driving a Web site's information. ©1998 Warner Music Group.

Organized by genres, the site features artist information, instant sound clips, contests, chat areas, tour dates, and live events, all covering a diverse array of artists across a total of 20 Warner Group labels.

The Ear1 site is a successful example of information design that reveals systems and content. It establishes and launches a new online brand. It relies on an Oracle database and middleware application development with custom Web publishing tools. The information and interface design are integral to this complex back-end database system.

### Good Design Can Help Businesses Transform

Well-designed interface tools have the potential to streamline business processes, build customer relationships, and open up entirely new business opportunities. The tools that need to be designed for businesses are creating new communications, opening new markets, and actually becoming new products and services themselves. For example, Razorfish works with Charles Schwab to develop new vehicles for trading online. Electronic trading is transforming financial institutions. In the following example, the Carnegie Hall site development illustrates how digital changes are transforming cultural institutions as well.

**Example: Carnegie Hall** (carnegiehall.org). Razorfish created Carnegie Hall's Web site, where visitors from around the world can virtually experience the treasures and history of New York City's famed concert Mecca (see Figure 4.10). We designed the site to serve the core audience of concert-goers while attracting a younger, more international audience. Visitors can tour the hall interactively, scan and sample Carnegie Hall's music repertoire, view concert and event information, and purchase tickets.

Razorfish designed and implemented a custom online ticket-sales system for Carnegie Hall as well as publishing tools to help staff update the

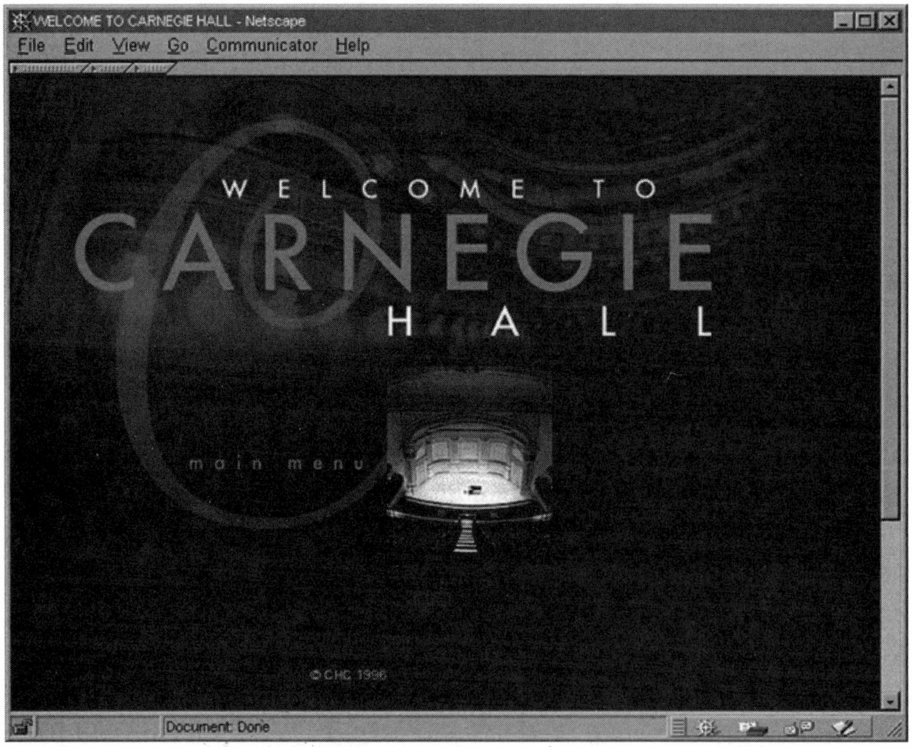


**Figure 4.10** Few concert venues elicit the awe of New York's Carnegie Hall. Successful design captures the aura and ambience for Web visitors. Copyright Carnegie Hall. All rights reserved.

site's content from any Web browser. The site's database also streamlines internal business functions. To facilitate Carnegie Hall's direct marketing to specialized audiences, Razorfish created a system that notifies interested users of upcoming events and offers real-time discounts on ticket sales (see Figure 4.11).

### Web Designers Create New Corporate Identities

A key aspect of visual interface design is its role in creating an overall corporate identity. Interface has introduced new issues in corporate identity. Perceptions of a company's presence consist of customers' thoughts and feelings about an organization. The quality of interaction on a company's Web site now gives visitors a new sense of the nature of the company. With multiple browser types and widely differing machines on which Web sites are displayed, controlling a corporate identity now poses new challenges.

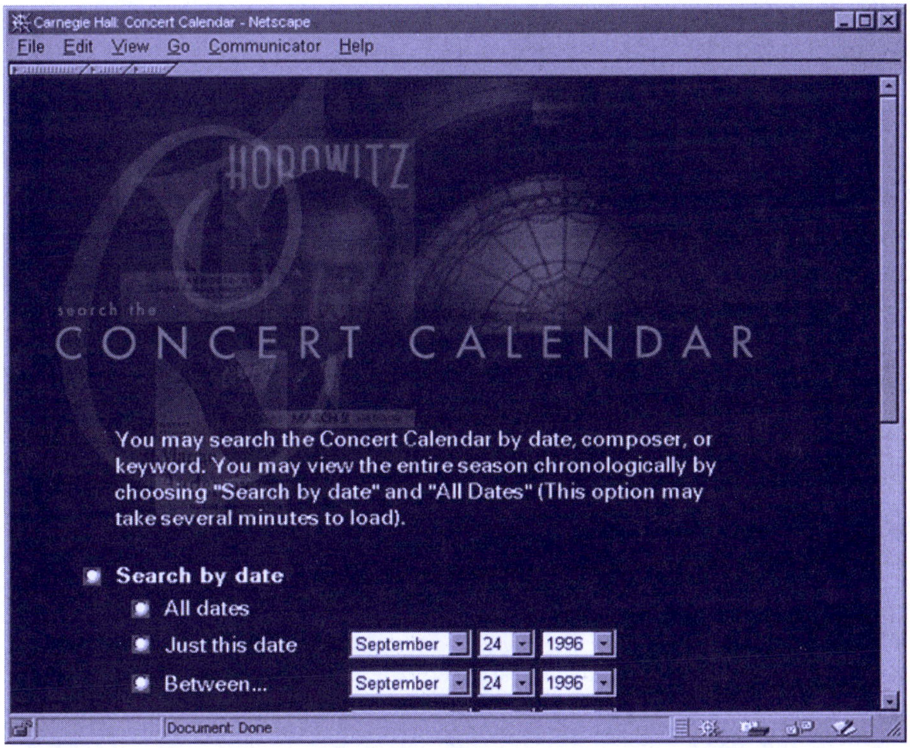


**Figure 4.11** The design remains consistent and elegant, serving as an interface to a searchable database of concert information. Copyright Carnegie Hall. All rights reserved.

The interface is a place where new identities are being developed (see Figure 4.12). The design process should give structure and form the clients' vision and take into account the spectrum of constituents. Mindful design practice includes attention to identity across many types of online audiences. Users arrive at perceptions of companies and products through both the content and feel on screen. These issues must be considered during the Web design process because they shape the company's communications.

### The Designer and Information Architecture

*Information design* refers to how data is grouped. Once a project's goals are defined, the designer organizes data into meaningful arrangements—that is, arranges content and sequences the experience, thereby prioritizing the importance of the information on the site. For example, information at the top is more important than information at the bottom of the screen.

Interface designers are charged with the task of giving form to business concepts and making those ideas understandable and functional. A distinct attribute of interface design is that it must be functional as well as visually appealing in order to accomplish business goals. Interface designers must work as information architects now that information products—those that can be distributed digitally—are becoming mission critical to business. Designers must create new frameworks upon which visual elements are built. The framework must organize data and quickly communicate a context and give a sense of the structures in abstract information space—ways of organizing information so that it becomes more useful. Interface design is successful when hierarchies are clear and the user can interact easily with data structures.

### The Fundamental Steps of Design Activity

In working with a visual user interface designer, it's helpful to consider the nature of the design process itself.

There are two structures that characterize the visual user interface design process. They can be characterized as *vertical* and *horizontal.* The vertical structure involves a chronological sequence of activities that are described

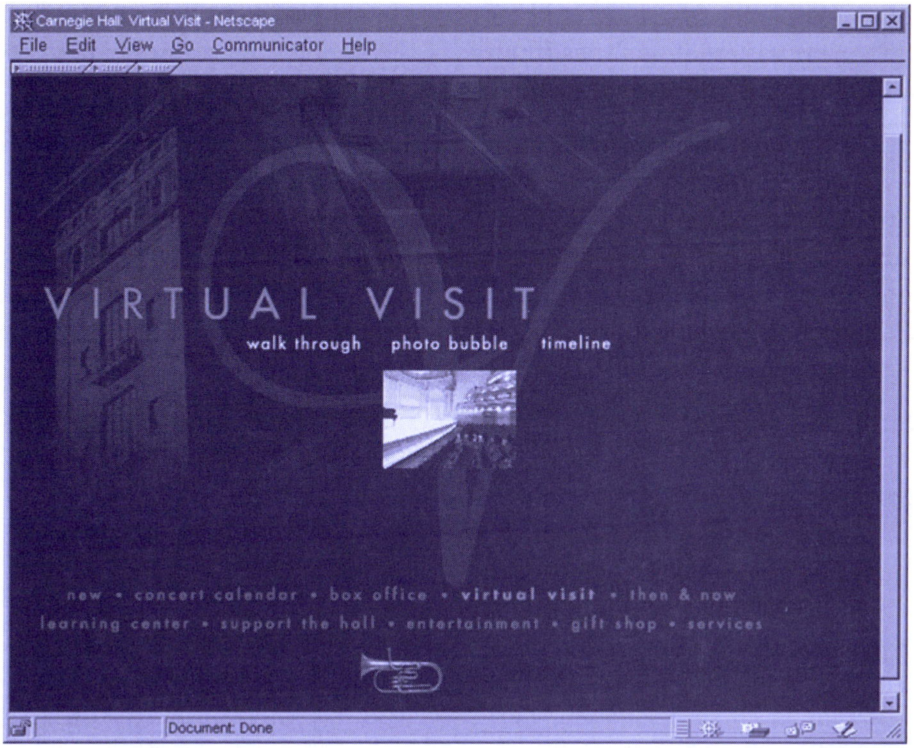


**Figure 4.12** For a global audience, the virtual visit to Carnegie Hall has the power to shape the actual perceptions of the concert hall to future customers who haven't yet set foot inside its doors. 

in this section. These activities are sometimes repeated during the course of a project's development and can happen repeatedly for multiple parts of a project. The horizontal structures form the decision-making cycle.

**Definition of Need.** In the realm of visual user interface design, there are well-defined and inadequately defined design problems. For many interface design problems, solutions are unknown at the outset. Usually, a client comes to the designer to build a Web site where the general thrust of the design problem may be clear, but team members must spend substantial time and effort working with the client to clarify the requirements. The client should expect the design firm to guide it through this process. A large part of interface design consists of defining (and periodically revisiting) problems. As an example, working from the creative brief at the start of the creation of the G-Shock site for Casio, Razorfish spent many weeks working to determine the nature of the Web site or the site's many different qualities (there is a section on creative briefs later in this chapter).

**Research, Incubation, and Immersion.** After the problem is defined, client and designer must allocate time for preparation of the design task. This incubation phase serves as a period of preparation for development, the time during which the designer collects information from as many related sources as possible. Such sources may include specific research results, imagery, graphic elements, audio samples, photography, text elements, visual data, and mental models.

During this phase in the design of the FAO Schwarz Web site, the Razorfish team spent many days in the FAO Schwarz stores, wandering the aisles, looking at the product from the point of view of the child, parent, and store employee. They went through archives of historical photographs of stores and the brand. They looked at the competition and gathered information on the toy design process. They surrounded themselves with merchandise from the store and gathered audio files of music for kids. Over a period of several weeks, the studio became a wild mess of photographs, toys, sketches, text documents, and store paraphernalia, all for the purpose of preparing for development.

**Preliminary Design.** In the preliminary design phase, sometimes called the *illumination* or *inspiration phase*, the designer becomes aware of potential solutions. Sometimes flashes of insight and intuition provide solutions; hunches provide leads to follow. During this phase, good designers allow free rein to thoughts about tasks and design elements. There are effective tools that a designer can use; for example, perhaps a circle is proposed as an organizing principle. Often, a guiding idea or rule of thumb can help solve certain design problems. Particular heuristic devices can help organize the problem space. For example, in designing the Web site for FAO Schwarz, we worked from the idea of an interactive toy box—an idea against which we tested designs. A heuristic employed in an interface design problem is often used briefly and then replaced, giving this phase of design an elastic quality.

As an example, during the FAO Schwarz design process a designer decided to use the giant robot elevator in the flagship store as a guiding theme. From this idea, he generated exciting graphical elements that the client approved and that eventually ended up defining the e-commerce area of the site (see Figure 4.13).

**Detailed Design Production Planning.** This is where concepts meet reality. Ideas are integrated and brought into line with specific limitations. Now design production planning can start—including verification of design features and testing of proposed solutions by comparing the design to the original project requirements. The means of production—that is, the authoring tools that we use and the process by which we will create the graphics and integrate them with the programming code—are determined. During this phase, we move incrementally from inferior solutions to better ones.

At Razorfish, this process happens both during team meetings, when all of the team members across disciplines get together to review each team member's work, as well as in smaller meetings between specific team members. Software engineers, Web developers, and information architects

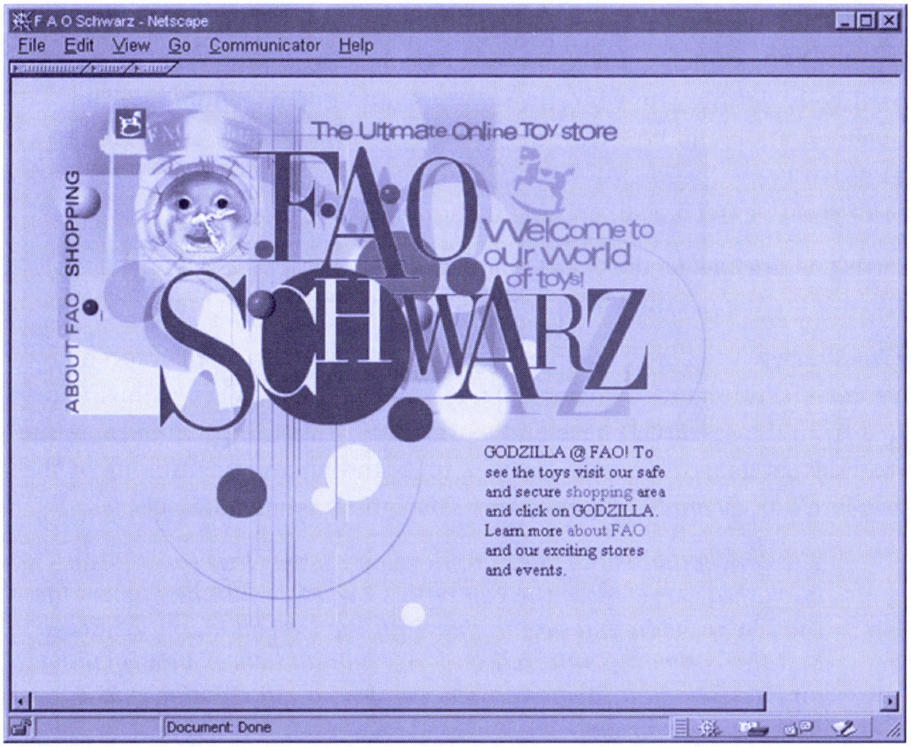


**Figure 4.13** Research led the creative team to understand and implement a look and feel that equates the FAO Schwarz Web site with the existing identity of the world's most famous toy store.

review proposed designs and discuss feasibility. Production works with the design team to map out specific graphics that are needed, and producers develop production timelines and budgets.

**Production.** Once established, the visual look and feel, interface, and navigation of the site are extended and developed. This phase includes development of all areas: icons, specific technical requirements, text treatments, navigation elements, and so on. This phase results in the creation of an overall visual style and a suite of graphic elements. Production refers directly to the design strategy document and the creative brief, which are described in this section, ensuring that the branding objectives are actualized in the design of the site.

### Supporting Documents for the Design Process

Experience shows that several written documents are important in the planning of any interface design project, including a creative brief, a design strategy, and a navigation document.

**Creative Brief.** Embracing a wide range of project goals, the creative brief specifically defines site concept, function, audience, technology, and implementation and how they mesh with the broad goals expressed in a design strategy document. A good creative brief provides the framework for all creative, technical, and navigational executions (see Figure 4.14).

**Sample Creative Brief for the Casio G-Shock Web site** (www.gshock.com). Table 4.1 contains the creative brief for the Casio G-Shock Web site.

**Design Strategy.** The research phase leads to formulation of a comprehensive design strategy document. This document presents key elements distilled from the research phase and extrapolates this information to define broad design goals. The main focus is on branding and positioning of the site. Here's an example of a very small design strategy statement:

> *The conceptual challenge is to develop an extranet for a large bank that serves both the company's broad communications objectives by providing design in line with the overall identity system and the company's internal and external audiences by providing an interface that facilitates accessibility to information and manipulation of data.*
>
> *In order to leverage the power of the company's new overall identity, we recommend a visual design that consistently extends the*

*company's communication objectives and style guide. The visual components of the company's new identity can be readily translated into the Web environment. Simple, bold, geometric fields of color; crisp, harmonious typography; and a strong compositional structure activated with unique attributes will both complement the company's identity and enhance usability.*

*The color palette should balance the strong primary red and black of the company mark with broad fields of color in softer hues and lighter values. The typography will consistently extend the type treatments advocated in the communications briefing material, expressing the company's attitudes of being unexpected, unique, simplified, and harmonious. The compositional structure will provide a fresh intuitive organizational system for complex information.*

**Navigation Document.** The navigation document graphically represents the structure of the site and includes a detailed explanation of the information architecture. The architecture includes such things as multimedia asset distribution (the way that the many types of media assets—text,

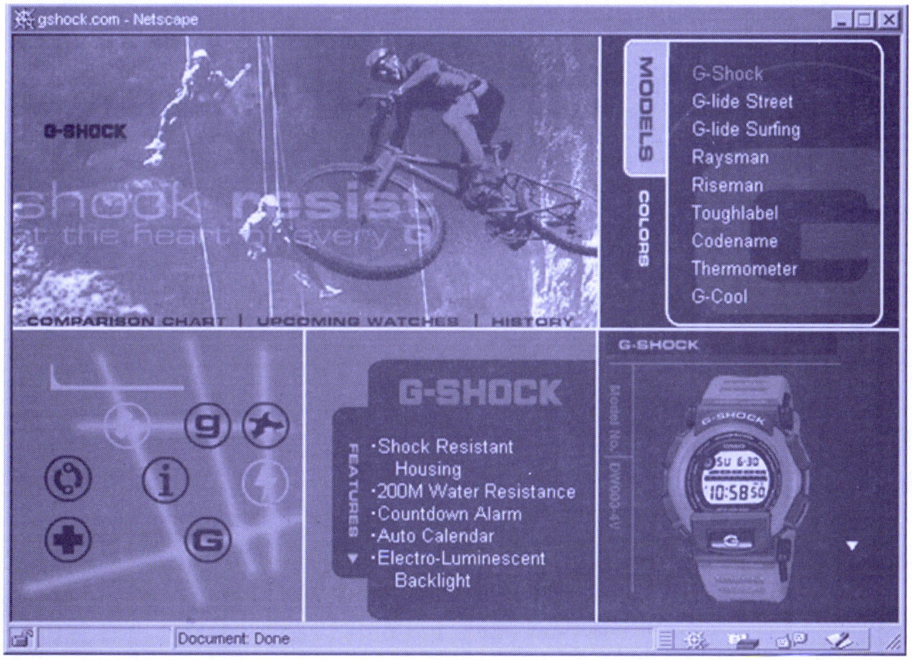


**Figure 4.14** Razorfish's successful translation from creative development to design reality.

**Table 4.1** The Casio G-Shock Creative Brief

| Factor | Details |
|---|---|
| Current situation | The Casio Web site currently has information on the G-Shock brand and on each product within the brand (www.casio.com). The information contained on this Web site was actually developed by, and links to, the parent company in Japan and is housed on their Web site. Casio, Inc., USA is now ready to create a G-Shock Web site for its U.S. customers. Currently, Casio does no Web banner advertising to drive traffic to the site. |
| Assignment | Develop a U.S. based Web site for G-Shock that conveys the essence of the brand, informs customers about current products, demonstrates each product's unique attributes, helps customers purchase the product, informs customers when new products are introduced, creates a dialog with customers, and gathers information for future use. Create and place online advertising to drive traffic to the G-Shock Web site. |
| Target | Men and women aged 14–30 (Gen-Xers) who lead an active lifestyle and/or are fashion conscience.<br>G-Shock: Men<br>Baby-G: Women<br>Extreme sports participants and fashion-minded consumers. |
| Objective | • To enhance the G-Shock brand with the target audience(s)<br>• To provide product information necessary to generate a sale<br>• To generate retail traffic<br>• To gain valuable insight from our current and prospective customers<br>• To develop relationships with G-Shock customers<br>• To lower marketing and operating costs |
| Barriers | • G-Shock is seen as bulky.<br>• G-Shock is attempting to create a new category of timepieces in an established market. |
| Strategies | • Create an interactive experience that motivates our target audience(s) to become connected to the brand<br>• Help guide the customer toward choosing the timepiece that makes a statement about him/herself and his/her lifestyle<br>• In a clean, clear, organized, and attractive fashion. provide the information necessary for the customer to make a purchase decision.<br>• Provide tools that allow customers to find, select, and buy the products that best suit their needs.<br>• Create online mechanisms that allow customers to interact with Casio and other G-Shock customers.<br>• Develop programs that begin to develop a relationship between Casio and its customers. |
| Net take-away | Owning a G-Shock timepiece is making a statement about the way I work, play, and dress. It tells the world that I'm different. Someone to be reckoned with. To be taken seriously. I work hard and play hard. Always pushing the envelope and taking no prisoners along the way. I live for the challenge and attack every day. It tells people about my taste in music, fashion, and activity intensity. My G-Shock watch is my gear for living. |
| Key messages | • G-Shock timepieces are built tough to handle the most active lifestyles.<br>• Owning a G-Shock timepiece is about making a statement about your lifestyle.<br>• G-Shock has a timepiece to fit every lifestyle. |
| Creative considerations | • Tagline: "Time for the 21st century."<br>• Keywords: Technology, Intensity, Durability, Resistance, Power, Resilience, Cool, Trendy, Different, Fashionable.<br>• Product is currently demonstrated in conjunction with extreme sports (surfing, snowboarding, rock climbing, rollerblading, etc.) and has a strong connection to the music world.<br>• G-Shock timepieces, although targeted to active lifestyles, must have mass-market appeal. |
| Products | • G-Shock Timepieces<br>– G-Shock<br>– G-Lide<br>– G-Cool<br>– ToughLabel<br>– Riseman<br>– Codename<br>– Mudman (Combi)<br>– Twin Sensor<br>– Rust Resist Tide Graph<br>– Triple Crown<br>– Baby-G Timepieces<br>– Baby-G<br>– G-Lide<br>– ToughLabel |

**Table 4.1** *Continued*

| Factor | Details |
|---|---|
| Call to action | • Visit your local retailer to purchase the G-Shock that fits your lifestyle.<br>• Talk to us or request more information online.<br>• Give us your thoughts, comments, or suggestions online. |
| Tone and manner | Edgy and irreverent, yet has mainstream market appeal. |
| Deliverables | G-Shock Web site, Web advertising banners ,and online advertising placement services. Banner effectiveness reporting (preferably from third-party measurement service). |

image, and sound—are presented, or "published," to the user) as well as how site traffic flow (how visitors interact as they move through the site) is represented (see Figure 4.15).

## Summary

The Web is a technologist's medium. It is the job of the design process to enable technology transparently for the end user. This chapter illustrates the concept that good Web site design is about the process of defining a creative strategy and working through the design process to translate that process into concrete interface design—screens that guide users

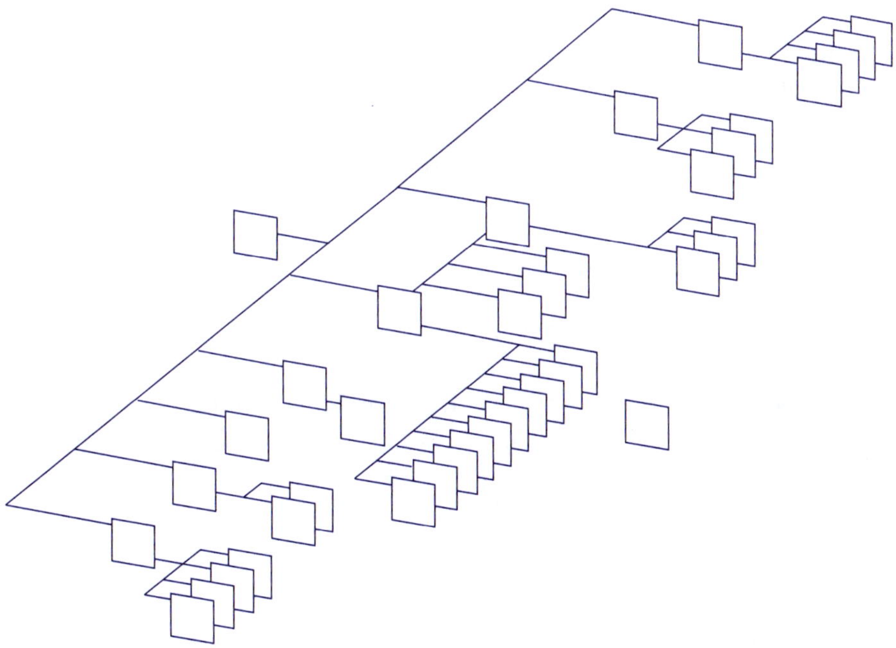

**Figure 4.15** An example of a typical Web site navigation document.

through experiences. Solid planning is also a prerequisite to Web site hosting. It's true that without good design, technology is unusable. It is equally true that without a successful site hosting arrangement, good design never reaches its intended audience. We tackle the complex and significant issue of Web hosting in the next chapter.

## Checklist

- ☐ Have you thought about your company's brand—that important identity moniker that defines who and what your company represents—to potential customers on the Web?
- ☐ What kind of context do you want your site to have? Have you developed a context for your firm's Web site? Do you want it to look like corporate headquarters? Or do you want to do a new and innovative look and feel?
- ☐ Have you created a document that addresses how the design process will be integrated with the content and the technology to be presented on your site?
- ☐ Have you carefully defined your end user and created a technical profile that will govern your design requirements?
- ☐ Brainstorm with your developer. Tell them what you like and what you don't like. Show them examples of marketing materials you like and you dislike, and tell them why. Penchant for the Baroque? Don't be afraid to list your 10 favorite fine artists, writers, and musicians and share them with your developer. The more you share, the more they'll understand who you are and what kind of tastes you and your company lean toward.
- ☐ Check your ego. You may have matched your tie to your swanky new suit—that doesn't make you a designer. Make sure that you say to yourself, "Everything I like is not good, there are things that I don't like that are good, and I need to be open to new ideas," at least five times before meeting your Web developer's design team.

- ☐ Review the design steps and discuss a plan for your involvement in each. These include definition of need, research, preliminary design, design and production planning, and production. Are you involved on a daily basis or only at key checkpoints? Let the designers know so they can have the time and space to create while you have the opportunity for adequate participation in the process.
- ☐ Create a design brief for your project with your developer.
- ☐ Develop a design strategy for your project with your developer.
- ☐ Develop site navigation and architecture for your project with your developer.

chapter

# 5

# Infrastructure and Site Hosting

**Chris Bryant**
**T3 Media, Inc.**
*Cbryant@t3media.com*

## About This Chapter

Few aspects of Web site development are as critical, complicated, and costly as analyzing your site's infrastructure and budgeting for site hosting. Every Web site has unique infrastructure needs, and every developer will approach those needs from a perspective that they have honed after years of creating and hosting Web sites. Of course, new hardware, software, computers, and telecommunications technology require the constant evaluation of infrastructure and site hosting options. As the Web becomes more central to your business and the complexity of your site increases, you can be sure that infrastructure and site hosting capabilities will grow along with it. Gone are the days in which you could call up an Internet Service Provider (ISP), register a URL, and fill 25 megabytes of server space with HTML files. Infrastructure needs and hosting capabilities require a great deal of understanding about the Internet, server capacity, and the technological needs of your current and future site.

This chapter begins with a look at proper infrastructure and hosting planning, takes you through the process of constructing a technology plan for site hosting, and provides a strategy that you can use to review your Web site's needs and map those needs to the appropriate site hosting options. While a good Web developer should help you handle this part of site development (after all, you did outsource your site, right?), it behooves you to understand in as much detail as possible the decision you make as well as the budget implications of those decisions. In fact, many of the issues addressed in this chapter (such as what percentage site hosting should be in your total budget) have not received much coverage in trade publications. Finally, this chapter takes you through the information you need in order to choose a host solution. The chapter concludes with an analysis of whether or not it is more cost effective to build your own infrastructure and host your Web site yourself, or buy site hosting services from a Web developer and/or ISP.

### About the Author

Chris Bryant is the CEO and founding partner of T3 Media, one of the most respected and largest independent interactive agencies in New York City. He has more than a decade of technology-related experience including five years of Internet-related development work. Chris is considered a pioneer in the New York new media community, and his company has produced some of the most notable Web sites across a diverse range of industries including technology, finance, media, and entertainment. Sites produced by his company include development projects for Microsoft, Digital Equipment Corporation, American Express, and Sir Andrew Lloyd Webber. Bryant is considered an industry expert on the topics of site hosting, database-delivered Web projects, and technology planning as well as client management, customer service, and the general business and financial state of the Web development industry.

**This chapter examines the process and exposes the costs of selecting a Web site hosting solution. Because this book focuses on outsourcing, this chapter will focus on Internet sites. In most cases, intranet and extranet sites will be at least partially hosted on your own network, significantly increasing the difficulty of presenting a meaningful generic analysis.**

This chapter also assumes a broad definition of a hosting solution. Typically, hosting refers to the cost of the space on a server and/or connection line charges. In order to provide you with as clear a picture as possible about site infrastructure and hosting, I include the hardware, software, ISP components, and issues involving your company's larger "technology plan" in my analysis of site hosting options.

While some sources have explored the costs associated with building different types of Web sites, the true costs associated with hosting have largely been ignored.

The chapter is divided into four sections. The first section describes the technology planning process within the context of the overall site development process. The second section discusses different types of Web sites and their hosting requirements. The third section explores the cost of the hosting solution relative to the Web site's total cost of ownership and examines the importance of making the right hosting choices initially. The final section provides a basic introduction to the Internet and its terminology and explores the process of finding and evaluating site-hosting solutions. The chapter concludes with a build-versus-buy analysis of site hosting.

## The Web Site Development Process: Technology Planning

The process of building a Web site is a relatively new experience. Unless you've been involved in large-scale project management in the past, you may not be prepared for what will ensue. Web site development involves some very different skill sets and requires managers to temporarily become experts in the fields of marketing, design, technology, and project management. This is obviously a tall order for any individual. Nevertheless, the creation of a successful Web site requires vision in all of these disciplines.

Fortunately, a new type of organization has evolved to fill this need. Interactive agencies combine much of the creative and marketing capabilities of traditional advertising agencies with the technology capabilities of system integrators. The best companies also add strong project management skills to the mix to form an organization optimized for creating Web properties.

As the industry is still young, there is very little information readily available about the process, costs, and pitfalls of building Web sites. Many managers begin the process of building a Web site without a clear understanding of what's involved.

The process of building a Web site typically begins with a thorough analysis and assessment of a company's needs. After determining the need for a Web site and the need to outsource, a manager prequalifies several firms. Prequalification generally consists of reviewing a vendor's capabilities, checking its client references, and establishing a preliminary rapport. After prequalifying a few, an RFP (Request for Proposal) is distributed to the vendors asking for a quote on a defined project. Some companies may begin the process with an RFP and skip the initial review process, while others may actually select a company from the initial review process to help determine their Web site requirements. Regardless of how the process is initiated, the object is to get several proposals for comparison.

Once the initial shock of development costs wears off, managers must begin evaluating each vendor's approach and pricing. It is important at this point to understand that the proposal will only reflect the initial development costs and not the additional yearly maintenance costs. It is also critical to understand the importance of the hosting solution and the impact it has on those maintenance costs.

So let's not focus on the costs involved just yet. Instead, let's jump ahead to the point at which the Web site planning begins. Assume we've already chosen an interactive agency vendor and now we've got to define the Web site's specifications. Requirement analysis and technology planning are crucial at this phase to ensure the appropriate ISP and technology-hosting solution are chosen.

Let's begin the discussion by reviewing a typical Web site development process. It will be helpful to differentiate between the planning process

**Table 5.1** T3 Media's Infrastructure Planning and Site Hosting Analysis Takes Place within the Larger Context of Web Site Development

| Process | Output |
| --- | --- |
| Analysis and needs assessment | Needs Assessment |
| Business planning | Site Business Plan |
| Strategic planning | Marketing and Strategy Briefs |
| Technology planning | Technology Plan and Specification |
| Creative design | Creative Brief |
| Functional design | Functional Specification |
| Technical design | Technical Specification |
| Quality assurance | Site Release Specification |

and the actual documents created as a result of the process. The process is important because it enables agencies to consistently produce high-quality Web sites. Table 5.1 outlines T3 Media's Web site development processes, and its respective planning documents. Other chapters in this book discuss processes in greater detail, but I felt it important to include a quick snapshot of them here so that you can understand how they relate to site hosting.

**What Is a Technology Plan?** The development of all Web sites can be broken down into three phases: pre-production, production, and post-production. What happens during each of those phases will differ between Web sites and development companies. To fully understand the role of a technology plan in a site's development, it is necessary to view it relative to the other Web site planning documents. The Web site planning documents used by T3 Media are listed in Table 5.1. Although they have been addressed in other chapters, I will briefly describe them to give you a basis for understanding how site hosting impacts all phases of the Web development process.

The Site Business Plan should be the first document created after the Needs Assessment. As the name implies, it contains the business justification for the creation of the site. It will project any anticipated revenues and/or cost savings against the development and maintenance costs of the site. Like all business plans, it is a living document. It will change and should be updated as assumptions and realities change.

The Marketing and Strategy Briefs identify the site's target audience as well as specific marketing and strategic goals to be accomplished by the site. It is not uncommon to include site performance metrics like "increasing the number of qualified leads generated by 150 percent" or "decreasing the number of inbound calls to a help desk by 25 percent."

The Creative Brief defines how the site's graphical and navigational design will help achieve the goals set forth in the Marketing and Strategy Briefs. It may also address more specific branding issues, colors, and font choices to be used in the site. It serves as a high-level document to frame the project's creative boundaries.

The Technology Plan is also derived from the Marketing Brief. It outlines the project's technology goals, and can consist of anything from a simple statement about how you plan to facilitate the future growth and expansion of your Web site to a complex document specifying hardware, software, and physical network and data designs. In general, a technology plan includes:

- How you plan to use your Web site today and in the future
- High-level requirements that may impact your technology solution
- Future functionality or site growth plans
- Estimated bandwidth and infrastructure requirements

The statement of your planned Web site usage can come straight from the Marketing and Strategy Briefs, and it will drive the site's functional and technical requirements. If your site will be used to sell products directly to your customers in the future, then it may need to interface with your inventory and billing systems. At the very least, it will need some type of online commerce (ecommerce) capability. These are important requirements that will impact your hosting solution.

The Technology Plan serves to mitigate technology risk to the extent that you can anticipate future Web site requirements. It will have a direct impact on the initial design of the system and will force system designers to accommodate the site's future growth potential. This concept is commonly referred to as *scalability.*

For example, if you know today that your promotional site will eventually contain an online sales component, you may choose a hosting solution that can easily scale to facilitate ecommerce. If you do not anticipate your site will ever be used as more than a promotional vehicle, there is no need to consider ecommerce.

Another requirement factor often overlooked is multimedia content to be included on the site. Large audio and video files that will be frequently accessed may increase your bandwidth and/or server requirements. Any streaming media such as RealAudio, RealVideo, or NetShow content will require additional servers with resulting additional bandwidth charges. These costs are generally variable based on usage.

Perhaps the most difficult task of all is to estimate the site's traffic. Because the picture of the Internet user base is still sketchy at best, this estimate is typically more intuitive than scientific. There are a number of factors that can affect site traffic, including frequency of content updating, advertising and promotions created to support the site, type of content offered, as well as the size of your traditional customer base. An interactive agency can be a great help here as much of the data available is experiential in nature.

Your best bet is to begin with comparisons of sites you know. To illustrate, consider another Web site within your industry that offers similar functionality and receives approximately 300,000 page views per month. I use page views here as a measure of traffic because it is a more objective measure with which to make comparisons between Web sites. For example, the calculation of visitors or unique visits is often calculated differently between sites—leaving page views as a more objective measure. Additionally, the most heavily trafficked site in the industry receives 2,000,000 page views per month. While it may seem unreasonable to assume your site traffic will approach the high end of the spectrum, you should optimistically plan for something in between. The Web site Functional Specification and Technical Specification are the development road maps for the Web site. The Functional Specification, generally augmented with online prototypes, describes in detail the site's functionality. It contains a statement of the project's scope, a map of the site's structure, detailed description of each site section including detail on all site interactivity. Online mock-ups are often created to show screen flow through interactive elements. The document should also define project terminology and browser and screen resolution specifications. You should expect to sign off on the Functional Specification before any development work begins.

The Technical Specification should detail site access and authentication, servers and applications to be deployed, hardware configuration, engineering systems, and database configurations. The document will be used as a road map for the programmers and engineers and will be based on the Marketing Brief and Technology Plan. Like the Functional Specification, this document will need approval before technical development can be started.

Both the Functional and Technical Specifications should be reviewed by a technical analyst or someone within the IT or MIS department. It is imperative that these documents accurately reflect your expectations before development work begins. Changes to the specifications after approval can have significant budget implications.

Finally, the Web site release document will contain all of the information you need to maintain the Web site, including final file and directory structures, image catalogs, all programming code created, a quality assurance test plan and results, and site bug and issue resolution.

Once you understand the site requirements that will impact hosting, you can begin preparing a requirements document or RFP to be distributed to ISPs. This document can simply be the Technology Plan with an introductory letter requesting pricing to accommodate the system requirements outlined in the plan. We will discuss the typical pricing components and evaluation criteria for choosing an ISP in the final section of this chapter.

### Assessing Your Web Site Needs

Now that we've explained the role of the Technology Plan in the process of creating a site, let's jump back to the initial determination of your Web site needs. It is important to understand some of the different types of Web sites and their particular hosting and technology requirements.

Companies often begin the process of building a Web site without giving much consideration to a hosting solution. Late-night television commercials hawking Web sites for as low as $19.99 per month have given many people the impression that site hosting is a commodity.

While consumer Web site hosting has to some extent become a commodity business, solutions suitable for your business Web site are quite another story. If you are serious about creating a professional presence for your company on the Internet, then a more customized solution from a qualified ISP will be required.

Custom solutions are almost always more expensive, but there are some very good reasons to choose them. While most managers consider domain name and DNS (Domain Name Service) issues to be the most important considerations when dealing with ISPs, there are many more important issues that must be addressed. The ISP's ability to meet your bandwidth requirements, server performance, backup and redundancy planning (in case of network and/or equipment failure), and customer service needs are often overlooked when selecting a hosting solution for your Web site.

As a manager responsible for your company's Internet presence, you need to understand the importance of choosing the right ISP and hosting solution for your Web site. Whether you choose your hosting solution yourself or rely on an interactive agency, it is important to understand your site's hosting requirements. The type of Web site you decide to build will play a large part in driving your hosting requirements. Therefore, it is important to decide what type of Web site you will build prior to selecting a hosting solution.

**Static versus Dynamic.** Before discussing the function your Web site will serve, we need to define some basic concepts. One of the most important factors affecting your hosting requirements will be whether your site will be primarily static or more dynamic in nature. Static Web sites consist of a collection of coded HTML documents organized and stored on a Web server. Each Web "page" has a discrete corresponding file. When a user selects a link, the corresponding HTML page is returned. In contrast, dynamic sites consist of sets of generic HTML templates that are populated with data from a data source at the time a user requests them. The data is added to the template on the fly. In other words, the data is not part of the page until after the user selects the link. Databases are the most common data sources used by dynamic sites. Other dynamic data sources include news and data feeds as well as streaming multimedia content like RealMedia and NetShow content.

To further illustrate, take a look at Figure 5.1. In the case of the static page, a user makes a request to the Web server for a specific page and the server returns it.

However, with the dynamic page, we can see that each request for a particular page is more complicated. The browser queries the Web server

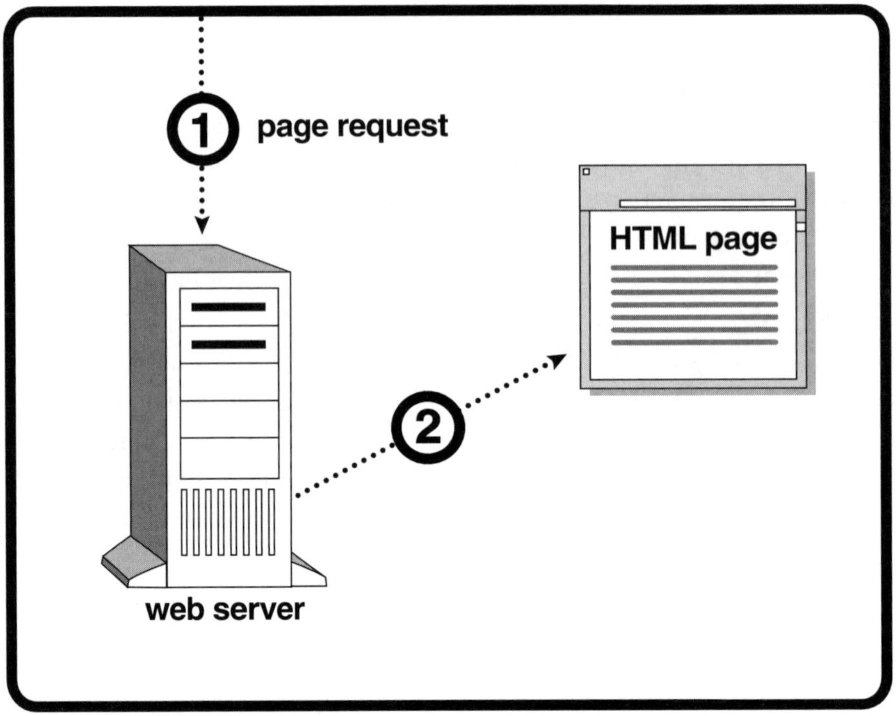


**Figure 5.1** The simple infrastructure and hosting needs of a site that is strictly delivering static HTML pages.

and the server returns a template. The template is then filled with appropriate content queried from the database. The Web server receives the data, adds it to the template, and returns a completed HTML page to the user.

Dynamic sites generally require a more complex hosting solution than static sites. Most dynamic Web sites are integrated with relational databases that typically require dedicated servers themselves. As discussed in Chapter 4, "Understanding Design," relational databases contain data that enable the user to extract information according to specific relationships. For example, a query that asks the database to show all dress shirts, all dress shirts that are blue, all dress shirts that are blue and are made of cotton, all dress shirts that are blue and are made of cotton and are button-down in style. One query in a relational database would allow this type of information to be extracted. To see what I mean, take a look at Figure 5.2.

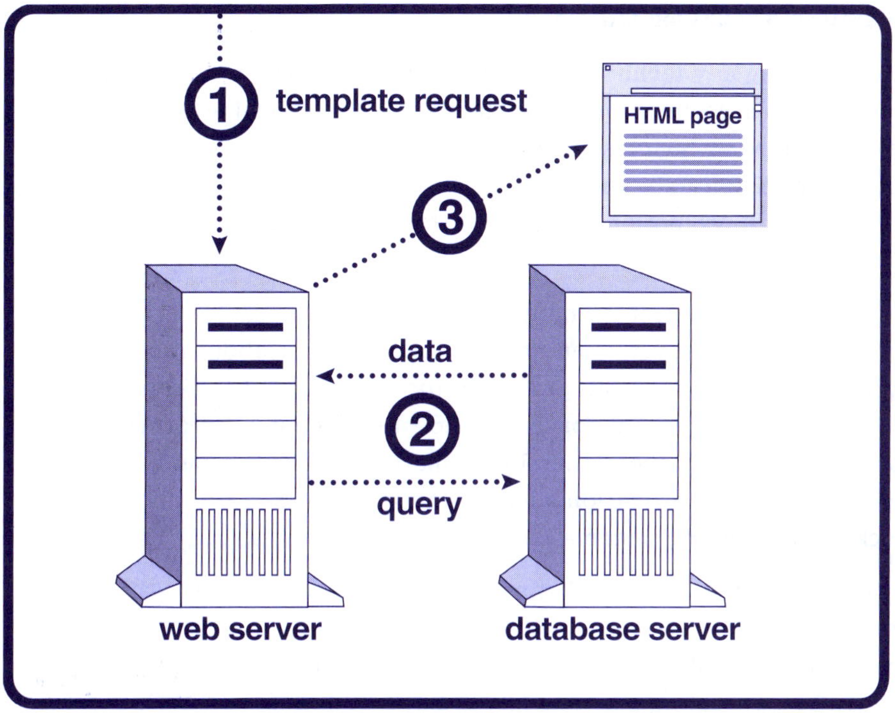


**Figure 5.2** The infrastructure and hosting requirements for a dynamic Web site. Note that a dynamic Web site can require two separate servers: one for the Web site and one for the database accessed by the Web site.

The process of retrieving a static page requires two steps: the document request and its return to the user. A dynamic request requires an additional query to a data source to create the page before it can be returned.

An additional data source is required to support a dynamic Web site. In our example, the data source is a database residing on a separate server. Although it is possible to host both the database and Web server on the same machine, it isn't recommended. Databases require a large amount of system resources and can negatively impact the performance of your Web site.

As you can see, the hosting requirements are more complex for a dynamic database-driven site. But how do you know if you need a dynamic site or not? Before you can answer this question, you must have a better understanding of the purpose your site will serve.

### Determining Your Web Site Needs

Before making any technology decisions it is important to go through a basic needs assessment process. The idea is to determine what type of Web site fits your business and marketing needs as well as your budget. The first decision to be made is whether your Web site will be primarily a marketing and promotional tool, or if it will be used to meet other specific business objectives.

For many businesses, it is enough to offer a site for customers, investors, and prospective employees to learn more about their company. Promotional sites can provide information about the company's products and services, history, office locations, contact information, job opportunities, and other general information. Public companies often include investor information such as annual reports, 10Ks, and annual stockholder meeting information.

A well-executed promotional site can be a good first step for companies experimenting with a Web presence. Building a Web site can create many unexpected problems (as discussed in other chapters), so minimizing your risks by creating a simple site is not a bad idea.

Promotional sites are most often static but can have interactive features like data collection forms and quizzes using simple CGI (Common Gateway Interface) scripting. This type of interactivity does not require additional servers.

To get a feel for what a well-executed promotional site will cost, let's take a look at an actual budget. Table 5.2 gives you insight into how much of your budget you should allocate to site hosting. For this example, I have taken a budget originally prepared by T3 Media for a large corporate client that required a static site for one of its divisions. The site was purely promotional and included five sections containing approximately 80 static HTML pages. The site contained a JavaScript ticker on the homepage that could be dynamically updated using a Web-based form.

While the focus of this chapter is on the Web site hosting solution, it is important to understand the hosting costs relative to the rest of the site. For this reason I have opted to include a complete site budget. There are two key points to note. As you can see, hosting comprises two of the

**Table 5.2** Basic Sample Budget for a Static, Promotional Web Site

| | |
|---|---|
| **1. Pre-production (2 weeks)**<br>Site development and planning<br>Marketing, Creative, and Technology Briefs<br>Functional Specification | **$18,000** |
| **2. Production (6 weeks)**<br>Design and production<br>HTML and scripting<br>Copywriting | **$37,200** |
| **3. Post-production (2 weeks)**<br>Quality assurance<br>Site marketing and promotion | **$8,750** |
| **4. Project management (10 weeks)** | **$15,000** |
| **5. Hosting startup** | **$5,000** |
| **6. Hosting monthly** | **$3,000** |
| **7. Monthly maintenance (beginning 2nd month)** | **$2,000** |
| **Total startup (includes 1st month of hosting)** | **$86,950** |

seven line items in the budget but makes up less than 10 percent (8,000/86,950) of the initial cost of a promotional Web site. Also, a promotional site of this size only takes about 10 weeks to develop, but its hosting solution continues on for the life of the site. These ongoing costs are typically not addressed within development budgets but make up a significant portion of a Web site's total cost of ownership. We'll explore this more in the next section.

To wrap up, promotional sites are the quickest and easiest to develop. They have the least-complicated hosting requirements and can be a good first offering for companies building their first Web site. On the downside, most Internet users expect more interactivity, and a promotional billboard in cyberspace may characterize you as lacking technology savvy relative to your competition.

**Business-Driven Web Sites.** Many companies already have promotional Web sites and for them the minimum requirement is no longer enough. Experienced managers who have addressed the issues associated with having an Internet presence will want to take the next step: A business-driven Web site solution that offers a solid ROI (Return on Investment). While there are not always technological differences between promotional and business-driven Web sites, the latter are typically more dynamic and thus have more complex technology requirements.

Business-driven Web sites are created to address specific business goals with ROI as the primary objective. Goals can include the creation of incremental revenue streams or the reduction of operating expenses. Either way, the objective is to realize a return on your Web site investment.

Although the promise of incremental revenue is still largely unrealized by companies on the Internet, there are a few highly publicized exceptions like amazon.com and Dell Computers. Many managers have rationalized their Internet budgets by citing these two companies as examples of what could be. For most businesses to date though, the growing cost associated with building and maintaining Web sites has outpaced the growth of revenues.

A much more successful, and less publicized, way to make money on the Internet is by lowering costs associated with servicing your customers. Companies have experienced cost savings by reducing the number of 800 calls requesting general information about their products and services. For instance, one of T3 Media's large corporate clients was able to reduce both the average number of calls per day and the average length of those calls by creating lists of the most Frequently Asked Questions (FAQs) online. Directing customers to online brochures and publications can reduce postage and handling costs.

Your goals do not have to be so ambitious for your Web site to be successful. Other examples of business goals include collecting qualified leads for your sales department, initiation of transactions online to be completed by a salesperson, or simply collecting more specific information about your customers to better serve them.

Now let's take a look at a budget for a more dynamic ROI-based Web site. This site was built for a client to sell approximately 15,000 different electronic documents online. These documents were frequently updated and the client needed to be able to add new documents, edit existing documents, and delete old documents from the site. The company had no staff capable of editing HTML documents. Additionally, the homepage needed to display the latest documents added to the site and also the latest updates to existing documents. All of this needed to be done on the fly.

The Web site clearly needed to be dynamic, so T3 Media proposed storing all of the content in a database. All of the pertinent information including statistics, synopses, and URLs (Uniform Resource Locators) about the actual documents was created and maintained on a separate database server. To allow the client to easily update the database content and upload new documents to the site, Web-based content-management tools were created by T3 Media. Users could add, edit, and delete records in the database through a browser form from the client's office. Finally, pricing, order tracking, and shopping cart databases had to be integrated with an ecommerce solution. ICVerify and SSL (Secure Sockets Layer) were used to process credit card orders. The budget for the project is displayed in Table 5.3.

As you can see, the budget for this type of Web site is more involved and the costs associated with it are significantly higher than for a static, promotional site. The total time required jumped from 10 weeks to 20 weeks, and the budget increased almost 450 percent. Oddly enough, even though the hosting solution was considerably more complex and expensive, the cost was about 10 percent (35,000/360,150) of the initial startup cost, which is consistent with budgeting for the promotional site.

Business-driven Web sites can help drive your company or department's bottom line by adding revenues or reducing operating costs. Dynamic sites can also add to overall customer satisfaction and may provide a competitive advantage over some of your less-savvy competitors.

**Table 5.3** Typical Site Hosting Costs Associated with the Delivery of Dynamic Web Sites

| | |
|---|---|
| **1. Pre-production (4 weeks)**<br>Site development and planning<br>Marketing, Creative, and Technology Briefs<br>Functional Specification | **$36,000** |
| **2. Production (12 weeks)**<br>Design and production<br>HTML and scripting<br>Copywriting<br>Engineering design and programming | **$174,150** |
| **3. Post-production (4 weeks)**<br>Quality assurance<br>Site marketing and promotion | **$45,000** |
| **4. Project management (20 weeks)** | **$70,000** |
| **5. Hosting startup**<br>Server hardware setup, software purchase/configuration<br>Ecommerce setup and configuration<br>Security configuration | **$30,000** |
| **6. Hosting monthly** | **$5,000** |
| **7. Monthly maintenance** | **$4,000** |
| **Total startup (includes 1st month of hosting)** | **$360,150** |

Depending on your specific objectives, dynamic sites can be much more expensive to build and usually require more complex hosting and technology solutions. Preliminary planning is more costly and time consuming as clear business objectives and measurement criteria must be developed.

**Extranets.** We have discussed some of the initial considerations in determining the business role your site will play. Once you've made the decision to create a dynamic rather than static site, you are quickly faced with another important question: Should you connect your clients directly to your business systems?

This question will have different meanings depending on the nature of your business. For companies selling a product, it could mean allowing customers to interface directly with your inventory, purchasing, and accounting systems via the Internet. For example, a customer could begin a transaction online by first checking your inventory system to make sure an item is in stock. Once the stock has been confirmed, your customer's credit card could be accepted with the resulting transaction entered directly into your accounting system. This type of dynamic Web site is commonly referred to as an *extranet.*

To fully understand what an extranet is, let's review some other networking concepts. By now, everyone should be familiar with the term *internet,* which is a collection of interconnected networks. Notice that internet is a generic networking while *Internet* refers to the public network we all have in common. More and more company managers are now being exposed to the concept of an intranet. An *intranet* system can best be described as an intra-departmental or intra-company network that is not connected to the public Internet. Now let's put the two concepts together to create an extra-company network. At its most basic level, an extranet is an intranet system connected to the public Internet.

While extranet systems can be technologically complex, they are the key to the successes Dell Computers and amazon.com have enjoyed on the Internet. While there is no such thing as a generic example of extranet hosting and technology requirements, suffice it to say these projects are an order of magnitude more complex and expensive than a dynamic Web site.

If your business is service based, you might consider offering something slightly different from what your competitors offer to your customers. For example, one of our large financial clients has been servicing its largest customer group, the Federal Government, for years via fax and telephone. The company offers managers within the Federal Government the ability to add new members, change their addresses, and create monthly spending reports by faxing account representatives detailed request forms. While the government is relatively happy with this service, there are a few problems. It costs the company millions of dollars to fulfill these services each year and the process is highly subject to error.

In October of 1997, T3 Media was hired to design and create an extranet site targeted at this government clientele. The idea was simple: Build a secure, private Web site that would allow government managers to make their own changes and create their own reports securely over the Internet, thereby saving customer service dollars and improving the government's experience with our client.

The site required the creation of *middleware* (software written to connect Web sites to legacy systems) to interface with our client's mainframe computers, making the budget extremely complex. And since our client operated its own data centers, hosting costs were not applicable. For those reasons, I have opted not to include it. For a relative comparison to the other two types of sites, though, the project cost approximately $1,000,000 and took seven months to complete.

Making a commitment to build an extranet site can substantially lower your customer service and sales transaction costs. It can also give your business a head start on your competition.

Of course, with the promise of huge upside potential comes risk. The most critical issue is the security risk of exposing your proprietary systems and information to the world and your competition. Integrating a Web site into your backend business systems can also be very expensive. The technical complexity involved in this integration is extremely high and qualified developers are difficult to find.

### Hosting: The Long-Term Budget Implications

We have discussed a few different types of sites, the reasons you might choose each, and some examples of typical budgets. As mentioned in the last section, analyzing the initial development costs does not tell the whole story. In this section, we'll examine the long-term impact site hosting will have on your Web site budget and what can happen when you select the wrong hosting solution.

We'll begin with our promotional site example from the last section. Remember that the site contained five sections with approximately 80 static HTML pages and an updateable JavaScript ticker on the homepage.

Our original budget (Table 5.2) included total costs through the launch of the site. Now let's take a look at what happens after the site is completed. Once the site is launched it will be updated monthly with new information. To keep the site fresh, it will be redesigned at the beginning of year 2, and then again at the beginning of year 3 (see Table 5.4).

Remember that less than 10 percent of the development cost was related to the hosting solution chosen. According to the budget, that included the hosting startup costs and the first month of hosting charges. This budget only told a fraction of the story.

To get the whole story, we need to take a look at the cost to maintain the site over a reasonable period of time. Let's project the maintenance, hosting and redesign costs over a three-year period (see Table 5.5). Because the site will take 10 weeks to build, we'll only have 9 months of maintenance charges during the first year. We'll assume that our two redesign charges will be roughly half the cost of the initial site, or $40,000 each.

As you can see in Table 5.5 the site will actually cost significantly more than the original $90,000. In fact, the largest part of your Web site's cost

**Table 5.4** Long-Term Budget Implications for Hosting a Promotional Web Site

| | |
|---|---|
| 1. Pre-production (2 weeks) | $18,000 |
| 2. Production (6 weeks) | $37,200 |
| 3. Post-production (2 weeks) | $8,750 |
| 4. Project management (10 weeks) | $15,000 |
| 5. Hosting startup | $5,000 |
| 6. Hosting monthly | $3,000 |
| 7. Monthly maintenance | $2,000 |
| **Total startup (includes 1st month of hosting)** | **$86,950** |

**Table 5.5** A Look at the Site Hosting Costs for a Static Web Site over a Three-Year Period

| | |
|---|---|
| **Total 1st year** | **$159,950** |
| 9 months of maintenance @ $2,000/month | |
| 11 months of hosting @ $3,000/month | |
| **Total 2nd year** | **$100,000** |
| $40,000 redesign | |
| 12 months of hosting @ $3,000/month | |
| **Total 3rd year (includes $40K redesign)** | **$100,000** |
| $40,000 redesign | |
| 12 months of hosting @ $3,000/month | |
| **3-year total** | **$359,950** |

will be realized *after* the site is completed. This promotional Web site is actually going to cost nearly $360,000 over the next three years.

But what does that have to do with hosting? Let's take a look at one more chart. Table 5.6 shows the percentage of hosting costs each year. Although it only makes up 9 percent of the initial costs, hosting averages over 30 percent of the three-year running costs.

With hosting making up such a large portion of the Web site's total cost of ownership, it is important to make sure you choose a solution that can serve your needs for the long term. Selecting the wrong hosting solution can impact your Web site as well as your business.

Let's assume you chose a comparatively cheaper hosting solution from a local ISP. Your site was well designed and offered lots of great content. It was also listed on many search and directory sites, and as a result it generated lots of traffic. Unfortunately, you realized later during the first year that your hosting solution was not sufficient for handling all the traffic. Six months after launching the site, you were forced (after many complaints from users about performance) to move the site to a new ISP. This change was not only very expensive but was also very embarrassing, as you had to explain the additional expenditures to your boss.

**Business-Driven Web Sites.** Now let's do the same analysis we just did for our promotional site on our business-driven Web site example.

To add context to the example, let's assume that ACME Reports, Inc. wants to build a site to sell about 15,000 different documents online.

**Table 5.6** The Long-Term Cost of Infrastructure and Hosting Is Likely to Be One of the Biggest Expenses You Will Incur in Developing Your Site

| | |
|---|---|
| **Startup (8,000/86,950)** | **9%** |
| **1st year (38,000/159,950)**<br>$5,000 startup costs<br>11 months of hosting @ $3,000/month | **24%** |
| **2nd year (36,000/100,000)**<br>12 months of hosting @ $3,000/month | **36%** |
| **3rd year (36,000/100,000)**<br>12 months of hosting @ $3,000/month | **36%** |
| **3-year average (110,000/359,950)** | **31%** |

Their Web site requirements include:

- Making all 15,000 documents available for sale online
- Allowing ACME employees to post new and edited documents to the site immediately and with minimal effort
- Featuring information about new and updated documents on the homepage as soon as they are available

In the second year, ACME would like to offer customers their own customized homepages at a cost of $80,000, and in the third year spend $100,000 for profiling software that customizes displays, showing only the documents that match users' historic browsing and purchasing profiles.

The site developer recognizes immediately that the site must be template based and database driven to accommodate the requirements. To enable ACME to update the database monthly, the developer offers to build Web-based update forms so that ACME can remotely add content to the database through any Web browser without needing to know HTML.

To support the projected growth in traffic due to the site's popularity and the additional processing requirements of the custom Web sites, the developer plans to separate the Web and database servers onto two separate machines in the second year, thereby increasing hosting costs by $3,000 per month. Because the update forms will allow ACME to do much of its own site content updating, monthly maintenance fees for site updating will only be about $4,000 per month.

The budget for the 20-week project is shown in Table 5.7.

**Table 5.7** A Look at the Costs Associated with the Development of a Business Web Site

| | |
|---|---|
| **1. Pre-production (4 weeks)**<br>Site development and planning<br>(Strategic, Creative and Technology Plans) | **$36,000** |
| **2. Production (12 weeks)**<br>Design and production<br>HTML and scripting<br>Copywriting<br>Engineering design and programming | **$174,150** |
| **3. Post-production (4 weeks)**<br>Quality assurance<br>Site marketing and promotion | **$45,000** |
| **4. Project management (20 weeks)** | **$70,000** |
| **5. Hosting startup**<br>Server hardware setup, software purchase/configuration<br>Ecommerce setup and configuration (does not include the costs associated with obtaining a financial institution and setting up merchant accounts)<br>Security configuration | **$30,000** |
| **6. Hosting monthly** | **$5,000** |
| **7. Monthly maintenance** | **$4,000** |
| **Total startup (includes 1st month of hosting)** | **$360,150** |

As stated earlier, the costs associated with business-driven Web sites can be substantially higher than promotional sites. ACME's site requirements are similar to many sites on the Web today. Before we make any judgments about the magnitude of cost difference, let's take a look at the three-year costs (see Table 5.8).

Once again, the costs of the Web site are realized after launch. This $350,000 Web site actually costs almost $450,000 in the first year and nearly $900,000 over three years.

Now let's see the role hosting played in these costs. Table 5.9 breaks the hosting costs down as a percentage of the entire project. Although hosting for a dynamic site makes up a larger portion of the initial costs, it is still small relative to the yearly cost ratios. Note that site infrastructure and hosting represents a major percentage of the budget.

As with the promotional site, the percentage of total cost that the technology solution comprises significantly increases after the site development is complete. At this level, choosing the wrong ISP can have significantly higher cost implications, and perhaps even some career implications for the unfortunate manager.

**Table 5.8** The Long-Term Cost of Infrastructure and Hosting for a Business-Driven Web Site

| | |
|---|---|
| **Total 1st year (includes 7 months of maintenance)** | **$443,150** |
| 360,150—development cost | |
| $28,000—7 months' maintenance | |
| $55,000—11 months' Web server hosting | |
| **Total 2nd year** | **$224,000** |
| $80,000—customized Web site module | |
| $48,000—12 months' maintenance | |
| $60,000—12 months' Web server hosting | |
| $36,000—12 months' database server hosting | |
| **Total 3rd year** | **$244,000** |
| $100,000—profiling module | |
| $48,000—12 months' maintenance | |
| $60,000—12 months' hosting | |
| $36,000—12 months' database server hosting | |
| **3-year total** | **$883,150** |

**What Does It Mean?.** There are two very important points to take away from these examples. First, hosting solutions account for a much greater percentage of total expenditures *after* a Web site is launched. Second, the costs associated with choosing the wrong ISP increase as your site becomes more complex.

Failure to recognize these two realities can be devastating to both the Web site project and, ultimately, to the manager responsible for its creation. It is easy to underestimate monthly hosting costs when presented with a budget that only addresses startup costs. Far too often, developers provide development budgets without giving appropriate thought to a three-year technology plan.

## Choosing a Hosting Solution

The first three sections of this chapter explored the importance of technology planning when creating a Web site, the hosting requirements of different types of Web sites, and the impact of hosting on your overall Web site budget. All of these sections assumed you chose an ISP to host your Web site.

In this section, we'll discuss some of the important Internet concepts you need to understand to make an informed hosting decision. We'll also take a look at some of the more popular hosting configurations offered by ISPs and evaluate the decision of whether to build hosting capabilities inhouse or outsource to an ISP.

**Table 5.9** The True Cost of Hosting a Business-Driven Web Site over a Three-Year Period

| | |
|---|---|
| **Startup (35,000/360,150)**<br>$30,000—hosting startup costs<br>$5,000—hosting first month | **10%** |
| **1st year (90,000/443,150)**<br>$30,000—hosting startup costs<br>$60,000—12 months' Web server hosting | **20%** |
| **2nd year (96,000/224,000)**<br>$60,000—12 months' Web server hosting<br>$36,000—12 months' database server hosting | **43%** |
| **3rd year (96,000/244,000)**<br>$60,000—12 months' Web server hosting<br>$36,000—12 months' database server hosting | **39%** |
| **3-year average (282,000/911,150)** | **31%** |

**The Internet: A Brief Overview.** It is impossible to talk about hosting solutions in any depth without some brief overview of the Internet, and at least a basic introduction to some networking concepts. Any in-depth discussion about Internet hosting involves the use of acronyms and can quickly get very technical. With that thought in mind, I will attempt to communicate a balance of conceptual and practical information to aid in the understanding of Web site hosting.

One of the most helpful, albeit most difficult, exercises when discussing the Internet is to develop a mental image of what it is and how it works. Picturing the physical model—a collection of "over-wired" equipment rooms around the world connected by routers and leased telephone lines—is not very helpful as it does nothing to help explain how it works. Picturing instead the logical model—what points are connected and where on the map—is much more helpful.

The first and most important concept to grasp is that a network is a logical entity rather than a physical entity. The telephone lines and cables that most people imagine to be the network are simply the physical medium over which data is transported. The network itself is actually the collection of protocols that define it.

The Internet, then, is a large logical network made up of many smaller interconnected networks (hence the term *Internet*). These different logical networks all run over the same physical wires. This, too, is a very important concept to grasp. The same physical telephone wire can carry data for many different logical networks. An example of this can be seen on most company LANs (Local Area Networks). For example, there is only one physical set of network cables within your company, yet accounting, financial, and production can all have their own separate networks.

The Internet is comprised of a three-level network hierarchy that includes *backbone* networks, *mid-level* networks (also known as *regional* networks), and *stub* networks (or *local* networks).

The backbone networks, often referred to as the *backbone*, form the primary traffic conduits between the regional networks. Proceeding down the chain, the regional networks are often referred to as *transit* networks because they connect the local networks to the backbone networks. Thousands of local networks exist all over the world connected to small ISPs and corporate LANs. Local networks are where most small ISPs enter the fray. When you dial into your local ISP through your modem from home, you are connecting to a local network that is connected to a regional network and ultimately to the network backbone.

Very large ISPs such as MCI, Sprint, IBM, and ANS own the backbone networks. These networks converge at major access points—called Network Access Points, or NAPs—around the United States and the globe. Figure 5.3 depicts the major U.S. NAPs.

National backbone service providers converge at these points (along with many other network providers) to exchange traffic through a process known as *peering* (Table 5.10). For example, in order for MCI to exchange traffic with Sprint at the Chicago NAP, the two companies must have a peering agreement in place. Connecting to these NAPs is synonymous with connecting to the Internet.

ISPs can be separated into two groups depending on whether they own or lease their networks. Tier-1 providers must have their own backbone network and have peering arrangements at many of the national NAPs. Generally speaking, a minimum of three diverse NAP connections is required to be recognized as a Tier-1 provider. Tier-2 providers usually buy their network bandwidth from Tier-1 providers.

Since many Tier-1 providers exist simply to resell space on their networks to other regional and local ISPs, we will separate them into two

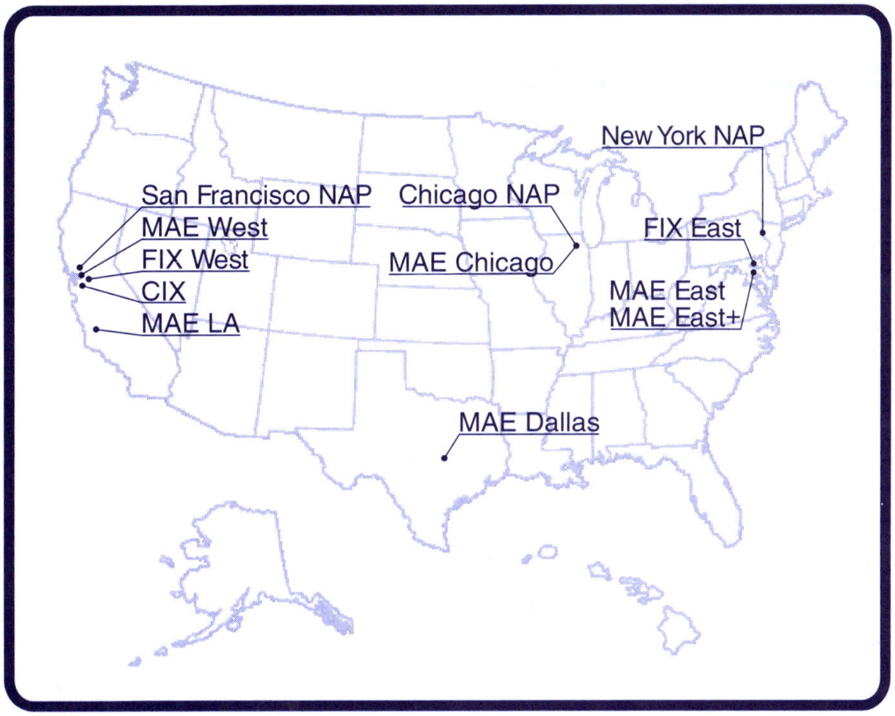


**Figure 5.3** Key Internet access points, or Network Access Points (NAPs) across the United States.

classes: those who offer Web hosting solutions and those who don't. Examples of Tier-1 providers that offer hosting solutions include Digex, UUNET, IBM, and PSINET.

**The Domain Name System.** Now that we've discussed the physical and logical network infrastructure of the Internet, let's talk about how individual computers are identified on the Internet. To begin, every single computer on the Internet has a unique Internet Protocol (IP) address. This number can be written as a 4- to 12-digit number broken into subsets in the form X.X.X.X, where X is a number between 0 and 255. For example, the IP address 154.167.227.112 is a valid address that identifies a single machine on the Internet. Likewise, the IP address 6.4.3.2 is also a valid address. No two machines can have the same IP address.

Fortunately, early network designers recognized the need for an Internet naming scheme, and in 1983 the Domain Name System (DNS) was created. Among other functions, DNS allows IP addresses to be substituted

**Table 5.10** A list of the Cities that Include Major U.S. Network Access Points to the Internet

| Name | Location | Operated by |
|---|---|---|
| San Francisco NAP | San Francisco, CA | PacBell |
| Chicago NAP | Chicago, IL | Ameritech |
| New York NAP | Pennsauken, NJ | Sprintlink |
| MAE-East | Washington, DC | Metropolitan Fiber Systems |
| MAE-East+ | Washington, DC | Metropolitan Fiber Systems |
| MAE-West | San Jose, CA | Metropolitan Fiber Systems |
| MAE-LA | Los Angeles, CA | Metropolitan Fiber Systems |
| MAE-Dallas | Dallas, TX | Metropolitan Fiber Systems |
| MAE-Chicago | Chicago, IL | Metropolitan Fiber Systems |
| FIX-East | College Park, MD | University of Maryland |
| FIX-West | Mountain View, CA | NASA |
| CIX | Palo Alto, CA | Commercial Internet Exchange |

with more easily remembered hostnames. For example, the IP address 206.67.227.2 can be reached by using the hostname www.t3media.com. The DNS database stores hostname substitutions for seven different Internet domains.

To facilitate growth of the domain name system, its designers created seven top-level domains (see Table 5.11). The registration and management of these domains is handled by the InterNIC (www.internic.net). The InterNIC is responsible for maintaining the domain name database as well as arbitrating domain name disputes.

**Choosing an Internet Service Provider.** Now that we have discussed the structure of the Internet and briefly introduced some basic networking concepts, we can discuss the factors involved in selecting a hosting solution. For your needs there are three basic types of commercial hosting solutions: *shared servers*, *dedicated servers*, and *collocated servers*. Each solution is appropriate for a different type of Web site.

Shared server solutions are the most common and are offered by almost all ISPs. The concept is simple: ISPs put as many different Web sites on a single machine as possible. This lowers their maintenance costs per client, and allows them to pass some of the savings on to you. Unfortunately, many ISPs take this too far, putting as many as 20 or more sites on a single machine. While your monthly hosting bill might be lower, your Web site will suffer in terms of performance.

**Table 5.11** Identifying Top-Level Domain Names

| Top-Level Domain | Reserved for |
|---|---|
| .edu | Universities and educational institutions |
| .com | Commercial entities |
| .gov | Government entities |
| .mil | Military entities |
| .net | Network service providers |
| .org | Nonprofit organizations |
| .int | International treaty entities |

The shared server solution is the least flexible, as you are required to use the software the ISP supports. This can be ideal though for static promotional Web sites that do not expect to get large amounts of traffic. Because of their relatively low cost, shared servers can also make good testing or staging sites. You can keep an exact copy of your site and test new features before adding them to your live site.

Another common hosting solution is the dedicated server. In this scenario, an ISP provides you with a dedicated machine, configured to your specification, and connects it to its network. The ISP will provide you with all the access you need to maintain the server remotely and will make sure the machine is running at all times. This option is the most flexible as you are free to install and configure any special software your site might need.

The least common of the three solutions, server collocation has become more popular of late with Tier-1 providers like Exodus moving to the forefront. This hosting solution requires you to buy and configure your own servers. All the ISP provides is a climate-controlled room in which to store your equipment and a powerful network for you to plug in to. As with the dedicated server option, the ISP will monitor your machines to make sure they are running.

Many companies have opted to outsource their data centers to collocation facilities. They have found it cheaper to rent the facilities, network bandwidth, and around-the-clock maintenance from a third-party provider than to build it themselves.

**Network Connectivity.** There are two basic principals to understand when evaluating an ISP's network offering: The more users sharing the same network segment, the less bandwidth available to your site, and a network is only as fast as its slowest link.

Many providers will try to impress customers with raw network throughput numbers like 10Mbps or 100Mbps network segments without mention of the number of servers sharing these links. In general, you should expect to pay more when there are fewer servers connected to your network segment. Savvy ISPs will generally offer different pricing plans based on the number of servers allocated to connections.

It is also important to understand the speed of the network link between the data center housing your server and the network access point. For example, you might be connected to a 10Mbps Ethernet segment within a data center that is connected via a T-1 (1.54Mbps) line to another provider that then connects to the network access point. Effectively, your network connection is 1.54Mbps, or the slowest link in the network. Nearly all Tier-1 providers offer high-speed access (45Mbps and above) from their data centers to network access points.

When evaluating competing Tier-1 providers, it is important to make sure you are comparing similar network offerings.

**Hardware and Software.** Today ISPs generally offer both Unix- and Windows NT-based hosting solutions. The pros and cons of different hardware and software configurations are beyond the scope of this chapter, but there are a couple of key points to consider when making the decision about your server platform. In general, development costs tend to be lower on the Windows NT platform, but there can be a performance and scalability trade-off. For most sites this will not be a concern; only the most heavily trafficked sites push these limits. If you plan to bring the Web site inhouse or connect it your company's network at some point, you may want to consider a platform that can be easily worked into your network configuration. You should work with your developer to determine the system that can best meet your requirements. Often this will be based upon your developer's skill set.

**Specific Service Offerings.** Perhaps the most confusing and difficult part of choosing a hosting solution is deciphering the product offering so you can compare "apples to apples." Cryptic terminology and confusing acronyms can seem daunting to the layperson. To add to the confusion, nearly every ISP has its own branded product offerings.

The services you should expect from your ISP can be broken down into six categories: customer support, facilities management, monitoring, system administration, backup and recovery, and security.

Because very few providers can claim any substantial technology advantage, customer service is the biggest differentiator between ISPs and by far the most important service to you. At a minimum, you should expect a dedicated account manager familiar with your business and hosting requirements with an emergency customer support line available 24 hours a day, 7 days a week, 365 days a year. The provider should also take care of any domain name registration and the DNS hosting for your site.

Facilities management and monitoring services are fairly standard with nearly all Tier-1 providers offering Uninterruptable Power Supplies (UPS) supported by diesel generators in case of prolonged power outages. $24 \times 7 \times 365$ server and network monitoring should also be a requirement. Most providers have Network Operation Centers (NOCs) that perform around-the-clock service.

The provider you select should offer hardware, software, and network maintenance at no additional cost to you. While this is typically part of the service offering, you should verify that there are no hidden costs. For sites requiring database or other special servers, some network providers will provide database administrators or qualified engineers at an hourly rate. This should be viewed as a value-added service and not part of a standard offering. The provider should also give you the ability to remotely update your content. This entails providing you with basic FTP (File Transfer Protocol) access for single Web server sites and more advanced administration privileges for database and other specialized servers.

All providers will offer a backup and recovery plan. The points that should be verified are that backups are conducted on a daily basis and that there is some provision in place for storing them offsite. This prevents fire and other potential disasters from destroying all of your data.

Finally, the provider should present you with several different levels of security from which to choose. Secure Sockets Layer (SSL)-enabled Web

**Table 5.12** A Handy Checklist of Issues that You Can Use when Selecting an Internet Service Provider

| Service | Yes | No |
|---|---|---|
| Customer service | | |
| Dedicated account manager | | |
| 24x7x365 customer support | | |
| Initial domain name registration | | |
| Primary and secondary Domain Name Service (DNS) | | |
| Facilities management and monitoring | | |
| Uninterruptable Power Supply (UPS) | | |
| Diesel generator power supply | | |
| 24x7x365 server and network monitoring | | |
| System administration | | |
| Hardware maintenance | | |
| Software maintenance | | |
| Network maintenance | | |
| System and network administrators | | |
| Remote content administration privileges | | |
| Backup and recovery | | |
| Daily tape backup | | |
| Offsite tape backup storage | | |
| Security | | |
| SSL-enabled Web servers | | |
| Other firewall products | | |
| Options | | |
| Email hosting | | |
| Virtual hosting | | |
| Site traffic reporting | | |

servers are considered to be a requisite security offering. Most providers will also offer you a choice of firewall application software to protect valuable data stored on your Web server. Most also offer some level of router-level packet filtering. You should expect to pay à la carte for the security options you choose.

There are a number of value-added services that ISPs can provide including email hosting, virtual hosting (multiple IP addresses on one machine), and monthly site traffic reporting.

Table 5.12 contains a handy checklist for making sure your ISP candidates meet certain minimum-level requirements.

**Table 5.13** A Typical Budget for Outsourcing Infrastructure and Hosting Costs for a Web Site over a Three-Year Period

| | |
|---|---|
| Server startup and configuration (2 servers) | $10,000 |
| Monthly hosting (2 servers) | $6,000 |
| Total year 1 costs | $82,000 |
| Total year 2 costs | $72,000 |
| Total year 3 costs | $72,000 |
| **Total 3-year cost** | **$226,000** |

**Should You Outsource?** Now that we have a considerable amount of data about Internet Service Providers and the solutions they offer, we can make the build-versus-buy evaluation. A simple analysis of costs can answer the question fairly quickly. Let's take a look at some comparative data.

Let's assume we have to make the decision whether to outsource the hosting of our Web site to a Tier-1 provider or to host the site internally. I assume that you have no hosting capabilities inhouse, but you can customize the analysis based on the resources you have.

Let's modify the ACME Reports example used earlier in this chapter. As you recall, ACME required a hosting solution consisting of both a Web and database server and an ecommerce solution beginning in year two. For this example, let's assume that ACME simply requires hosting for a Web and database server from day one (see Table 5.13).

As you can see in Table 5.13, our three-year costs total about $230,000. To make an accurate comparison, we need to build a capability similar to that outlined earlier. Specifically we will need to purchase all of the necessary networking hardware, lease a dedicated Internet connection, purchase and configure the hardware and software, and hire a small staff to provide support. Let's take a look at some line item costs (see Table 5.14).

As you can see, the outsourcing solution is much cheaper after you factor in the cost of salaries to maintain your network and Web site. Further, it is unlikely that you would even be able to match the level of service an ISP can provide. Again, you should customize the analysis based on the current scenario within your company.

**Table 5.14** A Typical Budget for Hosting Infrastructure and Hosting Costs for a Web Site over a Three-Year Period

| | |
|---|---|
| **Networking hardware** | |
| Router/hub | $2,000 |
| **Hardware and software** | |
| (2) Intel-based servers | $14,000 |
| Windows NT 4.0 | $1,000 |
| Microsoft SQL Server 6.5 | $1,200 |
| **Internet connection** | |
| Dedicated T-1 from Tier-1 provider | |
| Setup | $5,000 |
| Monthly | $2,000 |
| Local loop charge (monthly telco charge) | $500 |
| **Staff** | |
| Systems administrator (always on call) | $125,000 |
| Database administrator | $65,000 |
| Security consultant (part-time) | $30,000 |
| **Total year 1 Costs** | **$273,200** |
| **Total year 2 Costs** | **$250,000** |
| **Total year 3 Costs** | **$250,000** |
| **Total 3-year cost** | **$773,200** |

## Summary

Understanding the importance of analyzing and planning for your site infrastructure and hosting needs in the present—and three years down the road—is one of the most critical aspects of Web site development. Mistakes you make in the short term have the potential to seriously impact your site development budget. By assessing your site needs carefully and understanding the budget implications of your options, you can make good solid choices with your interactive agency right from the start.

And speaking of right from the start, understanding all of the legal issues involved in developing your site is also an important part of making your Web site development process a success. We move from technology to the law in the next chapter.

## Checklist

- ☐ Discuss the development of a Technology Plan with your Web development team and your Web developer.
- ☐ Is your site static or dynamic? Understand the difference.

- ☐ Prepare an RFP (Request for Proposal)and submit it to several major Internet Service Providers. Do this even if your Web developer is going to take care of it for you.
- ☐ Create a spreadsheet of your site infrastructure and hosting costs in the first year of your site's development. Compare the cost you researched with the cost submitted by your Web developer to be sure you are being charged fairly.
- ☐ Extrapolate your costs over a period of three years. How do the costs that you found compare to your developer? If your developer's estimated costs rise significantly, that's a sign the initial bid is being "low balled" and you can expect costs to increase over time.
- ☐ Register your own DNS, or have your developer do it for you, but register it in your name. That way you can be sure you own it, and if you later decide to change ISPs, you can do so quickly.
- ☐ Understand the difference between shared, dedicated, and collocated servers. Be sure you have the right one for your Web site and that the option you choose is a scalable one.
- ☐ Review the checklist presented in Table 5.12. Use this table to guide your comparison of site infrastructure and hosting options.

You might not want to host your site inhouse, but the exercise of figuring out the difference between inhouse hosting and outsourcing is an important one.

chapter

# 6

# Covering Your Legal Bases

**Jerrold B. Spiegel, Esq.**
**Frankfurt, Garbus, Klein & Selz, PC**
*jspiegel@fgks.com*

### About This Chapter

Covering your legal bases is one of the most important elements to consider when outsourcing your Web site. If you don't pay sufficient attention to the legal aspects of your Web business, you could end up in litigation or worse: Your business could lose valuable assets, including your logo, brand, or the site itself. In some cases, you could be sued and risk facing damages in court.

This chapter offers a look at all of the legal issues to consider as you develop your site, ranging from domain names and trademarks, data collection, privacy, libel, Web site jurisdiction, and Web site ownership to copyright, intellectual property rights, and other important legal considerations. Finally, this chapter presents a sample legal contract that you can use as a guideline for working with your Web developer.

### About the Author

Jerrold B. Spiegel, Esq., is a well-known figure on the New York Web development scene. Jerry has a reputation for working not only as an attorney but as business advisor, cheerleader, and friend for numerous start-up Web development firms in addition to a large corporate client base. He is a 1973 *cum laude* graduate of New York University Law School and a member of the New York-based law firm Frankfurt, Garbus, Klein & Selz, which represents clients primarily in the media and entertainment industries. Jerry is the head of the New Media Practice Group at Frankfurt, Garbus, which is involved in all areas of interactive media. He has advised software and online companies since 1985 and has written and lectured extensively on the impact of interactive media. Jerry currently edits the Frankfurt, Garbus, Klein & Selz *New Media News.*

## Why Should I Read This Chapter?

**The explosion of businesses marketed, promoted, enhanced, and increasingly conducted through Web sites presents every businessperson today with both the opportunity and the challenge of a lifetime. The opportunity is the chance to increase and enhance your business through a Web site designed to market and promote your goods and services and to communicate with existing and potential suppliers and customers (making the business more efficient to boot). For some businesses, having a Web site is quickly becoming a question of simple survival. Shifting business paradigms are forcing more organizations to successfully establish Web-based operations, either in conjunction with an existing, real-world business operated through retail outlets, mail order catalogs, or other traditional means or in lieu of the real-world presence entirely.**

This rapid growth is driving the need to understand and work with basic concepts of e-commerce at all levels of the business. A basic understanding of the rules of property and doing business in cyberspace is required. The purpose of this chapter is to explain the basic legal elements involved in establishing and operating a Web presence, including:

- Understanding what intellectual property rights are and how to make sure that yours are protected
- The legal issues involved in outsourcing Web site development and hosting services, including what provisions should be in your Web site development agreement
- The legal and regulatory issues involved in marketing, promoting, and operating a Web site and conducting e-commerce

In the days when ever-faster modes of travel were developing, people used to say the world was shrinking; in the virtual world of the Internet, the world has shrunk to a "singularity," to use the expression cosmologists use to describe both the moment immediately prior to the birth of the universe and what's at the center of a black hole. Just like on the Internet, you can be here and there, everywhere at the same time, disregarding geographical boundaries and physical limitations in the search for business. In the process, we are unwittingly undermining much of the basis on which our governmental and legal institutions have been built.

The Web is a virtual world. It is virtual in that there are no bricks and mortar, wood, metal, ceramic, or glass; no property in the real, actual, physical, atomic sense. There are, instead, bits of digital media that exist as electronic impulses in files stored on server computers connected to the Internet. These electronic impulses are summoned up on our computer screens, when requested (and sometimes even when not); text, images (real and graphic, still and moving), sound, music, and voice—all in some sense are designed to evoke real-world experiences. In cyberspace, business is conducted through intellectual property that can't be touched or physically possessed. Intellectual property has historically been the province of government and law. Without the common and statutory law that creates, governs, and protects copyright, trademarks, patents, and trade secrets, intellectual property would not be possessible or ownable (ownership connoting, with respect to any particular intellectual property right, the exclusive right to use, exploit, modify, and derive new works from, as well as the right to prevent others from doing so), because the essence of intellectual property is the absence of the restraints of the physical world. Intellectual property can be easily and inexpensively reproduced without limit, each copy the equal of the original.

Doing business on the Web is fundamentally different from setting up shop in the real world in that all of the assets you purchase, create, own, and operate to generate business and revenue consist of intellectual property rights (copyrights, trademarks, patents, and trade secrets). The security of that business and its future value are dependent in no small measure on the strength and certainty with which they are protected under applicable intellectual property rights laws.

The Web is also fundamentally different from the real world in that it "exists" wherever someone can access its files and display them on a computer screen. Thus, when you establish a Web site, unless you take steps to the contrary, the files comprising your Web site can be displayed on computer screens in places you never imagined. The downside to all this? Uncertainty and risk. No one can predict where this will take us, and at the moment we often can't be sure of which state's or country's laws apply (can a Web-based business choose the friendliest jurisdiction and thumb its nose at the rest?) or whether all of them apply (in which case the jurisdiction with the most restrictive or repressive laws will control behavior on the Web because no one will want to risk violating those laws).

One of the most significant consequences of e-commerce is that geographical boundaries are no longer limitations to conducting business. This not only opens the door to doing business with customers around the world, it also opens the door for governments and judicial systems to claim jurisdiction over even the smallest business, raising the specter of having to defend legal process in foreign jurisdictions in circumstances never before imagined. The complications are endless and, at least to lawyers, both fascinating and horrifying.

Given that this book is published in the United States, it seems appropriate to assume that in the event of any jurisdictional uncertainty, the laws of the United States apply to the intellectual property the book represents. Of course, in many cases, there will be no confusion, because the applicable law will be clear, either from the location of the parties or the terms of a contract.

Because so much of what you will do when conducting e-commerce involves developing and operating a Web site that concerns the creation, exploitation, and protection of intellectual property rights, it's important to have a good understanding of exactly what each type of intellectual property right is, what it protects, how it differs from and works with other types of intellectual property rights, and how to perfect and protect it. That's the aim of this chapter.

This is not a "do it yourself" project. Before I go on, I must advise you of what this chapter will *not* do. It will *not* enable you to proceed without expert legal counsel. The purpose of this chapter is to help you understand what you need from your lawyer—in short, how to help you help your lawyer help you. These are serious matters; I cannot overemphasize the need to seek expert counsel before you undertake any of the actions contemplated in this book. Failure to consult with counsel on any of these issues may result in substantial costs or liability to you and your business. Please use this material only in conjunction with your lawyer. Make sure your lawyer knows and understands these issues, or refers you to someone who does. Nothing is more valuable than consulting with experienced counsel who will not only be able to competently and efficiently answer your questions and make sure your interests and desires are adequately protected, but such counsel can frequently anticipate potential future problems, perhaps resulting in substantial savings down the road.

### Some Basic Internet Legal Issues

Let's begin by looking at some of the basic issues we need to address when it comes to understanding the legal aspects of Web development.

**Domain Names and Trademarks.** Securing and protecting your domain name (also referred to as a URL, or uniform resource locator, which is the exact file name that is indexed for your Web site—for example, www.yourwebsite.com) are the first steps in establishing a Web site. For a pure e-commerce business, this domain name is frequently the most valuable asset. In the physical world, your business name and trademarks identify your goods or services in the marketplace, but your customers can find you in lots of different ways, even if they don't know your company name or its precise spelling. However, on the Web, your domain name is the equivalent of your name, address, phone number, and trademark, all rolled into one. If your customers and potential customers don't know your domain name and its precise spelling or can't intuitively figure it out, it's much harder for them to find you. This fact accounts for the large number of high-profile disputes concerning ownership of domain names.

Trademarks are more important today than ever before. Therefore, understanding what they are, how they work, and how to secure and protect them is extremely important.

What exactly is a trademark? A trademark is a symbol (nondescriptive words, designs, names, or slogans) used to identify and distinguish the origin of goods or services. Rights in a trademark are acquired when it is used in commerce. Trademarks can also be registered with the United States Patent and Trademark Office and internationally with governmental offices in each country. Registration of a trademark always occurs for specific uses or categories. These standard categories were, for the most part, established before the digital era. Consequently, it is often difficult to identify the correct category for many of the new Web-based businesses, but your trademark lawyer will help you to figure out which categories are appropriate for business.

By registering the trademark prior to anyone else in a particular category with evidence of its use in commerce (i.e., an advertisement), the owner of the trademark acquires stronger rights, entitling the owner to recover fees and costs in the event of infringement. Or, prior to use, you can file an intent-to-use-trademark application, which will reserve the trademark in that particular category for up to 18 months, pending actual use in commerce.

The value of a trademark is a function of the perception of that brand in the public mind, and that perception is based on the quality of the products to which the brand is attached as well as the substantial sums spent on marketing, promoting, and advertising the brand. In the virtual world of the Web, brands are of paramount importance because they're the only edifice that your customers see. Brands constitute the only way your customers can find you. Today, the value of a well-known, international consumer products brand can reach into the hundreds of millions, if not billions, of dollars. On the Web, its value may be even greater.

A copyrighted work, such as a graphic design or a cartoon character, can also serve as a trademark. Mickey Mouse is a principal spokesperson for the Walt Disney Company, and the cartoon character is also one of Disney's most valuable trademarks. Even once his copyright has expired, use of Mickey's image for commercial purposes will still be subject to trademark rights. The importance of protecting the trademark rights in this mouse are of obvious importance. The same principle applies to all other potentially valuable trademarks on your Web site. So, if you're contemplating creation of an animated character for your Web site, remember to consider not only the copyright, but also the trademark implications.

In the United States, the federal Trademark Antidilution Act grants to the owners of well-known or famous trademarks the right to prevent the use of those marks for any purposes whatsoever. Similarly, if you build enough brand equity in your mark, you will be entitled to protect it for your exclusive use across all types of commerce.

Since 1995, Network Solutions, Inc. (NSI) has handled registration of domain names for the most frequently used top-level domains: .com,

.net, and .org. Under NSI's original rules, registration was on a first-come, first-served proposition. But as domain names quickly took on importance as identification on the Internet, trademark owners suddenly found themselves unable to register their marks as domain names. NSI found itself embroiled in numerous lawsuits, caught in the no man's land between the proverbial Hatfields and the McCoys, resulting in changes to the domain name rules to try to make NSI more impartial and a mere stakeholder.

The European Union has established an office to handle trademark registrations covering the entire European Union, but existing country-specific trademark registrations will continue to be valid. Trademark piracy is a way of life in some countries. How important all this will be in the future virtual world of the Web is unclear, because the successful Web businesses to date have relied on domain names ending in .com, which, while noncountry specific, have been administered by U.S. entities under U.S. law, treating U.S. federal trademark law as controlling the right to use specific domain names.

How the current discussions and negotiations over the Internet's domain-name scheme will be resolved is unclear, but the future will likely bring an expanded domain-name registration system, both as to the number of top-level domains and the number of registrars. The United States monopoly on the registration of commercial domains cannot and should not survive. The success of the Internet and the Web, as well as the realization of their value, are dependent on their internationalization.

Today, the issue of domain-name ownership is inextricably tied to trademark law—so much so that some experts have likened domain names to a quasi-trademark. Recent cases have explored the application of the law of trademark dilution to domain-name hijacking. However, because trademark dilution applies only to "famous" marks, it is of little help to most trademark owners. Frequently, the equities aren't clearly on one side or the other. The rules are still very much in flux, so the best advice is:

- Register trademarks you might use as domain names as soon as possible, preferably before use.
- Research possible conflicting trademarks before deciding which trademarks to use.

- Select trademarks that are unique and not descriptive. The term "non-descriptive" is a term of trademark law meaning that a trademark cannot merely be descriptive of the goods or services being offered.
- Avoid trademarks already taken in other categories; this practice may prevent you from expanding into that category under that trademark and could lead to confusion. Costs are the same for promoting a common mark and a unique one, but the value of that uniqueness may someday be far greater because unique trademarks are easier to protect.
- Check availability of desired domain names and register available domain names as soon as possible.

**Data Collection and Individual Privacy.** The Internet as an interactive medium is perhaps the greatest data collection system invented by man. In a sense, George Orwell's Big Brother has arrived in the guise of the Internet, because everyone can now be a data collector. The temptation to use it to gather demographic information has driven much of the growth of the Internet. It has also caused a backlash of concern by freedom activists and regulators. Business ethics demand respect for individual privacy concerns and full disclosure of all data collection activities and policies.

The U.S. Constitution was created on the fundamental premise that each of us living in a free society has the fundamental right to protect our bodies, our personae, and our lives from surreptitious invasion by busybodies, snooping merchants, or government agents. This right to "pull down the blinds" has been recognized in the United States and many other countries as a right to privacy.

In the old world of centralized media, the right that needed to be protected was the right of access to, and protection from, the media (for example, the right to freedom of speech and assembly). As media intruded further into our lives in fulfillment of Andy Warhol's 15-minutes-of-fame imperative, the law adopted concepts of protection of privacy that addressed the concerns of the time—the fear that the media would broadcast some aspect of our lives into other people's living rooms. Thus, as Professor William L. Prosser discussed in his seminal 1960 law review article on the law of privacy ("Privacy" 48, California Law Review 383, 1960) the law was comprised of four separate torts:

- Intentional intrusion upon one's solitude or private affairs
- Public disclosure of private facts
- Public portrayal of an individual in a false light
- Appropriation of one's name or likeness for commercial gain

Notice that each of these rights basically turns on the loss of one's privacy by exposure in the public eye through a mass medium. The concept of privacy thus was its juxtaposition to its opposite: the public. In each of these torts, one's private life becomes public against the plaintiff's will. But we don't necessarily have to be exposed in public to lose our privacy. Before computer media, and particularly the Internet, there was little need to protect one's privacy from invasion by snooping data hounds because there *were* no snooping data hounds—the technology that enabled their existence hadn't yet been invented.

Today's technology enables marketers to track your every move and every mouse click to try to develop a picture of you. One's privacy can be lost in many little ways, which, when aggregated, can be just as intrusive as having our private lives made public. This certainly suggests that all of us should be just a little more sensitive to each other's need for privacy.

Aside from the Fourth Amendment to the U.S. Constitution, which protects against unreasonable searches and seizures by the government, there are currently no federal laws specifically regulating or restricting the collection of data. The policy of the present U.S. administration has been to encourage industry self-regulation first, then address abuses that cannot be managed with self-regulation. Policies have been adopted by a number of organizations (such as the Direct Marketing Association) that encourage their members and others to disclose on their Web sites their data collection practices, including the kind of data collected, the uses to which such data is put, and whether the data will be sold to others. Some of these policies also encourage Web sites to provide the user with the opportunity to opt out of the data collection scheme. At this time, however, voluntary regulation does not seem to be solving the problem, and it appears like that there will be federal legislation of some sort. Internet marketing advocates, however, are raising concerns that blanket restrictions on information gathering online may stifle development of electronic commerce.

The Federal Trade Commission (FTC) has asserted jurisdiction over commercial Web sites under Section 5 of the FTC Act, which empowers the FTC to regulate unfair and deceptive trade practices. The FTC has announced that deceptive trade practices include the failure of a Web site operator to comply with posted privacy policies. Under current law, however, the FTC cannot force Web sites to disclose their privacy policies or practices. The FTC has also asserted that the failure to obtain parental consent before collecting information from children is an unfair trade practice. The FTC's position in one recent matter involving KidsCom, a Web site for children ages 4– 15 was articulated as follows:

> *...in order to be effective, any disclosure regarding collection and use of children's information must be made to a parent, given the limited ability of many children within the target audience to comprehend such information.... An adequate notice to parents should disclose: who is collecting the information, what information is being collected, its intended use(s), to whom and in what form it will be disclosed to third parties, and the means by which parents may prevent the retention, use or disclosure of the information. (FTC News Release: Center for Media Education, FTC File No. 962-3220, July 16, 1997)*

The Children's Advertising Review Unit (CARU) of the Council of Better Business Bureaus, Inc., has for many years maintained something called the Self-Regulatory Guidelines for Children's Advertising. They have added a section for Internet and online services called "Guidelines for Interactive Electronic Media," which establishes guidelines online advertising to children under 12 years of age.

Over 85 percent of children's commercial Web sites recently surveyed by the FTC collected data about children. Furthermore, in recent surveys of adults, a majority said that they would be more likely to use the Web if their privacy were more secure. At the same time, there are over 30 bills pending in Congress concerning online privacy. Thus, it appears likely that online privacy regulation by the U.S. government will be a reality in the not too distant future.

On October 25, 1995, the European Community (EC) adopted a directive concerning the protection of persons with regard to the collection and use of personal data. The aim of this directive was to establish a standard level of security as to the collection and use of personal data among the EC's member states before the end of 1998. Almost all of the

EC member states have already adopted legislation regulating the collection and use of personal data. The EC directive would also restrict the collection of EC residents' personal data by Web sites from nonmember countries unless the nonmember country has enacted legislation that establishes a level of security for personal data similar to that mandated by the EC directive. Given the importance of international exposure for Web sites, regardless of where they are developed, and the increasing importance of international commerce, careful attention will have to be paid to privacy regulations in other countries.

**The Basics of Libel Law.** The Internet has been likened to a giant copy machine. It is no surprise, therefore, that one of the first decisions involving the world of online business was essentially a publishing claim of defamation filed against CompuServe, a commercial online service. In that case, *Cubby, Inc., v. CompuServe, Inc.*, 776 F.Supp. 135 (S.D.N.Y. 1991), the plaintiff claimed to have been damaged by false and defamatory statements made by the manager of one of CompuServe's electronic forums. The Court held CompuServe was not liable for the statements made, because the electronic forum was like a newsstand that could not be held responsible for all of the statements made in the periodicals or books sold. Although this was good news for online service providers, what it portended was the expansion of the law of defamation in the information age, so that it now impacts day-to-day decisions in the operation of many Web sites. After all, every Web site is a publisher. So, you have to think as a publisher.

The law of defamation is a state common law right comprising the torts of libel, involving written communications, slander, and oral communications that involve false statements causing harm to a person's reputation. Since 1964, numerous cases have applied the First Amendment to the law of defamation, but the boundaries remain unclear. The First Amendment's general prohibition on government regulation of speech comes into direct conflict with the law of defamation, which effectively regulates the content of speech. The Supreme Court has thus been called upon to balance the legitimate public interests implicated by both.

Under common law, *malice* is a necessary element of a defamation claim. An improper motive, such as hatred or revenge, or conscious disregard of the truth can constitute malice. Under the First Amendment, the Supreme Court has held that public officials and public figures may not recover damages for a defamatory statement unless the statement was made ". . . with knowledge that it was false or with reckless disregard of whether it was false or not." (*New York Times Co. v. Sullivan*, 376 U.S. 254, 279-80 [1964]). This standard, known as *actual malice*, focuses primarily on the defendant's knowledge or attitude toward the facts, rather than the defendant's attitude toward the plaintiff.

The law of defamation is extensive and complex. The key issue for Web site operators is not to understand its intricacies, but to understand that every communication by your employees to others is a potential liability. Making sure that your employees understand the possible risks inherent in their communications is therefore of paramount importance. What they say via e-mail or in newsgroups about other people or companies or the products or services they offer may result in a libel claim.

If you maintain bulletin board or chat services on your Web site, there is the potential risk of liability for defamatory statements made by visitors to your Web site. In *Stratton-Oakmont, Inc., v. Prodigy Services Co.*, 1995 WL 323710 (App.Div. 1995), Prodigy discovered that it was potentially liable for defamatory statements made about plaintiff broker-dealer on one of Prodigy's bulletin boards. The Court reasoned that because Prodigy had publicly undertaken to screen the content on its service (not for defamatory remarks, which it could not possibly know about, but for obscenity and statements intended to disrupt the service), it was potentially liable for all such content. The seeming unfairness of this result has been reversed by provisions of the Communications Decency Act of 1996 (CDA), which now provides that an online service will not be deemed the publisher of information provided by someone else merely because it otherwise screens the content on the service for obscenity, violent, harassing, or otherwise objectionable material.

The protections against libel claims afforded to online services in the CDA will not, however, insulate Web sites from libel claims based on material prepared by or for them. Thus, in appropriate cases, you may want to consider having your Web site material vetted by your attorney before you publish it. Vetting is a standard practice in the publishing industry with a goal of avoiding libel claims and showing that the publisher acted in good faith and with due regard to ensure that the publication contained no defamatory material.

**Jurisdiction.** As stated at the outset of this chapter, geographic boundaries become meaningless on the Internet. On the Web, you can do business with customers wherever they may reside, so long as they have access to your Web site. Of course, business transactions sometimes go awry—one party to a transaction can fails to perform its obligations. In the real world, these actions would be remedied by the commencement of civil litigation or the commencement of criminal proceedings.

In the virtual world of the Web, these same remedies are being applied, but with some startling results. Courts are struggling with concepts that originated in a world of geographical limitations, but that are now being applied to the virtual world of the Web, where there are no geographical limitations. Thus, will a Web site (which can be accessed from anyplace) be subject to the jurisdiction of the courts and/or the governments of all jurisdictions with Internet access? These issues are just now being sorted out.

Courts seem to be making distinctions between active Web sites that contain interactive elements (such as the ability to order goods or services) and passive Web sites that are purely promotional (such as national advertising). In one of the more expansive cases, *Zippo Manufacturing Co. v. Zippo Dot Com, Inc.*, the defendant, Zippo Dot Com, was a Sunnyvale, California-based Internet news service and World Wide Web operator that owned the domain names zippo.com, zippo.net, and zipponews.com. The plaintiff, Zippo Manufacturing Co., was a Pennsylvania-based producer of ZIPPO brand tobacco lighters; it brought this suit seeking redress for trademark dilution, infringement and false designation under federal trademark law, and trademark dilution under Pennsylvania law. The defendant's contacts with Pennsylvania occurred almost exclusively over the Internet. Approximately 2 percent of the defendant's customers were located in Pennsylvania, but the defendant maintained no offices, employees, or agents in Pennsylvania. Nevertheless, the court held that the defendant was subject to jurisdiction because its Web site was targeted to citizens of Pennsylvania.

Among cases refusing to assert jurisdiction on the basis of a Web site is *Hearst Corp. v. Goldberger,* F.Supp. (SDNY 1997). In this case, the plaintiff, publisher of *Esquire* magazine, was located in New York, and the defendant was a New Jersey-based provider of an electronic law office infrastructure network, including information services. The Court, in refusing to find jurisdiction, held that where the Web site had "contracted to sell or actually sold any goods or services to New Yorkers, a finding of personal would mean that there would be nationwide (indeed, worldwide) personal jurisdiction over anyone who establishes an Internet Web site."

In another case, *Bensusan Restaurant Corp. v. King*, the famous Blue Note club in New York City sued a local club in Missouri for trademark infringement for using the same name. The Second Circuit Court of Appeals, in refusing to assert jurisdiction over the defendant, upheld the District Court's ruling that a Web site advertising a local Missouri cabaret business, by itself, does not subject that business to personal jurisdiction in New York.

More recently, in *Mallinckrodt Medical Inc. v. Sonus Pharmaceuticals Inc.*, the Court held that the posting of defamatory statements on an America Online bulletin board was not alone sufficient to subject the defendant to jurisdiction, where the plaintiff had failed to demonstrate that the defendant had conducted business in the forum state or had caused tortious injury in the forum state.

What we can determine from these cases is that if you operate an active Web site that targets customers all over the United States, you are likely to be subject to jurisdiction all over the United States in any litigation arising from transactions involving the Web site and perhaps even lawsuits not arising from such transactions, if the claim is somehow related to the Web site, such as a claim of trademark infringement.

On the regulatory side, the U.S. government in *United States v. SDB Global* (March 5, 1998) charged owners and managers of six offshore companies with illegal use of interstate phone lines to attract and take online wagers from Americans. Each of the defendants was involved in the operation of a Web site that permitted and promoted online wagering. The Web sites were all operated from servers outside the United States, but the defendants were all U.S. citizens or had other U.S.

connections. It is unclear how successful these actions will be in shutting down these Web sites.

This expansion of jurisdiction is not just affecting online businesses. In a case not involving the Internet, *United States v. BAJ Marketing Inc., et al*, a federal judge ordered four Barbados-based direct mail companies to cease and desist in pitching get-rich-quick schemes through the mails to elderly people in New Jersey.

Suggestions have been made that the Internet needs a new type of dispute resolution and regulatory mechanisms, such as online tribunals. Whether and to what extent these proposals, if implemented, will be successful is unclear.

### Web Site Ownership

The issue of Web site ownership is a complex matter which must be addressed right from the start of your site's development. Before taking your first steps, you should map out your strategy for ensuring ownership of the rights necessary to accomplish your objective.

The Internet is a *medium of expression*: words, images, sounds, and software. A Web site is a collection of computer files that, when summoned by a user, function together to display the Web site on the user's computer monitor provide any accompanying video and sound, and also provide the Web site's functionality, such as order processing.

Copyright is the *ownership of expression*, whether in the form of writing, images, sound, three-dimensional objects, or a computer program. Essentially, any medium recognizable by human senses, either directly or through the use of mechanical devices (such as phonographs, televisions, or computers), applies. Copyright, however, protects only the expression itself, not the ideas or concepts or facts incorporated therein. Thus, the law of copyright governs the ownership of all of the expressive elements of your Web site. It determines who owns your Web site. So, here is an explanation of how copyright works and how to work with it.

As discussed earlier, no one can own exclusive rights to intellectual property in the absence of an effective system of law, rules, and sanctions. That's what our law of copyright is: A system of rules and sanctions, civil and criminal, which establishes specific rights of ownership of certain categories of expression and rules for the use and exploitation of those rights and imposes sanctions, in the form of civil remedies and criminal sanctions, for specific violations of those rules.

Copyright vests in the author at the time the work is created and fixed in a tangible medium, whether on paper or on the screen. The author is the person who creates the work, with two exceptions:

- A work created by an employee within the scope of employment, in which case the employer is deemed the author
- A work created as a work-made-for-hire pursuant to a written agreement if it falls into one of nine specific categories: contribution to a collective work; part of a motion picture or other audiovisual work; translation; supplementary work; compilation; atlas; instructional text; test; or answer material, in which case the party who hired the creator is deemed an author for copyright purposes

Copyright is not just a single right. It is really a bundle of rights that are divisible and can be dealt with separately. Thus, copyright law grants to the author of a work the exclusive right to:

- Reproduce the work
- Prepare derivative works
- Distribute copies of the work
- Perform the work publicly
- Display the work publicly
- Authorize others to do so

In addition, the author has the exclusive right to control the first publication of the work: the distribution of copies by sale or other transfer of ownership.

You must recognize that copyright is a double-edged sword. Although copyright protects the text, images, graphics, sounds, music, and software created for your Web site, copyright also prevents you from using any existing text, images, graphics, sounds, music, and software unless you secure permission from the owner of the material. The stronger the law, the better protected your intellectual property rights may be, but the more likely you will infringe on other people's intellectual property rights. The weaker the law, the less well protected, and so on.

The term of copyright protection has increased dramatically over the years. Most recently, Congress passed the Copyright Term Extension Act of 1997, which increased copyright protection to the life of the author plus 70 years or, in the case of an anonymous or pseudonymous author, such as a corporation, 95 years from publication.

Derivative works include translations, dramatizations, fictionalizations, motion picture versions, condensations, abridgments, and other forms in which a work may be recast, transformed, or adapted. It also includes works consisting of editorial revisions, annotations, elaborations, or other modifications to an original work. A derivative work need not be in the same medium as the original. Indeed, some of the most noteworthy examples of derivative works include theatrical and made-for-television motion pictures based on the popular works of novelists Herman Wouk, Stephen King, and Danielle Steele. Because a derivative work involves additional creative work, it is frequently copyrightable independently of the original work.

Compilations are collections of other materials, whether copyrighted (such as an anthology of poems), in the public domain (such as a collection of Shakespeare's plays), or facts (such as a white pages telephone directory or a database of movie credits). A compilation is entitled to copyright protection as a separate work, provided it meets the minimal requirement of originality in its selection, coordination, and arrangement. What is protected by a compilation copyright is the totality of the work rather than its individual elements, regardless of whether the elements are entitled to copyright protection.

Many computerized databases are compilations of statistics or other facts. The Supreme Court has said that whether or not such compilations are protected by compilation copyright will depend upon whether there is at least a minimum of creativity in the creation of the database in terms of selecting and organizing the subject facts. But, as the Supreme Court noted in *Feist v. Rural Publishing Co.*, it is hard to find any creativity in a database of facts that by its very nature is supposed to be exhaustively complete and organized alphabetically. It may be even more difficult to meet the minimum requirements of creativity when you consider that a computer database, in fact, has no organization but consists of bytes of data that are organized only when searched by a database user.

Because databases are subject to copyright protection, permission may be necessary to use them. However, even if the database qualifies for compilation copyright protection, facts or other unprotected content are not protected. Anyone with access could copy facts from the database. The wholesale copying of an entire or substantial portion of a database, however, may subject the copier to a claim of copyright infringement or unfair competition.

Many database owners have resorted to contractual restrictions (which are in the nature of state trade secret laws), whereby access to the database is conditioned on the user's written agreement to use the database only for limited specified purposes and not to copy or otherwise use the database or any portion thereof. Frequently, databases are protected by shrink-wrap licenses (either on CD-ROM or online), which are presumptively enforceable. If a database is protected by compilation copyright, a license is required to copy and republish it.

A proposed Collections of Information Antipiracy Act would impose liability for the extraction or use in commerce of all or a substantial part of a collection of information gathered, organized, or maintained by another person through the investment of substantial monetary or other resources, so as to harm that other person's actual or potential market for a product or service that incorporates that collection of information. This is similar to existing European Union proposals to protect databases under the Berne Convention. Whether any of these proposals will become law is unclear, but watch this area for future developments.

**A Brief History of Copyright Law.** To understand the future direction of copyright law, it is important to understand how it has evolved.

Copyright started almost 300 years ago in England with the adoption of the Statute of Anne in 1710, which granted to copyright holders the exclusive right to copy a work for a 14-year period. Although copyright law today speaks in terms of protection of the artist or author, the genesis of copyright was to protect the established book publishers and the monopoly that they established over the publishing industry in 18th-century England.

In 1787, the U.S. Constitution mandated Congress to adopt laws "[t]o promote the Progress of Science and useful Arts, by securing for limited Times to Authors and Inventors the exclusive Right to their respective Writings and Discoveries." The concept is that government wants to encourage artists and inventors to be productive and, to such end, grants to them, for a limited time, the exclusive rights to exploit their work. In consideration of the grant of such exclusive rights, the public has the right to freely exploit such properties after the expiration of the exclusive time period.

Three years later, in 1790, the first copyright law was adopted by Congress.

In 1909, Congress adopted a comprehensive revision of the copyright law, which remained unchanged until January 1, 1978, the effective date of the Copyright Revision Act of 1976. Under the 1909 Act, copyright lasted from the date of publication (or the date of registration, in the case of unpublished works) for a period of 28 years and could be renewed for an additional 28 years.

The 1976 Act provided that all works "fixed in a tangible medium of expression" are entitled to federal statutory copyright protection from the moment they are so fixed, regardless of whether they are published or disseminated. In addition, the 1976 Act extended copyright protection to new types of expression, including recordings, cable and educational television programs, motion picture soundtracks, and computer programs.

The 1976 Act also eliminated the registration requirement as a condition of copyright protection, but continued the notice requirement, with provisions for curing the failure to provide notice under certain circumstances. Under the 1976 Act, protection for works created on or after January 1, 1978, commence upon creation of the work and continue for the life of the author plus 50 years. (Actually, the copyright expires on December 31 of the calendar year in which the copyright would otherwise expire. When the author is not a person, the copyright term ran for 75 years from the year of first publication, or 100 years from the year of creation, whichever expires first.)

On March 1, 1989, the United States became a member of the Berne Convention, the international treaty governing copyright law to which most countries are signatories. The treaty exacts conformity to certain common legal principles, but in exchange grants enhanced protection in other signatory countries. Reflecting the pro-author/artist sentiment that is the essence of European culture, the Convention prohibits the imposition of any impediments to copyright protection. Thus, in order to bring U.S. copyright law into conformity, notice became optional, rather than mandatory. The copyright law requires the deposit of copies of copyrighted works with the Library of Congress, but such deposit is not a condition to copyright protection. Today, a work enjoys copyright protection from the moment it is fixed in a tangible medium.

Most recently, the Copyright Term Extension Act of 1997 extended the term of protection to the life of the author plus 70 years, in the case of a living author, and 95 years from first publication, in the case of an author that is not a person.

**So, Who Owns My Web Site?** Now that you have a grasp of the complex world of copyright law, let's apply it to your situation. The people who write the code for your Web site will be the authors of that code unless they are your employees or they have signed an agreement stating that the code is a work made for hire and they further assign all of their rights in the code to you (a work-made-for-hire agreement). Likewise, the people who create the content of your Web site—the text, images, sound, graphics, and animation that appear on your site—will own their creations unless they are your employees or they have signed a work-made-for-hire agreement.

If you engage an outside firm to produce your Web site, that firm will frequently object to signing a work-made-for-hire agreement because it is in the business of building Web sites for others, and software developers reuse software tools that they have previously created for others to provide basic functionality. This is not illogical—it's sort of like the carpenter objecting to your owning his tools if he builds your house. The Web developer should be willing to grant you a perpetual, fully paid license for these software tools that are incorporated into your Web site and sign a work-made-for-hire agreement for the rest. This should give you ownership of the important parts of your Web site.

**Web Site Look and Feel: Protecting the Unprotectible.** I have represented many online businesses since 1986 and clients have often asked whether they could prevent others from copying some unique or unusual aspect of their online presence so that competitors would not gain unfair business advantage. An online retail store wanted to protect its interactive television service, which created a virtual store with aisles through which customers could navigate as if they were in a real store; an online bank wanted to protect its concept of a virtual branch, complete with distinguished wood paneling (the design and development of which they had paid significant fees); a CD-ROM developer wanted to protect his concept of the turning pages of a book for a work of interactive fiction; and an online database company wanted to prevent competitors from copying the layout of its online service. In each of these cases, the client was unhappy with my reply: I told them that although the actual text, images, sounds, and computer code that made up their online businesses would be protected under copyright law, they could not protect the "metaphor" the ideas behind the design of their businesses. That, I had to tell them, is unprotectible.

In a series of lawsuits over the past 10 years, the degree of copyright protection available for computer interfaces has been explored in some detail. In the case of *Lotus v. Borland*, it was finally determined that the command structure of the plaintiff's spreadsheet program was not protected and could be copied in the defendant's competing spreadsheet program in order to make it easier to convert users. In *Apple v. Microsoft*, Apple could not prevent Microsoft from using a trash can icon to evoke the function of erasing a computer file, as long as the particular image used by Microsoft was different from that used by Apple. Thus, the degree of copyright protection afforded to interfaces and Web sites today is relatively thin, requiring a very high degree of similarity before a finding of infringement can be made. You cannot own the metaphor itself.

Although you may not own the general look and feel of your Web site, your particular expression of that look and feel is protected by copyright law. Branding the Web site extensively with your company's trademarks and copyrighted material will help ensure its uniqueness and make it difficult for someone else to make unfair use of your hard work.

**Clearing Rights: The Lore of Copyright.** The law and lore that surround each type of media have evolved into varied and unusual concepts and principles. A basic understanding of how these work is essential for anyone dealing with rights issues or having to license content.

Whenever you desire to use content you don't own, you must secure the right to do so. Such rights, referred to as "subsidiary rights," are sources of additional revenue to the owner of those rights. You must usually secure the agreement of the rights owner or an agent to whom responsibility for management of the subsidiary rights has been delegated (for example, ASCAP licenses music publishing rights).

The most important word to remember when you're licensing rights is *indemnification*. Make sure that each party from whom you have secured any rights has agreed to indemnify you if anyone makes a claim arising from the permitted use of those rights. More important, make sure they will be able to indemnify you if the need arises. It makes no sense to get an indemnity from an indemnator who may not be around six months hence.

The following presents a brief description of how each industry has structured the ownership, use, protection, and licensing of its particular type of copyrightable material.

**Literary Property** Literary works include works of fiction and nonfiction such as books, magazine, and newspaper articles—essentially all written or printed works. The reproduction in whole or the excerpting of any portion of a copyrighted literary work requires written permission from the copyright holder, as does the creation of a derivative work based in any substantial part on the copyrighted work, such as a screenplay based on a novel.

Copyright ownership of a book generally resides with the author, usually subject to an agreement with a publisher that runs for the life of the work's copyright, or at least until the book has gone out of print. Newspaper and magazine articles could be owned (or controlled) by the author or the publisher, and conducting a copyright search may very well be impossible. Even though a third party, such as a publisher, may control the rights to a work in book or periodical format, the author may have retained some or all of the other rights to the works (either because the agreement with the publisher did not contemplate such uses or because the author negotiated to retain such rights). Sometimes the author has a right to require the publisher to revert certain rights to the work if the publisher has failed to exercise them within a specified period of time from publication.

A copyright search can resolve questions as to ownership, but probably not with respect to the terms of any publishing agreement. You may need to rely on the author's representation that your rights don't violate the publishing agreement. Ask the author first, of course, and if the author refuses, you may want to rethink your interest. You may also want to contact the publisher before you sign an agreement. Of course, if you've started with the publisher, you will probably have to rely on the publisher's representations as to its rights, but if it is a reputable firm (and financially solvent), that should not be a problem.

**Musical Compositions and Sound Recordings**

An arcane and confusing tangle of rights surrounds the music industry. Rights exist in the musical composition (which is the written sequence of musical notes) and any arrangements, recorded performances, and live performances, and the licenses for the use of each of these rights will vary depending upon the type of use, such as the right to incorporate a musical performance into an audio/visual work, such as a theatrical motion picture or a multimedia CD-ROM.

Copyright in musical compositions is owned by the music publisher, typically a corporation formed by the composer. Copyright in the sound recording of a musical performance is typically owned by the recording label, which maintains the master recordings for each of an artist's published works.

Mechanical licenses are required to manufacture and distribute physical objects (such as CD-ROMs) incorporating a musical composition.

Synchronization licenses are required to synchronize a musical composition with visual images, such as a motion picture. They are obtained from the music publisher.

Public performance licenses are required to perform the musical composition publicly. They are obtained from the music publisher, and they may be necessary for use of music on an online area. These licenses are typically administered by performing rights societies (ASCAP or BMI).

Master recording licenses are required to reproduce and distribute the sound recording of a particular musical performance. They are obtained from the record company or the owner of the master recording. Only recently was the copyright law amended to grant to performers a public performance right in their recordings.

Of course, figuring out which permissions you need requires a mastery of these intersecting rights—which is not a job for the faint of heart. Thus, for example, a Web site that incorporates an existing recording may require a mechanical license, a synchronization (or synch) license, a master recording license, and a public performance license. Better leave this one to the experts.

### Photography and Graphic Artists

Photographs and visual images are given a high degree of copyright protection. Although the idea behind each picture may not be protectible, commissioning a work to mimic another specific work could result in a claim of infringement.

Of course, to use a copyrighted photograph or graphic image requires permission from the copyright owner. Because photographers usually work on a freelance basis, they usually retain copyright ownership of their photographs. Frequently, a photographer will be represented by an agent or a stock photo house; similarly, graphic artists are often represented by syndication houses or agents. In such cases, it is important to obtain appropriate indemnifications from a reputable stock photo house or syndication house.

When using a photograph for commercial or non-editorial purposes, releases must also be secured from identifiable persons and the owners of trademarks that are identifiable in the photograph. A reputable stock photo house should know the release status of each of their photos.

**Motion Picture Clips**

The use of an excerpt from a motion picture requires permission, typically a clip license. One frequently sees clips from movies currently in release on the Web or commercial online services. Such clips are frequently secured from interactive press kits distributed by studios to promote their films. The use of these clips by online publishers is frequently based on an implied license. That is, the studio's submission of its interactive press kit to the online publisher is an implicit license to put online the clips contained in the interactive press kit. An implied license, if one exists at all, is subject to revocation at any time by the studio.

By their nature, movies and videos are inherently collaborative, involving at least one writer, one director, actors, camera operators, technicians, stunt doubles, and so on. The use of clips may require additional clearances and payments for music rights (if the clip contains music) or for residuals (to unions or guilds, such as the Screen Actors Guild) if it contains the voice or image of a member. This makes the process of clearing rights quite complex and best left to experienced clearance agents.

Appropriate clips can sometimes be obtained from a stock film house or library. Be sure to deal only with reputable companies that will be able to stand behind their clips and that are willing to give you an appropriate indemnity.

**News Footage** The use of copyrighted news footage for any purpose requires permission from the copyright owner. Normally, the copyright holder is the news division of the station or network, but sometimes an amateur takes the footage (for example, the Zapruder film of the JFK assassination). Many news organizations have made arrangements for licensing their footage, either through an agent or affiliate. Copyright could also be in the hands of a freelancer. Releases must also be secured from identifiable persons who appear in the footage, as well as from the owners of trademarked material contained in the footage.

Because of the inherently collaborative nature of such endeavors, there are frequently unresolvable rights questions with respect to older footage.

**Physical Objects** Physical objects may also be protected by copyright or trademark, requiring permission for their reproduction individually or as part of a larger image. This could include toys (such as a spaceship from one of the Star Wars movies).

**To License or Not to License: When Can I Use Copyrighted Material Without Permission?**

This is a trick question. There are no circumstances in which you have the right to use anyone else's copyrighted material without their permission. But when considering the use of existing material, you can encounter two circumstances in which you may use that content without permission: First, if it is not protected by copyright (such material is considered to be in the public domain); second, in those limited cases permitted under the First Amendment, which guarantees freedom of expression, and embodied in the doctrine of fair use. The complexities of rights clearance have resulted in the development of what are known as *rights clearance agents*. These individuals specialize in clearing rights to using copyrighted material and frequently have extensive contacts in the relevant industries. You would be well advised to consider using a rights clearance agent if you have any kind of sophisticated rights clearance issues. Again, be cautious when using this information and do so only in conjunction with your lawyer. A mistake in this area could subject you to substantial damages and attorney's fees.

**Public Domain.** Works considered to be in the public domain include works with respect to which copyright protection has either expired or been lost for some reason and works prepared by an officer or employee of the United States government as part of that person's official duties.

Under current copyright law, an author does not need to do anything to claim copyright in his work. The mere act of putting the work into tangible form vests the author with copyright ownership. However, prior to 1989, a work could have come into the public domain in the following ways:

- For works first published in the United States prior to January 1, 1978, failure to place proper copyright notice on the work and failure to comply with the registration and deposit requirements
- For works first published in the United States between January 1, 1978, and February 28, 1989, failure to place proper copyright notice on the work which was not properly cured
- For works first published in the United States prior to January 1, 1964, failure to renew the copyright at the expiration of the first 28-year term

Determining that a work is not protected by copyright can be quite difficult. With respect to works first published prior to January 1, 1978, the lack of a copyright registration indicates that the work is in the public domain. With respect to works published after that date, the lack of a copyright registration is not determinative. You may, however, want to conduct a copyright search (which can be performed by the copyright office or a private organization, such as Thompson & Thompson). The existence of a copyright registration will determine when the work comes into the public domain.

Even if a work is clearly in the public domain, you can't necessarily use it for any purpose. Other rights, such as the right of publicity (which restricts the use of an individual's persona for commercial purposes) and trademark rights with respect to characters or other elements of a work, may restrict the permitted use of the work. Works that have entered the public domain may also contain elements that are still subject to copyright protection. For example, the motion picture Rear Window may be in the public domain due to a failure to properly renew a copyright registration, but the script on which it was based is still protected by copyright. Thus, the owner of the copyright in the script can control the exploitation of the film as a derivative work.

As a consequence of certain agreements by the United States under an international treaty, the foreign owners of certain foreign works that came into the public domain in the United States, due to a failure to comply with some technical requirement of U.S. copyright law, are now entitled to have copyright restored in such works, further complicating the determination of which works are in the public domain.

**Fair Use**

The U.S. Constitution provides the mandate and authority for Congress to adopt copyright laws that grant exclusive rights to authors. The First Amendment, on the other hand, guarantees freedom of expression. How can this freedom of expression be reconciled with the right of an individual to prevent another from using his copyrighted material? The concept of fair use is an attempt by the courts to reconcile the two.

Fair use limits the exclusive rights granted to the author and permits the use of copyrighted material without permission in certain extremely limited circumstances, such as satire and parody, critical commentary, and education. Four factors are commonly referred to in fair use cases:

1. What is the purpose and character of the use? Is the use of a commercial nature or is for nonprofit, educational purposes?
2. What is the nature of the copyrighted work? Is the copyrighted work published or unpublished? Is it fact or fiction? Is it informational or entertainment oriented? Is the work available or out of print?
3. What are the amount and substantiality of the portion used in relation to the copyrighted work as a whole?
4. What is the effect of the use upon the potential market for or value of the copyrighted work?

It may appear that these factors can be used to determine when fair use is available. But the truth is that fair use always turns up as a defense. In other words, if you use the material without permission and you're sued, the only excuse you can come up with is that the First Amendment guarantees you the right to use it. Sounds a bit like kids who shout names at each other, then when confronted, argue that "It's a free country and I can say anything I want." But it's not and you can't, so discuss questionable material with your lawyer before you use it.

### Beyond Trademark and Copyright: Other Intellectual Property Rights

The development and operation of your Web site may also implicate other intellectual property rights, including the following:

**Trade Secrets.** What about all that confidential know-how and data generated during the development and operation of your Web site? What about all that confidential information that your competitors would love to get their hands on? These concerns fall into a kind of catch-all category of intellectual property rights: *trade secrets.* What is a trade secret? It can sometimes be hard to describe. You would probably expect it to include all the information and know-how related to your business that is possessed by your staff and that is not generally known outside of your organization. But you might be surprised. A classic example of a trade secret is the formula for Coca-Cola syrup.

The Uniform Trade Secrets Act defines a trade secret as information that has value, is not generally known or readily ascertainable by proper means, is valuable because it is secret, and is protected as a secret. Some companies maintain the source code to their software as a trade secret, refusing to file even a portion of the source code with the Library of Congress, as would be necessary in order to bring an action for copyright infringement.

Trade secrets may or may not also be copyrighted. Protection for trade secrets differs from copyright, arising instead from the common law theory of theft or misappropriation. Enforcement has been the province of state courts and legislatures.

As with all other types of intellectual property, trade secrets—once they become publicly known—are not protectible from others' exploitation except through a system of laws and legal sanctions. In the case of trade secrets, however, the law affords protection only so long as the trade secrets remain just that—secret. To protect your trade secrets, you must demonstrate to the world (and ultimately the court) that you regard them as valuable to your business and that they are, indeed, secret. To do this, you must exercise a combination of continuous and diligent efforts to maintain their secrecy, requiring written nondisclosure or confidentiality agreements from all persons who have access to them. Your failure to diligently require such agreements from each person who has access to them can be used against you if you ever have to sue to protect them. That is why requiring a written nondisclosure agreement from each and every employee is so important. That first employee who doesn't sign the agreement may result in the loss of protection for your trade secrets.

What actually constitutes trade secrets can vary remarkably from industry to industry. Many industries maintain that certain types of information, such as a customer list, constitute trade secrets, while courts have been hesitant to extend the umbrella to cover anything but the most clearly proprietary information and know-how. Thus, a customer list may not be protectible as a trade secret. That is all the more reason to carefully and jealously guard it. Once such a piece of information is in the hands of the wrong person, you've lost all control of it.

The recently adopted Economic Espionage Act of 1996 creates criminal sanctions for the theft of important trade secrets. However, the lack of a right of private action leaves enforcement to the U.S. government, so trade secrets protected from theft will be limited to matters of significance to the public interest. Sanctions include fines of up to $500,000 ($10 million for corporations) and imprisonment for up to 10 years. There have been a few prosecutions, typically involving the sale of trade secrets by an employee to a foreign competitor.

**Patents.** A *patent* is a government-sanctioned monopoly for a limited time on an invention or process. Ideas are not patentable; devices and processes are. In order to qualify for patent protection, an invention must be "reduced to practice" and must be new, useful, and non-obvious. A patent application must be filed within one year of public disclosure of the invention.

Under the U.S. Constitution, patent protection was intended to encourage practical development of the sciences. In exchange for a public statement and explanation of an invention, the inventor is entitled to the exclusive exploitation of the invention for a limited period of time, which, due to recent amendments to the patent law, is now 20 years from the date of filing of the patent application. This latest change is part of an effort to normalize U.S. patent laws with those of other countries.

The owner of a patent has the right to prevent others from making, using, and/or selling anything that is covered by the claims of the patent. The grant of a letters patent by the U.S. Patent and Trademark Office is not a guaranty of protection. Anyone challenging the patent can claim that it does not qualify for patent protection and introduce evidence to that effect. Patents are frequently made invalid on this basis.

Computer software is a unique type of intellectual property right because it qualifies for protection under both copyright and patent law. Copyright protection for software came first in 1978, when it was made eligible for copyright protection as a literary work, by virtue of the Copyright Revision Act of 1976. But the nature of computer software (instructions to the microprocessor to perform certain functions, including creation of the display or interface as a visual image) is so different from a book or poem that the Supreme Court, in 1982, finally accepted the notion that software, when combined with hardware, can also constitute an invention protectible under patent law. Since then, there has been an explosion of software patent filings. However, the lack of available precedent with respect to software technology prior to 1982, combined with patent examiners' the lack of familiarity with software, has resulted in some notorious patent grants that have been withdrawn (in the case of Compton's patent on the use of multimedia) or dedicated to the public domain (in the case of Optical Data Corporation, in the face of industry opposition to the enforcement of its patent.)

The conflict between the appropriateness of patent versus copyright protection for software continues today. Given the radical difference between the two schemes of protection, that controversy is likely to continue. For example, under patent law, Microsoft would have been entitled to 20 years of protection for the original version of MS-DOS.

Under copyright law, that term of protection would extend for 75 years from the date of the last material modification thereof.

**Moral Rights.** Moral rights are a kind of copyright law. They limit the ability of the owner of a physical work, or of the copyright if other than the author or artist, to alter the work in any way. The purpose of moral rights provisions is to preserve the integrity of the artist and his or her vision from tampering by anyone other than the author or artist. It entitles the author or artist, and in some countries their heirs, to enjoin the alteration of their works and the display of such works in those jurisdictions recognizing those rights. These rights apply generally to literary, visual, or audio/visual works such as books, paintings, limited-edition prints, and motion pictures. Moral rights give the author the right to the physical integrity of a work as a whole and the right to be identified as the creator of the work (or to disclaim such authorship).

Moral rights were first formally recognized by federal law in 1991 under the Visual Artists Rights Act, applying only to fine art such as paintings and drawings or limited-edition signed prints (up to 200 copies). The law protects rights of integrity and attribution. It does not apply to works-made-for-hire. Moral rights can be waived.

Some states, including New York, Massachusetts, and Maine, have moral rights laws. California has a resale royalty law, which grants a royalty on the resale of a work of fine art.

Internationally, the extent of moral rights varies from country to country. For example, in France, *droit morale* applies regardless of the country of origin of the work. In France, moral rights may not be transferred or waived and are perpetual.

**Right of Publicity.** The *right of publicity* is the right to control the use of one's personality or persona. It protects against the unauthorized commercial of a celebrity's name, voice, signature, photograph, or likeness against unauthorized commercial exploitation. Section 51 of the New York Civil Rights Law, for example, prohibits the use of an individual's name, likeness, or image for commercial purposes without permission. In California and an increasing number of other states, an individual's persona is protected after death as well as during life.

There have been a number of interesting court battles over the right of publicity. One of the earliest involved the undisclosed use of a Woody Allen look-alike in an advertisement, suggesting the endorsement of the product by him. Both Bette Midler and Tom Waits have won cases involving the use of singers imitating their distinctive singing styles. Perhaps the most interesting case involved Vanna White and Samsung. In that case, Samsung had secured the rights to use a Wheel-of-Fortune-like game in the future, but it did not obtain White's permission. They probably thought they didn't need her permission, because in the ad White was replaced by a very mechanical robot (which was admittedly dressed very nicely). But the court thought otherwise, holding that White's rights of publicity had been violated.

The right of publicity vests in the individual and his or her transferees and heirs. These rights exist during the individual's life and, in many jurisdictions, posthumously (they pass to the individual's heirs) and may also be transferred or divided.

Before using the image or other identifiable characteristics of a famous person, or any person for that matter, you may need a release from such person. Consult your attorney before you make plans or commitments based on such use. A release is not necessary in cases protected by the First Amendment, such as news or biographical coverage, in which case the concept of fair use generally permits such use.

### Legal Issues in the Operation of a Web Site

Online media is a revolution in the making. The Web was designed to enable a new level of communications—*hypertext*. And this new level of communications is challenging many of the assumptions of our legal system. As the Web evolves, conflicts with the existing legal system arise, defining the current landscape of Internet law. Here are some of the highlights that you should know about as you outsource your Web site. Remember, your developer might or might not know about them, and it is ultimately your responsibility to make sure your business is "covered."

**Linking to Other Web Sites.** Hypertext, the ability to jump from one page to another by clicking a mouse button, was the basis on which the Web was created. That technical feature, generally referred to today as *linking* or *hyperlinking*, is a fundamental feature of HyperText Transfer Protocol (the HTTP in every Web address). In the early days of the Web's development, the unrestricted right to link to any material on the Web reflected the academic community's influence. Although the free ability to link to any other page was the ethic of Web pioneers, as the Web has undergone commercialization, the unrestricted ability to link between Web sites is becoming an increasingly contentious matter.

The nature of the Web permits each site to control not only the look and feel of its own pages but also the appearance of pages from other Web sites accessed via links from such sites. As Web site operators start to earn increasingly significant revenue from advertising, the ability to link to other Web sites without permission is increasingly being seen as undermining the advertising business model. The issues discussed in the following sections have been raised.

**Framing**

*Framing* is the display of a linked Web site within an outer border of one or more sides of a third party's Web site. The outer border may contain navigational tools, branding, and advertising. Framing permits a Web site to control users' navigation by keeping them at the host site while still permitting the viewing of the framed Web page.

Certain Web sites have made framing a part of their look and feel. One such site, TotalNews, was referred to as a so-called "para-site," a central navigation site for news services on the Web. By accessing TotalNews.com, a Web surfer could have instant access to all of the main news Web sites. If the surfer clicked on a desired link, TotalNews displayed in the user's browser the desired Web page, surrounded by TotalNews' frame, which contained branding, navigational tools, and advertising.

In *The Washington Post Company, et al. v. TotalNews*, the plaintiff Web site operator charged defendant TotalNews with trademark infringement and unfair competition for framing the plaintiff's Web-based news service. Although the case was settled, a quote from the complaint eloquently states the plaintiff's claim:

*Simply put, Defendants are engaged in the Internet equivalent of pirating copyrighted material from a variety of famous newspapers, magazines, or television news programs; packaging those stories to advertisers as part of a competitive publication or program produced by Defendants; and pocketing the advertising revenue generated by their unauthorized use of that material.*

**Deeplinking**

*Deeplinking* is creating a link to a page on another Web site other than that site's homepage. For instance, Microsoft's Sidewalk Web sites established deeplinks to specific event pages within Ticketmaster's Web site. In *Ticketmaster v. Microsoft, Inc.*, the plaintiff (Ticketmaster) asserted that the defendant's practice of deeplinking was an unfair trade practice in that it deprived the plaintiff of the branding benefits and advertising opportunities that arise from the navigation of Web users from the plaintiff's homepage through the plaintiff's Web site. Microsoft has voluntarily disconnected the deeplinks to Ticketmaster's site.

**Metatags**

Search engines act as an index to the Web and are a favorite starting point for many Web surfers. One of the features of the Web are *metatags*, which are words placed in the coding of a Web page that are read by the search engines and associated with the Web site. When a metatag for a particular site is typed into a Web search, that Web page will be presented, along with all other Web pages containing the same metatag.

It didn't take long for some imaginative Web designer to realize that the name of a much more well-known competitor placed among the metatags of a Web page would bring lots of traffic. Such practices have resulted in a number of lawsuits, including *Oppendahl v. Larsen*, in which the plaintiff law firm's name was placed among the metatags of the defendant's Web site. The court granted the plaintiff's preliminary motion, holding that the defendant's actions, which were likely to be proven by the plaintiff, constituted trademark infringement and unfair competition.

**Gaming and Sweepstakes.** Gaming on the Internet has become one of the technology's leading growth industries. Numerous Web sites have been set up in friendly jurisdictions (those that offer greater flexibility when it comes to the law—generally nonregulated locations offshore). How long these sites will continue to thrive or exist is uncertain, because U.S. Government attempts to shut down gaming sites with a U.S. connection (such as U.S. resident shareholders) have not been very successful to date.

Sweepstakes have also taken the Web by storm. They are a powerful and popular way of driving traffic to a Web site and promoting Web activities. A sweepstakes as a type of gambling, however, is permitted only in compliance with strict legal and disclosure requirements adopted by each state. These requirements are beyond the scope of this chapter, but the simple concept is that gambling involves a game of chance in which consideration is passed in the form of a wager. To avoid running afoul of antigambling laws, a sweepstakes must be structured as something other than a game of chance, such as a game of skill, or there must be an absence of consideration on the part of the participant. The rules governing the operation of a sweepstakes are complex, so you should consult with competent counsel sufficiently in advance of the promotion to help you draw up a set of sweepstakes rules and to otherwise assist you in structuring the promotion so that you don't run afoul of the law.

### The Web Site Development and Hosting Agreement

One of the most important aspects of managing your Web site's legal matters concerns contracts. Properly prepared contracts protect your company and its relationship with a Web developer. Many people new to Web development struggle when it comes to working with an attorney to draft an agreement with a Web developer. This section presents a sample legal agreement that you can use as a starting point. Use this agreement to gain an understanding about the types of issues that you should discuss with your lawyer.

## WEB SITE DEVELOPMENT AND HOSTING AGREEMENT

AGREEMENT dated ______________ by and between ______________________________ ,
a ____________________________________________ corporation with an office at ("Developer"),
and ____________________________________________ , a corporation with an office
at ____________________________________________ ("Client")

BACKGROUND

Client desires to hire Developer, and Developer has agreed, to design, develop, implement, host, manage, and maintain on behalf of Client a presence (the "Web site") on the international computer network referred to as the Internet, accessible using HyperText Transfer Protocol and generally known as the World Wide Web (the "Web"). Developer has agreed to provide Client with development, design, and management services in connection with the Web site and to provide related services, all as set forth in this Agreement.

NOW, THEREFORE, the parties hereby agree as follows:

1. DEVELOPER'S SERVICES AND OBLIGATIONS.

   1.1 Developer agrees to furnish technical, creative, and ongoing management services in the design, development, and implementation of the Web site accessible using the address "www.______________________________". Developer's services will include (i) creative and technical design of the Web site, such as interactive elements and hyperlinks, as incorporated into the HTML and associated files for the Web site (the "Developer Material"), (ii) consultation services with respect to Client's facilities, equipment, and systems for access to the Web site, and (iii) such services as are more fully specified on Schedule 1.1 (collectively, the "Basic Development Services"). In addition to the Basic Development Services, Developer will provide such additional development services with respect to the Web site as Client may request, subject to agreement as to the additional costs to be paid by Client to Developer therefore (the "Additional Development Services" and, together with the Basic Development Services, the "Development Services").

   1.2 Developer shall develop and produce the Web site and deliver the deliverables (the "Deliverables") set forth on and in accordance with the delivery timetable set forth on Schedule 1.2 hereto (the "Timetable"). Client and Developer shall cooperate so that the Web site will be developed and launched substantially in accordance with the Timetable.

   1.3 Commencing with the launch of the Web site, Developer shall provide management and maintenance services in connection with the Web site as specified on Schedule 1.3 hereto ("Maintenance Services").

1.4 Commencing with the launch of the Web site, Developer shall provide all necessary Web site hosting services, including all required computer equipment, software, and telecommunications links in accordance with the hosting specifications set forth on Schedule 1.4 hereto ("Hosting Services" and, together with the Development Services and the Maintenance Services, the "Services"").

2. CLIENT'S OBLIGATIONS.

2.1 Client shall assist and cooperate with Developer in connection with the design, development, implementation, hosting, management, and maintenance of the Web site, including delivery of all copyrighted, trademarked, or other material provided by or for the Client for incorporation into the Web site (collectively, the "Client Material") and making Client personnel reasonably available to review all Deliverables.

2.2 Client shall provide the Client Material in the form agreed upon by Developer and Client for inclusion in the Web site in a timely manner to enable the Web site to be developed in accordance with the Timetable, and Developer shall digitize the Client Material to the extent necessary. Client shall secure all necessary rights to all Client Material.

3. COMPENSATION.

3.1 Client shall pay Developer a fee in accordance with Schedule 1.2 hereto (the "Development Fee"") for performing the Development Services, which shall be payable upon acceptance of Deliverables by Client in accordance with the Timetable.

3.2 Client shall pay Developer a monthly fee in accordance with Schedule 3.2 hereto (the "Maintenance and Hosting Fee") for providing the Maintenance Services and Hosting Services.

4. REPRESENTATIONS AND WARRANTIES.

4.1 Developer hereby represents and warrants that:

4.1.1 Developer has the power and authority to enter into this Agreement and to provide the Services and to perform its other obligations hereunder and, upon execution and delivery hereof, this Agreement shall constitute the valid and binding obligations of Developer, enforceable in accordance with its terms; and

4.1.2 The Developer Material will not violate the rights of any third party or give rise to any claim of such violation, including, without limitation, claims of libel, slander, defamation, copyright infringement, infringement of moral rights, trademark infringement, false designation of origin, disparagement, violation of privacy, publicity, identity, or other proprietary rights.

4.2 Client hereby represents and warrants that:

4.2.1 Client has the power and authority to enter into this Agreement and to perform its obligations hereunder and, upon execution and delivery hereof, this Agreement shall constitute the valid and binding obligations of Client, enforceable in accordance with its terms; and

4.2.2 The Client Material will not violate the rights of any third party and will not give rise to any claim of such violation, including, without limitation, claims of libel, slander, defamation, copyright infringement, infringement of moral rights, trademark infringement, false designation of origin, disparagement, violation of privacy, publicity, identity, or other proprietary rights.

5. INDEMNIFICATION. Each party ("Indemnifying Party") will indemnify, defend, and hold the other party ("Indemnified Party") and its employees, directors, successors, and assigns harmless from and against any and all claims, damages, liabilities, costs, and expenses (including, but not limited to, reasonable counsel fees and expenses) arising out of any breach by Indemnifying Party of any representation, warranty, or agreement made by Indemnifying Party herein.

6. RIGHTS.

6.1 Client hereby acknowledges and agrees that the Developer Material, exclusive of any Software Tools (as hereinafter defined) (the "Work"), has been specially ordered or commissioned by Client as a work-made-for-hire as part of the Web site, and Client shall own all right, title, and interest thereto. Client shall be considered the author of the Work for the purposes of copyright, shall own all rights in and to the copyright of the Work, and shall have the right to register and renew the copyright in the Work in its name. To the extent that the Work does not vest in Client as a work-made-for-hire, Developer hereby irrevocably grants, assigns, and transfers all of its right, title, and interest in and to the Work to Client. Developer shall secure and provide to client, concurrently with delivery of each deliverable incorporating any such material, all necessary assignments and releases from its employees and independent contractors to enable Client to use, distribute, and exploit the Work as contemplated by this Agreement. Developer also hereby assigns to Client and/or waives any and all claims that it may now or hereafter have in any jurisdiction to so-called "moral rights" or rights of "droit morale" in connection with the Work and shall secure the same agreement from all employees and independent contractors performing services in connection with the Web site.

6.2 Developer owns certain existing software, routines, and methods (the "Software Tools"), which will be incorporated by Developer in the Web site. Client agrees that any newly developed software routines and methods which constitute software tools used by Developer in the regular course of its business shall be deemed to be Software Tools and shall be and remain the sole and exclusive property of Developer. Developer hereby grants to Client a perpetual, irrevocable, fully paid license to use the Software Tools as incorporated into and as part of the Web site, as modified or altered by or on behalf of Client.

6.3 Developer shall cause its employees and independent contractors which perform services in connection with the Web site to execute confidentiality and work-made-for-hire agreements in the form of Exhibit 6.3 hereto and provide copies thereof to Client upon request.

7. TERM AND TERMINATION.

7.1 The term of this Agreement (the "Term") shall commence on the date hereof and shall continue for a period of one (1) year from launch of the Web site. The Term may be extended for a specific term or on a month-to-month basis upon the written agreement of the parties, and any such extension shall be part of the Term.

7.2 In the case of a breach of any material provision of this Agreement by either party, the other party may terminate this Agreement by giving written notice thereof, specifying the nature of such breach; provided that this Agreement shall not terminate if such breach shall have been corrected within thirty (30) days (ten (10) days in the case of non-payment) after such notice shall have been given.

7.3 Upon the expiration or prior termination of the Term or prior thereto upon written request of Client, Developer shall (i) return to Client all copies of the Web site (including all files and source code therefore), Client Material, and Confidential Information (as hereinafter defined), and (ii) cooperate with Client to transfer hosting of the Web site to such server computer as Client shall designate. In addition, In the event that such cooperation requires the rendering of any services by Developer after the Term, Client shall pay Developer for such services at Developer's standard hourly rates for such services.

7.4 To the extent that Developer has acted as Client's agent with respect to securing domain names, Internet addresses, unique telephone numbers for access to the Web site, or any other similar properties, rights, or matters ("Addressing Materials"), Developer agrees that it shall hold all of such Addressing Materials in trust for Client's sole and absolute use and shall execute any documents that Client may reasonably require to effect transfer of any Addressing Materials to Client or its designee.

7.5 Upon expiration or prior termination of the Term, Client shall have a perpetual royalty-free, limited-use license to use any Software Tools incorporated into the Web site solely as part of the Web site, as modified or altered by or on behalf of Client.

8. CONFIDENTIALITY.

8.1 Developer acknowledges that in performing the Services, Developer and its employees and independent contractors may have access to and will be provided with proprietary and confidential information of Client (including, without limitation, all Web site data and information, the terms and existence of this Agreement, and the performance of the Services), all of which constitutes Client's valuable trade secrets. This proprietary and confidential information of Client is herein referred to as "Confidential Information." In recognition of the foregoing, Developer covenants and agrees that Developer (i) will keep and maintain, and shall use all reasonable efforts to cause its employees and independent contractors to keep and maintain, all Confidential Information in strict confidence, and (ii) will not, directly or indirectly, disclose any Confidential Information to any third party, except with Client's prior express written consent; provided that Developer shall be permitted to disclose the Confidential Information (x) to its employees and independent contractors who shall have signed an agreement in the form of Exhibit 6.3 hereto, and (y) if disclosure is required by law, but in such event Developer shall notify Client in writing promptly upon receipt of notice of such requirement, and provide Client with copies of related information so that Client may take appropriate action to protect the Confidential Information.

8.2 Confidential Information shall not include information that (i) is or becomes generally known to the public otherwise than as a result of a disclosure by or through Developer or its employees or independent contractors; (ii) is rightfully in the possession of Developer or its employees prior to disclosure by Client, or (iii) is received by Developer or its employees or independent contractors in good faith without restriction from a third party not under a confidentiality agreement to Client and having the right to make such disclosure.

8.3 Developer acknowledges that the disclosure of Confidential Information may cause irreparable harm to Client and damages that may be difficult to ascertain. Client shall, therefore, be entitled to injunctive relief upon a disclosure or threatened disclosure of any Confidential Information in addition to such other remedies as may be available in law or in equity.

9. NOTICES AND CREDITS. The parties agree that the Web site shall include copyright notices evidencing Client's ownership of the copyright in and to the Web site and other legal notices in forms designated by Client from time to time. Client agrees that Developer shall be entitled to reasonable and customary credit for creation of the Web site, including a link on the Web site linking to Developer's Web site in such form, substance and placement as approved by Client. The parties agree that the Web site shall also include a copyright notice evidencing Developer's ownership of the Software Tools in form designated by Developer and reasonably acceptable to Client.

10. ASSIGNMENT. Neither party may assign or transfer its rights hereunder in whole or in part to any person, firm, or corporation, and any such attempted assignment or transfer shall be void ab initio; provided that Client may assign or transfer its rights hereunder in whole to any subsidiary, parent, or sister corporation, or any transferee or successor to the business or assets of Client; provided that no such assignment shall release Client from any obligation hereunder.

11. GENERAL PROVISIONS.

11.1 This Agreement shall be construed in accordance with the laws of the State of New York applicable to contracts made and fully performed therein. Any dispute or controversy between the parties with respect to this Agreement or the Services shall be subject to the exclusive jurisdiction of the federal or state courts in New York County, and each of the parties hereto hereby submit to the personal jurisdiction of such courts over such parties in any such action.

11.2 All notices required to be given hereunder shall be given in writing by personal delivery or by certified mail, return receipt requested, at the respective addresses set forth above, or at such other addresses as may be designated in writing by certified mail by either party. Notice shall be deemed given on the earlier of (i) actual delivery or (ii) three (3) days after the date of mailing postage prepaid. A copy of any notice to Developer shall be sent to

__________________________________________________ .

All notices to Client shall be sent to

__________________________________________________ .

11.3 This Agreement contains the entire understanding of the parties hereto relating to the subject matter herein contained and cannot be modified or terminated except in writing, signed by the parties.

IN WITNESS WHEREOF, the parties hereto have executed this Agreement as of the day and the year first above written.

[DEVELOPER]

By:____________________________________________

Title:__________________________________________

[CLIENT]

By:____________________________________________

Title:__________________________________________

SCHEDULE 1.1: Developer's Services

SCHEDULE 1.2: Timetable and Deliverables

Developer shall use the most recent versions of all application software. Developer shall design the Web site to be compatible will all commonly used browser technology and to minimize download times and the effects of latency.

SCHEDULE 1.3: Web Site Maintenance Services

Developer shall provide Web Site Maintenance Services including, but not limited to:

- Updating Web site contents
- Retrieving information with respect to usage statistics
- Database information retrieval
- Mailing list maintenance
- Data back-up and archiving

Developer shall provide Client with such statistical reports and user access data with respect to the Web site as Client shall, from time to time, request. As new tools are developed to improve monitoring of access to or usage of Web sites, Developer shall, at the request of Client, incorporate such tools into the Web site and add the information and detail gathered thereby to its reports; provided that Client shall pay the costs and fees in connection with the implementation or use of such tools in connection with the Web site.

SCHEDULE 1.4: Web Site Hosting Services

Server Specifications

Hardware:

Software:

Telecommunications:

All computers, software, and communications links shall be of first-class quality, and communications links shall be capable of operating at not less than T-1 speed.

Web Site Performance Criteria

Access Time/Traffic:

Client Access: Availability and Response Time

Technical Assistance and Customer Support

Response Time

Search Engines

Metatags

General

Sufficient capacity of communications links shall be maintained or added to meet requested access to the Web site; provided that if such requested access shall require additional computers, software, or communications links, then Developer shall quote Client a price for such additional computers, software, or communications links, and upon Client's written agreement to pay therefor, Developer shall promptly acquire and implement such additional computers, software, and communications links. Developer shall use commercially reasonable efforts to keep equipment operating and online. Developer shall use commercially reasonable efforts to minimize offline time by using backup equipment.

EXHIBIT 6.3: Form of Employee Confidentiality and Work-Made-for-Hire Agreement

## Summary

This chapter has provided you with insight into a wide range of legal information that you can use to identify key legal issues and gain a background about each. It can guide you as you consider addressing the legal aspects of your Web site. With your legal bases covered, your next challenge will be to set up systems to help you organize your Web project. That subject is covered in the next chapter: "Managing a Long-Term Outsourced Web Project."

## Checklist

- ☐ Find an attorney that can help you understand the legal issues involved in setting up a Web site and contracting with a Web developer.
- ☐ Register your company's domain name and address the issue of protecting your trademark.
- ☐ If applicable, review the privacy information presented in this chapter and draft a statement to be posted on your Web site.
- ☐ Do you understand application of libel laws to your Web site? Have you communicated your company's concerns to your Web developer?
- ☐ Do you understand the issue of Web site jurisdiction? Have your prepared an appropriate legal disclaimer for your Web site?

- ☐ Establish proper ownership of your site with your Web developer. Discuss this with your attorney and be sure that you secured all necessary paperwork to ensure that you own your Web site.
- ☐ Talk with your Web developer about clearing all rights to material presented on your site.
- ☐ Review the contract presented in this chapter. Discuss the chapter with your attorney, draft a contract to be used with your developer, and make sure that the signed agreements are retained in an accessible and safe location.

chapter

7

# Managing a Long-Term Outsourced Web Project

**Bill Seitz**
**Medscape, Inc.**
*seitz@mail.medscape.com*

### About This Chapter

Project management is one of the trickiest aspects of creating a successful, long-term Web site. It gets even more difficult when you add outsourcing to the mix. This is partially due to the fact that both client and developer are likely to have an infrastructure and procedures in place to manage large-scale, long-term projects. Outsourcing forces two distinct businesses to blend their approach to maximize efficiency when working with one another, which is easier said than done. Outsourcing also relies on outstanding and open communication—still a challenge in our high-tech, communications-savvy age. Software tools such as Microsoft's Project Pro offer some hope, but they don't often reflect the dynamic nature of constantly evolving organizations. Finally, good management is hard, and the volatile nature of the Web doesn't make it any easier.

Surprisingly, books and trade publications have not featured much discussion on the topic of Web site project management. This chapter is an excellent step in the right direction toward remedying that situation. It begins with advice on issues such as the evangelism of a project within a company to ensure its voice, presence, and survival in an organization (one of the many tasks that a good project manager must tackle). The chapter provides an overview of the project design life cycle and offers insight into procedures for ongoing site maintenance, semirepetitive site development aspects, adding new project components, and project portfolio management. Finally, the chapter concludes with an examination of how to manage the implementation of project elements that alter the structure of your Web site, incorporating less significant individual project considerations into your project, and covers the topic of "closing the loop" on Web site developments.

### About the Author

Bill Seitz graduated from Cornell University with a degree in operations research and industrial engineering and later earned his MBA in finance and marketing from Columbia University before going on to work at several health care, media, business, consulting, and technology firms. He was an initial founding member of Medscape (www.medscape.com), where he serves as vice president of technology. Medscape, generally recognized as the Yahoo of medical information, is a premier Web site delivering patient care information to physicians and other members of the medical profession.

## A Healthy Amount of Skepticism

**I'm extremely skeptical about outsourcing. Ronald Coase's theory of the corporation says that you build a company to perform multiple functions when it's too expensive to manage the communications about integrating those functions across company lines. In a new industry, where both technologies and strategies change quickly and significantly, defining a financial and operations relationship with someone outside the company is like "riding the whip" on a skating pond. The more important a Web site is to its parent business, the more important it is to have (1) long-term, hands-on stewardship of the operation and (2) integration with other parts and processes of the business. This two-part requirement is not inherently contradictory with an outsourcing process, but it creates an additional challenge.**

Yet outsourcing has been used by some major players (such as Charles Schwab). Are these organizations crazy? Well, sometimes. But there can be good reasons to take this approach, such as the cost of bringing talent and expertise in-house. You may need to start delivering results so quickly that you can't wait to develop the skills in your current employees. You might anticipate a highly specialized need that may be very rare and thus difficult to acquire through hiring or training. Or, despite the significance of your Web activities, they might still be sufficiently far from your core business that you don't want to build up a staff of people with skills too specialized to be applicable elsewhere in your business. Even if a number of these reasons apply to you, just remember that there are costs to outsourcing (beyond your contractor's profit margin) and that these costs should be considered in the planning stages.

My background is as the technical member of the team that founded the Medscape medical Web site (www.medscape.com/). We started doing research in late 1994 and launched the site in May 1995. We began as part of SCP Communications, Inc., a medical print journal publisher and meetings coordinator, but later spun off into an independent company now numbering 40 people (the technical team includes 8 people). We've contracted out development of some client sites and hired freelancers for some specialized client work. During our own site development, we used only one consultant, and that was to assist in managing the transition from our original Macintosh server platform to Windows NT. We are only now beginning to consider outsourcing for some non-integrated new features.

## Project Manager as Evangelist

To frame your thinking, start with defining your title or role. Think of yourself as both liaison and project manager. This image emphasizes the two major aspects of your job. On one hand, you are the link between your business and the contractor you're working with. At the same time, you must remember that you are *personally* ultimately responsible for the success or failure of this enterprise.

This may seem unfair, because you don't directly control the contractor's staff. This is the tension inherent in outsourcing. Still, you must define and maintain the vision for the project, set priorities for delivering specific results, and make sure that those results get delivered.

Most of this chapter focuses on the contractor and the project itself, but it's worth first considering how your role as project manager relates to your company. Recognize that your project is just one within the corporate ecosystem. (For background on the ecosystem metaphor, read Kevin Kelly's *Out of Control* [Addison-Wesley, 1994] or any of the other chaos/complexity or bionomics books.)

Before spending too much time on the vision for your project, consider the direction of your company. What major goal or value does your project support? For instance, if your company's strategy is based on low-cost manufacturing and your site makes more customers aware of loss-leader products that the company would rather stop making altogether, your project may not have a bright future.

In *some* cases, it's okay for a Web site's direction to be somewhat mismatched with the company's direction, as long as (1) your project is accepted from the outset as belonging to at least one group within the company with whom your project's vision is congruent, and (2) you report into that group. If you work in the finance department and show interest in the Web, then you find yourself running a site, but the project ends up with a marketing focus, you might want to feel out the idea of reporting into marketing. If marketing doesn't want it that way, who is really the sponsor for your work?

Be especially wary of having your project deliver nothing but strokes to the egos of senior management (just check out the annual report sites of many of the Fortune 500). At some point, those bosses might need tangible successes, might be replaced, or might be embarrassed by a scathing review in a magazine (see www.metoo.com).

How important is your project (explicitly or at least potentially) to the achievement of a goal? You probably don't want your project positioned as the *only* hope for achieving a crucial goal (this smells like being set up as the fall guy). If the outsourcing success of your project isn't going to matter to anyone, you are at risk. As companies redefine their focus and/or cut overhead costs, insignificant distractions become targets, and rightly so. Companies and departments change direction, or at least priorities, on a regular basis.

The keys to operating in a corporate environment are (1) always think in terms of what matters to the business and (2) maintain strong communication with the key players who can support or kill your project. Regularly review your thinking on what matters to the business and how your work supports that. Evaluate whether your project is making or will make a real contribution. Documenting this thought process will both clarify it in your own mind and communicate it to others.

Make sure both internal stakeholders and your contractor share your vision. If your vendor doesn't believe in what you're doing, he or she may end up undercutting you. When it comes to vision, you really must be partners.

Regularly remind both your internal stakeholders and vendors of how the vision for your project fits into the big picture and what your short- and medium-term plans are for fulfilling that vision. Try to avoid doing this in formal, large-audience, "dog and pony" shows (or, if such shows are important in the culture of your company, don't let such a performance be your primary avenue of communication); meet or chat informally. If short, chatty emails are part of the culture, then do that. If communications are a little more formal, focus on communicating when specific milestones are achieved. (An example of a specific milestone is "prototype completed and demonstrated to three focus groups"; a meaningless pseudo-milestone is "trading system 50 percent complete.") In these cases, make sure to place that announcement in the context of the planned overall schedule and how that contributes to the major vision.

Use the Web to document the various perspectives (overall vision, next small step, and so on) of the project. Keep individual documents concise and focused. One of the joys of hypertext linking is allowing the reader to re-achieve context. For example, a status update about a narrow issue can link to the higher-level project component it relates to, which links to the part of the vision it helps support, and so on. A big, long-term project has many complex components that relate in subtle ways, and anyone who is not involved on a daily basis is going to lose track of all those pieces.

To make this tactic effective, and for other obvious reasons, try to make sure that your key reviewers are comfortable with using the Web. A formal executive training program will probably not work. I recommend (low-key) guerrilla evangelism. Assuming such key people at least have PCs on their desk and use them regularly, you should get whatever applications and tools they need installed on their machines. Offer to show them things. Write little cheat sheets if necessary (such as "First, check that the modem is on—you should see at least one red light..."). Don't be condescending, but recognize that tiny details often get in the way of a new user's satisfaction.

Seek and maintain alliances with other players in your firm. Understand how the work you do relates to the goals they're trying to achieve. It's entirely possible that your goals may conflict with theirs (for instance, your attempts at direct sales online will not sit well with the manager of the reseller channel). Both your efforts should fit together somehow.

Listening is as important as talking. Listen carefully for signs that your audience disagrees with a key assumption behind your work ("Online support will result in fewer phone calls")—or, maybe worse, that they just consider your project and its goals irrelevant.

These recommendations are not about politics or manipulating executive egos. They're about recognizing that your work has to fit in with other people's goals and priorities. Without this process, you might find that you are meeting your self-perceived objectives, only to have your project canceled without warning.

### Project Design: The Life Cycle

Your project will pass through multiple stages. Work that you do early on will have to be maintained, integrated into later work, or discarded later in the process.

Begin with the "big picture" vision of what you hope to achieve and think about how long it might take to reach that point. Then consider whether you can wait that long to have any "deliverables" (launched features delivering benefits to users and your business). You might envision an online database-driven library of every product produced by your company, fully integrated with your sales support systems. That could take a long time to finish, but if a small number of less complex goals will deliver a lot of value with little effort in a short time, get those done first, even though you might have to redo that work later in a more elegant and scalable way. For instance, marketing or the tech support group may be able to identify a small number of resources that they know are greatly needed by users, and it would make sense to get those online quickly, even if they are later reorganized as part of a coherent and more expansive collection. Think of those first steps as prototypes and market research. They can help challenge or confirm your understanding of the audience's needs and clarify issues that you will face in the implementation of your more complex product. Plus, if all goes well, early success will reduce concerns that your project may be a pipe dream.

Another approach to life-cycle planning is to clarify the specific goals for various phases of the project. In *Crossing the Chasm* (Harperbusiness, 1995), Geoffrey Moore discusses a technology company that started out by concentrating on achieving "design wins" (favorable reviews, industry buzz, and such), then later revenue, and much later profitability. The danger with this approach is that it can be difficult to define objective or measurable goals in the early stages of this kind of project, but a reasonable spin on this idea is to focus on short-term deliverables that test the concept of your project (design wins) and begin delivering value (revenue), even if not through the most efficient (profitable) process. In Medscape's case, this has meant that we have skimped on automation of our production processes (a good deal of our HTML conversion process still involves manually cutting and pasting chunks of template code from cookbooks), because our development resources are better invested in features that are visible to our site's users (such as an improved search engine and greater personalization features), rather than in reducing our production costs.

The life-cycle planning process should help you refine your plan, but don't expect that you'll have a detailed road map of everything you're going to deliver over the next two years. Business changes too much, and the Web is still not sufficiently predictable. Again, discuss this plan with your contractor and the appropriate internal staff.

As you begin to move through the life cycle of your project, you'll find that your contractor's tasks will range from the repetitive to the new and unpredictable. You can think of this as a portfolio of activities that have to be managed. It is your responsibility to recognize the various management issues associated with these different types of activities.

A variety of skills are needed to perform different types of tasks. Some contractors excel at building complex applications but don't have the low-end staff to cost-effectively handle repetitive production tasks. Others design great static sites and can code HTML pages but cannot build an infrastructure that will grow with your site's scope and traffic.

Your monitoring controls must fit the various tasks. Repetitive activities can be measured in volumes of flow (for example, "Three new documents added per week") and/or unit cost (for instance, $20 per document). Development of significant new functions must be tracked against scheduled progress. You may even set up different fee schedules with your contractor to reflect the various components of the project.

As you discover the extent of the maintenance activities needed to sustain the site, you might even reconsider whether they should be outsourced at all. If your contractor has built the appropriate infrastructure for your site and you've found ways to integrate that into your company's internal activities, it might begin to make sense to "insource." Discuss the potential for insourcing with your contractor from the beginning, and be sure to structure the project and its fees so that neither of you has a vested interest in pushing the decision in one direction or the other.

**Managing Maintenance Activities.** The archetypal maintenance activity is content production. In a publishing or entertainment-model site, it's clear what content is. In other cases, like a technical support site, content might include product descriptions, product documentation, enhancements such as software drivers or add-on utilities, and records of previous customer questions and their answers. In yet other cases, such as financial data sites, online communities driven by discussion-forum software, or sites where the content varies so significantly in structure that its production is always a technical craft, this manually handled repetitive activity might not exist at all.

As previously mentioned, this type of maintenance activity is relatively easy to quantify. How many documents are added to the site each week? What's the average cost per document? How long does it take to get the average document through the pipeline? What's the backlog? Just because you're able to measure these activities, however, does not necessarily mean that the measurements are useful in every situation, but it's worth consideration, if only to evaluate the performance of your contractor or predict future costs or other metrics as your project's scale increases.

A variety of techniques and tools are available for managing repetitive tasks more effectively. Simple checklist-style production procedures both improve and help maintain the quality and productivity of repetitive tasks as the team faces staff turnover (see Figures 7.1 and 7.2).

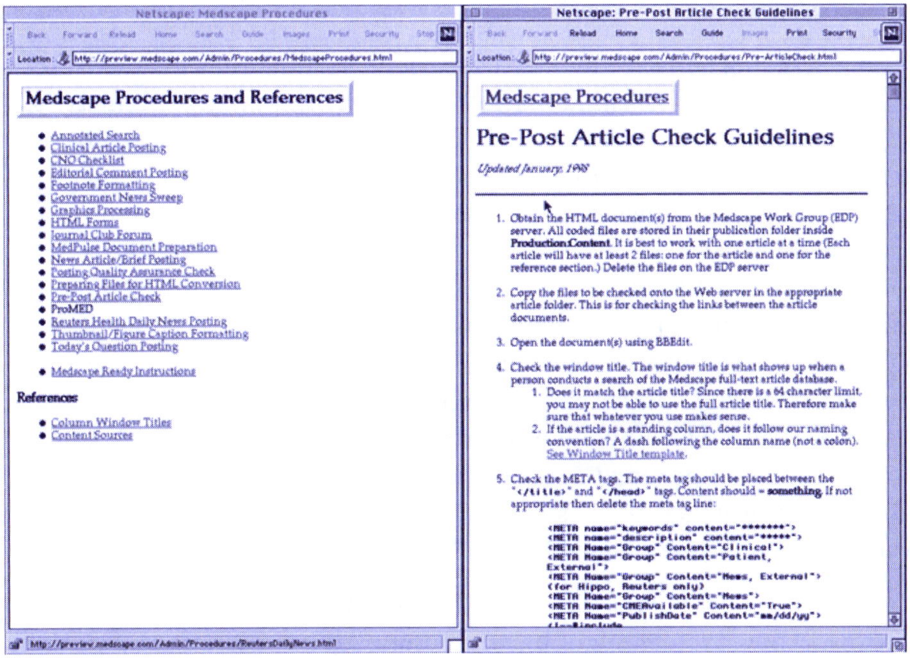


**Figure 7.1** A simple and effective checklist of how to post articles to the Medscape Web site. Documents such as these can be easily created in HTML and accessed by both internal and external teams working on a project.

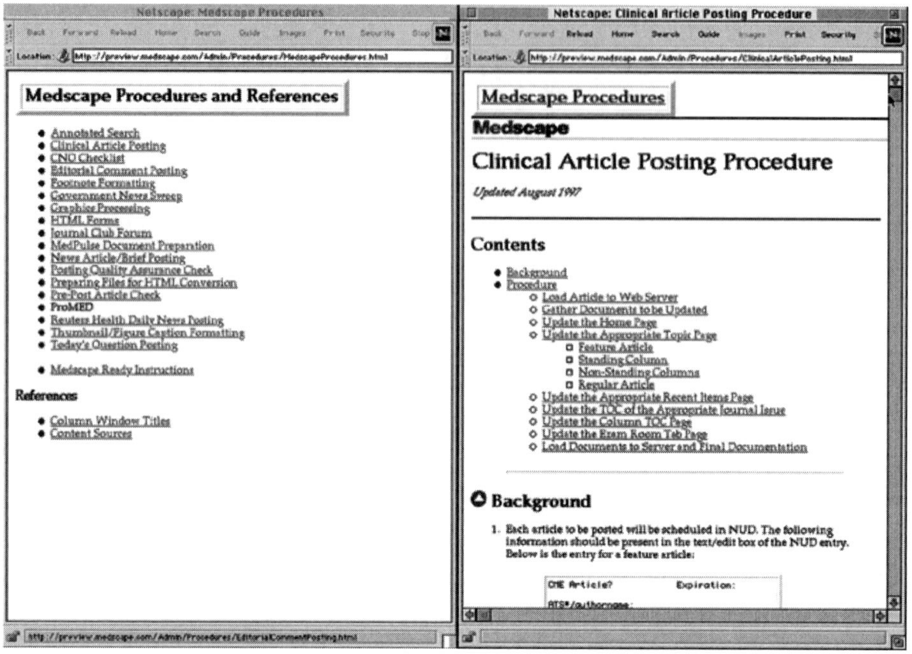


**Figure 7.2** A simple checklist for posting articles to the Medscape Web site. Because these documents are in HTML, they can be updated frequently as management processes evolve throughout the project's life cycle.

Various tracking software may be used to manage the flow of activity. Our production staff uses NowUpToDate (now called Eudora Planner) , a calendar scheduling program, to manage article conversion (much of our non-database-driven or static content such as journal articles is aggregated from print publishers). Content areas are assigned to various calendar categories (such as AIDS articles rather than clinical practice guidelines) so that they can be scheduled over the course of the month and moved around to maintain a consistent flow in each area. Then various flags are used in the short title of each article being added to communicate the status of various required tasks for that article (for instance, "Waiting for links to other sites"). This approach doesn't support structured reporting ("Show me all the articles waiting for copyedit"), but it provides visual support for the scheduled roll-out process, which is more important (see Figure 7.3).

For processes that take place over a longer period of time, a more structured workflow system might be appropriate, because it can help prevent delays at specific steps in the flow (for example, in getting final edits

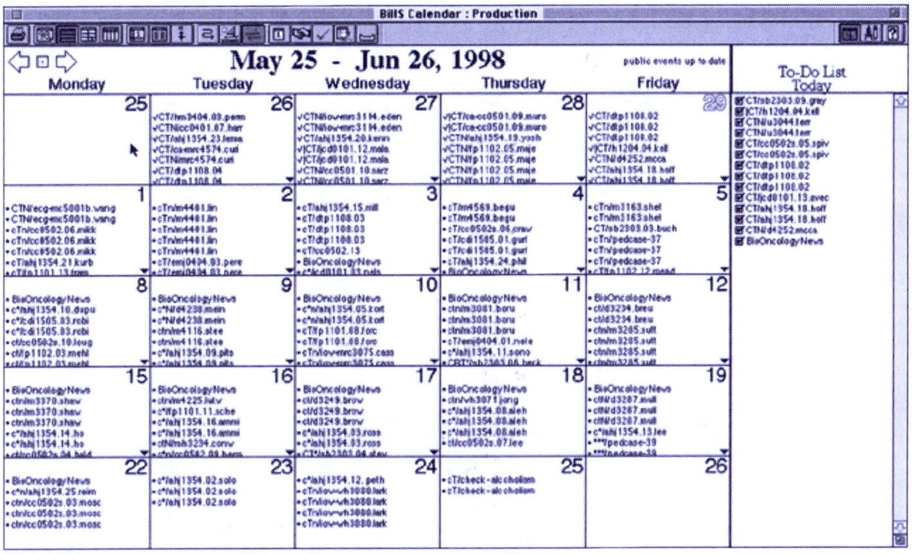


**Figure 7.3** Simple workgroup calendar tools, such as Eudora Planner, can be adapted to provide everyone working on a project with the opportunity to view due dates and milestones and stay informed about the status of a Web project.

back from authors). The original content we develop takes months from solicitation to the final production process, and there may be hundreds of articles at various stages in that process. Being able to report across articles to find those whose status hasn't changed in a long time avoids the sudden discovery that nothing's ready to go into production. Workflow systems are becoming more affordable, but you might still prefer to build a lower-tech system with a workgroup database like Claris FileMaker or MS-Access. Just remember that you want to be careful about turning management of the process into yet another project. Medscape uses custom database-driven software because it's tailored to our processes (see Figure 7.4). If workflow tracking is going to be a big activity in managing your site, you might want to select a contractor based on their existing workflow system.

At some point in the maintenance management process, increased automation opportunities might become feasible. Although we've put off writing programs to automate the production of our more complex content, we built the much simpler programs sufficient to make the production a nearly hands-off operation when we started working with a couple publishers of shorter and more simply structured bundles of content

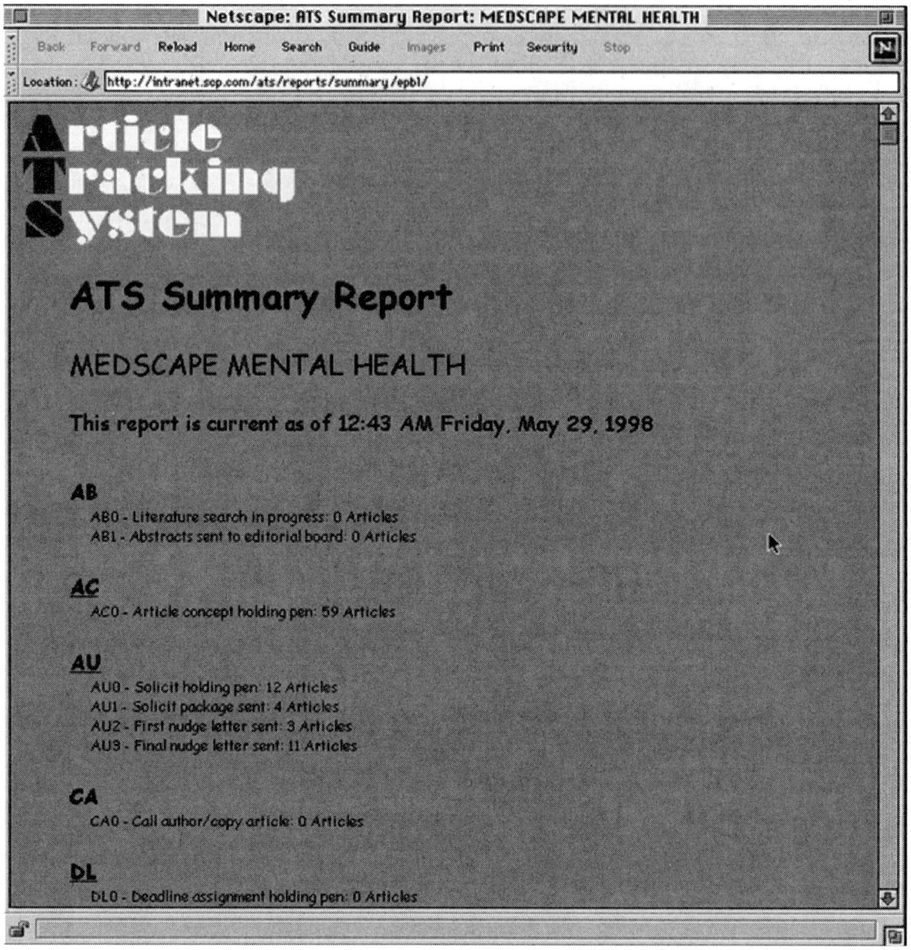


**Figure 7.4** Medscape's Article Tracking System uses an intranet to provide the status of each article being processed for uploading to its Web site. Medscape uploads several thousand articles a year, and current status reports can be generated dynamically by the company's system.

(such as news stories). In some cases, you might suggest that your contractor build (or buy) these tools on the basis that the results could be applied to other clients' projects, giving the contractor a cost advantage over the competition.

Make it clear that you expect the vendor to use an extranet (an Internet-based system run by a company to support confidential communication with specific outsiders such as vendors, customers, and partners) to make appropriate monitoring information available to you. If the vendor's group is generating production statistics internally, you should be able to get those online, rather than having to attend a meeting to get an update. This might not always be appropriate, so be flexible in your expectations.

You should look for opportunities to integrate repetitive tasks with related activities performed within your company. In other words, if you want to generate a customer support knowledge base from every single customer support case that your staff handles, it might be worth investing in building an infrastructure that manages this case information in a way that reduces manual management. Having support staff write small text files and save them into a search engine might work for a purely internal process, but having the files entered directly into a structured database and then indexed might eliminate a future conversion process for the public site.

### Semirepetitive Projects

Many projects run across various events analogous to a magazine's special issues. In other words, many projects share similar major issues and resource requirements, but each one can involve new twists that warrant attention. At Medscape, one of our custom services, Conference News Online, involves sending medical writers to a conference and publishing online session reports. A new client, for example, might pay for some special interviews with keynote speakers that require a different kind of preparation. In dealing with these new issues, you can get distracted from another milestone's deadline. We have a generic plan template to start with, but there are always changes, and sometimes making them can require some creative restructuring of the process if there is a particularly tight schedule (for example, when the client is a week late signing the contract, the conference doesn't get pushed back). We use basic traditional project-planning software (AEC Software's FastTrack Scheduler Pro, a cheaper and easier competitor to MS-Project) to track task timeline dependencies.

The key to managing semirepetitive tasks or projects is to have enough short-term, discrete tasks so that you're meeting milestones on a regular basis to confirm your progress toward the deadline.

Schedule frequent status meetings, either at regular intervals or based on scheduled milestones. Use these meetings to identify and resolve issues.

If your vendor is getting into deadline trouble, you can then redefine your expectations or find options that will benefit you both.

### New Project Components

Implementing new features is one of the greatest challenges of Web site development. This level of project management gets you into the heart of true software development. I'll assume that although you may be semi-technical, you've never been a full-time programmer or manager of programmers, so I'll focus on some of the macro issues involved. A great book to read next is Steve McConnell's *Software Project Survival Guide* (Microsoft Press, 1997); it covers the full breadth of project management and provides plenty of checklists.

### Managing the Components

No other area of software development requires a greater focus on "time to market" than Web feature development. Rapid development is an excellent form of risk management. In software customized for a specific client, the requirements are understood and structured in advance. In developing retail software, market research can offer insight into your target market, at least after your product's category has been defined (it was a lot harder to design VisiCalc than Excel). Great Web sites are still at the VisiCalc stage: Each one is trying to change the world. That's what makes Web site development so exciting, but the flip side is that it's difficult to figure out what customers want, or more accurately, what they'll use. Because standard market research activities don't apply in Web development, some people are trying to come up with better processes (see *Contextual Design* by Hugh Beyer and Karen Holtzblatt [Morgan Kaufman Publishers, 1997]). Still, the newer processes are very complex and require that significant time be spent one-on-one with potential users, which is difficult to achieve. In addition, Web projects rarely have the development budgets of, say, the Denver airport, so to tie up multiple programmers for a full year on a single project is rarely feasible.

Some businesses require the development of extremely complex systems that warrant a substantial investment in development. We can break these down into "rocket science" projects that break new conceptual ground and "nasty" projects that are complex due to the number of components rather than the complexity of any of those individual components. Management of both these categories of projects is beyond the scope of this chapter.

The most practical way to test a system's concept is to build and release a working version, then see how much traffic it gets. The first release should include a number of new features that should make it easy to measure how much traffic they draw; then you can decide which are worthy of the investment required to improve them.

Your goal, in other words, is not likely to be building a big system, but rather putting together a bunch of small systems over time. Think about the various stages your site will go through (design wins, then revenue, then profit) and match the types of projects to the stage. You are essentially a project portfolio manager, which begs the question of how best to build that portfolio. As discussed earlier in this chapter, score some early wins to satisfy the in-house skeptics.

Brainstorm by building a huge list of potential projects, even if you know that many of them will never be built. Then, a couple of times a year, review the list and categorize projects as "hot" (those you want to accomplish based on the resources currently available), "maybe," and "probably not." As a manager, you'll want to discuss the "hot" list with the people whose input you'll want or need. Doing the categorizing yourself will avoid a drawn-out consensus-building process. Of course, you should consider the needs of the various stakeholders involved and take others' input very seriously while noting that different people have different priorities, largely driven by subjective or personal criteria, and that nobody can really predict what people want.

After finalizing "hot" selections, decide in what order to attack them. By starting with the highest-priority items, you're more likely to deliver maximum value by the end of the year. At the same time, stay flexible enough to adjust priorities according to unforeseen factors. A project that might not seem to be a priority may be a good test of, say, a technical architecture that needs to be built for a more valuable but complex project. By starting with a simpler and lower-priority deliverable, you can test the architecture and hash out some of the unpredictable issues in a project that can be rebuilt relatively easily. Staying flexible might also mean delaying a valuable project because resources outside your control (designers, editorial content, outside partners) might not be available when you want them, and you don't want to spend time pushing resources that are out of your control.

Priorities will change and resources will change, but the planning process serves two important purposes: First, it forces you to think through what's important to your site's success; second, the "hot" list gives you ammunition against *inappropriate* changes to the plan. For example, people will often come to you with new ideas, and your prioritized list gives you a basis for thinking, "Well, this might be a good idea, but is it a better use of scarce resources than these previously planned projects?" You can also ask that question of other people and challenge their thinking. Again, I'm not recommending knee-jerk following of a plan; just make sure that deviations from your plan are conscious and justified rather than reactionary.

### Selecting Your Site's Architecture

Project scheduling may be significantly affected by the architectural decisions made at various stages of your site's life. Whether you're considering operating systems, development environments, or shrink-wrapped software, there are similar factors to consider (cost, quality, reliability, ease of integration with other systems, stability of vendor). Of course, all these decisions are related, because some applications are only available under certain operating systems, for example. Ideally, you want to consider all your major decisions at the same time so you can make a coherent integrated choice, but because many significant elements of your architecture are things you don't even know you need yet and many of the products you'll eventually evaluate don't yet exist, you'll have to make some very rough guesses about future markets for software.

You might think that these decisions should be made by your contractor, but your input into these issues should be significant. If you feel your contractor's recommendations are based more on his or her familiarity with certain products than on your needs, it might be time to revisit your contractor selection. In fact, a good case can be made for working with a consultant to help you in some of the architectural decisions, then finding a contractor who agrees with you.

Also note that I'm talking about architecture after talking about project prioritization. That's because having a sense of what types of systems you expect to buy/build/integrate on your site will help you to think about trade-offs.

We ran Medscape on Macintosh servers for a year and a half. As mentioned earlier, we started out as part of SCP Communications, which had Macs on every desktop, and we saw integration of the production process as being important to our ability to bootstrap the operation. By the time we moved off the Mac, we were running two production Web servers, plus a dedicated server for our AppleSearch engine (we still run our email, DNS, and FTP on Macs). I don't regret the decision to use Mac servers, considering that Windows NT was in its infancy when we were getting started, so UNIX was really the only other alternative. I was the sole tech person, both systems administrator and programmer, for that first year; managing a more complex UNIX environment was not a realistic expectation. Limits to file input/output speed curtail the Mac's scalability, and as more people build new sites around SQL back ends that render and deliver content dynamically rather than as static standalone files, the Mac becomes untenable due to its lack of high-performance database servers. (Although it's possible to run a Mac Web server connected to a SQL back end running on another platform, that just creates another variable to worry about.) But when you're trying out a business model that's untested, I still think the Mac is a great Web-prototyping platform.

Once scalable performance and reliability became significant issues for us and we realized that we'd want to be able to buy certain high-end dynamic capabilities (ad servers to dynamically insert ads according to business rules rather than just randomly, template-based middleware for developing SQL-based features, and so on) that were never going to be available on the Mac, we knew we had to switch. I found a consultant who had been working with Time Inc.'s Pathfinder site; he had the chance to see many of our options already in action, because Pathfinder had the budget to buy things and spend time trying to make them work. We ended up settling on Windows NT, a decision I'm still pretty comfortable with. Note that I didn't say "thrilled." We knew then that Windows NT was not as scalable as UNIX, but we were comfortable that we wouldn't run into problems based on our traffic forecasts. (Make sure that you do capacity planning calculations based on peak load, not average weekly or even daily load. Medscape doesn't have a huge daily variation: Our peak load is typically double our steady daytime traffic, but some sites see huge peaks, based on either special events or time of day, such as lunch hour.) We also knew that Windows NT wasn't perfect and that the stability of UNIX systems is highly variable, so there were risks on either side. Having covered those concerns, we chose NT based on hardware cost, software cost, support labor cost, and expectation that Microsoft's dominance in the corporate market would extend into intranet servers, driving many application developers to switch from UNIX to NT as their primary target platform. Software cost differentials have actually decreased as NT's strength has forced down UNIX pricing. Many vendors still start with UNIX, but the momentum of Windows NT is there.

When it came to Web server selection, it was clearly a Netscape vs. Microsoft decision. Performance was comparable. We chose Netscape because we suspected that its philosophy of open standards would make for easier integration with third-party applications (such as the previously mentioned ad server), although we knew Microsoft would always be torn between working with vendors and competing with them. At times, I still question whether Netscape was the right choice, but less because of any current dissatisfaction than from fear that Netscape will be marginalized over time as Apple was.

We bought two major server applications during our initial platform migration: the Verity search engine and the NetGravity ad server. Search engines are rather complex, and you certainly don't want to build one. Many of them are available for free, but you probably don't want to spend a lot of time maintaining or tweaking it. On the other hand, you might find that the vanilla search engines are inappropriate for your purposes. For instance, we define some custom fields in our documents to allow searching based on area of the site, publication date, and whether continuing education credit was available on the content. In addition, we were able to entirely exclude certain pages (such as navigation) from the search engine.

Ad serving was a technology we were tempted to build rather than buy, because we had specific requirements that would be tough to implement in a shrink-wrapped application. Ultimately, we needed the application on such short deadline that we decided to buy it. An added benefit of buying an ad server is that you'll have a legitimate excuse for not providing an unnecessary number of customized features (which salespeople tend to request) because a shrink-wrapped application has limited capabilities. (Salespeople have a right to ask for what they want, but they also tend to hyper-focus on narrow areas of functionality that aren't crucial to their business success but increase the risk of project failure as the software gets overly complex, so it's in your mutual best interest to avoid this.)

We evaluate other application categories (workflow or content template systems, personalization technology) periodically but so far have found those applications expensive and the benefits unproved. Also note that the applications we bought come from reliable vendors with proven track records; you don't want to buy software to implement technology that's key to your site, then spend all your time worrying about whether your vendor will go out of business (or get bought out by Microsoft).

To integrate these applications and build new custom features, we needed a variety of development tools. But we didn't want too many tools, because that would be a burden on our development staff. The code, such as that handling our authentication control (to use our site, you must create a free account and sign in at each visit) and issuing of cookies, which has to run in the NSAPI (the Netscape API which allows you to customize the core functionality of the server with high performance) at high load, is developed in C or C++; luckily, there isn't too much of this; it's the most expensive code to maintain or change because C++ is an overly complex language. We've found that applications that are driven primarily by access to SQL-based data (such as our drug database) are best handled with Allaire's ColdFusion, which allows us to focus on the SQL logic rather than having to write a lot of code. And for the applications that don't fall into either of these categories (such as middleware that communicates with a partner's site to grab and reorganize Medline searches), we write server-side (pure) Java because it's a well-structured and productive development language. We avoid browser-interface programming because of the unprofessional behavior of the browser companies in consistently supporting any language. On an intranet, you can try to force everyone to use the same browser (and the same version of that browser); on a public site, though, code that works with one version of Netscape will break with Internet Explorer, forcing you to write many things twice and spend a lot of time testing.

Again, note that we tend to stick with relatively mainstream, well-supported technologies. This makes us less nervous about vendor viability and gives us a reasonable chance of hiring staff who are already experienced in a given technology. For instance, I'm often tempted to use the Python scripting language, which is supposedly as productive as Perl but more amenable to building well-structured, maintainable code, but I always stay away because of the scarcity of Python programmers.

### Managing Individual Projects

My approach to managing individual projects can be summed up as follows: Plan for a multiphased delivery and try to avoid ever getting to the second phase. In other words, because we're attempting to deliver a large number of projects with limited resources, we'll settle for delivering "good enough" software (see the article by James Bach at www.stlabs.com/testnet/docs/good.htm), then getting on to the next project. Again, this doesn't mean we produce buggy software; it means we create applications that deliver the core benefits to the bulk of target users. James Brooks, in his classic book *The Mythical Man Month* (Addison-Wesley, 1995), describes a consultant who was renowned for coming into projects that looked like they'd never end and bringing them to closure. When asked what his secret was, he said, "I just keep throwing out requirements until I get down to a project that can actually get completed."

Start applying this approach before you even begin programming a project: when you write the requirements for it. You should have done some thinking about this during the process of prioritizing your projects for the year, because the complexity of requirements will define the cost of the project and thus the evaluation of whether it's worth doing. But now it's time to get into the details.

The requirements might result in realizing that a project is much more expensive than you originally thought, forcing a reconsideration of its priority or even its cancellation. One of the dirty secrets of the development world is that a huge percentage of projects are never successfully completed (and few are finished on time and within budget). So, canceling a project that's unlikely to be completed before significant resources are invested in it can be a good decision.

Document all the features you plan to deliver. Distinguish between those that must be included in the first release and those that can be held off for later releases. Then describe explicitly those features you have no intention of delivering. (This process also helps you brainstorm about features you don't want to forget about.) Structure your requirements around the series of interactions between your system and its various users (these are referred to as *scenarios* or *use cases*, and there are a number of complex books available on their structure).

According to some formal development methodologies, you'd first finish the requirements document, then start on the design process (data structures, interface, and so on), but I find that making the design part of the requirements process helps keep everything consistent. So I typically cycle through different parts of the plan (what does the user want to do? what does the system have to do? how should it look? what needs to be happening behind the scenes?) one requirement at a time.

One of the joys of HTML is that you can easily build a prototype of your system simply by creating a series of static HTML documents for each use case, showing how the user progresses through the scenario. (If there are significantly different paths the user might take or special exceptions that need to be recognized, you might have to make a nearly duplicate set of pages for each sub-case.) Then you can link the documentation of each requirement to its prototype. This technique will both improve the thoroughness of your planning (you will discover special cases your system must react to or you might realize that your user is going to be confused halfway through a process) and communicate your design to your company peers and the people building the system.

This type of process may not work as well for you, because you may not have the skills and experience to think through the details of the interface and data structures, and your contractor's project manager might want to manage these parts of the process, so the two of you might need to work on this together. Try to avoid the "I'll finish the requirements by myself, then toss them over for you to do the design" scenario, because you'll end up having to cycle through plan changes anyway, so it's best to avoid overformalizing what is bound to be just a first draft.

Once you (both) think this document is completed (it's never *really* done until the project is over), you should review it with the appropriate parties. You should have been discussing many of the issues during the writing of the document, but review the final results again anyway.

Another outcome of the requirements analysis and design should be a rough task list and schedule for the project. In "nasty" projects, you would go through an extremely complex estimating process, building up an estimate of "function points" from which you would predict total development time and so on. But I've found that our projects are too small to warrant that analysis investment and too likely to run into ugly surprises due to the immaturity (bugs) of the development tools or applications being integrated. Breaking things down into a reasonable level of detailed tasks (to the extent that they are predictable), however, will help build a calendar of progress.

By the time the task list is ready, the actual programming is taking place. The more complex your project, the more important a role the contractor's processes play. But it's difficult to evaluate this from the outside. You could take Steve McConnell's *Rapid Development* book, go through its list of best practices, and ask your contractor a series of questions: "Do you do code reviews? Do you having coding standards?" and so on. However, he or she could easily lie, or go through the motions of some of these practices without actually getting the benefit. It' difficult to generalize about which practices are most valuable. Therefore, it's probably best not to meddle too much in your vendor's internal operations.

I'm going to immediately contradict myself and mention two particular practices which I've chosen to implement in our group, just because I thought they were the most important place to start.

Version-control software lets developers track changes in source code or other files (such as documentation) as the project progresses. The software can analyze differences between the various generations of code. This makes it easier for the contractor to resurrect draft code that worked but was abandoned in favor of a new approach, retrace the steps of a programmer who leaves so his or her replacement can see what was built over time, and create an audit trail for tracking when a particular component was built or changed and sometimes why that was done. In the case of project documentation updates (like changes in requirements), it's handy to have an audit trail. The Versions product from StarBase (www.starbase.com/) is probably the most affordable market leader.

A defect-tracking system is helpful for managing bugs, from the point at which they are discovered through various cycles of repair. Even in relatively small projects, it's easy to forget about a bug (the programmer might remember to fix it, but the tester might forget to retest it), so some sort of structured log is helpful. A variety of high-end systems are on the market; we chose to build a custom system using SQL and ColdFusion so that it would support our chosen level of complexity and be Web-based (see Figure 7.5). But, again, it's easy to have this type of system and misuse it, so evaluating a contractor's development processes from outside when you don't have programming experience is rarely a good idea.

One of our system's customized features for tracking bugs is to tie them to a test's "phase." Certain types of testing can be time-consuming and you might want to evaluate them only after other tests have been passed. For instance, we start by using other members of our development team to test a system and fix all the bugs found during that process before anyone else in the company tests it. Later, we get to more complex challenges such as retesting an entire system on a variety of browsers, versions, and platforms and load testing the system to see whether it breaks when run with high frequency. Then, when the system goes live (in other words, when it's installed on the production server for use by the public), we test yet again (at least some of the basic features) and watch error logs carefully for the first couple days. We also write some code to count the volumes of known error codes in our daily server error logs (to catch a sudden increase in frequency) and list new codes.

Encouraging feedback from users provides many benefits, from discovering bugs experienced only by browsers you didn't test to finding that people can't figure out how to use certain features that you think are obvious. (Despite our best efforts to make it obvious that our site is free, we still get email asking, "But how much does it cost?").

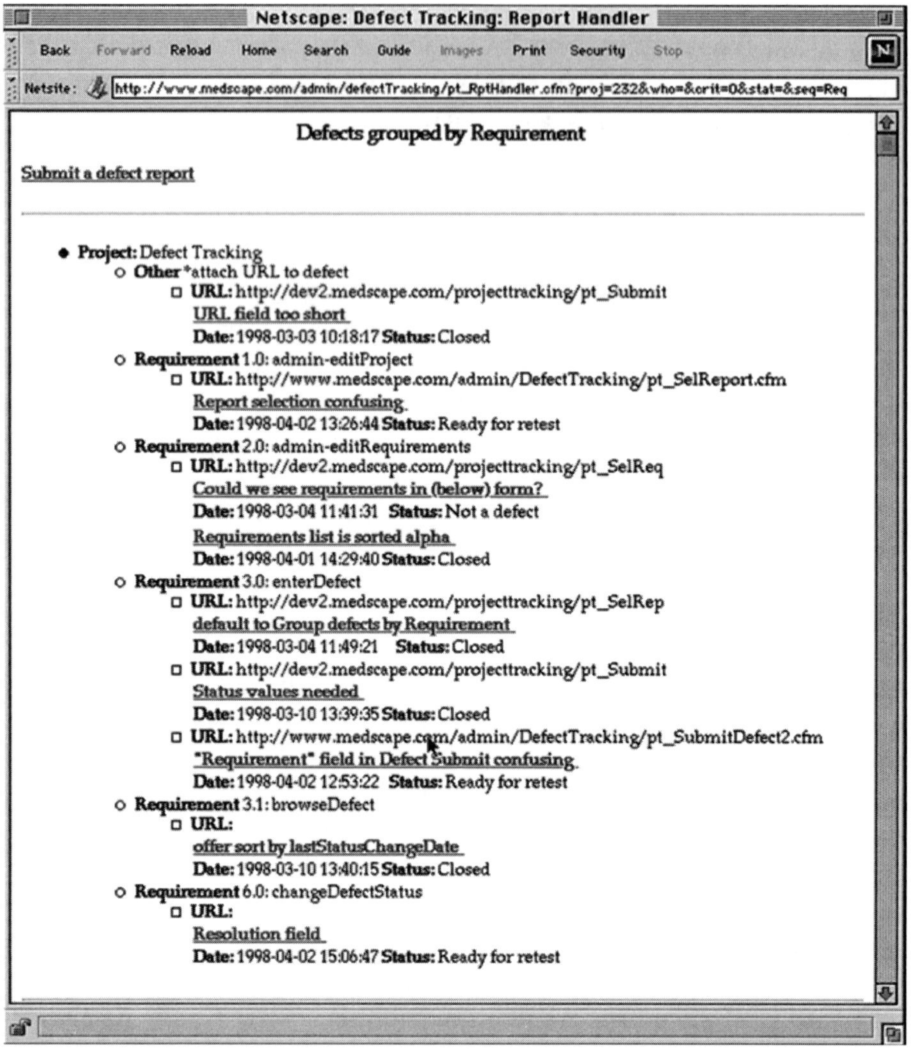


**Figure 7.5** A report that groups Web site defects by requirement, enabling project managers to zero in on defects by importance, complexity, and date.

On many sites, you'll see a "mailto" link on a page, which makes it easy to send a message to an identified support person in the site's group (or its contractor's group). We've gone a bit further, creating a feedback link on every page, which takes the user to a form which will generate the email. This allows us to grab the URL of the page the user is coming from, which helps make clear where they were; grab the name, version, and platform of the browser they're using; let them direct the message to the appropriate specialized support person, depending on the nature of the question (content vs. technical); and provide a few different entry fields to structure the information they give us, helping to get a more specific, and therefore useful, question.

By the way, handling this email can easily become a significant maintenance activity—don't forget to plan and budget for it.

In addition, we've created even more specialized service request forms ("I forgot my password," "Help me unsubscribe from the 'what's new' email broadcast list," and the like) for cases in which forcing a certain structure to the email message will let us write programs on the other end to automatically process a batch of similar requests.

## Closing the Loop

As I've repeatedly mentioned, the reason for my "portfolio" approach to site development is the difficulty in predicting what people will like. It's almost as hard to figure out whether your site is successful (and why) *after* the fact! The portfolio approach helps set appropriate and realistic expectations. For example, sites that are designed as profit-making ventures (as opposed to those that promote an offline business activity or reduce its costs) face a particular challenge. Despite the "make money fast" aura of the Web, the only people getting rich so far are those who cash out after their unprofitable company is foisted onto an unsuspecting public or the groups servicing those unprofitable sites (ad agencies, lawyers, investment bankers, consultants, headhunters). This doesn't necessarily mean that those companies won't be profitable someday. But nobody can accurately predict how long it will take, so measuring progress toward that goal is impossible.

To set clearer expectations for your site, start with a "future perfect" vision (Luke Hohmann describes this process a bit in *Journey of the Software Professional* [Prentice Hall Computer Books, 1996]). Studies have found that people generate more vivid visions if, instead of thinking from the present to the future ("How will your site succeed?"), they think from the future to the present and near future ("Imagine it's two years later, and your site is a huge success—what makes it a success, and how did you get there?"). The more you expand your vision into a story, the more detail you'll be able to create. (Looping back to the beginning of the chapter, this story should help you define the goals of your site and come up with ideas for what to add to it.) This vivid detail is especially helpful in creating a sense of how things might progress in stages from the current time to that successful future. Having your present-time, critically thinking self interview your future self can help build the bridge between the two phases.

Having described a progression toward a successful future, you must then try and define quantitative stages of progress. Recognize that a bottom-line budget number can be met or not met for a variety of reasons, so you'll probably want to develop a series of less direct but more descriptive measures. Some of these measures might be based on traffic figures (analyzing your server's log files), but others might be gathered through other means. For instance, if your site is intended to provide customer support, you might have your existing phone staffers ask customers whether they've tried finding the information on your site yet. For an annual goal, you want big ranges of values that you associate with levels of success ("If, after six months, less than 20 percent of customers calling in have tried the site, we're in trouble. Anything from 20 percent to 50 percent qualifies as on-track. If we're above 50 percent, we're lucky—or heroes").

As time progresses, compare reality to your planned indicators, then figure out why you got the result you did. This is where things get challenging: Lots of explanations are possible, and it's difficult using *any* data source (traffic logs, surveys, and so on) to *prove* a particular theory. Likewise, figuring out what to do differently in the future to improve your success is more difficult than creating your original vision, especially if your original vision hasn't been successful (how can you believe your next plan?).

The most credible process for figuring out what to do in the future is, again, to trade numeric precision for broad-stroke indications either supporting or challenging a mental model (back to the story concept). The way to drive this process is through external communication (asking site users, through whatever medium possible, without regard for measurability) and internal discussion (arguing about the implications of feedback gathered so far, asking the next question to be put to the users, and so on).

If you can master the process of investigation and discovery, everything else in this chapter (and book) will fit together.

## Summary

Many companies that outsource their Web site fall into what we call the trap of unmanageable moving targets. The way companies fall into that trap is by believing that, because the Web is evolving so quickly and forever morphing into greater and more exciting areas, it is best to keep the management of a Web project loose as you move forward in your efforts.

This chapter suggests just the opposite. Many aspects of Web development need to be managed, and they can and should be addressed through organized and efficient systems set up and agreed upon by you and your Web developer.

Of course, sometimes the best plans do not work as intended. In our next chapter, "When Things Go Wrong," we take a look at the likely fail points on a Web project and suggest strategies for avoiding them before they happen ... and coping with them if they do.

## Checklist

- ☐ Have you identified clear goals for your project? Share these goals with your developer and your staff.
- ☐ Identify a list of key people in your organization who need to approve and support your project. Find out how those key people define the success of a project, and let them know about your project.
- ☐ Create a list defining maintenance activities and discuss strategies for managing them. Are there procedures in place, and are those procedures accessible to your staff and your developer?
- ☐ Create a list defining semirepetitive tasks and discuss strategies for managing them. Are there procedures in place, and are those procedures accessible to your staff and your developer?
- ☐ Create a list defining new Web site projects and components and discuss strategies for managing them. Are there procedures in place, and are those procedures accessible to your staff and your developer?

- ☐ Create a list defining activities that alter your site's structure and discuss strategies for managing them. Are there procedures in place, and are those procedures accessible to your staff and your developer?
- ☐ Create a task list and work with your developer to set up a schedule.
- ☐ Create a testing schedule and work with your developer to set up a process for implementing it.
- ☐ Create a process for soliciting and evaluating feedback for your site.
- ☐ Institute a formal procedure to review your deadlines, successes, and failures. Always remember the key to project management is to "close the loop."

chapter

8

# When Things Go Wrong

**Julia Rubinic**
**R/GA Interactive, a Division of R/GA Associates**
*juliar@rga.com*

## About This Chapter

"Anticipation" is perhaps a more appropriate title for this chapter because Web development experts recognize that it's better to anticipate potential problems than attempt to manage them "when things go wrong."

This chapter provides a framework for creating an environment and a set of procedures that will help you work with your Web developer to reduce potential problems as you build your site. Many of the steps you can take to prevent problems—such as planning and prioritizing your goals, getting over the production bumps, and confronting problems—can be made by communicating effectively with your Web developer. This chapter takes a look at the key problems that are likely to occur as they relate to the issues of design, technology, and usability and suggests strategies for anticipating and managing them along the way.

## About the Author

Julia Rubinic began her career in interactive media for the consumer and commercial market more than six years ago. She started out as a CD-ROM producer on topics such as the Civil War and Shakespeare. For the past two years, she's concentrated on working with corporate clients seeking to enhance their presence on the Internet. She is currently a producer at R/GA Interactive, a high-end, Web developer that is a subset of the well-known special effects film, video, and imaging firm, R/GA Associates.

## Confronting and Avoiding Development Problems

**There is a general fear that when you embark on a Web project, you're risking a place in the history of great, failed projects. Finding the perfect developer, gaining a thorough understanding of the technology, communicating your goals to a wide range of professionals—including artists, programmers, and writers—and ensuring that a complicated project is neither late nor over the original budget are not small tasks, so the fear is understandable.**

Fortunately, there are many experienced Web developers in the market who have overcome the hurdles of creating Web sites. The key is to find a company that has a solid production process in place that helps you avoid costly and unnecessary problems. In this chapter, I'll point out the problems that often appear and recommend methods of anticipating and avoiding them. If roughly categorized, these problems are usually related to issues of technology, design, usability, and, on a more global scale, misunderstanding. Within each of these categories lie specific challenges that can be successfully met with the proper procedures in place.

There is no one perfect process that should govern the development of a Web site. Procedures should reflect the particularities of each project, including complexity, client involvement, and the like. You should, however, ensure that your Web developer prioritizes the need for a process that prevents things from going wrong. A good developer incorporates into documentation many procedures that have worked well in the past and adjusts them to match the needs of each client and project. This includes consideration of what works well for other media, such as television, film, publishing, and print. New media is, after all, an amalgam of different media, each of which has specific operations in place that facilitate development. A smooth process should blend checks and milestones that play a traditional role in related industries.

### The Developer as Partner

Keep in mind one general rule that can help prevent disasters from befalling any project: Good developers should see themselves as partners in your project, with an equal interest in producing a high-quality Web site with minimal development problems. Assuming you have a developer who has this attitude about the client/developer relationship, you should foster this partnership as much as possible. If your developer truly feels a vested interest in your Web site, keeping the lines of communication open will be easier and can only work to the advantage of the project. It can also prevent the majority of mishaps and misunderstandings that lead to a disappointing or defective Web site.

### Planning and Prioritizing

Establishing your working relationship as a partnership with your Web developer is especially relevant in the planning phase. Careful planning is what helps avoid costly mistakes and missed deadlines, and open communication is the only way to carefully plan a project.

When scoping a project, consider what could go wrong and how grave these potential outcomes may or may not be for your project. Make a list of priorities and share them with your developer. For example, although you may want the Web site to display an appealing graphic design, your Web site is targeting users with the slowest modems; therefore, you have to be more concerned with the speed at which graphics download. Perhaps the Web site launch is pinned to a specific date, such as the beginning of the holiday shopping season. In that case, your priority has to be your deadline because, no matter how easy your developer makes it to order chocolate Christmas trees online, there won't be many takers on December 26.

You may be wondering why you should share a list of priorities with a developer; after all, he should be considering *every* step of the development process as though it were a priority. A good developer will not see this list of priorities as an opportunity to fall behind in areas that are lower on the list. Instead, he'll see this list is a valuable tool that allows him to assist you in making decisions that work within your expectations and constraints. For example, you may have a tight time frame in which to complete a Web site for your interior design firm. Communicating a deadline will provide your developer with a milestone, but little else. With limited time to build the site and no information about your priorities, the developer might make uninformed decisions about which areas to be scaled down in order to meet your deadline. In this case, you may end up with a Web site that includes an elaborate catalogue of your furniture, but little overall visual appeal, when you'd been hoping for something with more pizzazz that reflects the cutting-edge approach of your interior designs.

In that case, if you had told the developer that in addition to the tight schedule, you also consider a sleek graphic design to be a priority, you would've gotten results that more closely matched your vision for the Web site. Your developer would've worked with you to ensure that resources were properly allocated so that the visual aspect of the Web site was given the proper attention. Your developer might've told you that your tight time frame and the extra attention paid to design wouldn't allow for other features, such as the catalogue of furniture. By discussing the priorities and possibilities up front, you retain greater control over your options. In the end, you would have opted for a snazzy-looking Web site that launched on time, and you would have sacrificed only the catalogue, a feature that wasn't very important to you anyway.

I once had a client who was eager to launch his site as quickly as possible. We agreed to a very aggressive schedule that necessitated a dedicated, full-time team of designers and programmers. We scoped the project carefully, building a set of milestones that required the quick turnaround of pages from the development team and materials from the client. However, once production was rolling, the client soon learned how difficult it was for us to deliver his materials (which included new logos, copy, and product shots) according to our milestones. When the materials finally arrived, the haste with which they were created was reflected in their poor quality, such as copy with grammatical errors and poorly lit product shots. These materials, along with the increasingly distressed messages he left on my voicemail, were clear signals that something had to be changed in the production phase if we wanted to see both a valuable Web site and a sane client. After sitting down with the client, I learned that the aggressive schedule was more a whim than a necessity. By pushing the schedule and reallocating my internal resources over several projects, we were able to produce a high-quality Web site within the originally agreed-upon budget. A better discussion of priorities up front, plus the knowledge that the initial deadline wasn't one of them, could have spared everyone a few headaches.

## Getting Past the Bumps

Let's assume that you have clear specifications in the form of documents, such as functional specifications and design documents, as well as an understanding of the priorities, and you are currently in production. You and the developer hit a snag, resulting in a minor bump in the development process (or what seems like an airbag-inflating stop). Whatever the problem is, this is the point at which both partners must practice a little common sense.

Even with the best planning, there is a high probability that something could go awry in the development process. Once again, there are several compelling reasons to regard your developer as a partner. A good developer should assist you with a quick confrontation of the problem, a thorough analysis, a plan of action, and a post-mortem to ensure that the situation is not repeated. These steps are common sense because they are not exclusive to the new-media industry and in most situations can be applied toward the resolution of problems.

**Confronting Problems Early.** First, confront the problem early on. Even if you are simply anticipating a potential problem, as long as you are sensitive to maintaining an environment of open communication, both you and the developer will appreciate having time to solve a problem before it becomes a disaster.

I once produced a Web site that suffered major setbacks as a result of a delay in addressing a serious problem. The Web site was for a product that was geared toward users with expensive computers and high-speed Internet connections. The assumption agreed to with our client was that users would have the necessary technology that would allow us to add more bells and whistles in the site. It wasn't until several weeks into the design phase that we learned of a new direction from our client's marketing department: The Web site would have to reach a broader audience, including users who would not be able to properly access the Web site's information as currently designed. If we had been privy to this shift in direction earlier, we could have spent more time inventing new and accommodating design ideas, instead of continuing the production of profitless design.

**Problem Analysis.** Once you've acknowledged a problem, analyze the situation with your developer so that you have a shared understanding of its origin and potential impact. One of the most common results of a lack of communication is a misunderstanding about whether a situation has become problematic. What seems glaringly irreparable to the client may only require a small tweak by the developer, or what appears trivial to the developer could mean disaster for the client.

For example, you may notice that an application controlling your Web site's navigation system runs very slowly on your browser. Each time you click to get to a new page, the application takes a long time to readjust to its new location. You have been accessing the development site for weeks but haven't noticed an improvement in this application, even though the site is due to launch in a few weeks. When you point this out to the developer, she is much more calm about it. What you didn't realize was that the developer was about to complete the relatively simple portion of the application that detects which browser you are using. Browsers that cannot handle applications built in Java, such as the browser you've been using, have a slightly different navigation structure. The only problem in this scenario is that you spent time worrying needlessly.

A similar situation may arise from the developer's misunderstanding of a potential problem. Perhaps the developer created a design that doesn't work well on earlier versions of browsers. Images aren't lining up in the browser you're using the way they did on pages that were sent to you for approval. Your developer may then spend weeks trying to tweak the HTML coding to fix the disparity. After painstaking attempts to find a solution, the developer believes that the only alternative is to present you with a new design. The developer may not realize that compatibility with early versions of browsers is not important to you. Your company's research has provided you with data that shows a vast majority of your target users browsing with the most recent browser releases. Having a small percentage of your market view unaligned images is not the problem that the developer thought it would be.

Naturally, not every confronted problem turns out to be a simple misunderstanding. You might often call your developer to report a situation and hear that, yes, you've uncovered a problem. This leads to step three: building a plan of action with your developer. This is tricky, because the plan may often involve resolutions that thrill neither you nor the developer. A resolution to the problem can sometimes involve delaying schedules, sacrificing features, or additional costs. For example, the problem may be that your Web site must be launched earlier than the original schedule due to increased competition. For the developer, this could mean having his programming team strung out on Jolt cola at 4:00 in the morning. As for the client, you may have to sacrifice precious features by narrowing the scope of the original design.

I've noticed that my clients tend to perk up a bit when, instead of thinking in terms of features being lost, they begin to see them as planned features for "Phase 2." Even if there never is a second phase, it's the perfect consolation for struggling through problems that arise in Phase 1.

**The Problem-Solving Plan.** Solving the problem is the third step in working toward resolution. Once again, it illustrates how essential it is to work with your developer to create a plan of action. Your developer may have ideas about various approaches to solving the problem that only someone close to the development process could conceive. For example, a Java applet that looks cool because it has rollovers can be built as straight HTML without the rollovers. This would reduce production and testing time drastically without detracting from navigability. The only loss would be a little pizzazz, which may not be that important to your Web site. By working together to devise an action plan, you and your developer can bounce ideas off one another to test for feasibility on his part and acceptability on yours.

**Preventing Future Problems.** No problem is too small to merit a post-mortem. It's a step that I always take, regardless of whether or not the client participates. Often, if a problem has been particularly stressful, those involved want to leave it as far behind as possible. Asking a team that has been working weekends to meet a new deadline to stay one hour longer to assess what went wrong is not easy. It is equally difficult to convince a client to rehash what may have been a tense process of resolution. The point of this last step, however, is a significant one: to ensure that it doesn't happen again.

Make a list of events that may have led to the problem. Was there a miscommunication? Did the developer promise a technology that wasn't properly tested without a safety plan? Did you approve something that had to be changed when someone in another of your company's departments saw it? Keep in mind that this is not an exercise in placing blame.

The second half of this step involves supplementing the list with ideas about how to prevent the problem from occurring again. Maybe the project requires the developer to write weekly reports to the client in order to maintain effective communication. Perhaps a longer scoping phase is necessary for applications that have not yet been programmed into the site. Consider suggestions from everyone on the team and distribute the final list or ask your developer to distribute it. On some of my more complicated projects, I've kept a list next to my desk of even the smallest potential mishaps, such as making sure I'm delivering materials to the correct location of a client who travels often. By keeping this as a checklist, I've been able to quickly smooth the bumps that often appear at the beginning of a project by making sure they happen only once.

### Avoiding and Managing Design-Related Problems

One of the most difficult messages to communicate is the look that you're envisioning for your Web site. Even the most specific directions regarding a graphic treatment are subjective. Think about the last time you had to rent a movie for someone who was in the mood for something "funny." Chances are that you spent a while trying to determine what this person would think is funny. You probably weren't completely confident in your choice until after the movie was over. Now imagine that the person you have to amuse is someone you've just met who has high expectations and, instead of asking you to rent a movie, is requesting that you film a comedy from scratch. That's what a developer can often feel like at the beginning of the design process.

There are a few steps that you and your developer can take to ensure that you'll be happy with your Web site's look. First, sit down with the designers and communicate any information that you think may be of value, even if it seems trivial. At worst, trivial information will be discarded after the meeting is over. At best, it can inspire a designer. If you have relevant materials, such as company brochures or annual reports, pass them along to the designer, with your assessment of what works and what could be improved. You may even reference design work that is not related to your company to give examples of what you're trying to achieve. The point is that you should be as clear as possible about the direction you expect to see in their design. Keep in mind that this is a dialogue; the designers should be prepared with questions for you to help get closer to a mutual understanding.

The second recommendation toward avoiding future design-related problems is to request a number of approaches to the design. Before moving into full-fledged design, your Web developer can mock up one page in two or three directions. This provides you with an opportunity to show the designs to colleagues who may have an interest in the Web site's overall look. Someone in the marketing department, for example, may want to ensure that the look complies with the company's overall branding. Although it is difficult to get a number of people to agree on how to direct a Web developer, it should be easier to encourage participation by providing several design concepts. Once a direction is established, the individuals who gave their input may not have to continue to be as closely involved, as long as the look has been well defined and is adhered to.

Finally, design disasters are often technical in nature. During the planning phase, it should be made absolutely clear, and then documented, what areas of the Web site must be easily updated—for instance, the headings of a product catalogue for a company that changes its products weekly. The plan for dynamic areas (areas that will be refreshed often) should be perfectly clear to both you and your developer before a design is completed.

Despite these planning precautions, you may still run into a problem with the design, even after a look has been established. A design approach that may have worked well last month may not be in line with the company's new approach to positioning itself this month. (As a member of an industry where even the biggest of companies must be able to quickly turn around their strategies in order to survive, I am familiar with companies having to rethink their identities. Where else but in the computer industry can a behemoth like Microsoft go from dismissing the Internet one year to being accused by the U.S. Government of attempting to monopolize Internet software the next?)

Another potential problem may arise from a shift in personnel, where a new manager coming into the project late in the process has clear, resolute ideas about how a company's image should be portrayed on the

Web. What do you do when a great, already agreed-upon design, for which most of the art assets have already been completed, is suddenly unacceptable?

The solution refers back to my original recommendations regarding approaching problems by working with your Web developer. Meet with your developer to analyze this new situation, determine the potential repercussions, negotiate a resolution that cuts losses, and set up an action plan. Don't forget to incorporate the lessons learned from the post-mortem into the action plan. Let's use my redesign scenario as an example for executing the problem resolution.

It's clear that the original design no longer melds with the company's new branding. What may not be clear to you is how to approach a redesign and how much work has already been done. These questions can only be answered by your Web developer. In order to get an accurate assessment, you must supply as much information as possible about the new design and what elements no longer work with it. Perhaps the redesign requires only a new color palette, which wouldn't affect the layout and treatment of icons too severely. Maybe the redesign issues are more general, such as a shift in tone from cutting-edge to warm and fuzzy, which would require a complete overhaul. Whatever the feedback—and the more, the better—the designers need ample information in order to assess the situation. The outcome of the analysis may be better or worse than you had imagined, so avoid making assumptions until you speak to your developer.

Let's imagine that the color palette is no longer suitable. The good news may be that the creation of a new palette is relatively straightforward for the senior designer. (Please bear in mind that I do not mean to undervalue the importance of a color palette, nor am I implying that a changed color palette is a small design task. I am constructing a world in which it is a small design matter for the sake of this example; I'm sure that the many designers who have struggled with palettes would like for me to construct this world for them.) Because this is a new design, you should go back one step in the production process and have your developer create three treatments from which to choose. Finally, take a peek at the post-mortem notes that you have dutifully taped to your computer and see if there is anything that could have prevented this from happening the first time. Sure enough, you note that you were supposed to run the design by the person in charge of overseeing the focus group that determines the direction of the company's logo. (Bear in mind that this is what it looks like from the developer side of the fence.) You promptly include him or her in your approval process.

Another result of the analysis of the redesign problem is that the majority of the art assets, based on the original design, have already been created. Your Web developer tells you how many resources have to be allocated to recreating these assets, which in this case may not be so vexing, because only the icons' color palette (now approved) has to be altered. There is a realistic shift in the schedule by two weeks, which you agree to offset by losing another feature. So the action plan that has been carefully discussed is as follows:

- The developer and client build a new schedule, including consideration of the shift in design and loss of the specified feature.
- The developer creates three treatments using different color palettes.
- The client selects the new palette after receiving internal approvals.
- The developer recreates original art assets.

Once broken down in this manner, what once seemed like a problem becomes more like an unforeseen, but manageable, phase of the development process.

### Avoiding and Managing Technology Problems

The technology that drives your Web site can be the most exciting aspect of your overall design, but also the most precarious if not designed correctly. The technology is a crucial aspect of a Web site, the integration of which demands a serious consideration of the strategic approach, thorough processes throughout development, and cautious testing before completion. When selecting from among the countless new products that are released every week, you must weigh the product's exciting features against its stability and long-term viability.

Many of the technical problems that afflict a Web project could be avoided with adequate planning. The Internet boom has inspired a vast number of companies and individuals to build software and hardware tools that push technology to its limit. Your Web developer should work with you from the very beginning to determine your needs. The technical design should consider all aspects of the project, including time frame, audience, and target audience's machines. Disasters often occur when the technology doesn't adhere to the project's goals.

One possible outcome of choosing inappropriate technology can be schedule delays due to a few lingering technical bugs. I'm frequently amazed at how an entire team can rally behind meeting deadlines, completing the content and design assets ahead of schedule, only to wait helplessly while programmers struggle with difficult code. This is not to blame the programmers, because writing code is a complicated, time-consuming process. The point is that choosing an appropriate technology design means finding one that can be implemented by the specified deadlines.

The technical design must also consider the target audience. During the planning phase, let your developer know the characteristics of your intended audience, especially the type of equipment they're likely to be using to view your Web site. Do they have recently released browsers? Would they have downloaded plug-ins that the technical designer is planning to use? How fast are their Internet connections? These are all essential questions to answer before solidifying a technical approach.

Creating documentation for your Web site, such as a technical specification that maps out the technical design, is extremely important. The documentation should be detailed enough so that programmers on your developer's team, as well as technical personnel on your side, can address potential flaws. It should also include text that translates the limitations of the technology and explains the constraints that must be followed by designers, writers, and other team members in order to adhere to any limitations imposed by the technical design. Once this documentation has been submitted by your developer and agreed upon, the Web site must be produced according to the criteria established in the technical design.

Let's assume that you're supplying art elements from your company's graphics department to your developer. You may be building templates for a product catalogue that the technical design specifies as containing one picture of a specific size per product page. If you ask your designer to crop the product pictures to the right size, you shouldn't run into a problem. However, you may have overlooked letting the designer know the limitations that she must adhere to in order to comply with the developed technology. If your designer hasn't been alerted to the required size for the product shots, she may deliver product pictures that are not useable. The worst-case scenario is that the pictures don't fit inside the templates and are unacceptably cut off, and the designer would have to repeat the task again.

Another important planning point involves the prudent use of new technologies. You may have determined in your planning phase that you want to experiment with a new software program. ("New" is a relative term in the new-media industry, so we'll define it as referring to a product that is in a beta release at the inception of your planning phase.) Perhaps you want your site to appeal to a technically savvy audience that demands breaking features, such as increased interactivity or higher-resolution video. Maybe the usefulness of your Web site would double if you included a feature that's available only in a beta product. Whatever your reasons for using it, extra care must go into the integration of untested (or less tested) technology.

Ask your developer to help you understand the potential results of incorporating a product that fails to deliver what it promises. What is the likelihood of something going wrong? How much of the overall Web site will it affect? Your developer can recommend a backup plan, whenever possible, that mitigates the damage. For example, you may want your Web site's navigational graphics to respond to interaction in a lively manner. This could involve a new product that makes it easy for designers to build responsive, animated graphics using code that once had to written by a programmer. Let's say that your Web developer predicts that there is a 50 percent chance that this solution won't work on all browsers, which proves to be a correct assumption. However, you and your developer have already decided that this is an important feature to implement and worth the additional cost of assigning the graphics animation task to a programmer. Your backup plan, then, might be one that sacrifices the animations, replacing them with static graphics.

The point is, don't become overly dependent on an inadequately tested product. Although it is often rewarding to use your project as a showcase for new technology, you should understand the risks and create a rescue plan that fits within your original budget and schedule.

Finally, I repeat my mantra: Work with your Web developer as a partner. Programmers are in the tricky situation of making recommendations about software and hardware that they may not have created. This means they have less control over the programming process going exactly as planned and may run into snafus that were not easily predicted. At R/GA, we often joke that we serve as unpaid beta testers to the computer industry, reporting bugs to companies such as IBM and Microsoft that they may not have caught. We often uncover problems that contradict the promises stated in product manuals. The best method for resolving these types of situations is to understand the ramifications, come up with alternate solutions, and agree to an action plan for everyone to follow.

### Avoiding and Managing Usability Problems

Usability is a broad term that includes everything from the architecture of the entire site to the intuitiveness of the site's navigation. The wide range of Web sites serve myriad purposes, whether to entertain, provide a service, or deliver information. Whatever the goal of your Web site, you want to be sure that it is intuitive, allowing users easy access to pertinent information. There is little that is more frustrating to a visitor than a Web site that is confusing to navigate.

A Web developer must consider several issues in order to avoid usability conflicts. One priority involves organizing information so that users have access to the information that most interests them. This priority incorporates the challenge of understanding your target audience's interests. If you don't understand what information your user will be searching for, you will not know which information to make accessible in your site's architecture. This lack of understanding may result in the mistake of burying the content that is compelling to your user underneath content that is more relevant to a third party, such as your marketing department. Although your marketing department may be satisfied that its materials are prominent on the site, the department may not realize that if the audience isn't interested in that marketing information, the site's impact is reduced and frustrated users will abandon the site.

Another usability issue to consider involves the ease of navigating through a Web site. Easy navigability seems like a fundamental concept, yet some Web developers still create paths from which there is no return. A straightforward example of this problem is a Web site that branches off from a main menu into subcategories, with no clear indication to the user of how to return to the main menu. Visitors often revert to using their browser's Back button, the tracing technique of which may not conform to the path established by your site's architecture.

Finally, you may have a well-planned architecture with an easy-to-use navigation scheme, the value of which is lost because of the design treatment of the navigation elements. When users enter a site, they look for visual clues about how to proceed with finding the information they seek. If the visual representation of the tools available to the user is unclear, the user may become more confused than if there been no tools at all. For example, many Web developers try to project a certain image on their Web sites by borrowing from design elements found in other media, such as broadcast or print. This appropriation of style can produce a Web site that has a feeling consistent with a print campaign, but that consistency may detract from the intuitiveness of the design. For example, your designer may design a table of contents that borrows stylistic characteristics of a printed page. Although the table of contents looks nice, it may not tell the user that it is a clickable element.

One very effective way of avoiding usability problems is to build a prototype. Many companies shy away from prototypes due to the mistaken perception that they add more time and money to a project. I would argue that building a well-planned prototype up front ends up saving both time and money in the long run.

A prototype is a sampling of your Web site that allows you to make development decisions based on feedback from your prototype users. It should provide enough direction for users to accurately judge features and functions, but it should not involve so much production investment that making changes based on feedback becomes counter-productive. In addition to giving insight into usability, a prototype can answer questions about technical approach, scripts, and other aspects of the Web site that have not been completely established and can prevent problems (ones that may not have been foreseen until the site's launch) early, at a point at which they may not be as expensive to remedy.

Prototypes don't have to be very complicated, but in order to get the most value from them, they do have to be adequately tested. You must determine the reasons you are building a prototype and what you hope to learn from it. In the case of assessing usability, you could gather a focus group of individuals who best represent a sampling of your target audience. Your Web developer should have experience in conducting effective usability testing, which involves more than asking colleagues at the office for their opinions. Approve the methodology that will be used in the focus group, such as the questions that will be asked. Decide whether or not the answers to the proposed questions would fulfill the prototype's original goal.

After you have the results of your usability testing, analyze what you've learned and how it should affect design changes. Did your users find it confusing to figure out their location within your site? Maybe it would help to have the same global commands appear on each page of your site. Did your users spend a lot of time clicking art elements that weren't interactive? Perhaps you need to develop a consistent treatment of interactive elements. What information were your users trying to access? Did they skip past the information provided on the home page to search for information that you assumed to be trivial? If so, you should consider restructuring the site's information architecture.

The feedback you receive about the prototype should provide enough insight into the site's weaknesses to inspire solutions from your Web developer. If you have the luxury of a second round of user testing, rebuild the prototype with the proposed solutions updated in the design. If your Web developer has a solid grasp on the prototype's flaws and how to address them, the new prototype shouldn't take long to implement, and it will produce a more satisfactory user experience.

Usability is one of the most important attributes of a well-designed Web site. When R/GA began building interactive products, we realized that ensuring successful usability, including information architecture and intuitiveness of interface, is a discipline that requires a dedicated approach. We created an Interaction Design department that operates somewhat independently from the Graphic Design department and gives the usability of a Web site the proper attention. Often, a confusing and ineffectual Web site is the result of a developer not giving usability enough consideration during the development process.

You should ask your Web developer to provide documents that reflect the development team's thought process regarding interaction design and usability. These documents can range from overall site flow to very detailed navigation specifications. These documents will provide the structure from which designers, programmers, and writers work, so they should be created early in the development process. They force you and your developer to consider issues that are best thought out in the beginning of the project, before you've committed to a technical and graphic approach. Once finalized, the documents provide a blueprint that can be handed off to team members in order for them to conform to the site's proposed architecture.

## Summary

This chapter provided insight into how to anticipate problems before they begin and how to manage them as they occur. Certainly, companies that anticipate what could go wrong from the outset have a better chance to establish the type of open communication they need with their Web developers to simplify the difficult process of building Web sites. In the next chapter, we discuss the unique types of challenges that arise from working with multiple subcontractors to build your site.

## Checklist

- ☐ Establish a partnership. Web developers want you to succeed—their business depends on it. Be sure to meet with your developer early on and be clear about your desire to keep the lines of communication open throughout the development process. Your efforts will help your developer relax and perform at his or her best.
- ☐ Establish priorities. Create a document that indicates your company's priorities—for example, what's more important, having the site completed by a certain date or carefully reproduced product shots?

- ☐ Is there a problem? Meet with your developer early and often to communicate any problems you see arising during the development process. Bad news only gets worse the longer you wait.
- ☐ Set up a procedure for problem solving. This will provide a forum for constructively addressing important issues.
- ☐ Meet regularly. Schedule a regular meeting during which you and your developer can address not only how the project is going, but the future direction of the project as well.
- ☐ Set up a design review. Make sure that you set up a specific date to review your Web site's design. Be sure the date is set early enough in the development process to allow for any necessary changes. Set up the same type of review process to address technology and usability issues.

chapter

9

# Working with Multiple Contractors

**Matt Carmichael**
**Advertising Age**
*mattc@netb2b.com*

## About This Chapter

There are times when working with one Web developer will not meet your needs and it makes sense to work with multiple developers in order to accomplish your goals. For example, say your company already has a firm that's programmed and maintained your database for years, providing exemplary service. What do you do if you want to continue using that company as you move to the Web, but they aren't designers and can't come up with an eye-catching creative look for your site? You'll quickly find yourself on the hunt for a solid design studio and along with that you will be in the midst of working with multiple subcontractors. It's a process that presents its own unique management challenges. Navigating those challenges is the subject of this chapter.

## About the Author

Matt Carmichael is the online editor for *Advertising Age* and *Advertising Age's Business Marketing* magazines. He is the main editorial contact at www.adage.com and netb2b.com. He also conducts NetMarketing's Web Price Index, a monthly survey of Web development costs, and writes for Ad Age's *Interactive Media & Marketing* section.

The little gray box on your desk seems to be the center of your life sometimes. The disembodied voices of two or three database engineers and system administrators are projecting from it in a language you don't really understand. The designers are crying out for some sort of spec to work with. All the voices from seven states and several companies half joke about how this project will ever get off the ground when even the limited technology of setting up the conference call breaks down and takes forever. And everyone is curious about when the contracts will be signed. Can this setup really be the best idea of how to get a project done? You bet.

As the Web development industry continues its rapid germination and maturation, the cream is rising to the top of the grande triple latte. If your project is large scale, it sometimes becomes necessary to call in teams of specialists rather than one catch-all shop.

If you thought keeping a relationship with *one* Web developer was a tightrope and a seesaw all at once, you were right. But nothing compares to the challenges of managing several of them at the same time.

## Why Work with Multiple Subcontractors?

**There are two types of scenarios for having multiple Web shops involved in a project. The first is having several contractors all working on the same project, but in different ways. For example, you might have one shop doing frontend design, another doing the backend work of creating databases and software tools, and a third hosting the site. The other scenario occurs for a large umbrella-type site, when different developers work on the individual parts and pages of the site.**

## The Challenge of Working with Multiple Subcontractors

Take a deep breath. This won't be easy no matter how you cut it, but we're going to give you some pointers from people who have been through the process, finished their projects, and lived to tell you about it. They'll all tell you that the more time you spend planning, the more smoothly the process will go. So we're going to devote the bulk of this chapter to the predevelopment stages and helping you to get them right.

We're going to take a look at a some of the issues that are constant when working with multiple subcontractors. We'll present some case studies of major projects by Fortune 500 companies with the budgets and time to do it right, and see what lessons we can learn from their experiences.

Why should you do it? "It depends largely upon the individual company, its product or service, goals and motivation," says Lisa Bertelsen of vivid studios, San Francisco. "The benefit of using numerous developers is that they bring in different creative solutions to the problem."

Say you have a small project to build into your larger site—some sort of add-on module or feature, or an annual report. Or maybe you just want a part of your site to have a different look and feel and want some fresh minds to work on it. If you already have a relationship with a developer, it's possible that he or she is swamped with other work from you or other clients, and the nature of the project and budget mean that it would be considered a low-priority job. It's the same in the offline world. If a building contractor is gutting and rehabing a house for one customer and gets a call for a quick installation of some duct work for another, one job will clearly get more priority.

Perhaps you do most of the work for your site inhouse, but you have a project that would overburden the staff, or is beyond the realm of their expertise. These types of situations often create the need to parcel out some, if not all, aspects of a project to another developer. Realistically, one of these scenarios is likely to crop up at some point in your Web business, and it's not a bad idea to experiment with other Web shops along the way for a project that's not mission critical.

Another reason to work with multiple shops is if you're putting together an initial site that has enough complexity and a large enough budget to justify hiring several shops to do it. These types of relationships will almost always be more costly both in terms of time and money, mostly because of the increased man hours needed to manage both the client and developer staffs. Sometimes your branding strategy is complex enough to merit multiple groups of developers as well. If, say, you're a large package goods company and each of your products has its own branded identity, you might want to have separate teams developing their online presence to ensure that each product's site will have as distinctive a feel as the rest of their marketing approaches.

The same thoughts, caveats, and processes apply for the most part under these circumstances. In this type of setup, however, you can be much more honest up front. Hinting that you might not give one developer all of your business could lead to a bit of strain with the developers about the kind of relationships you're looking to build with them, and can set up the parameters for the working relationships.

When shouldn't you work with multiple subcontractors? When your needs are simple enough to be met with one shop. If you're happy with a one-to-one relationship, stay with it. There is no reason to add complexity, management time, and costs to your Web budget if you don't need to. Don't go to an outside developer that specializes in chat just because you want to add chat to your site. If your existing developers can do the work in a timely and cost-efficient manner, let them. Keep it simple. "It's easier to do it all inhouse if you have the skills and the people to do it," says Fran Middleton, production manager at Thunderhouse, Cambridge, Massachusetts.

### Hiring

Don't forget everything you already know about hiring a developer just because you're hiring several at once. Do some research. Find out which shops either specialize or have experience in the type of project you're working on. Do some surfing. Run through their client sites and evaluate if they work well and look elegant.

Approach several shops and go through a bidding process. Let them know up front the scope of the project and the nature of the rest of your Web development relationships. If this might be the first step in a longer relationship between your companies, dangle that bait as well. See if they're interested and can meet your timetable.

How you handle this with your existing developer can be a bit tricky. There's a good chance the news will not be well received. But if your developer can't adequately handle the project, he or she will realize that it's in his or her best interest to smile and accept your decision gracefully. It might be a good idea to offer your existing developer the work first, and let him or her decline it if the work can't be completed on time.

On the other hand, some shops enjoy the challenge of working closely with others in their industry. Developers may find themselves working with people and companies that could turn into future allies. "Many of our strongest professional and personal relationships are with creatives and engineers we've teamed up with in the past," says vivid's Ms. Bertelsen.

Developers might also have worked with other shops before that they can recommend for the bidding process. Regardless, work this out with your contracted developer up front. Be honest and don't just spring it on them when it comes time to have them integrate a project into your existing site. That's when the egos might get out of control.

"We've been up front from the beginning about our desire to work this way, so we really haven't run into [too many ego problems]," says Lynne Pollard, business operations manager for Nike Interactive. The first rule of managing multiple subcontractors is that meetings will breed exponentially, not linearly. Be prepared for this, have your travel agent's number on your speed dial, a conference call bridge account set up through your favorite telco, and a detailed calendar handy at all times. This is a complex way to go about running a project, but it can be done. Both marketers and developers will admit that this kind of setup is more work than a one-to-one client-to-Web-shop relationship, but they also agree that the benefits are there as well.

Since the public only sees the end results of your site, and not all the headaches that go on behind the velvet curtain, creating the best site possible with the best companies possible can pay off in helping to achieve your business goals, be it a brand- or community-building project, a full-service commerce project, or a hybrid of the two.

The second rule of managing multiple subcontractors is to take every equation you know about the development process and multiply it by the number of groups involved. Everything—from pitching to planning to producing product—takes longer. What you can and must control is how much time you put in up front with the contractors planning the project. You'll find that the amount of preplanning at the start of a project will pay exponential dividends later on.

### Top-Ten Issues

Let's flag the top-ten issues to be on the lookout for as you begin the project. The most important task you can accomplish is to get all of these issues cleared up before work begins.

- **Who will host the site?** Will this be done by one of the developers, your corporate IT department, or another subcontractor? Will one developer be responsible for all the work on the server, and will therefore need to interface directly with all the other contractors, or will each group have root-level access to the server?
- **Which operating system will your project use?** Do all the developers have expertise working with your chosen hosting OS. Do all the different software packages (including the search, ad manager, database, and media streaming software, etc.) work on that platform?
- **Get the contracts signed.** You've already read about some of the legal pitfalls in Web development, but there are issues with multiple contractors that don't come up in one-to-one relationships. What happens when one developer fails to meet the timeline, and thereby holds up other stages of the process? Who is responsible for maintaining/

bug-checking each area of the site? Does one developer do that for all aspects, or is each ultimately responsible for his or her own work? Get it all in writing, ideally before you begin. Who has the rights to the code, the design, the content, etc.?

- **Create a design spec.** Get all the developers on the same page. Make sure they're working under the same parameters, that their code will integrate smoothly, etc.
- **Ownership.** Make sure someone has ownership of every aspect of the project and that you, as the client-side manager of the project, have the list of who owns what.
- **Deadlines.** Put together as detailed a time line as possible and make sure everyone involved in the project understands not only their role, but how their role fits into the whole project.
- **Travel.** Figure out how much travel will be needed when you're setting up the time line. Someone (let's bet it's the client) needs to pay for it, and it will always take time. If all the contractors are in one city, this isn't a problem, but chances are that they won't be. For the record, much of this chapter was written on airplanes as the author went to meetings with multiple subcontractors.
- **Approval.** Delineate what the approval process is, and who in each group has the final word for each group. Keep in mind that the more voices that have to agree at any stage, the longer it will take. Empower as few people per group as possible, but if timeliness is important, empower those people fully.
- **Hardware.** Who needs to buy what equipment? This includes, but is certainly not limited to, servers, bandwidth, and software licenses. At what point does that get factored into the budget (i.e., who pays for it up front)?
- **Maintenance.** Once it's finished, who keeps it working? And equally importantly, for how long? Do the subcontractors wash their hands of their piece of the pie once it's delivered?

Got those all answered now? If not, don't sweat it just yet. The answers to all those questions will almost never be settled up front. And for a while at least, every question you answer will raise 13 more in the development process. This is normal. Keep track of them, keep a paper trail, and keep plugging away at them. It's the only way you'll get through this.

### How Two Companies Handle the Issues

Now that we've got the issues on the table, we'll take a look at two companies and how they've addressed them.

First, we'll examine Intel's process for managing projects. Intel began using what it calls "Map Days" to coordinate groups inside Intel for projects ranging in size all the way up to chip design—where hundreds of engineers work together on a single project with tight responsibilities and timeliness. Intel feels that at the start of a project, it is necessary to get all of the subcontractors together and working from the same page. This is especially important if you've got different developers working on design, technology, content, and so forth. Few companies do more of this kind of project than Intel, and the company takes the management of these relationship seriously. Intel has found that Map Days are so successful that they are now used in almost every project, both internal and Web-based.

The process is both regimented and chaotic. Scheduling is the first hurdle because all the parties must attend in person, which almost always means some travel. Once the time is set, supplies must be ordered including about 100 feet of butcher paper, rolls of adhesive tape, Sharpies, and Post-it notes. Lots of them. In four colors. Memos are sent out to all the developers explaining what the participants are supposed to do to prepare for Map Day, including the proper way to format the sticky notes. Each color has a purpose: yellow is for the deliverables that your group is responsible for providing, green is the major milestones both for the project as a whole and your group, blue is the dependencies that your group has on other groups in order to get your work done on time, and best of all, pink is for "issues" or questions that your group has before it can deliver code, content, graphics, and so forth.

Eric Allen, a product development manager at Intel, has facilitated many Map Days over the years. He says that the process usually takes about a day, and is used to set the course for an average of five to seven companies on a project. He is a believer in the process, as are those who have gone through it. "Everybody from the different groups proactively makes comments about how valuable it is," he says. The benefits for Intel are obvious. It gets a chance to fully delineate what is expected from all the groups involved and develop the timeline with the groups so that all factions are confident that it can be met. The goals of Map Day are realistic in themselves; the post-meeting goal is 80-percent confidence in the timeline. When managing projects with the levels of complexity Intel and others face, getting everything clear up front is of paramount importance. The better informed all participants are, the more smoothly the project will run.

"Vendors in general are often left out of the overall planning so they don't always feel a part of the process nor get the entire context," warns Mr. Allen. "They don't have a holistic understanding of the project."

In a best case, Map Day helps foster a sense of togetherness from the outset as the participants focus in on the task at hand. Tempers can start to flare, however, as people grasp all that is in front of them in constructing the Web site. Conflicts sometimes result from what Mr. Allen calls "mismatched expectations of the project," where one person or group has begun work on an aspect of the site only to find out that they've been headed in the wrong direction, and have to scrap what they've already done. Voices get louder. From a management perspective, that's why it's valuable to have these pink-sticky-noted issues raised at the outset. "If you see that kind of passion early on, it definitely means there is something to be dealt with," says Mr. Allen.

The end result of Map Day is a piece of butcher paper with a timeline along one axis and the groups along the other. The yellow and green stickies are posted in place in the box for the week that the particular group needs to have finished a deliverable. The groups have discussed the blue and pink stickies, and ownership of projects and issues have been assigned to the proper person in the proper group, which is a key to smooth management of the Web development process.

And, of course, more meetings are scheduled. "You start to dive into the project so you spawn into all kinds of regular meetings," says Mr. Allen. One type of meeting that tends to spring out of Map Day is meetings that are internal to the individual group organizations. Sometimes meetings are scheduled months in advance with no set agenda just so the participants have time cleared. Some of the groups may not need to attend once the agenda is set (sometimes as little as a week in advance), but it makes sense to have the dates cleared rather than try to coordinate a schedule at the last minute.

Finally, someone from each group copies down their part of the grid, and the physical Map is rolled up and shipped somewhere. "You may never do anything with the Map itself; it's the process that matters," says Mr. Allen. "One of the powers is to be able to visualize it as a whole and move stuff around."

Intel's process works very well for its projects, where many groups work together to create one final product. That is only one kind of multiple-developer scenario, however. With some Web sites, each developer is responsible for just one facet of a much larger product. One example of this kind of multideveloper relationship is at work in the production of Nike.com.

One strong reason to have multiple developers working on a site is if your company has multiple brands or divisions, and you want to ensure that each has a separate identity on the Web. For some applications, having different designers, or even different teams either internally or within a Web shop tackle a project is enough. Situations like this are perfect examples of why retaining multiple contractors can pay off.

Nike uses as many as 10 shops to develop all the different areas of its Nike.com site. One of the best-branded marketers, Nike faced the challenge of having multiple brands, each with its own unique and strong identity. Many of the Nike brands, such as the Air Jordan shoes and apparel, have images that are distinct from the omnipresent Nike Swoosh brand. Nike, therefore, felt it important to maintain that branding strategy across all media, including the Web. Nike also sponsors many high-profile sporting events such as the U.S. Open tennis tournament, and builds separate Nike-branded sites for those as well.

"We felt that we would have a greater creative range if we used more than one agency, and we'd be able to better manage a rapid production schedule, and our experience has proved this to be true," says Nike's Ms. Pollard.

For other companies, this might not be the best or most fruitful approach. Many companies will want to keep a consistent look and feel across all of the areas of their site. This creates other issues as you dictate to one shop what might well have been developed for you by one of their rivals. For example, they might think their ideas are better. In the end, you know your company best. Developers will work with you. Don't be afraid to give them your fonts, or dictate color schemes.

If consistency is your goal, you might want to have the lead shop set up templates or style sheets for the subcontractors to work with. One way to alleviate these kinds of issues while still adhering to your goals is to have one shop handle all the user interface design for all parts of the site. That will give visitors a sense of consistency.

Nike's setup is one used by many companies that rely on a stable of Web developers. It has one developer of record, in this case, San Francisco-based Organic Online, and several other shops that it uses for different modules of the site. Each of these developers interface with Nike's inhouse Web team in different ways, all of which are delineated in advance. Other companies will let the lead agency handle and manage all the subcontracting relationships themselves.

How you go about finding the shops is, of course, up to you. Nike chooses the shops based on its experience or on recommendations. You can also have the lead developer take over the selection of the subcontractors, if the developer is more qualified to navigate that part of the development process than anyone on your internal staff.

"We rely on our primary agency for the bigger site picture, with contributing agencies and developers adding different experiences within the site," said Ms. Pollard. Of course, this approach has its problems. "It probably takes more time. There are simply more people involved, and it's more difficult to manage all the integration issues, as each piece needs to work as part of the site as a whole," she says. It's a position that Organic likes: "Total comprehensive control of very complex situations," defines Ms. Horner.

The developers who work with Nike understand the importance of being part of a team as opposed to the one-and-only Nike shop. "The soul of Nike is innovation," says Ms. Horner. "It takes several developers to continue to innovate at the level Nike wants. It requires injection of new types of ideas and emotions into the work."

"The enormity of the project was challenging for both teams," says Lisa Bertelsen of vivid, which has worked with Nike in the past. "We were executing two or three site builds per day on multiple sites; 24/7 coverage of the site; navigating legal issues with star athletes, handlers, and the NCAA; managing many on-location teams; and dealing with "acts of nature" (the rain-out of the U.S. Open) meant that both the Nike and vivid teams had to come up with new process solutions and constantly think on our feet."

Nike has different contact relationships with each developer. Some work directly with Organic, some only work through Nike. Most have just one point of contact between Nike and the developer, but the complexity of Organic's relationship necessitates several points of contact.

Even with all the work that Nike shops out, it still does much of the day-to-day updating and content development inhouse. Just like any developer relationship, it's important for each company to examine its own needs and work with the developer to get them met. Nike needs timely and continuous updates for its site, so having an inhouse staff as well makes sense.

"It all depends on what you're trying to achieve," says Organic's Ms. Horner. "It has to map back to your strategy." For Nike and others who have a need for current and constantly changing content, she suggests that marketers "use the most efficient, best talent for what you need. Invest in a remote publishing tool from your developer if you do daily work on the site."

The result is a site at Nike.com that has all sorts of different modules. Each has its own feel. Each has its own look. Each has a different set of core functionalities. All take Nike's careful branding and relate it to the Web while never losing sight of all that has come before it in the offline world. Some of it is built by Organic, some by CKS Partners, some by Red Sky, and others. All of it is managed by Nike. Most of it gets done on time and within budget. And all of it is painstakingly planned out beforehand.

Of course, once your timeline is mapped out, contracts signed, and all the issues are dealt with, you're still not finished. You haven't actually built anything yet.

## Keeping the Project Moving

So once you've got the project moving, how do you *keep* it moving? Beyond meetings, conference calls, reams of email and fax page proofs, many developers set up a sort of online proving ground. Some are as simple as password-protected areas of their Web sites where project managers from the various groups can look at mock screens during the design process. Others take this a few steps further by including an online discussion functionality so people can comment directly on what they see in front of them as well as read what others have had to say about it. Keeping the feedback consolidated and recorded can help avoid communications conflicts that could arise later. It also makes it clear who hasn't looked over a project yet and whose input is still needed.

Some new issues will start to come up and you'll begin to see just how well you preplanned. Some of them will be unique to your particular project, and some will apply to many different types of issues.

We'll stress this again: "It goes smoothly when you have a clear definition of who does what," says Ms. Horner. "Without the definitions, people get a little funny and battle over turf." Nike claims to have had no real turf issues for exactly that reason: the company plans, delineates, and does it all up front.

You'll see your timeline get pushed back a few times. You'll see just how well the chain of command can agree in a certain time frame so that you, as the client, don't wind up delaying the developers' work because they're waiting for approval, copy, logos, or whatever it is that you're responsible for providing. You'll see all the things you missed in the first place, some hidden, some obvious.

Thunder House's Mr. Middleton worked on an ecommerce solution in conjunction with Silicon Reef, San Francisco, for a software distributor, Mobilesoft. His experience mirrors that of many other developers involved in projects with multiple contractors. And he points out one of those details that sometimes gets left out when looking at the big picture: time zones.

"[Geography] was not a problem at all—except for the time difference, which kept the East-coasters up an extra three hours," he says. "There will always be a couple of bumps in the road."

So, be ready for the bumps. They are in the road, and not always clearly marked. Hopefully you have an idea now of just how complex a multideveloper relationship can be. Prepare yourself, prepare your staff, ask questions and keep track of the answers.

Eventually, all the business travel will be done, the phone calls made, the bugs exterminated, and you'll have a working Web site. You will know which of the several contractors you work best with, and which you might not want to further a relationship with.

Just in time to redesign.

### Summary

Working with multiple subcontractors can be challenging but the rewards can, if properly managed, be great. This chapter walked you through the rationale for working with multiple subcontractors and helped you determine whether or not it made sense for your project to "divide and conquer." We also took a look at the 10 issues you should address prior to working with multiple subcontractors and offered two case studies—Intel and Nike—that illustrate the challenges in having multiple companies build your site. With this background, and hopefully, a successful site in the works, you are now ready to market your creation—a topic addressed in Chapter10, "Search Engines, Marketing, PR, and Advertising."

### Checklist

- ☐ Stop! Why are you working with multiple subcontractors? Are you sure that each contributes in a unique and positive way to your end goal?
- ☐ Stop again! Have you mentioned your decision to your current developer?
- ☐ Have you carefully addressed the issues of site hosting? Does each developer understand what is expected?
- ☐ Clarify which operating system the project will be completed on—UNIX, NT, etc. Have clear instructions been sent to your developer?
- ☐ Do you have specific contracts signed with each developer?
- ☐ Has the issue of ownership been addressed? Does each developer know what it is contributing to the project and who owns the final results?

- ☐ Have you declared and shared your deadlines?
- ☐ What is the system for approval? Is there one between the developers and then your company?
- ☐ Have you set protocols for meetings—places, times, etc.—that work for companies in different time zones?
- ☐ Review each of the 10 steps that you must address before starting your multiple subcontractor relationships. Have you meet with all the developers together to be sure that they understand your goals and expectations?

chapter

# 10

# Search Engines, Marketing, PR, and Advertising

**Daniel J. Barrett, Ph.D.**

## About This Chapter

After much hard work with your Web developer, your business's Web site is finally designed, debugged, and hosted. Now it's time to attract visitors. What's the best way to publicize your site? Potential customers must know about your Web site and be able to find it, or else the site won't be able to help your business, no matter how many bells and whistles the site has. You can expect that Web developers have some basic knowledge of Web site marketing, but you can't be sure they will know all of the ins and outs of effectively using search engines, marketing your site, and managing public relations and advertising. By now you might realize that the more you know, the more successfully you can manage your relationship with your developer. Besides, in some cases, the task of marketing your business online might fall to you, and even if you've contracted your developer to do it, you will still want to know as much about the process as you can. It is, after all, your business.

This chapter provides background information on how a Web developer might publicize your Web site and market your product or service online, through both traditional means (i.e., advertising) and Internet-only techniques. The major topics we'll cover are

**Internet search engines.** What they are, how they work, and how to make them a realistic part of your marketing strategy.

**Online marketing and public relations.** How to publicize a site effectively while remaining sensitive to the Internet community's unique customs. We'll cover the three basics of Internet marketing: emphasizing information, adding value, and building a reputation.

**Advertising.** Dos and don'ts for the online world. We'll cover both commercial and free techniques for hawking a product or service on the Net.

**Directory of online resources.** Where to find more information on the topics in this chapter.

### About the Author

Daniel J. Barrett, Ph.D, is the author of the incredibly useful "NetResearch: Finding Information Online"(O'Reilly & Associates, Inc., 1997). He is also the Internet columnist for *Keyboard Magazine* and serves as the head of system operations for a Wall Street financial software company.

## Search Engines

**On the Web, the primary means that your customers will use to find your Web site is through a search engine. The more you know about search engines, the more successful your marketing effort will be and the more realistic your requests to your Web developer. In the end, you can't blame your developer if your site doesn't appear at the top of every search engine. So what is a search engine? A *search engine* is a special Web page that can look up and locate other Web pages. Search engines are similar to Yellow Pages telephone books, enabling Internet users to locate commercial and noncommercial Web sites by category. But the capabilities of search engines go beyond those of Yellow Pages, permitting users to locate Web sites by more powerful search criteria.**

Suppose you want to locate sites that sell widgets. A search engine could find Web pages that

- Contain the word *widget*
- Contain the words *widget*, *dealership*, *sale*, and the phrase *San Francisco*
- Mention your company's major competitor, Widget Universe, Ltd.

In response, the search engine displays links to Web pages that satisfy these criteria. These links and their associated pages are called *hits*. If a business sells widgets, a potential customer could simply select the hit (a Web link) to be led directly to the business's Web site.

From the perspective of your business, search engines can be a terrific, low-cost conduit for leading potential customers to your Web site. Search engines have free listings and are visited by millions of users worldwide. So what's the catch? Well, search engines typically have millions of listings, so there is much competition for a user's attention, and a listed business has little or no control over its hits. In other words, you cannot simply order your Web developer to register your Web site with a search engine and assume that customers will successfully locate the site. A search can just as easily generate hits for your competitors' Web sites, or even completely irrelevant hits that distract users.

In a Yellow Pages book, a business can pay extra for an eye-catching advertisement that's larger or more prominent than its competitors' ads.

Search engines, however, are largely noncommercial entities that do not accept payment for listings, and everybody's hits are displayed with the same look and size. (Some search engines do accept payment for ads, however, as we'll discuss later.) The goal, then, is to work with your developer to arrange for your business's hits to be

**Displayed often.** When users search for relevant criteria, hits should be displayed for your business's Web site.

**Displayed early.** When search engines display many hits, yours should appear early in the list, ideally in the first position.

The following section explains how search engines work, the issues of registering with them, and how to make effective use of a search engine in both a business-wise and socially responsible manner.

**How Search Engines Work.** Search engines do not literally search the whole Internet in response to users' requests. Each search engine maintains a *database* or *index* of the Web pages it knows: a subset of the pages available on the Web. When a user requests a search, the search engine checks the database for matches, displaying them as hits.

Some search engines build their database automatically, sending special programs called *spiders* or *robots* out onto the Web to gather URLs. Others rely on users to register their pages with the database, and many search engines do both. As a result, every search engine may have a different database, which means a site that's easy to locate with one search engine might be completely invisible to another due to differences in the two databases. Additionally, no search engine's database indexes the entire World Wide Web, which grows too rapidly for any spider program to keep up. Despite these limitations, search engines are still a great resource for users and businesses to look up information on many topics.

Users conduct searches by typing requests, called *queries*, to locate Web pages with particular content. For example, to locate Web pages containing the word "hotel," an appropriate query would be *hotel*, and hits would be displayed as in Figure 10.1. More complex searches can be requested with queries that string together multiple words or phrases. For example, a query for pages containing the names of fast-food restaurants might be *"McDonald's" OR "Burger King" OR "Kentucky Fried Chicken."*

1. Hotel Discounts
[URL: www.hoteldiscount.com/]
BRAND NEW FEATURES!!! New Booking Engine! HUNDREDS of new hotels! ...Orlando's Days Inn Suites for only $59.95! ...Reno/Lake Tahoe only $39.95 at Sands...
Last modified 30-Mar-98 - page size 18K - in English [ Translate ]

2. Hotels Wirdum : Hotel DUHOUX DE GRAND COUR (Wirdum - Netherlands - HotelInfoPl
[URL: hotelinfoplus.com/wirdum/duhouxdegrandco.htm]
Wirdum : Hotel DUHOUX DE GRAND COUR (HotelInfoPlus, Worldwide HotelInformation)
Last modified 5-Mar-98 - page size 2K

3. Hotels Linz : Hotel CITY (Linz - Austria - HotelInfoPlus).
[URL: hotelinfoplus.com/linz/city.htm]
Linz : Hotel CITY (HotelInfoPlus, Worldwide HotelInformation)
Last modified 5-Mar-98 - page size 2K - in English [ Translate ]

4. Discount Hotel Reservations for Business and Pleasure
[URL: www.abctravel.com/]
ABC Premier Hotel Plan | Hotel Database Search and Reservations. Please direct any comments and suggestions to: ABC TRAVEL VOICE: (888) 800-6157 FAX:...
Last modified 30-Mar-98 - page size 2K - in English [ Translate ]

5. Välkommen till Hotel Tylösand
[URL: www.tylosand.se/]
Box 643, S-301 16 Halmstad. Telefon: 035-305 00 Telefax: 035-324 39. E-mail: info@tylosand.se.
Last modified 23-Mar-98 - page size 508 bytes - in Swedish

6. LUNGARNO ALBERGHI S.p.A. Firenze Pontevecchio hotel in Florence hotels in Fi
[URL: www.lungarnohotels.it/]
Lungarno Hotels Firenze Pontevecchio, the heart of Florence: the magic atmosphere that surrounds our Hotels. Windows like frames around masterpieces,
Last modified 1-Apr-97 - page size 3K - in Italian [ Translate ]

**Figure 10.1** Typical search engine results for the query "hotel."

There is no standard language for writing queries; each search engine has its own rules and permits different kinds of searches. Instructions are found at each search engine, usually behind a link called Help, Search Tips, or something similar.

**Relevance and Rankings.** Search engines can index tremendous numbers of pages, but they aren't very smart. In response to a query, a search engine merely looks for Web pages containing text specified in the query, with the assumption that these pages will be relevant to the user's needs. But text-matching is no guarantee of relevance. For instance, a search for *hotel* could find pages about hotel reservations, hotel construction techniques, John Irving's *The Hotel New Hampshire*, rap song lyrics that contain the word "hotel," and numerous other topics, most of which are not relevant to the user's needs.

If a query generates a lot of hits, the search engine displays them in some order, attempting to guess which ones are the most relevant to the query. This is called *ranking* the hits. Some search engines even display a numeric score or rank next to each hit. The top-ranked hit is the most likely to be followed by the user; therefore, the best situation for an online business is to be ranked first in any search relevant to its business. Unfortunately, this goal is unrealistic with today's technology, and you cannot expect your Web developer to be able to change this reality for the following reasons:

**Queries can be complex and ambiguous.** Queries can be phrased in many ways, and search engines don't understand meaning, just text. If a user searches for the phrase "CD vendor," is this a request for compact disc stores, or banks offering Certificates of Deposit? Which should rank more highly? A search engine isn't capable of making such distinctions.

**Ranking schemes are often proprietary.** The creators of many search engines guard their ranking schemes like trade secrets. This is unsurprising when you consider that the usefulness of a search engine is determined by its ability to find the most relevant hits, and it's nearly impossible to tailor a Web page to rank highly on all the major search engines.

**Search engines index millions of pages.** Most queries produce multiple hits, decreasing the chances that your pages will be ranked highly. Even if your site ranks highly one week, new pages are added constantly that can bump a site from a top slot.

**Increasing Your Ranking.** While there is no guaranteed way to send your pages to the top of the hit list, your developer can employ some standard techniques that may help raise their rankings. Remember that your developer is likely to be focused on building your site and in many cases might not be the best person to help you market the site when it is complete, so the more you know, the more you can effectively manage the process. First, ensure that your site gets ranked by registering it with multiple search engines. This can be done by having your developer manually visit each search engine site and go through its registration process. Alternatively, you may hire a registration service, a company that registers sites with search engines (see the *Directory of Online Resources* at the end of the chapter).

However, be prepared to pay for another technique that follows the old maxim, "If you can't beat 'em, join 'em." Locate the top-ranked pages in your field of business and advertise on them. Once again, you can have your developer do this for you, but in the end you are the one who best understands your business and industry. You can achieve this by taking the following steps:

1. At each of the major search engines, conduct searches using queries related to your business. Search for your business name, your type of business, and the products or services you engage in—anything that might attract the public to your site.
2. Make a list of the pages (URLs) that are top-ranked for each query.
3. Contact the maintainers of the top-ranked pages and pursue advertising on them, using the techniques covered later in this chapter (e.g., free link exchanges, commercial banner ads).

Another common approach is to have your developer incorporate *metatags* into your Web pages. These are special HTML instructions inside a Web page that advise search engines on how to index the page in their databases. Create a list of words or short phrases (the more specific, the better) that are highly relevant to your type of business. Then ask your Web designer to turn them into *metakeyword* tags in your Web site. Although a complete discussion of metatags is beyond the scope of this chapter, any competent Web designer should know how to incorporate them into your site.

Finally, be skeptical of Web marketing businesses that claim they can put any site into the top-10 hits on every search engine. It ain't so. If you are still intrigued, it should be easy to check their claims. Ask for references of previous clients, verify that the clients were satisfied with the service, and then look up the clients yourself at the major search engines. Are they in the top 10?

### Marketing and Public Relations

You might be tempted to approach marketing online in the same way as in more traditional media. Here, you might be in for a surprise. Traditionally, for example, a beautiful, glossy brochure might attract positive attention. On the Web, however, large pictures take a long time to download and can turn off users quickly. The Internet breeds impatience and a hunger for information, and successful marketing must take this into account. While you can expect that your Web developer understands what Web surfers will accept, it is important for you to understand Net culture so that you don't make unfair or unacceptable demands on the company you hire to build your site.

An online businessperson's dream is to whip together a low-cost Web site that attracts many customers immediately. More commonly, however, an online presence grows gradually. A fancy Web site with 3-D animations might garner some short-term attention, but long-term success requires a longer-term view of the online marketplace.

Don't fall for sensational claims that the Internet is an instant gold mine for businesses. Success in online marketing is often characterized by slow ramp-up of interest from users, not a sudden blitz on your Web site from around the Net. Payback is usually not immediate; however, if you remain patient and incorporate online techniques into your business's overall marketing strategy, you will likely see return on your investment.

In this section, we'll cover the three basic truths of Internet marketing:

**Emphasizing information.** Users grow bored of hype and want more useful information rather than pretty pictures.

**Adding value.** Give people a reason to return to your site.

**Building a reputation.** Be socially responsible, and you'll win in the long run.

**Emphasize Information.** On the Net, information is king. This is not just a cliché but also a mantra for marketing. Glitz and hype rarely work well online because customers want facts more than flash. A site with 3-D rotating hieroglyphics might attract attention initially, but if it's difficult to navigate or is missing vital data, visitors will move on to other sites. Gimmicks produce only short-lived publicity. The sites that attract the most *repeat* visitors emphasize content and easy access. Make sure that you understand this and that your Web developer respects it as well. Too many sites have failed because the developer was more focused on creating a site for its portfolio that was not in its client's best interest.

Whether your business is software, auto sales, politics, or meat-packing, effective Web sites tend to share the following features:

**Quick loading.** Pages that appear rapidly on the user's screen are more effective than ones that are slow to download. Unnecessarily large images, animations, and audio should be avoided on the main page; if they appear on other pages, they should be clearly labeled so users will be alerted to a longer download time. Images should be used like spices—a little here, a little there—to make the final product tastier. Unless your business is primarily graphics or animation, images should complement, not dominate, a Web site. When hiring a Web designer, ask to see sample pages and notice how quickly—or not—they download and appear in your browser.

**Easy navigation.** A well-organized site is a usable site, and a usable site gets lots of visitors and gains a loyal following. Links should be clearly visible and divided into appropriate categories and subcategories. Ideally, a search engine is also present, indexing only the site's contents. Excellent organization cannot be overemphasized; the structure of a growing site should be regularly reevaluated to make sure it's still effective as the number of pages increases. For an example of a site that meets all of these criteria, pay a visit to www.cnn.com—navigation is easy, links are clearly visible, and a search engine is readily available.

**Uniqueness.** To the extent possible, a site should offer something not found anywhere else. It could be the content (for example, the world's best source of rare coins), or it could be unparalleled ease of use (for example, photographs of a company's entire line of merchandise combined with a super-smooth online ordering system). Spend a few minutes on the Web site for Amazon books (www.amazon.com). Notice how easy it is to browse and order? Uniqueness may also be achieved by excellent organization, such as the link directory at Yahoo! (www.yahoo.com), possibly the most well-known site on the Internet.

Yahoo!, in fact, provides a good example of all these features. The pages are attractive, but load quickly since they are mostly text with some small, well-placed images as accents. Yahoo!'s directory is intelligently organized for easy navigation. Finally, while dozens of other search engines have emerged over the years, Yahoo! (which is the oldest) is still in wide use for its information-rich directory and diverse features.

**Add Value.** Commercial Web sites may need to turn a profit, but if you want repeat visitors, provide added value online that customers cannot get in your physical place of business (i.e., your store or office) or from your competitors.

Recall some ways that businesses add value in more traditional markets. Bookstores invite authors to give lectures and autograph books. Hospitals offer courses on health topics. Beer manufacturers sponsor sporting events. And, of course, most businesses offer discounted prices from time to time. Similar techniques can be used online to attract customers.

Just as bookstores invite authors, online businesses can invite relevant guests to contribute to a Web site. The simplest example is to conduct a traditional interview and post it on the site (over time, a large archive of such interviews could be compiled, and this itself could become a resource to attract customers to your site). Alternatively, a business can arrange online chats between guests and visitors to the site. Speak with your online service provider to discover what options you might have for running an online chat.

Just as hospitals offer courses on health topics, your site could contain instructional material within your domain of expertise. For example, a store specializing in rare coins could post articles on buying coins intelligently, detection of counterfeits, a history of minting through the ages, or even a virtual museum filled with photos and a cartoon animal as a tour guide.

Just as beer manufacturers sponsor sporting events, your business can sponsor other Web sites. Sponsorship could be as simple as advertising, but a more intriguing technique is to construct a second Web site—noncommercial—that's affiliated with your business. For example, suppose a statistical consulting business has a commercial Web site at www.stats-are-us.com. It could create a noncommercial site, say, www.math-for-fun.org, devoted to helping students learn probability and statistics. Sprinkled throughout the site would be sponsorship messages ("brought to you by Stats-Are-Us") with links leading to the commercial site. Since the noncommercial site is of high quality, it gets noticed by journalists and Net users who spread the word, generating free publicity for the commercial site in the process. Noncommercial sites can also be more easily advertised in noncommercial forums, such as public discussion groups, in which users welcome relevant announcements about information resources. This technique—creating a free and useful resource to help attract customers—is a powerful force not only for improving sales but also for improving the Internet. It enables companies, at low cost, to be socially responsible and give back to the online community, while at the same time increasing their visibility and attracting customers.

Just as businesses offer sale prices from time to time, your business could offer additional discounts to customers who visit (or order from) your Web site. Similarly, you could run contests on your Web site to win free merchandise. At some point in the Web development process you should talk to your developer about what type of value-added service you are willing to make available on your site. Are you willing to make available free products for a contest? Can you link your Web site to an event in your sales showroom? Present a list of your promotion ideas, and your developer should be able to build them into your site. Again, here you need to be more proactive than you have been in other areas of Web development. Usually site marketing takes place at a time when the development of your site is winding down. Don't fall into that trap. Be proactive and guide your developer.

**Build a Reputation.** The most valuable asset in your online marketing arsenal is your reputation. If users recognize and respect your online persona, any product or service you market online will be helped immeasurably.

At the same time, the speed and scope of the Internet also allow a negative reputation to spread like wildfire. Any communication made by your business might reach millions of potential customers. Not only that, but your words could get stored in online archives for years, indexed by search engines in their databases, and eventually viewed by potential customers who search for your company name. Ill-placed advertisements, thoughtless comments in a mailing list, factual errors, and even poor grammar can inspire potential customers to disregard your online business overtures. Here's where you, and not your Web developer, have to take action to extend your company's reputation onto the Web.

To preserve and spread a good reputation online while publicizing your business, here are some tips:

**Participate.** Join public discussion groups in the domain of your business and answer users' questions. Treat the Internet and its subcultures as communities, not just a medium for marketing, and in return you'll be treated (and respected) as a fellow citizen.

**Know your audience.** Spend time observing any online group before entering into conversations. Read the FAQ (Frequently Asked Questions document) for the group if one exists. Get to know what constitutes acceptable behavior in this group: which topics are acceptable, which are off limits, and so forth.

**Be accurate.** Make sure your online statements are well-researched. Since online communication is usually not real-time, you'll have an opportunity to check facts before responding to users' questions. A reputation for accuracy will help your image as an expert, and will sometimes bring inquiries from journalists and more free publicity.

**Be clear.** Make sure your online representatives have outstanding written communication skills. Remember that online communication is more than just correct spelling and grammar: It also means being in tune with jargon, abbreviations, and acronyms in common use on the Net. Regular participation will keep your staff familiar with the latest Net-speak.

**Avoid flames (online insults and shouting matches).** Even if another user insults your business, your mother, and your dog, keep your response 100-percent professional, or don't respond at all. When flames escalate in public discussion groups, the only way to win is to stop. No matter how right your responses might feel, the other users will remember only that you kept arguing, and not who was right or wrong. If your responses are always calm and professional, people will remember this and respect you for it.

**Avoid form letters.** Internet users are tired of impersonal, obviously mail-merged messages extolling the virtues of some product they've never heard of. Whenever possible, write a personal reply to any question.

**Thank people.** Yes, it sounds like advice your mother gave you, but it really works. Always thank people for contacting you. Begin your email responses with some variation on "Thanks for your note," answer the user's questions, and end with a final thank you.

**Be patient.** Building a good reputation takes time.

### Advertising

The Internet is a unique medium for advertising. Millions of potential customers are available to be contacted at low cost. Nevertheless, the Net has informal but important traditions of conduct: Violate them at your own peril. An ill-placed advertisement could result in hundreds of thousands of complaints by email, and the deluge could overwhelm your electronic mailbox or even your Internet Service Provider (ISP). On the positive side, a well-placed ad can generate tremendous revenue at almost no cost to the advertiser.

The following section provides an overview of several types of online advertising, and discusses recommended and nonrecommended techniques for reaching Internet users with commercial messages.

**Paid Advertising.** Although a Web site can exist in isolation, promoting itself via search engines and offline advertising techniques, additional exposure can be gained by purchasing advertisements on third-party Web pages. You might want to consider outsourcing your Web advertising to a special consultant since Web developers might have less experience in this area.

A typical ad is simply a link from a third-party site to your business's site. Such ads come in several flavors.

**Text.** This is the simplest: an ordinary text link, perhaps with the name of your business or a catchy slogan.

**Banner ad.** This is the most common type of third-party ad. It is a horizontal picture, typically several inches across, with an eye-catching picture or slogan. The picture is a link to your site.

**Animated banner ad.** Just like the banner ad, but instead of a static picture, a brief animation is used.

Anything that can be placed onto a Web page—larger pictures, fancy animations, audio—can be turned into an advertisement linked to your Web site. The only limitation is what the advertising site will accept. Find out what forms of ads are acceptable, and any limitations on measurements (e.g., perhaps their banner ads must be exactly 468 by 60 pixels in no more than 32 colors).

Various kinds of sites accept paid advertising. *Online malls* are Web-based storefronts for a collection of unrelated businesses. They exist only to advertise. *Specialty sites* advertise a related group of businesses; for example, dentists in Massachusetts, or limousine services throughout the United States. *Search engines* frequently accept advertising, even keyed to the topics being searched. For example, if a user searches for *hotel*, the search engine could place an advertisement for a hotel chain or an airline above the list of hits. Many other sites accept ads as well. Use a search engine to locate potential advertising sites in your domain of business. For example, if you run a compact disc store, visit sites devoted to particular musical artists, run by fans.

With tens of millions of Web pages available on the Net, it's important to choose an advertising site carefully. Before purchasing advertising space from a third party, three important categories of questions should be asked.

- How popular is the site?
- How often will your ad be displayed?
- What statistics will be reported to you?

We will address each of these in turn, beginning with, how popular is the site? If a site isn't popular, there's not much sense advertising on it. Popularity is measured in *Web accesses* (i.e., number of times a site's pages are viewed by visitors). Unfortunately, many sites exaggerate their number of Web accesses, so here are some questions to ask when obtaining measurements from a site.

**How are Web accesses measured?** The unit of measurement should be "Web accesses" or "hits," not "visitors" or "people." Web servers don't measure how many people visit a site, only how many Web pages are viewed. Fifty accesses could be due to one person, 50 people, or anywhere in between.

**How is a Web access defined?** Some definitions lead to inflated figures. When one page with 10 images is viewed by a user, this should be considered a single access, but some sites will count it as 11 accesses, since 11 files were downloaded: 1 HTML file and 10 image files. Here's another situation: Suppose a single page is accessed 10 times by the same remote computer within two minutes. This is probably a single user browsing the site and reloading the same page; good statistics consider these 10 viewings to be a single access.

**What are *average* measurements over a *known period of time*?** A good example gives both the average and the time period, as in: "this site has averaged 30,000 hits per month for the past six months." Disregard claims of maximum hits, such as "up to 50,000 hits per month," as they are less meaningful than averages. Likewise, an average measurement without a time period, such as 30,000 hits per month, isn't sufficient; for all you know, the measurement represents the site's most popular month and nothing else. The bottom line is to request meaningful statistics of a site's popularity.

In the end, you'll still be relying on a site's honesty to disclose accurate statistics. The Internet provides no other, reliable way for a third party to measure Web accesses.

Next, consider how often your advertisement will be displayed. Sometimes an ad is made a permanent part of a Web page, but more commonly, advertisements are *rotated* by software. For example, six advertisers could rent the same ad space on a Web page, and each one's ad would be displayed one-sixth of the time. Rotation can be random (e.g., each time the page is visited, one of the six ads is selected randomly) or predetermined (e.g., each ad appears exclusively for four hours per day). If your ad is in random rotation, make sure to get a guaranteed minimum in writing; for example, your ad is guaranteed to appear at least 15 percent of the times the page is accessed. Likewise, if your ad is appearing for a set number of hours per day, get a guarantee that the ad will be displayed during popular hours of use, not just when your customers are asleep!

Finally, consider what statistics will be reported to you by the advertising site. At a bare minimum, you should receive a regular report of how many times your ad appeared, and how many times it was clicked on by visitors. But more sophisticated statistics are possible with current technology. For example:

- A daily or hourly breakdown of the times your ad was viewed and your link was clicked. This is useful for learning the Internet usage patterns of potential customers.
- The Internet domains of the people who saw your ad or clicked your link. This tells you where your potential customers are coming from and helps to gauge international interest in your company.
- The previous Web page visited by people who saw your ad or clicked your link. This can provide clues to the personal interests of your customer base.

In addition, find out how often you can get these reports: quarterly? monthly? daily? An ideal site would even provide a private Web page for instant feedback on your advertising statistics, 24 hours a day.

**Free Advertising.** The Internet offers many opportunities for free advertising, provided you know how to pursue it. A common technique is the *link exchange.* Two sites agree to advertise for each other by creating links to each other. Use a search engine to hunt for sites relevant to your business, or simply make deals with business acquaintances. *Banner exchanges* are the same as link exchanges except the link is accompanied by a picture. As tedious as it may sound, this approach works and you, not your developer, must take the initiative to make it pay off.

In addition, every time you send email, you have an opportunity to advertise. Many users place a *signature* at the end of an email message, containing their name and return email address. Use this space to include the name of your business and the URL of your Web site. It's possible to include more information about your business, but beware of going overboard. Large signatures—more than four lines long—become annoying to readers if seen frequently. For example, if you participate in a mailing list or discussion group, a large signature rapidly becomes a turn-off for other participants, thereby defeating its purpose. Consider having two signatures: a small one for use inside discussion groups, and a larger one for personal email. Examine other users' signatures for ideas.

Short, tasteful ads can be safely posted in relevant, public discussion groups. For example, if you run a software company, it's appropriate to post fact-filled announcements of new releases in discussion groups devoted to your kind of software. Nevertheless, beware of crossing the line between privacy and commercialism. Discussion groups are for discussion, so frequent or hype-filled advertisements will turn off users and can negatively impact your business's reputation online. In addition, *never* send advertisements by email blindly to large numbers of users. It might seem free, but it comes with large risks, as discussed later. Internet junk mail is a quick road to destroying an online reputation.

A final technique is known as *guerrilla marketing*. Internet users frequently discuss products and services they've enjoyed. Guerrilla marketing capitalizes on this by offering free samples to selected Internet users in the hopes that these users will enjoy and review the products or services online. For example, if you are a publisher, send free books to outspoken members of relevant mailing lists or public discussion groups. Keep a list of those users who review your products, and cultivate good relationships with them. This does *not* mean paying them, which would create a conflict of interest; guerrilla marketing is not about reimbursement, but about being on good terms with vocal users who like your business. Here again, you, and not your developer, are the key to making this happen.

**Nonrecommended Techniques.** Some advertising styles are instant turn-offs for many Internet users and you need to be aware of them. The use of all capital letters and excessive punctuation is generally not a good idea in ads, as in *FREE PRIZE* or *CHECK IT OUT!!!* Traditionally on the Internet, capitalization stands for shouting and is considered impolite, particularly in discussion groups and email messages (including their subject lines). Overuse of capitals and punctuation is like carrying a large, blinking sign that reads, "I am clueless." Also, beware of clichés. Information gets around so rapidly on the Internet that catch phrases quickly become overused. For example, avoid calling a Web site "hot." Finally, steer clear of "cyber," the oldest advertising cliché on the Net.

The preceding stylistic blunders are ineffective but relatively harmless. Every business makes a few mistakes online. Other techniques can actually harm your business, and the rest of this section will take a look at the seamy underbelly of Internet advertising. The techniques discussed in this section *do not work*, and you should be *strongly* discouraged from using them. They could seriously damage the reputation of your business on the Internet. Nevertheless, some irresponsible businesses will be delighted to sell you these techniques. Do not be fooled. If anyone offers you any of these services, then the offerer is at best, confused, and at worst, trying to scam you.

**Junk (Bulk) Email**

Email can be an effective and perfectly acceptable medium for advertising; for example, alerting your customers of upcoming sale events. Unfortunately, commercial email can also hurt your business if not used carefully. *Junk email*, also known as *bulk email* or *Unsolicited Commercial Email* (UCE), is a high-risk, low-return technique that initially looks attractive but in the end can damage a business's reputation. This chapter strongly recommends that you do not contract with a company to perform this anti-marketing function.

Junk email is the sending of unsolicited email advertisements blindly to thousands or millions of users. Since email is cheap and fast, junk email might seem like a very practical way to reach large numbers of users with a message. However, junk email has several important, hidden costs.

**Users hate it.** In the early days of junk email, users would deluge the senders with complaints. So the senders got more clever and started using fake return addresses so users couldn't reply. In response, computer system administrators started tracking down the senders using more sophisticated techniques and complaining to the senders' Internet Service Providers. So the senders started using more fakery to make the path less traceable . . . and so on. The war between junk emailers (trying to hide their identities) and consumers (trying to locate them) continues to escalate. Unless your business wants an adversarial relationship with its customers, don't send junk email.

**ISPs hate it.** The Terms Of Service agreement for most ISPs expressly forbids their users from sending junk email. A business can lose its Internet access over this.

**The Internet suffers from it.** Junk email might seem nearly free, but it takes its toll on the Net as a whole, clogging email gateways (computers that route email to the appropriate destination), slowing down networks, and burdening ISPs.

Senders of junk email are typically fly-by-night con artists who use fake email return addresses and operate out of post office boxes. Occasionally, however, a legitimate business new to the Internet will be attracted by the low cost of junk email and not know about the risks.

Despite the risks of junk email, regular email is great for staying in contact with customers. If customers willingly provide you with their email addresses, it's entirely appropriate to add them to your electronic mailing lists for announcements. Just remember:

- **Keep it brief.** Put the details on your Web site instead of filling an email message with commercialism.
- **Keep it factual.** Internet users appreciate facts and figures rather than hype.
- **Keep it relevant.** Advertisements for dish detergent won't be welcome in a mailing list for coin collectors or Boston Red Sox fans.
- **Respect requests to unsubscribe.** If someone asks to be removed from your electronic mailing lists, do the removal promptly.

**Newsgroup Spamming**

*Spamming* is the practice of posting massive numbers of duplicate articles—commercial or noncommercial—in online discussion groups, such as newsgroups or "boards." Previously used on the Net by pranksters and crackpots, spamming was turned into an advertising technique in the early 1990s when two attorneys, Lawrence Canter and Martha Siegel, posted an advertisement in over 6000 newsgroups on Usenet. This action spawned tens of thousands of complaints from users, but rather than cease the practice, Canter and Siegel turned their experience into a "how to" book, paving the way for thousands of fly-by-night spammers to follow in their footsteps. Today, newsgroup spamming is rampant. Many newsgroups, formerly rich resources of information, have become so overrun with spammed messages that the regular participants have all left. These newsgroups are the

Internet equivalents of ghost towns—abandoned houses buried under a steady stream of junk mail.

Newsgroup spamming is universally disliked not only by Internet users but also by most ISPs, since spammers' duplicate articles waste vast amounts of space on providers' hard drives. Spammers are the litterbugs of the Internet. Unless you want to damage your business's online reputation, don't hire someone to spam.

**Search Engine Overload**

As explained earlier, search engines use proprietary formulas to rank the relevance of Web sites as hits. The following tricks (which do not work) are sometimes used in an attempt to increase a site's ranking with a search engine. Beware of businesses that advocate these techniques.

The *repeated words trick* is based on a simple but flawed concept: if a Web page contains a certain word many times, then (supposedly) a search engine will rank the page highly when users search for that word. So if a Web page contains the word "widget" a hundred times, then the page will be ranked highly in a search for widgets.

This trick is pointless for two reasons: First, modern search engines tend to disregard heavily repeated words when ranking a page's relevance to a search. And second, search engine maintainers know about the trick and explicitly forbid it. A page containing massively repeated words is likely to be rejected upon registration. Even worse, any Internet domain that consistently violates the rule might find itself banned from the search engine entirely. In other words, all pages from the domain would be deleted from the search engine's database so they could not be found by any search. Obviously, this would be bad for business.

A variation on the preceding trick is the *invisible text trick*. Repeated words are placed on a Web page to try to increase its ranking in searches, but the words are not visible. This is usually accomplished by setting the words' foreground and background colors to be the same (e.g., white text on a white background). Search engines, however, don't care about color or text size. They'll treat the page just as they would for the repeated words trick.

The use of *multiple domain names* is sometimes hawked as a technique for increasing a site's ranking in a search engine. Here's how the trick (which doesn't work) is done. First, purchase several additional Internet domain names for your Web site. So if your site was formerly www.your-company.com, it's now also known as www.company2.com, www.another-company.com, and so forth. Then register your site with search engines under all the domain names. The claim is that your site is now more likely than before to be located by a search.

Why doesn't this trick work? Because most search engines rank the relevance of a page by its *content*, not its URL. If ACME Widgets was ranked #65 in a search, and the site then is duplicated under five different URLs, the ranking cannot improve because the page content has not changed. At best, the same page at five different URLs will be ranked 65, 66, 67, 68, 69.

In addition, the multiple domain name trick is socially irresponsible. Imagine if every company in the telephone Yellow Pages listed itself five times instead of once. The resulting book would be five times as thick as the original, but with no additional value for the consumer. Likewise for search engines: Filling the database with references to duplicate pages will provide consumers only with redundancy and slower searches.

## Directory Of Online Resources

### Major Internet Search Engines

| | |
|---|---|
| AltaVista | www.altavista.digital.com/ |
| Deja News | www.dejanews.com/ |
| Excite | www.excite.com/ |
| HotBot | www.hotbot.com/ |

| | |
|---|---|
| InfoSeek | www.infoseek.com/ |
| Lycos | www.lycos.com/ |
| Webcrawler | www.webcrawler.com/ |
| Yahoo! | www.yahoo.com/ |

### Search Engine Registries

Links to search engine registration services.

www.yahoo.com/Business_and_Economy/Companies/Internet_Services/Web_Services/Promotion/

### Advertising and Marketing Tips

ClickZ Today: Daily editorials about online commerce.

www.clickz.com/

Four Corners Effective Banners: How to create effective banner ads.

www.whitepalm.com/fourcorners/

Internet Advertising Report: News from the online advertising world.

www.internetnews.com/IAR/

Internet Advertising Resource Guide.

www.admedia.org/

Microscope: Online magazine devoted to online advertising, including banners ads of the week.

www.microscope.com/

Many links for site promotion.

www.yahoo.com/Computers_and_Internet/Internet/World_Wide_Web/Information_and_Documentation/Site_Announcement_and_Promotion/

### Junk Email and Spamming

The Coalition Against Unsolicited Commercial Email, an anti-spamming organization.

www.cauce.org/

"Bandits on the Information Superhighway" Information Center, including links about spamming and junk email, and online risks in general.

www.oreilly.com/catalog/bandits/

## Summary

Effective online marketing is an art. At times, it's a precarious balancing act between commercialism and users' privacy. But when done properly, it can be extremely rewarding, both for businesses and customers. Remember that you, not just your Web developer, bear responsibility for effectively marketing and advertising your site—it is your business. We'll conclude with a checklist emphasizing the chapter's major points.

## Checklist

- ☐ Register with all major search engines, or hire a registration service.
- ☐ Advertise on top-ranked sites in your business category.
- ☐ Emphasize informational content on Web pages, and avoid hype.
- ☐ Design Web pages that load quickly.
- ☐ Spend time making your site easy to navigate.
- ☐ Offer added value on your Web site so visitors return often.
- ☐ Create and/or sponsor noncommercial sites to publicize yourself.
- ☐ Participate in online discussion groups.
- ☐ Proofread all official communications that reach the Internet; a bad one can stick around for years.
- ☐ Thank users who contact your business.
- ☐ Avoid form letters in email.
- ☐ Carefully evaluate sites before advertising on them.
- ☐ Add your email address and URL to your email signature.
- ☐ Participate in link exchanges.
- ☐ Post short, tasteful ads in public forums.

- ☐ Participate in guerrilla marketing.
- ☐ Avoid spamming, junk email, and search engine overloading.
- ☐ Build a mailing list for your regular customers who want to be contacted.

chapter

11

# Going Forward: Next-Generation Sites and Building an E-Business

**Devajit Mukherjee, IBM Corporation**
*dev@us.ibm.com*

## About This Chapter

This chapter is about what happens *after* you've built your first Web site, a process that is often referred to in books and magazines as the creation of the "second-generation site" or "next-generation" site.

Second-generation sites are much more than marketing bolt-ons, they are fully integrated into your core business, forming a significant channel to key company stakeholders (customers, employees, partners, shareholders or all of the above). This chapter walks you through the challenging process of evolving your Web presence from your first-generation Web pages to a fully integrated, value-adding second-generation site, transforming your business into an e-business. Throughout, the author offers insights and suggestions regarding what it takes to make your company an e-business, how to decide what you want, establish and plan for site infrastructure, and develop and choose a plan for technology selection. Some parts of this chapter focus on how experts at IBM have approached this important process. That's no surprise given that it was written by an employee of IBM, and the fact that IBM is, I believe, the world's largest Web developer and technology supplier. In fact, IBM was one of the creators of NSFNet, the starting point for today's Internet. While some of the examples are indeed "IBM centric," the lessons to be learned are universal.

Planning to be a fully integrated e-business is likely to be the most important step as your Web development efforts grow. This is the point at which you really begin to change how you do things and reap the real benefits of the Internet: new customers, reduced costs, streamlined operations, and additional revenue.

### About the Author

Devajit Mukherjee is currently at MIT's Sloan School of Business with plans to return to IBM in mid-1999. Dev has held a number of positions at IBM, and most recently was director of internet marketing in IBM's server group. IBM's server product line extends from Intel-based NT servers to mainframe-class machines, including the infamous IBM SP—or Deep Blue—system that beat Kasparov at chess and powered the official Super Bowl and Olympics Web sites.

Before the server group, Dev ran Internet operations for IBM's personal computer and consumer divisions. This included the development of a publishing system to support local country Web sites around the globe, community Web areas to deliver customer service, support, and electronic commerce. These initiatives were some of IBM's first steps toward becoming an e-business.

Prior to moving to the United States, Dev led the launch for and ran IBM's ThinkPad business in Europe. Before joining IBM, Dev worked for Stratus Computer and Citibank's European Technology Office.

**The good news/bad news story on the Internet is that it is very easy to put up a Web site. A good ISP, an HTML editing tool, and you're in business. But are you really?**

Sites that get the most attention, and traffic, tend to either break new ground or provide a valuable set of interactive and dynamic services for their target audience. Most sites, however, are usually static pages that don't change very often—the online equivalent to a flyer, brochure, or annual report.

While static information can be useful, the true promise of the Internet is its ability to help us transform the way we do things, both in business and personally. At IBM, we use the term *e-business* to describe businesses that are transforming the way they deal with customers, partners, and employees to truly leverage Internet networks and technology.

Building a static, promotional Web site is only the first stage of becoming an e-business. Stage two is adding interactivity, where users can access information such as the status of an account or trace a package. Stage three is moving to transaction-based Web sites—not just buying and selling, but all the processes that require a dynamic and interactive flow of information. Think of this process as actually moving your business onto the Net.

This chapter outlines the major business functions that you can move or extend to the Web, the architecture choices you should make as part of your implementation plans, and some of the key technologies that are being used to make sites more effective. The ideas and opinions expressed in this chapter are the author's and not necessarily those of IBM or the other companies mentioned. We have, however, used IBM's Network Computing Framework in order to describe the major technical components you may need as you extend your site, whether or not you buy products from IBM.

Why include a chapter on Internet technology in a book on outsourcing? After all, when you hire a caterer, you don't start taking cooking classes. However, as you move your business to the Net, the architecture and technology choices you make will significantly affect the success, cost, and ability to scale of your site, now and in the future.

A first-generation "promotional" site tends to be an incremental effort designed as an add-on marketing or promotional project undertaken by the ad agency, marketing, or IT department. A second-generation site will be a core part of your business, affecting customer satisfaction, revenue, and profitability. So, while outsourcing is a good idea, it also pays to keep your hands on the reins for strategy, technology selection, and overall architecture to make sure the technology will support your business now and in the future.

The fuel to develop your e-business is the intellectual capital–information and know-how that is built into systems and processes that are part of how your organization does business. A lot of this may have been developed before you even thought of building your Web site. How you link the Web to your legacy environment is an important policy decision, one that will have future implications for IT investments and business strategy across your business. It will be easier (and more accurate) for you to inventory information and skills assets, determine which functions should be moved to the Web first, and establish how to measure success than it will be for your developer. Resist the temptation to abdicate responsibility—this will be the future of your business.

While most Web development firms are technically savvy, their primary skill is not your business strategy, customers, or current information systems. Web developers will also have a natural bias towards technologies they've used before. Since the products and technologies used on your site should be driven by your business objectives to support future integration and growth, the more you understand about Internet technology, the easier it will be to communicate your goals to a developer, and the greater your chances for a successful site.

### Making Your Business an E-Business

Imagine an early TV show with actors behind big silver microphones, as used on radio, simply talking to the audience. The technology had advanced, but the content remained the same. Many early Web sites struggled with the new Internet medium in much the same way. They focused on promotional materials that mirrored traditional "one-way" marketing strategies such as direct mail, brochures, and advertising. The focus was on creating visually attractive sites or using the latest technology, rather than on appealing to the majority of users with valuable information and services. As the Web matures, however, we're finding that the value of the content and the ability to interact is what keeps visitors coming back.

That's not to say that the experience should be strictly functional, however; the focus (and funds) needs to be directed to the function, not the look.

Bringing your site into its second generation is the time to stress the function of your Web site rather than the aesthetic virtues. The highest-volume, most-celebrated Web sites (e.g., amazon.com, Charles Schwab, and Fed Ex) are well designed to make them easy to navigate, but have relatively few images, reducing the load time, burden on the servers, and arguably making the sites easier to use.

In Figure 11.1, you will see the script of one of IBM's e-business commercials. In a humorous way, it points out that while snazzy graphics and logos may be cool, they won't transform your business into an e-business.

As you start to increase the function of your site and the level of integration into the rest of your business, there will be a new set of factors to consider. Different people to talk to in your organization, new skills you'll need to get the job done, and new technologies that you'll want to use. As you start to do more on the Web, you will be tempted by people to take leaps of technological faith in order to enhance the creative design of your site.

The mantra to always keep in mind as this happens is function, function, and function. Neither the user of your Web site nor management will give you extra brownie points for using the latest and greatest technology or redesigning your Web site every month, if the site doesn't do something useful.

The rapid evolution of the Internet, coupled with the growing number of users and investment dollars, has resulted in boatloads of new startups

**Manager:** What are you doing?

**Webmaster:** I'm figuring out what our Web site should be. We've got the spinning logo like this one or a flaming logo. It's cool.

**Manager:** You know what would be a great idea? If people with PCs anywhere could order our products and that was all tied together. Inventory, billing, vendors; you know, the works, then that would change everything.

**Webmaster:** I don't know how to do that.

**Figure 11.1** The real challenge is not building a Web site, but building a useful Web site.

and technologies. According to press releases, each of these technologies is about to transform the Internet by fixing the bandwidth problem, enabling commerce, and so forth.

The Gartner Group, specialists in technology planning, information, and consulting, describes the phases technologies go through before delivering on their initial promise.

The Gartner Group traces these technologies through five phases:

1. **The technology trigger.** A breakthrough, public demonstration, product launch, or other event generates significant press and industry interest.
2. **Peak of inflated expectations.** During this phase of over enthusiasm and unrealistic projections, a flurry of well-publicized activity by technology leaders results in some successes, but more failures, as the technology is pushed to its limits. The only enterprises making money are conference organizers and magazine publishers.
3. **Trough of disillusionment.** Because the technology does not live up to its inflated expectations, it rapidly becomes unfashionable and the press abandons the topic.
4. **Slope of enlightenment.** Focused experimentation and solid hard work by an increasingly diverse range of organizations lead to a true understanding of the technology's applicability, risks, and benefits. Commercial off-the-shelf methodologies and tools become available to ease the development process.
5. **Plateau of productivity.** The real-world benefits of the technology are demonstrated and accepted. Tools and methodologies are increasingly stable as they enter their second and third generations. The final height of the plateau varies according to whether the technology is broadly applicable or benefits only a niche market.

This is not to say that you should only select proven technologies; being an early adopter could give you a competitive advantage. A strong relationship with the provider, and maybe a lead in deployment (being the first to deliver your company's product or service on the Net) provides significant "first mover" advantages. Yahoo!'s stock price has gone from

$20 to $200 in the last year, not because it has the only useable taxonomy for the Web, but it was the first. The question to ask yourself is, "will the advantages of helping a new company develop its product be worth the investment?" This assessment should be done from a financial standpoint and in terms of the learning you'll gain from developing a new product.

As we developed IBM's PC Company and Consumer Division Web sites, we learned that Web users want to interact when they get to your site. Stepping through pretty pages or wrestling with a new technology may be fun once, but they won't keep an audience coming back.

A simple user interface and the functional features that help your audience achieve a goal or task will make your site the one they want to bookmark. The questions to keep asking yourself is, "why would my customers, employees, or partners want to use my Web site? How is this better than traditional methods?"

The following steps will help you understand the requirements necessary to bring your site to the next level and start transforming your business into an e-business.

**Step 1: Decide Which Functions You Want to Make Available on Your Web Site.** The trend towards network computing and the Internet will continue and will have a growing effect across all business functions in most industries. It is important, however, for you to select the functions that make sense for your company and your industry now.

Even if customer service is the most important function in your business, you should still ask, "will making this available on the Internet help my customers?" Are your customers already on the Net? Is your customer service department open to investing time and money to make this a success?

The following overview will help you think through which functions—specifically, customer service, technical support, electronic commerce, publishing, and integration—may be most important for your business and Web site. For example, which functions in your organization are likely to be most interested in making an Internet project successful? Who will benefit the most? Our customer service organization immediately understood that the Internet could improve support without the escalating 800-number costs by putting information online that our customers could access themselves.

Electronic commerce has received much attention since it means companies can give direct access to their end customers. For example, airlines can sell tickets over the Internet without paying for the costs and profit margin of travel agents, thereby increasing the potential gross margin on each transaction enormously. There are, however, a number of business issues (in addition to costs) to consider before embarking on an electronic commerce project. How will your current partners feel about being disintermediated? Will their reaction be more detrimental to your business than the new channel will be beneficial? How will your customers feel about doing business on the Web? Are they concerned about security? How much training will they require?

Customer service could be a more attractive first step, with a focus on providing enhanced service and saving money rather than trying to make it. Customers and partners can benefit from better support and, with an 800-number call costing upwards of $25 when the cost of providing the same information online can be just a few cents, there is plenty of opportunity for savings.

> According to a recent Booz-Allen and Hamilton study, a traditional bank transaction costs $1.07; the same transaction on the Web costs about $.01.

As you approach the task of deciding which functions to make available on your site, it is important to gather input from all the members of your organization responsible for business, marketing, and service strategy. Assembling a cross-functional team will help you broaden the level of Web awareness across your organization. With that broader input you will be better able to judge which projects will have the best support and the greatest return. Most importantly, a cross-functional team will ensure that you have buy-in to the project across your organization.

First-generation Web sites tend to be built using the company's product brochures or annual report as the main content. While this approach doesn't require much investment, it offers only limited returns to the business. Will more customers go into a store to buy your product after seeing a picture on the Internet, or should you provide online ordering?

The two main factors to consider are what resources you have that can be deployed over the Web, and which business levers will have the greatest impact on your bottom line. Resources that are useful on the Internet can come from surprising places. In addition to the standard material you provide your customers today, you may have additional "internal use" information that your customers would love to have. Before the Internet, it was probably not cost effective to distribute this material or maybe you couldn't identify which customers would be interested. Now, the incremental cost is zero and customers can serve themselves. In the Century 21 example that follows, the company had lots of information that was only available to the realtors; by making it available on the Web, Century 21 created an extremely useful site and generated new business. This is also an example of a key business lever. You cannot move your entire business to the Web overnight, so work out which pieces will create the biggest impact In their enthusiasm to get on the Web, many companies have forgotten to consider the return on investment of their Internet initiatives. You can avoid this trap by examining your resources and focusing on areas that will generate the greatest return.

For example, in real estate, generating leads (people interested in buying a property) is one of the more significant business functions. The more leads, the more business, and the more business, the greater the revenues and profits. This observation led Bob Pittman, then CEO of Century 21, to sign a deal with America Online. He realized that enabling customers to interact with Century 21 online would create a new source of leads.

Century 21's approach treats the Internet as a new channel for leads, linking the existing business process to the new medium. Other approaches take advantage of the nature of the Internet to adopt an alternate business strategy.

To take an example from a different industry, banking used to be a "high touch" relationship business. With the advent of ATMs, people stopped going into their bank branches at all. Suddenly, older banks with high-cost real estate in the center of town were at a disadvantage compared to newer financial institutions that were providing services without a fixed cost base. This industry is now using technology to adopt an alternate business strategy as other banks, discount brokers, and new entrants into financial services. For example, Intuit provides an excellent service with their Quicken software and Web site, giving their customers a broad range of information and personalized service without a physical presence and large staff. Banks have to follow suit, while at the same time leveraging their existing assets in new ways.

Banking strategy has shifted as that industry realized one of the major differences between the physical world and cyberspace: Once you have created them, digital assets are almost free, the cost of providing extra bandwidth or server capacity is much less than adding people or facilities. Web technology can enable you to build a "high touch" experience, dynamically created for every one of your customers with little or no intervention.

To select the right function, you should start by making an inventory of the following information:

- Who are the current users of your Web site?
- What do they want? We found that regular visitors to our site were much more willing to respond to a short set of online questions than to direct mail, and a questionnaire is easy to create.
- What digital assets do you have?
- What information on your products or marketplace would your target audience find useful?
- What are the key levers that will drive the success of your business?

To complete this section, and to help you select which functions you want to add to your Web site, we have included an overview of each of the major functions you should consider: customer service, technical support, electronic commerce, publishing, and interaction.

**Customer Service**

A real estate business like Century 21 has large amounts of information that prospective customers would find useful. This information may only be available to employees and partners because up to now it has been too voluminous and difficult to distribute.

By using the Web as a distribution mechanism, it's easy to give customers access to the information they want. What's the return? Like technical support, a customer service site can cut costs by allowing customers to browse data that previously would have required the time of a sales rep or service agent. The associated costs of handling information in physical form—printing, copying, and mailing—are also saved. Customer satisfaction improves as customers only receive the material they're interested in. A side benefit of this self-service approach is that at the end of the interaction, customers have a much better idea of what they want than from reading a brochure or pressing endless keys in response to a touch-tone voice response unit. For example, a customer might use the Web site to diagnose that her PC has too little memory for Windows 98 and all her new applications. If we know which machine she purchased, we can recommend the upgrades that she should purchase to increase memory capacity. The result is a better-educated and qualified customer before she calls.

This provides the following benefits:

- Improved customer satisfaction as customers can easily find information, even if they are not entirely sure what they need.
- Reduced demands on customer service and sales reps for general information.
- A shorter sales cycle, as the customer is better informed.
- Better service for customers who use traditional communication methods.
- Your company name and brand will be uppermost in the site visitors' minds when they are ready to buy.
- Reduced operating costs from printing, copying, and mailing.

Century 21 (www.century21.com) provides an excellent example of a customer service site. Visitors to the site can access such information as the demographic profile, income levels, and percentage of families with children in an area that they may be thinking of moving to. After the prospective homebuyer has selected an area, the site also contains links to information on applying for a mortgage and answers to frequently asked questions. When the customer is ready to buy, he or she can even search a list of properties before finding the local Century 21 office.

**Technical Support**

At the IBM Personal Computer Company, we found that we had information including hints and tips, frequently asked questions, and bug information that could help our customers and partners handle many of the difficulties they normally run into using personal computers. We also offer downloadable fixes and upgrades that can help our customers and partners to enhance their systems and avoid problems.

As PCs became less expensive yet more complex, the demands and cost pressure being placed on technical support organizations were increasing. Most of our technical information was readily available to our technical support staff. A customer or partner, however, would either have to call our support center or scroll through long lists to find the information they needed.

To maintain the level of support IBM customers expect, the IBM PC Co. support team developed a Lotus Notes-based system that made all of our support information available online. To avoid deluging visitors to the site with too much information, registered users are presented with a tailored view of the information relevant to the systems and configurations they've purchased. For example, as I enter the support site using my ThinkPad 560, I'm shown all the latest news, information, and upgrades for that system. Further support is provided through the use of discussion groups, which are segmented by product type and area.

The discussion groups allow customers to talk to each other and receive informal support from IBM technical staff members who monitor the forums.

The benefits of creating a technical support site are as follows:

- Greater customer satisfaction for customers who browse the service information themselves.
- Reduced load on our technical support staff, reducing wait times and allowing them to focus on more complex or critical problems.
- A direct channel to users for important news regarding their specific system.
- Better distribution of information that enhances the product experience (e.g. hints and tips, fixes, and product upgrades). This information increases product satisfaction and consequently the likelihood of repurchase.
- A simple mechanism to suggest new products or accessories for the customer's current system.

The IBM PC Company site (www.pc.ibm.com) demonstrates technical support for both registered and nonregistered users. This is also an excellent example of dynamic, database-driven pages, as many of the pages are created uniquely for each visitor to the site.

**Electronic Commerce**

Electronic commerce includes a number of separate activities. While the focus in the press tends to be on transactions (should we enter credit card numbers or not?), creating a successful electronic commerce area will require attention to the following components:

**Catalog.** The creation, management, and navigation of the product catalog, including keeping information on which products are in stock and price updates. This requires linking the site to a backend product database or inventory system. In an online environment, the last thing you want to do is to contact your customers after they've placed an order to tell them the product is out of stock.

**Maintenance of customer information.** Customers should not have to retype all of their account and address information every time they place an order. Hence, as much information as possible should be saved securely without violating the customer's privacy rights. For example, amazon.com offers one-click ordering to registered customers.

Customer information from the electronic commerce area of your site may be useful, allowing you to get fast input on what is selling and what's not. More sophisticated systems may also enable you to track which products customers are searching for or looking at, but not buying. Or, track which products customers tend to buy together (many of the current electronic commerce sites use this information to provide a customer service, prompting customers to buy products other customers with similar buying habits have purchased).

**Order processing.** Capturing a customer's order may require interaction with a number of different backend systems and processes in order to, for example, retrieve the customer's account information (including credit limit).

As the order is confirmed, these systems may require confirmation, and access to other systems, or new processes may also be invoked; for example, to perform a credit check. It may be critical to ensure all confirmations happen together, or if any fail, that the entire transaction is rolled back.

This type of activity has long been the preserve of large centralized systems (e.g., banking systems). As order processing is linked to the Web, you should pay special attention to ensure that neither the integrity of the transaction nor the security of the systems is compromised. This will involve reviewing all possible cases: What happens if customers do not complete the order? What if they don't receive their confirmation? What if they make a mistake?

Forethought in this area is particularly important, given that once the system is operational, it will probably run mostly unattended. Errors in the order processing area are time consuming to fix and very likely to cause customer dissatisfaction. Implemented correctly, however, the opportunity exists to provide a high level of service with relatively low cost.

**Payment.** There are a number of different payment options on the Internet depending on the type of transaction and the parties involved. For closed or business-to-business systems (for example, doctor to HMO), the Internet transaction can be completed using the electronic equivalent of a purchase order.

For broader reach, particularly where consumers are involved, different methods are appropriate. Credit cards are being used extensively on the Internet today. There is considerable unease, however, amongst consumers, merchants, and card issuers given the security issues. Giving your credit card number to a Web site may be similar to handing over the card to a waiter or gas station attendant. Yet neither of these cases create the same risks for a third party to copy the information or gain access to a large number of transactions as the Internet.

Protection from "snooping," the practice of snatching financial information as it traverses the Internet, can be improved using SSL (Secure Sockets Layer). SSL is used to encrypt the data between the client and the server as it travels over the Net (you'll know you're on an SSL page when the padlock icon is closed in your Browser window. Yet, this does not stop the data from being tampered with, nor does it give any assurance that any of the parties at the client or the server end are who they say they are. You don't really know that it's Dev Mukherjee accessing your site and I can't prove that the site I'm connected to is yours.

To mitigate the threat of snooping, and confirm that a site really belongs to the organization it claims to, a number of approaches are emerging involving the use of digital certificates. Using digital certificates, the identity of the consumer, merchant, and financial institution can all be authenticated, and sensitive parts of the transaction (e.g., amount or account number) can be hidden. The broadest initiative, supported by MasterCard and VISA, is called SET (Secure Electronic Transaction). IBM as a SET supporter provides systems that can authenticate and encrypt the messages as they travel between customer, online merchant, and the financial institution (e.g., VISA).

Although traditional methods of payment are working today, they will come under increasing attack due to a new breed of criminals. Payment is obviously a critical piece of electronic commerce, and pressure from financial institutions, merchants, and customers to implement new standards will increase. Implementation of these systems will provide greater security and other benefits.

While it may be difficult to implement the standards that will make your site more secure, you'll gain another opportunity to capture more information and learn more about your customers and their shopping habits.

**Publishing**

You are probably already publishing information on a Web site. However, as we look at moving towards a second-generation site, it is important to also look at how publishing can be extended and improved. There are three major areas of improvement that can be explored. The first is to allow a greater number of individuals to publish content on your Web site. Second, access to more data, perhaps located in centralized databases, can be provided. Finally, the information on the site can be personalized for the individual visitor.

Allowing more people to publish content can make your site much more valuable and interesting for visitors since they'll find information from a more diverse set of contributors as opposed to reading content developed solely by the central Web team. There are, however, a number of risks to consider. For example, losing control of the look and feel of the site, possible legal exposure from inaccurate content, and adding confusion caused by duplicate or unstructured information. These risks can be limited by developing a publishing or content management system.

Many organizations are now using Lotus Domino or Allaire's Cold Fusion to manage the publishing process (e.g., who has to sign off on new content, the look and feel, using templates, and the navigation of a site). At the IBM PC Company, this type of approach enabled us to have one or two staff members, with limited Web experience, publish their own Web sites without our central Web team having to relinquish control.

Providing access to more data can be achieved by using "connector" technology to access central databases. Technology topics will be covered later in this chapter.

Personalization means creating a customized view or views for each visitor to your site; for example, managing the content according to the user's browser type, or changing the default language according to where he or she is entering the Internet.

Personalization can be extended to deliver more value by using the visitor's own information to dynamically change the content that is sent to him or her. The content could be selected based on age, sex, or topics of interest that allow you to deliver information requested (e.g., the weather in Boston, new information on a specific product, the best performing mutual funds, etc.).

Although it is difficult to demonstrate the ROI (Return on Investment) of evolving a Web by site using financial metrics, it should be possible to justify the expense based on the benefits of improved customer service, technical support, electronic commerce, and content publishing—benefits that include increased customer satisfaction and loyalty. It is important to set specific objectives in each of the areas you target, milestones based on function delivery, customer response, and cost savings.

**Integration**

So far, we've reviewed four important functions—customer service, technical support, electronic commerce, and publishing—that can help evolve your Web site, and transform your business into an e-business. Although it is possible to implement each of these functions on its own, one of the important attributes of Web technology is its ability integrate many different content and transaction sources. A site that pulls together advanced publishing ideas, customer service, technical support, and electronic commerce will provide significant value to its visitors. Each function will benefit from the traffic brought in by the others.

The ability to leverage common technologies will make visiting the site a richer experience and potentially save infrastructure costs. For example, a voice response unit to serve customers and a dedicated dial-up system (e.g., bulletin board) for salespeople or resellers to make stock inquiries is likely to be more expensive than a single Web site servicing both. Logon and security may be different for the two types of users; however, the integration reduces costs and creates new opportunities to cross leverage the information and services that were originally targeted at only one group. For example, customers could leave messages for their sales rep, resellers could poll customers on their preferences or promote special offers in their areas.

Lotus Notes and other Dynamic Web environments (e.g., Cold Fusion) provide much greater opportunities for personalizing the user experience of the Web site. This can be based on previous visits, registration, or simply the order of their interaction.

**Step 2: Review and Plan the Infrastructure.** Once you've decided which functions you want to make available through your Web site, examine the assets you currently have available and the assets you'll need to develop.

Assets consist of your existing Web site, databases (e.g., the Century 21 example), other systems, or the employees' skills that can be better leveraged by making them accessible through the Internet. For example, service people may be able to answer customer questions online rather than make unnecessary service calls. Any knowledgeable group in your organization may be able to create a list of Frequently Asked Questions (FAQs) for a particular product or service, even if they never normally see a customer.

Your promotional site is probably maintained on a standalone Web server. As you add more function, you'll have to make decisions on whether to maintain the current Web server, connect it to where your legacy applications and data reside, or integrate the Web serving component into your core systems(the larger system or mainframe on which your primary data processing is done).

Most promotional Web sites (i.e., those that provide static information, such as annual reports, rather than interactive features) consist of standalone Web (HTTP and maybe FTP for large files) servers on a company's own premises or at an ISP or hosting company. This may be a dedicated server that only supports a single firm or department's Web presence, or one shared by multiple entities. The server is either managed by a small inhouse staff or outsourced to the ISP or an agency.

To add function to your Web site you will need to identify the key assets you want to leverage, and then decide how to link to your existing systems and processes. In this section, we will discuss which assets might be useful as you evolve your site and become an e-business. We'll discuss three architectural approaches to achieve the appropriate integration.

**Assets** In addition to your current Web server, your organization probably has a number of different computer systems handling transactions and data for customers, employees, and partners. Once you have decided which new functions to add to your Web site, it is important to do a complete inventory of all the people, systems, and processes that are related to this function. For example, if you plan to add a customer service function to your Web site, review the current resources used to deliver this function by phone or in person. This includes lists of common questions and answers, databases of resolved problems, and so forth. Recruit a set of people who understand the current process and the types of issues customers face. This group will be able to help validate the Web-based service and suggest additional features to improve the current setup.

The next step is to lay out the various systems that need to be connected to provide the new service. These systems will need to be connected to your Web server based on the architecture you select (architecture options are discussed in the next section).

Bear in mind that the current form and structure of the data may be inappropriate for your site. For example, the language may have been originally created for an internal support rep rather than a customer, or the layout may be difficult to display on a Web page.

After you have selected the assets you want to use, you'll need to decide on the architecture that will pull those assets together.

**Web Server Architecture**

The three architectural approaches you can use to extend the function of your Web site are a standalone server, a Web server interface to legacy systems, and integrated Web and core system functions. The trade-off you face when selecting a Web server is short-term expedience versus longer-term cost. Making incremental changes to your existing Web infrastructure may take you forward; however, as you move toward becoming an e-business you'll eventually need to fully integrate your Web and backend systems. It is possible to view this as a phased transition as long as you're very clear on the direction in which you're headed.

**Maintaining a stand-alone server.** This is the easiest step to take, as it creates the least short-term disruption. All the new data and services you want to add to your existing environment, however, will need to be transferred or developed on your Web server. The advantages of this approach are simplicity, easy migration from current systems and assets, and a degree of operational security by keeping the Internet physically separate. The disadvantage is that this is potentially the most expensive solution. A duplicate copy of your data will be created as it is transferred from your current systems to the Web servers. This creates a data integrity issue (which view of the data is the most current?). If I can update my account details online *and* on the phone, which one should be trusted? New technical development may also duplicate functions already in place. For example, credit card authorization may need to be implemented on both the Web server and your current system. In addition, information transfer between the legacy environment and Web server is not necessarily secure from outside access.

**Web server interface to legacy systems.** This approach can offer a good initial compromise between the two other options. Using this architecture, you can maintain the static pages already in place on your promotional site and add higher-level functions that access databases on other systems. By using CGI scripts or Java to extend the functions on a standard Web server, you can issue Structured Query Language (SQL) calls, such as "SELECT customers FROM DATABASE accounts WHERE BALANCE > $1,000" to a database on a legacy system. IBM DB2 and other databases use SQL to allow users and applications to easily find and manipulate the data within the database.

The Java standard libraries, extend the basic language to provide additional services. One of these libraries includes a series of JDBC (Java Database Connectivity) calls to facilitate these connections and allow Java programs to access SQL databases. Many database vendors, including IBM, have announced add-ons and packages to make these connections simple to build and secure.

A Web server interface to legacy systems provides a simple migration path, and allows both static content and interactive pages to be hosted on the same server. There is still, however, an issue of duplicating information on the Web server and in the legacy environment, and complex dynamic pages or personalized applications will be difficult to build using this architecture.

**Integrated Web and core system functions.** The latest Internet technologies allow Java-based Web applications to access and interact with core applications. For example, IBM's Connector Series or NetDynamic's products make it easy to connect Web applications to CICS or MVS applications on a mainframe. This enables the development of a three-tier architecture, in which the client (tier 1) runs Java-based applications, the Web server acts as the second tier channeling requests from multiple clients and running its own applications to access databases and other core applications running on the third-tier mainframes or other centralized systems. I have often described this as an evolution of what used to be called "*client-server development*," except this time it's client-server without any client development, installation, or maintenance. All you need is a standard Web browser; all the code (Java) is pulled from the Web server as required.

This approach provides the greatest flexibility and scalability, allowing you to leverage the investments you've already made in applications and databases, as well as providing an open environment that makes it easier to add functions later.

Most applications and database vendors are now providing Internet extensions to their applications, which simplifies the task of connecting to the Internet. Most of the "Web pages" in this architecture will not exist until they are requested, which means the pages are more dynamic and personalized than standard HTML pages. Templates are used to maintain a common look and feel, but the content is pulled from the application or database to create the Web page based on the user and the action he or she is requesting.

We used this approach for most of the IBM PC Company and Consumer Division sites, and a similar approach is used by almost all of the major sites because it allows the greatest control over the look and feel while enabling content to be generated that best fits users' needs, cutting down on the number of clicks they need to make. Changing a common page element, like a logo or privacy reference, requires a change to a single template, not multiple pages. Tailoring content, such as providing information to visitors based on the machine they're using, makes it easier for customers to use the site, which increases their likelihood to return and reduces the server load since fewer pages are accessed.

**Step 3: Select the Technology.** After deciding which business functions to add to your site and planning your infrastructure architecture, you're ready to select the appropriate technology for your needs.

As you make the selection, be aware of the constraints of your current environment and the skills that are available to you. Are you willing to discard your current investments, or would you prefer a slower, more evolutionary approach? In this section, we will use IBM's Network Computing Framework to describe the critical components you will need to develop a second-generation Web site that works well today and provides a solid base for future growth.

There is no shortage of Internet technologies from which to choose, as we discussed earlier using The Gartner Group's hype cycle. Whether or not you choose the latest technology, it's helpful to use some type of framework to guide your decisions.

The role of the framework is to help you select technologies that will work well together, even as your needs change, and even if you choose products from different vendors on different platforms. Given the pace of technological change, as well as environmental factors (such as acquisitions and mergers), it is important to be able to plan regardless of the platforms and software being used or added. This is called a *heterogeneous* environment and it's the most common environment in many organizations.

IBM developed the Network Computing Framework (NCF) to simplify the transition to e-business through the integration of different products on different platforms, whether they are existing systems or new Internet applications. The NCF helps developers answer the following questions:

- How does a company choose the right Web server foundation and build e-business applications fast enough to stay ahead of the competition?
- How are new and existing applications connected when they are on multiple platforms?
- How are intranets created and network environments extended to suppliers?
- How should constant availability of every mission-critical application be managed?
- How can the transition to e-business be fast, painless, and profitable?

The framework is summarized in Figure 11.2.

Any Java-enabled client—a PC running a Web browser or a dedicated Java NetStation that can render the HTML, and has a Java Virtual Machine to run Java applets and JavaBean components—is capable of being the front end to an NCF-based system. This is an important component of the overall system, even though it may not be owned by your organization or located on your premises. Defining your target client, either by adopting the NCF or by making up your own standards, is a critical first step. This

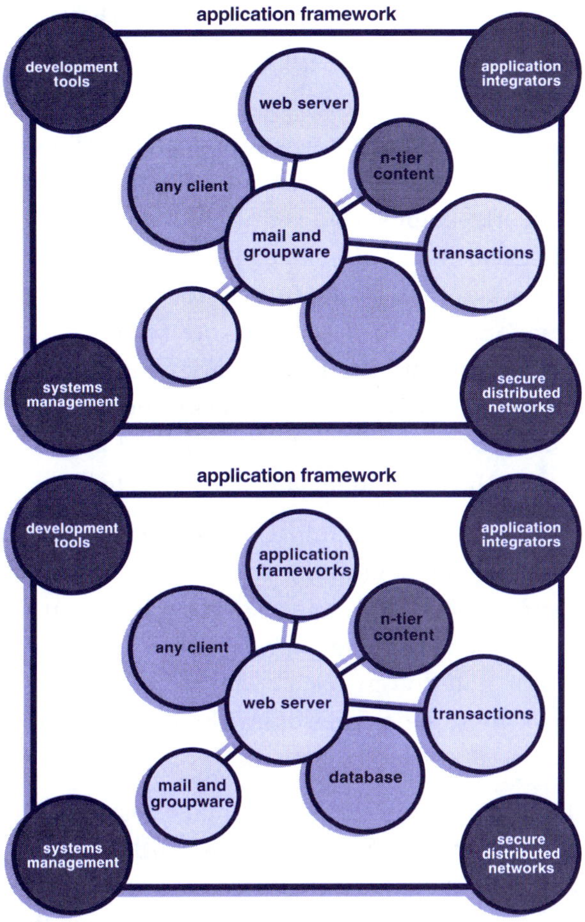


**Figure 11.2** IBM's Network Computing Framework (NCF) provides one example for companies looking to model the technology foundation of their future Internet plans.

choice will define the range of content and Internet applications you can use on your site. In addition, there is a set of client protocols that provide access to other services (for example, directories, news, and mail).

The diagram also shows the key server component's services and tools required to deliver e-business applications.

IBM's Network Computing Framework is based on two core ideas: the use of Java across all clients and servers, and the use of open standards. These new standards are designed to be independent of any product or supplier. Technology developers, such as IBM, who sign up to the standards "open up" their products by making the interfaces consistent, so that they can work with other suppliers' products and services. That's why IBM's Network Computing Framework is useful whether you use IBM technology or not.

Adopting the framework as the base for your Internet applications allows flexibility in the choice of components and services for each part of your Internet application. The framework establishes a set of guidelines for the key attributes a component or service must offer in order to work well with the rest of your applications, now and in the future. You can use these attributes to evaluate components and services before selecting them as part of your application. Each attribute is summarized in the following sections (more information on the NCF is available on the IBM Web site, including the latest framework description, IBM and non-IBM products that meet the criteria, at www.software.ibm.com/ebusiness/ncf).

One of the strengths of the NCF is its basis in industry-standard technologies. By using the NCF to guide the technology you select to build your second-generation Web site, you can leverage the technology that best meets your needs in each of the services or infrastructure areas discussed next. In addition, you'll be able to replace a component or add a new one (provided it adheres to the same standards) without having to rewrite your application.

As you select products to fit into your architecture, you should test the specifications against the NCF to ensure the appropriate standards are being met. During development, even though nonstandard extensions are available in most products, it is important to stick to the core functions that are included in the framework, as this will ensure the maximum flexibility.

Finally, using the framework and open standards to develop your application will provide significant opportunities for reusing code, both at the client and on the server, which can increase productivity and reduce costs.

**Clients: Browser Running on a PC or Network Appliance**

The Web client is important to keep in mind when building Web applications, as this is the delivery vehicle for your application whether it's written in HTML, Dynamic HTML, or Java. The browser or appliance should be capable of supporting these development environments and linking to the server using standard Internet protocols to invoke server-based objects and access services like mail, news, chat, and directory services. In addition to providing access to these services, Java offers standard mechanisms for "just-in-time" delivery of applets and applications. This means Java can be downloaded from the server when a particular service is required, in much the same way as a Web page is downloaded when selected by a user.

**Server Foundation Services and Infrastructure Components**

Foundation services and infrastructure components describe how applications should access database and transaction services using industry standard interfaces, as well as systems management and application services to support specific environments (e.g., SET for electronic commerce). The server environment is more complex than the client in that it defines the software to run Java applications as well as the necessary foundation services and infrastructure components for a complete business application, either as a gateway to a backend server or as a complete solution.

The NCF programming model describes how applications, Java applications, or servlets (server-based applets) should access the services using Java classes and JavaBeans. A number of software vendors, including IBM, have already delivered Java class and JavaBean components to provide access to their applications. This is being extended as companies start to adopt the Enterprise Java Beans standard, which extends the JavaBeans standard by adding additional features to support business applications.

**Web Server**

The Web server is the core component in the NCF foundation services definition. As messages or requests come in from a client, the Web server either executes HTML or Java code directly, or forwards the request to another server running on either the same or a different system.

To provide these functions, an NCF-compliant Web server should support standard HTML, 100% Pure Java, and provide ORB (Object Request Broker) services to allow JavaBeans to identify and communicate within the same server or across multiple servers.

By bringing together a number of associated standards to form the NCF, Web servers and associated code that meet the NCF definition can be sourced from a number of different vendors to build an application across multiple platforms.

**Mail and Groupware Services**

The NCF mail and Groupware services definition includes the standard mail (SMTP, POP, and IMAP 4), news (NNTP), chat (IRC), directory (LDAP), and certificate (X.509) services, as well as calendar and group scheduling protocols. By adopting the NCF definition, developers can flexibly interchange different product offerings for each of the services. As long as the new product adheres to the standards, the change should be invisible to all other parts of the system.

Groupware services provide a shared virtual workspace and enable the description of the document workflow (how documents should be handled as part of a business process). This includes actions or agents that can be used to define how information is presented, processed, protected, and distributed. Collaboration includes the management of different types of documents that are related to a particular project or activity. This could be a library for a reengineering project as well as discussion groups in which members of the project team can exchange updates and ideas.

**Database Services**

The NCF database services definition describes extensions to the Web server environment that support access to data and multimedia content. This support is to be provided using Java, SQL, and the JDBC (Java Database Connectivity) standards. Adhering to the NCF definition will provide a framework to build client- and server-based applications that can access file systems and relational databases. Using these methods, and the transaction services described next, will enable you to develop applications that integrate the data and services delivered by multiple backend systems, such as your current customer database or accounting systems.

**Transaction Services**

The NCF transaction services define how the Web server can be extended to provide access to transaction systems; for example, financial environments in which multiple activities must be completed as a single transaction.

By using the Enterprise JavaBeans support for transactions, application developers can declare when a transaction begins and ends. These calls are propagated through other called systems, ensuring the transaction integrity. If the transaction fails, all systems involved in the transaction will "roll-back" any updates or changes, returning all systems back to their original state.

In addition to these components, you should also consider the services and tools that your Internet applications will use or depend on. Given their importance, these elements are also included in the NCF.

**Secure Distributed Network**

The Internet is far from being a homogeneous entity. Where and how you connect is an important part of the service you are delivering.

For internal users there are a set of intranet standards that you should adopt to provide the desired level of performance and security you require. Current Internet protocols on their own do not extend to what is referred to as Quality of Service levels. This is where the network "guarantees" the throughput (how much data) and/or speed of transfer through the network. This and other new services are included in the latest definition of the underlying Internet communication protocols referred to as IPv6 (also IPNG or IP Next Generation). However, adoption of IPv6 has been somewhat slow as people have found new ways to extend the capabilities of the current IPv4 products.

As IPv6 is unlikely to be available to you for external customers, it's important to discuss with your network supplier, ISP or internal IT organization how information will flow from your servers to your customers, employees, and partners around the globe. Additionally, you may also want to contract with a monitoring service that reports regularly on what performance your users are actually seeing in terms of site responsiveness and page load times.

**Systems Management Tools**

Your IT organization or ISP may already have defined its own systems management approach and selected a set of tools. Although these tools are only loosely connected to your application, starting and stopping functions, and monitoring performance, it's essential that they are in place and suitable for the task.

As your site grows, the simple tools used to monitor a single server will not be sufficient to manage multiple servers, perhaps in multiple locations. As you develop your second-generation site plans, review the systems management support.

Specifically, review what happens if a part of the system becomes overloaded, or if a component fails. Ask questions regarding how failure or load problems will be detected, and assess how much human intervention may be required. Given the global nature of the Internet, 24 hours a day, 7 days a week operation is a must—the systems management tools are critical in achieving this level of performance.

**Application Integration**

As discussed earlier, a second-generation site will almost certainly require access to processes and data in the core backend systems. Application integration products, such as IBM's Enterprise Connectors, make it easier to connect your Web environment to these systems.

These products also reduce the level of change required in legacy systems, in effect insulating the core systems from the Web development.

Careful selection of application integration tools and products can reduce development time and provide future flexibility.

**Development Tools**

Your Web developers will have a set of tools that they use today. While most tools are capable of generating standard HTML and Java many also produce code that can only be run on specific Web servers or platforms.

This may not be an issue given the current level of activity on your site. However, you should consider what your needs will be as the load grows and you need to change platforms or add new systems. Your architectural and infrastructure plans may also influence which platforms you would like to use.

Hence, it is important to review which tools you want to be used in developing your site and set guidelines on which of the features are acceptable to ensure the site can be migrated to a different platform if required.

Each of these technology areas represents a critical set of policy decisions for your organization. IBM's NCF provides a framework and guidelines to help ensure that you have considered the key elements necessary to make your site successful. Even in an outsourced environment, these policies should be carefully developed to support the business strategy and technology constraints. Not doing so, or abdicating these responsibilities to the developer alone, is a recipe for future troubles. The right attention to these points at the beginning of your second-generation development will put you in a strong position to support efficient development and future scalability and growth needs.

## Summary

Planning and developing your second-generation site are important steps in evolving your Web presence. Whereas your initial, first-generation site was exploration into what the Internet could offer your business, the second-generation site should benefit from the experience you have gained and a more structured approach to development, as you move core pieces of your business onto the Net.

The Internet offers significant opportunities for you to differentiate your business by making customer service, ecommerce, interactivity, publishing, and technical support available on your Web site. Choosing which functions you move first should be based on your industry, your customers and partners, and your organization's assets and capabilities.

Once you have decided which functions to move to the Web, it's time to plan your architecture. From a single standalone Web server you should decide on how to increase your Internet infrastructure and connect to existing systems. This may result in a multitiered system or migration of the Internet services into your core systems.

Given the pace of change in the business environment and Internet technology, product selection to implement the architecture of a second-generation site should be done according to a defined framework and open standards. This approach will provide greatest flexibility in the products and services that can be used, and scalability as usage grows.

Finally, even in an outsourced environment, your organization should maintain control and a full understanding of each of these areas as you continue to evolve your Web presence, fully integrate the Internet into your business, and become an e-business.

## Checklist

- ☐ Create an inventory of the intellectual capital, know-how, and services that you could make available on your Web site.
- ☐ Identify which functions support your key business drivers, are useful for your target users, and will be supported by your organization.
- ☐ Review each function with the relevant group in your company. For example, specifications for the customer service component of your Web site should be developed in conjunction with your company's customer service department. Don't reinvent the wheel, and focus on function, not the art or the technology.
- ☐ Work with your MIS group and your Web developer to define the architecture for your site. Decide if you want a one-, two-, or three-tier architecture and which systems will need to be interconnected.
- ☐ Use the Network Computing Framework to define your organization's policies for technology selection.
- ☐ Work with your developers to establish guidelines for development to ensure future flexibility and scalability.

chapter

# 12

# Web Resources

**Felix Kramer**
**Constructors**
*felix@constructors.com*

## About This Chapter

You're already a busy person, and now you've got a new assignment: get your company or institution online (or revamp an inadequate Web site). Depending on where you're coming from—top management, marketing, sales, information systems, or human resources—your level of knowledge can vary greatly, as can your budget and in-house resources.

You've probably already checked out publications, Web sites, vendors, and consulting services. But chances are, unless you've been living and breathing HTML for the past few years, you'll need more help to find out the latest wisdom. Nowadays, the issue is no longer how to get information—it's how to navigate your way through the data overload to find what you need.

In the old days, you would start out by deciding whether to look for technical guidance offline or online. When you *really* want to concentrate on a complex or technical subject, you're likely to choose a book or magazine. Yet more and more often, you'll find a hyperlinked, interactive exploration helpful. Fortunately, most publications now have online versions, in which you can find more up-to-date information and useful details that didn't make it onto the printed page.

What follows is a selective list of starting points, not a comprehensive list. We've tried not to clutter this chapter with physical addresses and phone numbers; many of them won't work a few months from now, anyway. Instead, whenever possible, we give you a URL (of course, they change too, but a few minutes with a search engine should bring you what you need).

### About the Author

Felix Kramer has a background in business development and promotion for innovative products and services. His company, Kramer Communications (www.nlightning.com), specializes in online promotion and marketing. In 1997, he started Constructors, an online service linking Web developers across the nation with companies researching firms to assist them in "constructing" their Web sites, intranets or extranets. (Constructors is one of the resources listed below.) A long-time New Yorker, Felix is one of the many converts to West Coast life and is currently a resident of Silicon Valley. In addition to having an excellent pulse on the best information sources for the Web development industry, he is also the author of the first definitive guide to making money on desktop publishing.

### Specialty Web Sites and Hotlists

Most of these resources are intended for developers—but buyers can find much useful information at these sites:

- **Builder.com** (www.builder.com) is C|Net's superb repository of technical information, evaluations of tools and trends, and conferences.
- **CMP Netguide's WebBuilder 101** (www.netguide.com/special/internet/webbuilder/home.html) includes tutorials, tips, and resource lists and is directed to a business audience rather than developers.
- **DevEdge**, Netscape's developer community, features Open Studio (developer.netscape.com/openstudio) and offers tips, tools, news, special discussion areas, discounts, showcase areas, and other services.
- **Developer.com** (www.developer.com) from Earthweb (creators of the Gamelan Java site) provides a community for developers, with conferences, resources, and software.
- **Mainspring** (www.mainspring.com) is aimed at people who plan, design, and build large Internet and intranet sites. It includes very useful editorial material, templates, and conferences. Annual membership is $500.
- **Microsoft Site Builder Network** (www.microsoft.com/sitebuilder) provides resources for all Microsoft Internet-related products, such as ActiveX.
- **Mining Company's** Web design page (webdesign.miningco.com) is one of the largest sets of links to many useful resources on Web development; it also includes features and conferences.
- **Project Cool** (www.projectcool.com) provides thoughtful features about content and technology, advanced tutorials, and conferencing areas. **Devsearch** (www.devsearch.com) is a searchable index of resources at several dozen key developer Web sites (including many that appear on this list).
- **Sun Microsystems Developer Connection** (www.sun.com/developers/developers.html) provides technical support and information for Solaris and Java users.

- **Virtual Promote** (www.virtualpromote.com) offers information about Web site promotion techniques and pointers to resources for Webmasters.
- **Web Review** (webreview.com) provides information services for Web developers, including a design "studio" development workshops, reference guides, and tutorials.
- **WebDeveloper.com** (www.webdeveloper.com) from Mecklermedia offers a newsletter, forums, links to site-authoring tools, and tutorials.
- **Web Developers' Virtual Library** (www.stars.com) offers tutorials, examples, and links to resources for Webmasters and Internet developers—including more than 10 other virtual libraries!
- **Webmonkey** (go.hotwired.com/webmonkey) is HotWired's resource for Web developers. It provides tutorials, lists of recommended tools and books, and links to other developer resources.
- **Web-Vantage** (www.web-vantage.com) tracks emerging technologies for developers and includes a Site Builders Emporium of resources. Annual membership is $89.

### Specialty Services for Web Site Owners Seeking Developers

Currently, the marketplace nexus between buyers and sellers of Web development services is relatively underdeveloped—especially online, where it should be exploding! Here's what's out there right now:

- **Constructors (**www.constructors.com) connects Web site owners and a broad universe of vendors with match-making and follow-up "handholding" services. It includes a searchable database of Web shops and WhoBuiltIt?, which enables visitors to find out who gets the kudos for existing Web sites as well as industry discussion areas. Other resources under development include Web shop profiles.
- **Cyberjunction** (www.cyberjunction.com) offers Web site owners Interactive Blueprints (requests for proposals) and matches them with a group of participating developers.
- **Digital Talent** (www.digitaltalent.com) also matches customers with a selection of participating developers.

## Books

Begin at your bookstore, where you'll find dozens of volumes on most Internet topics. Many cover similar content, yet they differ in presentation, style, audience, and price.

You can also explore the online bookstores. Use Amazon and Barnes & Noble's capabilities to "show me more like this one" and "show me what else people who like this book have liked."

What follows is a series of starting points and personal favorites. The business categories are of primary interest, but because it's difficult to make knowledgeable choices without understanding the tools, we've also included a few top choices in technical areas.

### Business Strategies

- *Inside the Tornado: Marketing Strategies from Silicon Valley's Cutting Edge* by Geoffrey Moore (Harper Business, 1995) and *Crossing the Chasm: Marketing and Selling High-Tech Products to Mainstream Customers* (Harper Business, 1995) are basic texts for anyone interested in the intersection of business, marketing, and technology.
- *Net Gain: Expanding Markets through Virtual Communities* by John Hagel and Arthur Armstrong (www.hbsp.harvard.edu/netgain, Harvard University Press, 1997) is a primer on organizing online communities.
- *Webonomics: The Nine Essential Principles for Growing Your Business on the World Wide Web* by Evan Schwartz (www.webonomics.com, Broadway Books, 1997) is the classic "what works/what doesn't—and why?" primer on e-commerce.

### Design

- *Designing Excellent Websites: Secrets of an Information Architect* is the latest book by useability expert Jakob Nielsen (www.excellentsites.com, New Riders Publishing, 1998). It provides specific guidelines and approaches to effective design.
- *Information Architecture for the World Wide Web* by Louis Rosenfeld and Peter Morville (O'Reilly & Associates, 1997) focuses on incorporating

principles of architecture and library science in designing large sites to improve their useability through understandable hierarchies, design, and searchability.

- *Creative HTML Design, A Hands-on HTML 4 Web Design Manual* by Lynda Weinman and William Weinman (www.htmlbook.com, New Riders Publishing, 1997) is the latest by an industry leader and is a start-to-finish training course for Web design.

### E-Commerce

- *Customer Service on the Internet: Building Relationships, Increasing Loyalty, and Staying Competitive* by Jim Sterne (www.targetmarketing.com, Wiley, 1996) is a key book by a top marketing expert; it includes detailed cost/benefit analyses.
- *Electronic Commerce: A Manager's Guide* by Ravi Kalakota and Andrew Whinston (Addison-Wesley, 1996) is about management and business models, not technology.
- *Web Security and Commerce* by Simson Garfinkel and Gene Spafford (O'Reilly & Associates, 1997) focuses on technologies and strategic steps to reduce risks to systems and individual privacy.

### HTML Language

- *Cye's Definitive HTML Book List* (www.iz.com/books), although not currently being updated, is a useful starting point for finding books on this subject.
- *HTML 3.2 Manual of Style* by Larry Aronson and Joseph Lowery (www.laronson.com, Ziff-Davis, 1997) is a most readable update of one of the first and best guides.
- *Teach Yourself Web Publishing with HTML 4 in 14 Days* by Laura Lemay (www.lne.com/lemay, Sams, 1998) is the latest version of a very popular HTML manual.
- *HTML Sourcebook* by Ian Graham (Wiley, 1998) is another excellent HTML cookbook.

### Intranets and Extranets

- *Building an Extranet: Connect Your Intranet with Vendors and Customers* by Julie Bort and Bradley Felix (www.wiley.com/compbooks/bort, Wiley, 1997) is a relatively nontechnical overview.
- *Building the Corporate Intranet* by Steve Guengerich, Douglas Graham, Mitra Miller, and Skipper McDonald (Wiley, 1998) includes checklists and case studies.
- *The Corporate Intranet* by Ryan Bernard (www.wiley.com/compbooks/bernard, Wiley, 1998) is a very practical and specific introductory overview of intranets.

### Management

- *A Guide to Web Content and Design: 8 Steps to Web Site Success* by Roger Parker (www.rcparker.com, IDG Books, 1997), author of leading books about electronic publishing. This volume goes well beyond design to cover marketing and management as well, from the basics up.
- *Secrets of Successful Web Sites* by David Siegel (www.secretsites.com, 1997) concentrates on 15 in-depth case studies on project management.

### Marketing

- *Web Marketing Cookbook* by Janice King, Paul Knight, and James Mason (Wiley, 1997) includes a CD-ROM with templates and resources.
- *Online Marketing Handbook* by Daniel Janal (1997) is written by one of the industry's top experts.

### Promotion and Measuring Results

- *Getting Hits: The Definitive Guide to Promoting Your Website* by Don Sellers (Peachpit, 1997) is very specific and useable.
- *Increasing Hits and Selling More on Your Web Site* by Greg Helmstetter (www.monsoon.org/book, Wiley, 1997) has many tips that complement Sellers' book.
- *Measuring the Impact of Your Web Site: Proven Yardsticks for Evaluating Customer Impact, Site Evolution, Revenue Growth, ROI* by Robert W.

Buchanon Jr. and Charles Lukaszewski (www.siteimpact.com, Wiley, 1997) focuses on conceptual issues rather than tools.

### Periodicals: Magazines, Newspapers, and E-Zines

Virtually all of these publications have frequently updated versions on the Web, and many have subscription-based weekly e-zines. Publications marked with an asterisk are free to qualified subscribers who fill out an application form. Discounted subscriptions are often available by filling out cards in the magazines or from one of the companies listed at Yahoo under "magazine subscription services." Many of the e-zines are available both by email and at a Web site.

- *@NY* (www.atnewyork.com) is a weekly e-zine from New Paradigm Communications with news and profiles of the entire New York metro area's Silicon Alley community.
- *Alertbox* (www.useit.com/alertbox) is a weekly e-zine by Jakob Nielsen, one of the most perceptive analysts of trends in technology and content on the Web.
- *Business Week* (www.businessweek.com) frequently profiles emerging technology companies, tools, and trends. It charges for some of its information online (at a discount for print subscribers).
- *Byte* (www.byte.com) from McGraw-Hill provided thoughtful, non-hyped, big-picture views of current and future technology. Recently shut down after being acquired by CMP, it may be relaunched.
- *A.Clue* (www.a-clue.com) is a weekly e-zine from journalist Dana Blankenhorn directed at online managers and strategists, exploring who is clued in and who is clueless in bringing businesses online.
- *Computerworld* (www.computerworld.com) is a semitechnical weekly from International Data Group (IDG) covering business and technology.
- *Fast Company* (www.fastcompany.com) profiles "smart businesses" with an emphasis on networks and technology for a general business audience.
- *Fortune* (fortune.com) hosts the perceptive Stewart Alsop, veteran commentator on emerging trends and technologies, twice a month.

- *Infoworld** (www.infoworld.com) from IDG is a platform-agnostic industry weekly featuring pull-no-punches columnists Bob Metcalfe, Nicholas Petreley, and others, for anyone interested in staying on top of the latest developments in computing.
- *Internet Standard* (www.internet-standard.com) from IDG is a new weekly competitor to *Internet World* that is directed at business readers.
- *Internet Week,** formerly *Communications Week* (www.internetwk.com), from CMP Publications focuses primarily on networks; for technically advanced readers.
- *Internet World,** formerly *Web Week* (www.internetworld.com), from Mecklermedia remains the industry's leading publication for business and technical audiences.
- *Retro-push* (www.theobvious.com), a weekly e-zine from Michael Sippey for online managers and technologists, explores what does and doesn't work online.
- *NeTProfessional* (www.NeTProLive.com) focuses on tools and techniques and is directed mainly at Macintosh-based developers.
- *Profit** (1-800-672-2531) is a nontechnical quarterly from Oracle Corporation focusing on case studies about saving money using database software and technology.
- *Red Herring* (www.herring.com) covers technology for investors and periodically produces *Hits,* a supplement profiling successful businesses on the Internet.
- *San Jose Mercury News* (www.mercurycenter.com) has extensive Internet-related reporting in its "Business" and "Technology" sections for general business and consumer audiences.
- *Silicon Alley Reporter* (www.siliconalleyreporter.com) has a daily e-zine bulletin and a monthly magazine covering the entire New York metro area's Silicon Alley community.
- *The New York Times* (www.nytimes.com/yr/mo/day/cyber/indexcyber.html); the print version features media on Mondays and technology on Thursdays, for general business and consumer audiences.

- *Upside** (www.upside.com) reports on technology companies, with an emphasis on startups, for general business readers.
- *The Wall Street Journal* (wsj.com) features technology on Thursdays and runs a periodic "Net-Interest" section. It charges for some of its information online; charges are discounted for print subscribers.
- *Web Techniques* (www.webtechniques.com) from Miller Freeman covers technical issues for developers.
- *WebMaster** (www.web-master.com), from IDG's *CIO Communications* publication, focuses on case studies of Web sites, primarily for business readers.
- *Wired* (www.wired.com) offers profiles of industry leaders and technology trends for general business and consumer audiences.
- *ZD Inter@active Week** (www.interactive-week.com) is a relatively nontechnical publication and is a must-have for anyone tracking Internet technology, content, and commerce.
- *ZD Internet Magazine* (www.zdimag.com) presents comparative product reviews, case studies, and surveys of trends for business readers.
- *ZD TV,* "your computer channel," promises 24 hours per day of computer information, linked to its Web site at www.zdtv.com; for business and consumer audiences.
- *ZD Yahoo Internet Life* (yil.com) is a consumer monthly about popular Web sites.
- *ZD's e-Commerce Alert* (www.ecommercealert.com) is a print and online monthly publication highlighting new market trends and technologies for business strategists.

## Daily Intelligence Sources

You have to decide how you like your news served. You can customize the topics and organization of your news at Excite (myexcite.com) or Yahoo (my.yahoo.com) and at some of the sites listed below:

- **Headliner** (www.lanacom.com/hlnewsdown.html) provides customized streams of headlines from only one source, NewsEdge, to your browser.

- If you want to get your news by email, check out **Infobeat** (www.infobeat.com) and the three-times-weekly **Edupage** (www.edupage.edu).
- Providing a stream of the latest news from single sources are **C|Net** (www.news.com), which is perhaps the most easily navigable site, or **CNN** (cnn.com/TECH) and the daily newspapers listed previously.
- Computer publishing giants **CMP** (www.cmpnet.com), **IDG** (www.idg.net), **Mecklermedia** (www.internetnews.com), and **Ziff-Davis** (www.zdnet.com) provide both central news areas and specialized sites for each publication.

Roundup sites that pull information from many sources are found at these locations:

- **Internet Wire** (www.gina.com) tracks and archives technology news.
- **Newshub** (www.newshub.com/tech/bytime.html) is our personal favorite for its range and speed in loading.
- **Newsbot (**www.newsbot.com) tracks technology news and offers a downloadable personal agent to customize news.
- **NewsPage** (www.newspage.com) from NewsEdge gives you many ways to customize what you see, specifying particular industries, products, and companies.

### Trade Shows, Conferences, and Seminars

There's no better way to get the pulse of this industry than to go to a trade show or a large conference with an exhibits area. Most trade shows have a large accompanying program of seminars, workshops, and tutorials. Increasingly, all but the most technical events have a strong business focus. Be sure to bring a small stapler with you to the show to keep product info and business cards together, as well as some file folders if you're out of town, so you can organize your notes and papers back in your hotel room.

For a rundown of events, check **WebMaster's** all-in-one-list (www.cio.com/WebMaster/wm_calendar.html), **IBM's** customized Java-based

ConferenceTracker (www.conferencetracker.com), or **CMP's** categorized TechWeb Calendar (www.techcalendar.com/).

Top events include the following:

- **Internet and Electronic Commerce Conference and Exposition** (www.iec-expo.com) is sponsored by dci.com every April in New York.
- **Internet Commerce Expos** and **Extranet Expo** (www.idg.com/ice), sponsored by IDG, are held twice yearly.
- **Internet Engineering Consortium** hosts interactive online tutorials on technical topics, sponsored by major corporations, at (www.webproforum.com).
- **Internet World** is the leading Internet general interest trade show. Mecklermedia holds local versions in several dozen countries. In North America, locations and schedules are usually Toronto in February, Los Angeles in April, Chicago in July, and New York in October.
- **Java One, the Worldwide Java Developer Conference** (java.sun.com/javaone) is held annually in San Francisco and is primarily for technologists.
- **Seybold Seminars** (www.seyboldseminars.com), held in New York and San Francisco, focuses on all facets of information delivery.
- **Web Design & Development Conference** (www.mfweb.com) is sponsored by Miller Freeman and held twice yearly, most recently in Boston and San Francisco.
- **Web.Builder** (www.webuilder.com), C|Net's conference primarily for technologists, is held periodically in various locations; most recently, Web.Builder was held in New Orleans and San Francisco.
- **Web-X** (www.shownet.com/webx/webx.html), sponsored by Miller Freeman, is held yearly in conjunction with PC Expo in New York City.

### Industry Analysts

Industry analysts can help you decide what technology trends are significant and which are flashes in the pan. If you can't afford their high-priced reports, you may get some insight from the free summaries and excerpts offered at their Web sites. To understand their specialties and services, check out these sites:

- **Aberdeen Group** (www.aberdeen.com)
- **Forrester Research** (www.forrester.com)
- **Gartner Group** (www.gartnergroup.com)
- **Giga Information Group** (www.gigaweb.com)
- **International Data Corporation** (www.idcresearchl.com)
- **Intelliquest** (www.intelliquest.com)
- **Jupiter Communications** (www.jup.com)
- **Meta Group** (www.metagroup.com)
- **Yankee Group** (www.yankeegroup.com)
- **Zona Research** (www.zona.com)

### Trade Associations and User Groups

These organizations are evolving almost as rapidly as the Internet. They are generally good places to get a view of industry trends. If you persist in your search, from these groups and discussion areas you'll find a place that meets your needs: for professional contacts to get work or find freelancers; for colleagues to share experiences and war stories; for experts to help you out of a jam or check out your latest brainstorm.

Many of these organizations have both online and physical incarnations in the form of mailing lists (listservs) and regional or local chapters or events. You may find that attending local chapter meetings will be the best way to determine the value of their services:

- **Association of Internet Professionals** (www.association.org) is the leading effort to organize people in the industry. It was formed by a merger of the Internet Developers Association, the International Society of Internet Professionals, and the Webmasters Guild. Don't miss their Qualifying Document (www.association.org/english/services/esp/q1.html) for purchasers of services from Web developers.

- **HTML Writers Guild** (www.hwg.org) is an international user group serving the needs of individual Web designers rather than Web development companies.
- **International Interactive Computing Society** (www.iics.org) has been in existence longer than any other group of multimedia developers and has several dozen chapters worldwide.
- **Internet Professional Publishers Association** (www.ippa.org) is a user group that highlights outstanding Web design efforts.
- **Lynda Weinman's Web Design List** (www.webmonster.net/lists) has over 2,500 subscribers and provides tips and job listings for Web professionals.
- **National Association of Webmasters** (www.naw.org) is directed at individuals and organizations who create, manage, or market Web sites.
- **SigGraph** (www.siggraph.org), the Association for Computer Machinery's Special Interest Group on Computer Graphics, provides information on national conferences, local chapters, and other useful resources.

### Regional User Groups

Regional user groups usually combine face-to-face meetings, networking events, and listservs. You may find additional pages by searching Yahoo for Internet user groups:

- **NoEnd** (www.noend.org) is a small San Francisco Bay area group that holds meetings and has a medium-traffic listserv.
- **Multimedia Development Group** (www.mdg.org) is a San Francisco Bay area interactive media trade association with a list of members and other services.
- **New Media Association** (www.nynma.org) is a New York area networking organization with frequent meetings and an annual printed member directory.
- **Worldwide Web Artists Consortium** (www.wwwac.org) is a high-energy group that holds general and special interest group meeting in New York City and has a high-traffic listserv.

- **NW Cyberartists** holds meetings in the Northwestern United States and has a medium-traffic mailing list. To join, send email to listproc@u.washington.edu; leave the subject blank, and in the message write "Subscribe cyberartists [Your Name]."

### Discussions and Communities

Usenet newsgroups, including comp.infosystems.www.authoring (and others in the infosystems.www hierarchy), are places to search for specific topics and to post queries—but with no guarantee about the professional level of anyone who responds. They have in large part been superseded by conference areas at such Web sites as these:

- **Netscape's Professional Connections** area (form.netscape.com/directory/community/html/pc_unreg_main.html) holds conferences to discuss technology, content, and what does and doesn't work online, for business and technical audiences.
- *Online Insider* e-zine (www.onlineinsider.com) from Robert Seidman is supplemented by provocative Insider Talk discussions, for business managers and strategists.
- **ProjectCool's Peoplesphere** (www.projectcool.com/peoplesphere/forums) hosts discussions, mostly on technical issues.
- **Builder Buzz** (buzz.builder.com) from C|Net hosts discussions on technical and business issues.

### Vendor Lists

You can find lists and directories of major vendors online. These lists can be especially useful because they are more frequently updated than print equivalents:

- *NETMarketing NetB2B Directory* (www.netb2b.com/cgi-bin/cgi_dd) from *Ad Age* publishes city-by-city listings of Web shops that include the companies' self-descriptions.
- **Channel Seven** (www.channelseven.com) provides a list of the top 100 interactive ad agencies.

- **Clickz** (www.clickz.com) includes profiles of leading interactive agencies.
- **Constructors** (www.constructors.com) sponsors a searchable list of Web development companies. They are currently working on profiles of companies as well.
- *Directory of Interactive Marketing* (www.adweek.com) from *Ad Week* lists many Web site development companies and is available in print or on CD.
- *Internet Media Sourcebook* (www.hi-techmedia.com/main2.htm) is a book with an online version, covering many categories of vendors.
- *Internet World's* (previously *Web Week's*) **Second Annual Web Design Survey** (www.internetworld.com/print/1997/12/01/undercon/19971201-webdesign.html) lists over 100 Web shops with Fortune 1000 customers.
- **Ultimate Webdeveloper List (**www.webdesignlist.com) is a database of Web shops and their specialties.
- *ZD Internet Computing* magazine (www.zdnet.com/icom/content/anchors/199804/06/best.20) includes profiles of leading Web shops.

# chapter 13

# The Web Roundtable

**June 5, 1998, New York City**

The goal of the Web Roundtable is to provide a forum to discuss practical nuts-and-bolts business policies and practices taking place in the Web development community today.

The Roundtable was initially launched to offer some of the authors in this book the chance to comment on subjects that were outside the scope of the specific chapters that they wrote for this book. We also had as a goal the notion that we could get more than one opinion on some of the topics covered in this book—an important consideration, given that anyone who has ever built a Web site knows that there are dozens of ways to accomplish the same goal. We also wanted to see what type of ideas about our industry would evolve from a more in-depth group discussion. Although the panel for the Web Roundtable, for the most part, consisted of the authors in this book, we did add two individuals to the discussion for the purpose of attempting to get as diverse a range of opinions as possible.

The Web Roundtable transcript presented in this chapter is part of an ongoing series of discussions that, in the future, will include such topics as the role of traditional advertising agencies in the Web development process, budgeting and billing Web services, developing sound legal contracts, and more. Transcripts from future discussions will be made available either in print or on the Web. For more information on the ongoing Roundtable discussions, send an email to jpfrenza@earthpledge.org.

## Participants

**Moderator:** J. P. Frenza, editor of *Buying Web Services: The Survival Guide to Outsourcing*

**Panelists:**

Jerry Spiegel, attorney and author of Chapter 6, "Covering Your Legal Bases"

Dev Mukherjee, author of Chapter 11, "Going Forward: Next Generation Sites and Building an E-Business"

Julia Rubinic, author of Chapter 8, "When Things Go Wrong"

Vlad Edelman, senior producer of new media at CBS

Chris Bryant, author of Chapter 5, "Infrastructure and Site Hosting"

Lara Stein, president of IXL New York

Peter Seidler, author of Chapter 4, "Understanding Design"

## Overview: Key Issues in Outsourcing

**Frenza:** This book is about the process of outsourcing Web development services—from developing a concept, understanding design, and crafting a legal contract to project management and technology assessment. I'd like to go around the table and ask each of you to take five minutes and outline your top three keys that every client should pay attention to when outsourcing their site—things they should look out for, issues they should look to their Web developer to address, and so forth.

**Bryant:** I'd like to address what I see as some of the issues that clients are likely to fail at when it comes to the Web development process.

I think the first and most important failure that a client can make is to fail to set clear business objectives for their Web site. I think the second potential failure concerns the failure to do the appropriate planning in terms of the strategy for the site and how that strategy takes into account the issues of creative, business, and technology development.

Finally, and I am starting to see this one become more and more prevalent as of late, is the failure to recognize that once your Web site is complete, it is not actually done. What I mean by that is the fact that a Web site doesn't end when a contract with a Web developer ends—and the costs don't end when you perceive that you are done with your Web developer. In fact, they've just begun. Failure to address the ongoing nature of Web sites, whether it is from the perspective of content or budget and cost, is becoming increasingly acute.

**Seidler:** Chris has a list remarkably similar to mine.

I would say the first, biggest failure that I see happening with regard to how clients are going about outsourcing their sites is the absence of some kind of an Internet strategy which cuts across all of the divisions of the company.

Second, I would say the failure to develop the idea of a "scope's document," which is critical. The client should expect to work with the developer to produce a scope document that details every aspect of the project and the plan for the implementation of the project. If those things are not created at the outset, there are likely to be problems during implementation.

Finally, I would add, this idea that the Web site itself, or let's say any digital change that is happening to the company, is something that is going to keep going and that it is not a one-time process. Transformation is ongoing, and that fact needs to be recognized.

**Frenza:** I should note for the record that many Web shops use the term "scoping," which refers to the process of working with a client to define the exact nature of a Web site or the final Web site's definition in the form of a document that can be shared with both the client and the developer.

**Stein:** I would say the first problem is not setting a long-term vision for a project. I think that many companies going into this medium right now are looking at it from a very short-term perspective. It is almost like they have a knee-jerk reaction to the Web. They are looking around and they are seeing everybody getting into it, and they know they need to be there, but they are not taking the time out to look at their business and get a good understanding of where the whole industry is going and how to leverage it.

**Frenza:** Do you have any thoughts on how many years a company should include in its plan?

**Stein:** I think three to four years, which is really making them look into a crystal ball, but at least they are blue-skying. They can always step back from there.

I also believe that documentation and creating a very specific scoping document is key because it definitely does set expectations on both the client and the developer side.

Finally, an important part from the client's perspective is really looking at what the project is and where the balance between technology and creativity lies and using that balance to determine the type of partner they need based on that. I say that because I think that from a marketing standpoint a lot of entertainment clients, for example, are targeting a very different set of people, and having a developer that can create and develop the right sensibility and the right technology is very important.

**Edelman:** I'm going to split my thoughts a little bit between clients and developers.

I think that on the client side, one of the biggest problems is unrealistic expectations. You have to come into this process with basically what you want to accomplish, what you are willing to spend on it, and be completely open to discussion as to how much it is going to cost. That, in my mind, is the biggest problem on the client side.

The second is not really thinking far enough ahead. Too many clients come in thinking of Web sites in the short term, or technology solutions in general, that are in the short term. Too many developers let clients get away with that. They are not telling the client that they are thinking in the short term and that a certain solution is only going to work for three months and that they will be back asking for another contract. I think the client would be better served if the developer said, "This is extremely short term, we recommend a better long-term solution."

On the developer side, I just want to add that I think the biggest problem is the overstated ability to deliver and poor project management. I think the key on the developer side has to be an unbelievable ability to manage the project. Remember, as a client, I am farming something out for the specific reason that I don't want to have to manage it.

**Rubinic:** I think that managing expectations with respect to both the time element of a project as well as the budget aspect of the project are important.

Also, I think that clients need to know that this process is not easy and they should be open and willing to hear about a project's potential limitations and really make an effort to understand what they might be. Speaking entirely from the client's point of view, I would say that, in a way, during the pitch, I would rather hear about potential limitations up front rather than, "Sure, we can do that." And I would advise clients to probably pick their developer, whoever it may be, based on the realities that they are telling me that I have to understand as well as on timeline and on price issues.

Second, I think it is also important for clients to educate themselves about the process of Web development and gain an in-depth understanding of their project and the ramifications of decisions that they might make along the way. As a developer, we know that we are an industry where a lot of people do not completely understand the technology. We have an obligation to not only tell our clients about the key things that they have to approve, but also we have to go a step further. We have to be willing to say, "This is an important issue, this is what we are doing, this is what we are going to do next, and more importantly, this is what happens if you change your mind." I think it is the client's responsibility that if they are missing that information, if it is not conveyed or they don't completely understand it, to really, truly seek it out and try to understand what the ramifications of every decision are for the project as a whole.

Finally, and I write about this in my chapter, is the issue of treating the developer as a partner. It doesn't necessarily mean micromanaging them, but if the company decides upon a branding initiative, then the people who are building your Web site are just as important to that initiative as any group internally in the company. Clients need to be sure to view their developer as a partner and to convey important information to them. In some sense, Web developers are as involved in the company's initiative at a lot of levels as their ad agency, maybe more so.

**Mukherjee:** I think every client should set very specific business objectives, but not just a general objective—I think it should be quantifiable.

Maybe not a complete return on investment—for example, "I am going to spend a million dollars, here's how I am going to make a million dollars back." Something more realistic: "I expect to get 5,000 leads, or 200 new partners, or 50 new sales from my site." You may end up changing those goals, but at every step of the project you should, at the very least, have objectives and have them perfectly communicated within your organization and to your developer partner.

Second, I think there should be very clear ownership within the client. Step one should be to pick the smartest, most Internet-savvy person you can within your organization and say, "You are it, and if this Web site fails, you are fired." I say this because it is too easy to get distracted, it is too easy to have fragmentation within your organization and have five or six months go by with no results. Unless you anoint someone to do the job, the project is going to fail. As a continuation of that thought, if I was starting our Web development all over again I would, Day One, appoint an interactive architect to manage the structure of the project. Whether that was someone I hired in my own company, or someone that I essentially pinched, borrowed, or rented from my developer doesn't matter. The point is, there should be someone who is paid to be separate from the development activity and would serve as the architect of the project.

Third, I would, from the beginning, set technology standards for the project. Because this industry is moving so quickly, I would try as be as open as possible right now so that I don't lock myself into a non-open standard—whether it is an IBM product or a Microsoft product, it doesn't matter. Openness is important in an industry where flexibility is key and we don't know where we are going to end up.

We and our partners, and even some of our competitors, have taken Web sites or other applications, where there are say a hundred, fifty, or twenty-five NT servers, and migrated them back to mainframe solutions. This is necessary because what happens is that some small part of the organization starts this Web thing and then all of a sudden, the business says, "Hey, we are really dependent on this Web thing," and then they have to apply the same standards that they apply to the rest of their core systems. The thing has to work, there should be data integrity, and there should be security.

**Spiegel:** Just yesterday, I heard something that I hear not too infrequently, which is that people don't really like lawyers. I don't understand why [laughter].

But seriously, the nature of this industry is such that whether you realize it or not, you have placed in the hands of lawyers more power than they have ever had before in the history of man. This is true because every asset that is created today on the Web is a virtual one, and it exists only by virtue of intellectual property law. The idea that some people used to have about the Web being this great anarchy with no law is the most absurd concept, because the Web really exists only because intellectual property laws exist. Otherwise, it would be pure chaos.

So I think it is important that clients find a lawyer that they are comfortable working with, someone that they can pick up the phone or send an email and get a useful and intelligent response to their questions. So, I guess my first point is: Find a lawyer. You really cannot exist or function in this business without one.

Number two, make sure that your lawyer understands what is going on in the industry and also understands the dynamics of the relationship, the dynamics of the medium, and also the dynamics of how business models are changing as a result of the digital revolution. This is important because a client wants to get a certain job done in the middle of all of this change and uncertainty, so they need someone who understands the rule of law, but also the needs of business. It is important to get the job done, but you want to also make sure that you are protected.

I think the third thing is that at some point everyone needs an understanding as to what intellectual property is at some fundamental level. It is an essential aspect of business and life going into the 21st century. I think that bringing this education to youngsters would go a long way toward training the work force for the next generation in these fundamentals. At the very least, clients should be familiar with these concepts because they are the business tools they will need to use.

**Mukherjee:** If I could jump in—I agree. As information workers, all we have is not our manufacturing skills, but virtual knowledge. The other thing that I would mention is that anyone getting on to the Web should consult a lawyer on the issue of privacy. There are a lot of people who are going to get sued in this medium because they don't have adequate privacy protection policies in place.

**Spiegel:** Absolutely! But there are lots of issues that remain to be resolved. Back in 1990, I think it was, the Cubby case was decided (*Cubby vs. CompuServe*), which is the first real online libel decision. No one paid any attention to it, but it was the only piece of law that existed until 1994—the only piece of law that addressed any of the issues we are discussing here. The explosion of law, and I use that term very broadly, is astonishing, and that is going to continue, and we are all going to have to learn to live with that and run our businesses within that context.

### The Process of Web Development

**Frenza:** I would like to shift the discussion to the issue of process, because this book is really about educating businesses about the process of building a Web site. I'd like us to focus our discussion on what we perceive as the most important processes involved in Web development. For example, is the design process the most important? Technology on the back end? Site infrastructure?

**Mukherjee:** I think that clearly one of the most important processes that a client needs to concern itself with is the whole issue of developing and defining a company's business objective in this medium. What is the return on investment (ROI)?

I recently read an interesting report from Gartner which indicated that by the end of this year, most of the so-called experimental Web projects—and by that I mean the ones that up until now have really fueled the industry; for example, those projects where no one is worried about the business objective or the ROIs will come to term. People will be asking, "What is happening here? What are we going to get out of this?"

We are now at the point where a number of companies are going to have to really start answering the question of, "Okay, we've spent five million on our interactive strategy, what are we really getting in return?" You are also starting to see a number of companies taking a long, hard look at their competition and asking what are they doing, what is their big play, and what does that mean for their business.

**Stein:** This is interesting to me because I have been on both sides of the fence here—as a buyer at Microsoft and now as a developer at IXL.

I think the biggest challenge in an outsourcing relationship is the process of setting clear expectations for both the client and the developer. On the developer side, it is very important to listen to the client and to, more importantly, listen to what the client says its expectations are and clearly define those expectations in a manner in which both sides are comfortable.

In this business, it is very easy to get "creep" in a project—that is, the scope of the project continues to grow. The more documented you can be up front and the more specific you can be up front—whether that is a comprehensive scoping document or not—you have a better chance of making sure that important expectations have been met.

On the flip side, clients have to make every effort to be as clear as they possibly can, and it is often very difficult because so many of the larger Web projects are governed by committees, so you have a lot of different voices that must be taken into account.

What we have found at IXL is that a successful project has to have a one-to-one, point-to-point contact, and responsibility for both the client and the developer is probably the best way to ensure objectives are met.

**Rubinic:** I totally agree with that. At RGA Interactive, we are always demanding a single point of contact, and that single point of contact should be responsible for incorporating and managing all of the input from everybody on their team. You can't try to satisfy everyone on the client's team individually.

**Edelman:** I have to agree that the process of setting expectations Lara talks about is really important. I'd like to add that in a lot of the cases, it is the fault of the buyer in shifting the objectives of the project. For example, the client walks into a conference room and says, "We want this and that," and two weeks later what the client wants is completely different.

But I would like to add that the biggest problem that I have encountered is managing expectations on the developer's side. Developers who don't know what they can deliver are, in my mind, the biggest problem. You have a great deal of cases where there are developers who promise they can meet expectations, when in reality, they can't deliver.

**Mukherjee:** I find that interesting given that one of the reasons you are outsourcing is to take advantage of some previous experience that the developer is supposed to bring to the project.

**Seidler:** The process of setting expectations is really about the process of developing a relationship. When you think of the entire team being made up of the client and the supplier, then we need to understand how these different thinking styles work together to create something new. There needs to be an understanding on both sides.

**Stein:** I think that part of the reason you see this roll-up strategy going on in the industry is because of this issue of expectation. Clients come to a relationship with a certain set of expectations, and they want to partner with a developer that has the specific skill set they want to meet their goals and objectives. We are living in a world where there are so many types of technologies that for one small shop to be able to be an expert in all of those different areas is very, very difficult. Larger Web developers have the ability, for example, that if we don't have a specific skill set in New York in a certain AT&T solution, our office in Atlanta may.

**Bryant:** Our experience has been that those client expectations are best met by documentation. The most important thing that we, or any developer, can do is to create documentation to set expectations up front and make sure that expectations are clearly addressed in writing.

For example, when we work with a client, we give them a project scope document that clearly defines roles and responsibilities on each side. You also get a number of other documents, straight down to a functional specification that clearly indicates this is the definition of the project.

With that definition comes a clear delineation of the expectations. Right from the beginning, the precedent is clearly set that if requirements, and hence expectations, change from what we have agreed upon, then there will be additional costs, and that may affect other aspects of the project as well. But it is all in writing, and it is all clear to the client. I would encourage every client to get that sort of documentation from their developer.

I think there is one other additional issue which needs to be addressed, which is also similar to what we are calling "the expectation consideration."

Many times, when you contract with a developer or supplier to do a job, you get a scope of costs set over a fixed period of time. For instance, you have a relationship with a client, and the client says we are going to work with you over the period of a year and it is going to cost X amount. The thing that a lot of clients don't realize is that once that period ends, the costs associated with that product do not. In fact, they may increase. We try to approach our clients from a longer-term perspective. A lot of times when you are trying to make the sell, it is not the most advantageous thing to say, "By the way, over three years the site is really going to cost you five million as opposed to three million." That is another aspect of setting expectations that is equally important. Clients would do well to look long and hard at the cost expectation up front as well.

### Finding the Right Developer

**Frenza:** I think that another difficult challenge that clients face in regard to outsourcing their Web site has to do with the simple process of finding a Web developer. There are places in New York City and San Francisco where you can throw a rock down the street and there will be a good chance that you will hit a Web developer. The real trick is finding the right Web developer. What advice would this group offer to companies looking to find the best outsourcing partner?

**Stein:** I think clients need to recognize that it is a balancing act between creativity and technology that they should be looking for.

Often, shops—whether they are small, medium, or large—specialize in very different kinds of services. I was talking with one of our clients the other day, and they had a definite interest in working with a cutting-edge shop. But at the same time, they need somebody at the end of the day that is going to be able to do legacy integration and various other skill sets they require for their business.

So I think that for the client it is a constant dichotomy—do I go with a cool, hip shop, or do I go with something that is a bit more staid but stable? I would say that as a client, I would want to know that the developer I am working with has processes in place and they have been delivering solutions over a long period of time. A demonstrated ability to make on-time deliverables is probably the most important thing to consider when picking a developer.

**Edelman:** It is a tough issue and one that as a buyer of Web services I address with my colleagues at CBS on a frequent basis.

What we have found is that a lot of developers will come in and tell you how great the design is going to be and how phenomenal the technology is going to be, but those are issues that are less important for our goals than one would think.

We really need a developer to come in and say, "What do you want to say?" so that we can work with them effectively to figure out the best way to say it. It is like the great IBM commercials where the two people are sitting in front of the computer talking about how they can make their logo spin, catch on fire, and attract people's attention. Then they stop when they can't answer the simple question of how they can sell stuff on their Web site.

**Mukherjee:** Well, thanks for the great plug [laughter].

I do think the client is responsible for misdirecting the nature of the search. If the client is unfamiliar with the real value of the Web as a medium, they are the ones that encourage developers in the wrong direction when they are impressed not by solutions but by those spinning logos. If you are an auto dealer, you really want to work with your Web developer and focus the discussion on how you can use the Web to structure and extend your business. The discussion should not be about the technology. It should be about who you are and where you are going.

**Stein:** But I do think expertise should be an important question that clients should ask. For example, at IXL we focus on a couple of verticles where we go very deep—we have two companies that just focus on the travel market. When we go into a meeting with travel clients and we've already worked with lots of hotel chains and lots of airlines, we know their business intimately—to a degree that is a huge advantage for our clients. Understanding a client's business as best you can and going in with an intelligent pitch that really tells your client how to use the Web as a marketing tool is essential. That is what clients should be looking for.

**Frenza:** Should a client be looking for a developer with an expertise in their specific industry?

**Stein:** Well, as developers we are expected to know such a broad scope of businesses, and it is not like you are in the advertising business, where you might only be responsible for the development and projection of something like brand. Often, you are digging very deep into the core of a company. You might be involved in their IT strategies, their infrastructure, their sales, marketing, and so on. You are really fundamentally changing how that business is going to operate into the future. In order to do that in an intelligent way, you have got to know their business as well as they know their business, to create the vision they need for the next century.

**Rubinic:** It depends on how involved you are. Sometimes you work with the ad agencies for the client directly and they handle the branding the creative platforms, and all of that documentation is given to us to implement. Sometimes we do take a step back and include an account rep who understands their industry. It depends at what level you are when creating the strategy.

**Seidler:** I am not sure that it is necessary for the developer to have the experience with the same type of client, but I do think it is important to find out whether or not the developer has the team with the capacity to develop the knowledge necessary to do the work in order to understand the business.

**Mukherjee:** I think every client needs to be told that they are going to have to invest an awful lot to help the developer understand a lot more about your business than just what industry you are in. In fact, it appears the Web is so much the integration point across so many aspects of a business. Your Web developer or Web partner is going to end up knowing more about your total business than your ad agency or any other partner that you might have.

**Edelman:** You also look for, specifically, not people who have experience in your industry as much as people who are known to have done certain things well. For example, who does the best database?

**Stein:** At the end of the day, you want your site to be able to function. You want to make sure that it is an easy site to use and that people can navigate through it and there isn't a big wait. If it is a database-driven site, a huge part of that is database integration, and at IXL that is one area where we also have a huge amount of specialties. But at the same time, I think that, for especially an entertainment client, having a great front end that extends their brand is also a crucial part. So a client must really weigh the technology versus the creative and making sure that you are picking a partner that can deliver both. Or you can go to two different companies: one for functionality and integration and the other one for design.

**Spiegel:** This is one of the ways in which the world is changing because of the convergence of media and transaction.

Historically, when you look at the advertising industry, there developed over time relationships between certain agencies and certain clients, some of which were incredibly successful and went on for twenty, thirty, forty, fifty years, and some of them are still going on today. There are fewer today than there were ten years ago for various reasons, but I think that what is going on with interactive media raises that to a whole new level.

It really is a question of bringing your media partner—the Web company—in more than just as a media partner. You are really asking them to be part of your business strategy. This means, I think, that just as I have to understand what business my client is in so that I can be a good lawyer, developers will have to really learn and understand their clients' business. I think this is necessary because they have to make decisions, offer up recommendations, and give advice which really affects the nature of the client's business.

**Bryant:** I think that what is happening right now is a function of the youth of the Web industry and its relative newness. People right now are differentiating by skill sets, whereas in the future there is going to be a vertical segmentation of companies by type of industry. Technology integration is simply going to be a minimum level of entry.

**Stein:** IXL right now is focusing on five verticles, and we have a breadth of products—everything from laptop presentations to database integration. I've also spent the last few months that I have been on board layering and putting into place some world-class designers, so we have that aspect as well, and we also have rather extensive client services. So, at the end of the day, we can go to a client and say, "We know your business extremely well and you can come to us regardless of what your digital needs are."

**Mukherjee:** I don't think it is going to be possible for a company to do that successfully. At the risk of making a prediction, I think you will see, in the next two to three years, separate companies. There will be those who are interactive architects and those companies who specialize in understanding the business transformation side of it who will act as integrators to the services that Web developers provide today. The reason I say that is that is that it is clearly too big a stretch for one company to do all of that well.

**Stein:** Well, we don't look at ourselves as a Web developer, we look at ourselves as a technology company, and we layer the other services on top of the core strategy of what we do.

**Mukherjee:** But it is like saying to Ogilvy & Mather, or any other ad agency, "I want you to be responsible for business transformation as well as brand stewardship." The people are just too different. It won't work.

**Stein:** I understand your point, but IXL's culture did not grow out of a design agency.

**Mukherjee:** True, but still you can't have your design folks and your technology folks and these business transformation experts under the same management. The businesses are too different.

**Seidler:** Dev, I think what you are touching on is this idea which is floating around in our industry regarding who specifically owns the client relationship. Is it the consultant? Is it the ad agency? Is it the developer? On top of that, there is an emerging kind of company that will be the integrator, while at the same time, there will continue to be these very focused database shops, design shops, and the emerging information architect company as an additional layer.

**Mukherjee:** Peter, that is a very interesting thought. And, in some companies, those information architects will also work for the same company. By that I mean they will work in a different group at the client's company.

It is a very difficult thing to pull off under one roof. As we say in the pure consulting area, all of those businesses that try to have that and accounting, or have that and something else, have ended up fragmenting, splitting, or just fading away.

**Bryant:** I think that is very insightful. As our companies try to transform to the next level, I think that is something we are all struggling with: how do you become an integrator and a developer under the same roof? Their motives should be very different. And the question is, how do you maintain that autonomy under the same umbrella? I don't know that I agree with you completely that it can't be done; I think there are some ways, but it definitely needs to be looked at as two separate businesses.

**Seidler:** I agree, and I think that it is because, in a way, we are really talking about two separate functions. One is the business strategy side, and the other is the implementation side. On the implementation side, my opinion is that you can't separate technology and design.

**Rubinic:** This all might be true, but I don't think the industry is ready for that until clients become more savvy with how to manage all of these different aspects if they are going to go to different companies.

One thing that I find very interesting about working at RGA is that we have a great studio side that does special effects, broadcasting, and commercials—they are pretty well known. Their big joke is that unlike the interactive side, they have clients that have been doing this for years and there are processes in place. So on their side of the business, to go to different shops for different things is very simple because they have been doing it for years. And then they look us and we are just trying to teach a client what a Web site means in some cases and there are no processes in place—there aren't even conventions developed yet.

So you have to get to the point where there is an understanding. Skills on the client side are tantamount to the skills in organizing where we would like the industry to be.

**Mukherjee:** That's interesting. So the evolution on the client side is to know enough so that they can hire directly or enough that they can successfully hire a consultant.

### But Do Clients First Need to Know What They Want?

**Frenza:** After they have picked the right developer, does a client need to know what they want to do on the Web? I've heard some developers express the idea that it is preferable if a client has a pretty good handle on what they want to accomplish before they start working with their developer.

**Rubinic:** I disagree with the idea that a client has to come to you with knowledge of either the Web or what they want to do there. I think that is part of the challenge. It's not that we encourage it because it is more of a challenge, but when you can think of structuring the business relationship with a client so that you can encourage them to be a part of the creative process, you will ultimately have a better product.

**Edelman:** Conceptually, it is a good idea to educate the client about what they want, but that is part of the problem of how bad contracts get structured.

For example, I have seen a several situations where a client comes in and doesn't have a confident idea as to what they want to do on the Web. Typically, they wind up with an agreement that had to be continually adjusted almost every week, and they wound up six months behind on their project.

**Spiegel:** I think the scoping idea—which I've recommended to many clients on both sides—is a helpful contractual technique. It enables the client to take the necessary time to develop the concept for what it is that they want to do on the Web, and at the same time it protects the developer by setting the terms of the relationship and defining exactly what the project will be. In that scenario, you really have two phases of the project, with the first phase being essentially the creation of a contract for the scoping document and the second phase being the actual development of the site.

**Seidler:** I agree. From our experience, the Web development industry is moving in that direction—where you have the development of the concept of what needs to be done as a separate process from the actual implementation of the work. In other words, in terms of scoping out the project in the form of a document, it is not simply a one-way conversation—it is part of an ongoing dialogue between the client and the developer.

**Stein:** But I think the separation of the scoping from the project is more possible in some industries than in others. For example, in advertising, I think if you walk in the door and say, "You are going to pay me to scope out your project," it is not going to work. There, you generally tend to bid on jobs. That's the same with the entertainment industry. Unfortunately, developers are out there doing a lot of work before you get any kind of a contract.

**Mukherjee:** But if I am one of your clients and I say, "You need to come in and pitch me five ideas of what you can do to help me," the developer might come in and say, "Well, here are some promotional things that you might do," and so on. So you have a few key ideas to start the process and that then leads into a proposal.

**Stein:** Yes, but certain businesses are more open to that idea than not. I think for the financial institutions, consulting is normal for them. That they would need to spend millions of dollars on consulting is something that they are used to doing. So, if a developer were to come in and say, "we need thirty thousand or fifty thousand dollars to develop a scoping document," it isn't such a big stretch.

**Bryant:** I think the point is that there is a time in which the Web site actually begins to be built and a lot of time before that, before the client brings a developer into the process. We all know that there is this tremendous amount of planning that goes into the Web development process, whether the client does it themselves or whether they hire someone to do it with them. I would just make the case to all clients that it should be done.

**Edelman:** The problem is whether you are talking about designing the site from the ground up or whether you are talking about outsourcing bits and pieces.

We worked with, for example, Razorfish, on the enormous redesign of our site. That was a very long contract, and there was a very intensive scoping period before that. We brought them in early enough so that they had an idea about what we wanted.

Unfortunately, a client can't always do that. Sometimes you are constrained by deadlines, by how fast you have to get the site up and who you have to answer to in your company.

I've had to actually outsource to two or three developers different pieces of one site, and that is where you enter into a mess. Developer A has an idea as to what the site should be, and that is different from what developer B might believe the site should be, and you wind up with a patchwork site that looks a little odd and doesn't function well.

**Seidler:** Along the same lines, Vlad, these sites are no longer discrete units. It used to be that we would do the Elecktra site, and it would be a self-contained autonomous thing that would be on the Web. But now it actually is linked to and involved in all of these different business units and it is an ongoing consumable thing that needs to be addressed.

**Bryant:** My only point was that the planning has to be done, and I would recommend all clients take the time to do it. I prefer to do it with my client than have them do it by themselves, and that is not strictly because of the idea that planning is part of the revenue-generating process. We don't build Web sites for our clients as much as we focus on becoming their partner—it is the only way that you can solidify a business objective. The best way to do that is to come in at an early stage with enough time to have it benefit the client.

**Rubinic:** It is also a little frustrating when you come into a project and you get an RFP and you understand what the client's goals are, but with your knowledge of the industry or the medium, you would like to recommend something that might be much better—but because it is completely different, you can't.

**Mukherjee:** I think we all agree that you have to do the planning. You have a better chance of success if you do the planning with the vendor that you want to do the project with. But that brings us to the issue of the financial relationship—is this a retainer-based relationship where I am going to contract with you for the next two years to continue to build my site, or is this a straight work for hire, one-off job?

### Outsourcing: The Financial Relationship

**Frenza:** Dev raises an important point here. We all agree planning is good, but how is the relationship between a client and a developer structured financially during that process? It seems like there is no standard method for determining that aspect of the relationship.

**Seidler:** Several years ago, we always worked on fixed-fee projects, and now we have transitioned to only working on the basis of time and materials. Generally, that involves estimating projects, but it is time and materials which set up the possibility of having an ongoing relationship which will last as long as it is still positive and productive partnership.

**Mukherjee:** For the first year, your relationship with any developer has to be on a time-and-materials basis. I say that because probably, if you are being honest, you are going to fire them. The chance that you stay with the first developer that you select is pretty slight. But once you get a good relationship working and that partnership established, a retainer makes sense for both sides. So my position is, do not start out with a retainer initially, but have the relationship grow into that.

**Edelman:** For us, we are not in a constant relationship with the developer. There are different partnerships that we have with various companies that are helping us manage various pieces of our technology. We work with Oracle, Razorfish, a whole different group of people who come and go. It is not necessary to have a developer, at least for us, under contract. We sort of farm it out when we need it.

**Bryant:** Going forward, I think the way to have successful projects is to establish longer-term relationships with a developer.

I can speak for the development side when I say it is much more difficult to come in on a one-off basis on a project and hit everything right off. The client has a history, and as a developer coming in, you get an RFP or a description and you go in and do the best that you possibly can for what you think the client wants, but you don't have the background on what drove those requirements. So you get halfway through the project and the client has a committee that has to make decisions and you have to make decisions on the fly—and frankly, in our industry, as in all industries, sometimes you make good decisions and sometimes you make bad decisions.

So I think that at least we are seeing it in our business with our clients, that it makes more sense that we get not necessarily a retainer, but some kind of flexible contract over a period of time where there is some kind of float. For example, it could be between this number and that number, and it is time and materials between that.

**Edelman:** I think that might be fine, but I do think we are being unrealistic.

I think that one of the biggest problems that we face in the financial relationship is that a lot of companies get into trouble on the money side, for example, because they have completely unrealistic expectations. They are not realistic as to what it is going to take to design something or to integrate something, so they start to parcel it out bit by bit, paying as they go along. They are unlikely to opt for a retainer-based relationship. Then you get into trouble because a lot of developers, especially smaller developers, will come in and pitch completely unrealistic prices, and that is a huge problem because you start having expectations, and those expectations are not because it is physically impossible to meet them under any circumstance.

**Bryant:** There is an interesting thing that is starting to happen in our industry with this consolidation that is taking place. With the current wave of "roll-ups" that are happening, there is this tremendous land grab going on. It is important for these companies that need to hit fifty, sixty million in revenues because they have investor expectations to grab as much revenue as they can.

One of the things that we are seeing is that suddenly these companies that have been historically the high bidders are coming into projects tremendously low. I think it is something that is a trend that we are likely to see going forward.

**Frenza:** For the record, Chris is referring to the strategy of some of the larger Web developers to purchase smaller companies that might have a specific expertise or be located in an area where the large Web shop perceives that they will need to be able to offer client services.

**Stein:** I don't think that is entirely it, Chris. It is also that clients are becoming more savvy. They know what their projects should cost and what is realistic. If we go in and we low-ball it, they get it. Also from the entertainment standpoint, a lot of times going into a project within these corporations there is a resistance to spend too much money in the space.

Instead of looking at the long-term vision of, "where should I be five years from now?" Web work is far more piecemeal.

**Mukherjee:** But that is quickly changing. Within a very short period of time, say six months, all of your major clients are going to have a VP of interactive marketing, or VP of interactive services. If I think back a year ago, if I tried to find my peer in one of our clients, it was pretty difficult. We are quickly coming to the point where I think shareholders will revolt in a couple years' time if companies don't declare what their interactive strategy is going to be. It is that important.

**Rubinic:** I think you are right. IBM is doing a great job of that—and I am not saying that just because I am working on a project for IBM! [laughter]

IBM is doing what I don't see a lot of other companies doing—they are taking their interactive side seriously enough to incorporate it in all aspects of the company, right down to the branding messages that get moved around throughout the company.

It is one of the things that I can't change as a developer. But I would love to advise a client to change the support structure for the Internet at any company because often they are segmented away in a small office and they are not incorporated as much into the company as a whole. Whereas you may have coordination with print and TV, you don't see that when it comes to the Web on the Web sites.

**Mukherjee:** I think you make a good point. One of things I would like, part of the pitch I would like from a Web developer, would be to say, "Here's the organization you should have on your side." Before we start this process, or maybe part of the consulting engagement, is to look at my organization and determine who should be the lead interactive person and where you should put interactive people in your structure—sales, marketing, management, and so on. I think that would be a very powerful model for ensuring success.

### Legal Issues

**Frenza:** Let's talk about the legal issues that every client, and their developer, should address. It is, after all, becoming far more important, is it not? What aspects should clients consider when it comes to legal issues of Web site development?

**Spiegel:** Having a clear written legal document that sets forth the requirements of a project is crucial to starting a relationship with a Web developer. Those things are always a function of a particular situation, and Íve never seen the same exact situation twice. Each one is slightly different, and what I advise my clients is that you want to do business so you have to be accommodating, and that's where you have to be creative. My job is to help the client be creative in solutions to satisfy what the client wants as far as structuring an arrangement, how the contract relationship is going to work, at what point parties can opt out, make changes, and so forth.

I'd like to hit a slightly different point and throw this out to the table for discussion because I've been involved in what we traditionally call new media for fourteen to fifteen years. In the old days, my clients tended to be what everyone else would perceive as crackpots. You had to be a crackpot to be in this business back in 1985.

One of the things I remember most vividly from those days was being told that copyright is dead. I remember everyone feeling—now it is a good laugh but back then it wasn't such a crazy thought—you had this gigantic copying machine that would exist and it seemed pretty obvious that you couldn't control copying of intellectual property, and therefore copyright couldn't exist.

And, of course, what we've learned over the last several years is that more people are aware of these issues today than ever before. If anything, copyright is more critical to our lives and critical to the success of business because, indeed, what we see going on right now, and what will go on for the foreseeable future, is the creation of more intellectual property assets than ever before in our history.

I think that the businesses that will be successful—the survivors—will be the ones who understand what intellectual property is and how best to exploit it, to identify those things that are significant and make sure that they are protected for their use so that they can generate revenue from them. I rarely talk to people who have any sense of that issue. But when you talk to people on the application side about technology, they have plenty to talk about. I think the law and the issues of copyright—and all intellectual property—is equally important.

**Mukherjee:** I agree. As a client, this is where you need a lot of input from your developer—and developers need to be able to provide this service to their clients. Whether its finding intellectual capital in your organization that can be used on the Web, right on down to advice in managing privacy, for example, where there are a number of issues that someone building a large Web site might not have any idea about. It is the developers that are the thought leaders that can advise their clients on what to do and what traps to avoid.

**Stein:** I agree, and those issues, of course, change depending upon who the clients really are. For example, we are doing a big Web site for kids, and there are a lot of issues in the television and the entertainment world that are pretty traditional limitations put in on that space. At this point, in the Web space, there are less-specific limitations, and you create your own limitations based on not wanting to potentially get into areas where you think there is a vulnerability, whether it is perceived or real.

**Spiegel:** That leads to a phenomenon that you see happening every day. You have a convention in traditional media that is not taking into account the possibility of what can happen in new media. So new media ends up as a driving force, which causes a rethinking of the convention in traditional media to the point in which traditional media is no longer bound by its former restrictions.

**Edelman:** As a client at an entertainment company, I have to agree wholeheartedly. For us, these issues are some of the biggest stumbling blocks to creating a successful Web site. I work specifically on special projects, which is Web sites specific to a particular show on the network, such as David Letterman, and for us, these legal issues are perhaps the most significant aspect of our development process.

**Rubinic:** Fortunately, there are a lot of institutions that are becoming more open with their content. In the past, they may have been very closed, guarded, and secretive about it and generally suspicious of the whole Internet. Now, while they might still be protective of their content, and rightfully so, they are much more open, and there is the potential that you can work with them.

**Edelman:** Still, a huge part of my day-to-day operations center around the management of content issues. If I had to make an estimate, I would guess that thirty percent of my time is taken up by trying to figure out where my content came from and where it can be used. And that is something that should be pointed out to clients that are building Web sites. They need to be careful about their developer making assumptions about what can be used on a Web site, especially given that they might not be expert enough to make such claims.

For example, with media companies, content can only be used on one specific context. We might get the rights to use one Bettmann Archive photo only on a page that we create in conjunction with *Time* magazine and only on the third page for only one month.

**Seidler:** It is important, no question, for but us as a developer, a lot of what we are creating is the tools for business to change the way that they do business. These are very literally the businesses themselves that we are creating, so we have to come up with innovative ways to actually transform or convert existing traditional business practices into a digital environment. For instance, for Schwab, where we are building their trading environment, it is actually coming up with ways to structure that information and making determinations about whether or not to buy or build software, not so much content acquisition.

On the flip side, Razorfish has a very narrow client focus—financial institutions, media and entertainment, cultural institutions, and technology companies—and we are not developing sites where the site itself is not the business. For a lot of the media companies, the kind of content that's being produced is the business. Razorfish Studios, which is a separate company, is in fact working from the point of view that the idea comes first, and how it's actually delivered is second. Whether it is a book, music, or a Web site, what is more important is the end view of getting the message across.

**Bryant:** Outside of the media and entertainment industries, however, content is not an issue in the same way. We actually license content for some of our clients to enhance the offering available on their Web site. So in that sense we are having to face those issues up front. We are approaching the hurdles to begin with. We are not putting up a large amount of content on our site and sorting out the details later. The details for us, and I assume for most corporate sites, come up front, so it is handled differently.

**Stein:** I think that when it comes to what we call the entertainment vertical, a lot of the sites are an extension of the existing puppy—that is, they are more of a marketing-driven site. With the financial institutions, you are often building tools for them or things that require a certain amount of functionality.

On both sides of it, what we are looking at a lot at IXL and the company that IXL originally grew out of in New York City was a company that specializes in self-generated content. They had what amounted to the largest sports game on the Web, called Small World Sports, which is a site all about dynamic content—database-driven content.

So I think that in order to cut costs, avoid potential legal issues, and make it beneficial for entertainment companies to be able to put content up on the Web, you have to find efficient ways of developing original content—content that is not too expensive and cost prohibitive because, at the end of the day, we still don't have a mass-media platform. You can't justify spending the kind of money you could on television, for example.

**Rubinic:** The situation has changed a lot also from five years ago in the sense that companies that we work with are getting electronic rights up front, and that is a big difference from where we were. Five years ago, it was a big challenge, and we had to cut content because a company didn't have the research staff to do the kind of research or renegotiate and even track people down in the first place. Now what you see is the rights are already taken care of and addressed up front. So, overall, rights are not the big issues they once were.

**Spiegel:** I think a big part of the problem is this continuing concern about protecting those assets and the sense that once something is digitized and made available to people over the Web, it has a life of its own, which indeed it does at some level. It is unquestionable in my mind that it is something that needs to be carefully addressed. I also firmly believe that no one has come up with a solution that will work in the future for all media—text, pictures, video, sound.

**Mukherjee:** I think that if I were advising someone who is building a big Web site that they do actually try to get as much of their own content—and they can license content as well—because it is so very useful to users who visit their site.

To take the example of an insurance company, the site that has the requisite product information and rates as well as how to choose an insurance policy and some of the other things that people might really want to know is definitely useful. We all have to be sensitive to the intellectual property rights of our own content as well as the content that we license. But the reason that we are having this conversation is that it is useful to our audience, and that cannot get lost amid the discussion of legal issues. Content might present legal challenges, but we can't not have it.

**Spiegel:** I agree. I am a lawyer and I deal with these concepts daily—they are my tools. But I also understand that business people don't function like I do, and they have other needs. The legal requisites, as important as they are, have to be placed in perspective to the overall situation and what the client is actually trying to accomplish.

One of the things that I try to do is to help the client think through a sense of perspective when we have to deal with issues. So, for example, if there is a particular problem—say, they want to use a piece of material and there is a problem—I think the most important thing that I can do is identify what the problem is and look for a potential solution. What I would say to the client as good business advice is, "You are not in the interactive business and you are not in the computer business; do you think you can assess content and build a great Web site yourself?" The answer is that if you do, you are out of your mind. You need expert help, and you don't even know where to go for that. What you really need to do is go out, talk to people, research and educate yourself. And then try to find a company that shares your values and what you are trying to accomplish. Hire them and make them part of your team. You can't let the legal issues stand in the way of growing your business.

**Bryant:** I would like to add one last note on the legal discussion.

Today, Web developers are building more than Web sites—they are building business solutions. For example, we just built an extranet for American Express.

The big concern for us is, where does liability begin and end? For example, suppose there is some kind of security infiltration of a system or some kind of damage to a client because of something that a developer did or failed to do. That is a really huge issue that is not adequately being addressed. As we move into these larger, more far-reaching projects, that is where the greatest risk is.

**Frenza:** Sounds like a great topic to start off our next roundtable!

# Index


## A

Account manager, 51, 54
Accountability, 18–19
ActiveX, 46
Advertisements
 rotation, 287
Advertising, 274, 285, 294. *See also* Free advertising; Paid advertising.
 nonrecommended techniques, 289–293
Advertising agency, 77
Agencies. *See* Internet; World Wide Web development.
 consideration, 82
 defining, 61
 formal presentation, 61
 location, 99
 size, 99
Animated banner ad, 285
Animated GIFs, 37
AppleSearch engine, 225
Application integration, 326
Architecture. *See* Information; World Wide Web server; World Wide Web site architecture.
 options, 316
Association of Internet Professionals, 341
Audience, knowledge, 284
Audience profile, 69–70

## B

Backbone networks, 152
Bad proposal, signs, 99–100
Banner ad, 285. *See also* Animated banner ad.
Banner exchanges, 288
Brand, 13–14
Brand identity, establishment, 105
Branding, 70–72
Browser, 243, 322. *See also* World Wide Web.
Budget, 63, 64, 97. *See also* Project strategy; World Wide Web site.
 contents, 98
 implications. *See* Long-term budget implications.
Budget range
 identification, 81
 provision, 82
Bugs, 230
Builder.com, 333
Bulk email, 290
Business
 goals, 66–70
 innovation, 80
 plan, 69
 transformation, design usage, 116–117
 vision, sharing, 80
Business strategies, 333
Business-driven web sites, 141–143, 147, 149–150

## C

CARU. *See* Children's Advertising Review Unit.
CDA. *See* Communications Decency Act of 1996.
CGI. *See* Common Gateway Interface.
Children's Advertising Review Unit (CARU), 173
CICS, 318
Claris Home Page, 38, 44
Clearing rights, 185–189
Client/developer relationship, 239
Clients, 322
 needs, 359–362
Client-server development, 318
CMP, 341
CMP Netguide's WebBuilder, 331
C|Net, 341
CNN, 341
ColdFusion (Allaire), 231, 313
Collections of Information Antipiracy Act, 181
Collocated servers, 154
Common Gateway Interface (CGI), 43, 46, 140
 functions, 44
 scripting, 33
 scripts, 37, 317
Communications Decency Act of 1996 (CDA), 175
Company
 culture, 12–13, 64–66
 expertise, 64–66
 investment, 80–81
 understanding, 28–30
 weaknesses, 81
Competence, 16–17
Compilations, 180

Conferences, 339–340
Connectivity, 45–46
Consensus-making process, 7
Constructors, 334
Content developer/content strategist, 52
Content requirements, 72–73
Content/technology, integrating, 105
Context, creation, 105
Contracts, signatures, 262–263
Copyright, 178–181, 185–196
  law, basics, 181–183
  protection. *See* Software.
  usage permission, 189
Copyright Revision Act of 1976, 182, 194
Copyright Term Extension Act of 1997, 183
Core business, 9
Core system functions, 318–319
Corporate identity creation, web designer contribution, 117–118
Cost, 16, 96–98. *See also* Hidden costs.
  breakdown. *See* Proposal.
  factor, 8–9
  phase approach, 96
Creative Brief, 134
Creative director, 54
Creative lead, 51
Criteria, choice, 59–64
Customer information, maintenance, 309–310
Customer satisfaction, 307, 309
Customer service, 14, 304, 306–308
Cyberjunction, 334
Cyberspace, 165, 166, 306

**D**

Data collection, 171–174
Databases
  services, 324–325
Deadlines, 263
Debabelizer, 38
Decisions, 83–84
  award, 84
  criteria, definition/explanation, 81
Dedicated servers, 154
Deeplinking, 198
Defect-tracking system, 231
Delivery specialists, 33
Derivative works, 180
Design, 333–334. *See also* Preliminary design; Project; User interface design.
  activity, fundamental steps, 120–126
  clash. *See* Technology.
  examples, 107–112
  function, 105–106
  group, 52
  multidisciplinary approach, 106–112
  production planning, 121–122
  spec, creation, 263
  usage. *See* Business.
Designer, 34–36. *See also* Information architecture; Interface designers; World Wide Web designer.
Design-related problems, avoidance/management, 245–248
DevEdge, 331
Developer, 95, 239–240, 350. *See also* World Wide Web developer.
  appropriateness, 92
  choice, 89–92
  finding, 354–359
Developer.com, 331
Development. *See* World Wide Web development.
  tools, 327
Development problems
  analysis, 242–244
  avoidance, 239
  confrontation, 239, 242
  plan, 244
  prevention, 244–245
DHTML, 38
Digital Talent, 332
Direct Marketing Association, 172
Discovery meeting, 61, 63–65
Discussions/communities, 343
Distribution mechanism, 306
DNS. *See* Domain Name Service; Domain Name System.
Domain Name Service (DNS), 137
Domain Name System (DNS), 153–154, 225
  hosting, 157
Domain names, 168–171. *See also* Multiple domain names.
Dreamweaver, 38
Dynamic web environments, 314
Dynamic web sites, 137–139, 144, 160

**E**

E-business, 297, 299
  conversion, 300–327
EC. *See* European Community.
Economic Espionage Act of 1996, 193
Editorial, 39–41
Edupage, 339
Electronic commerce (E-commerce), 90, 92, 134, 165, 167, 309–312, 336
  payment, 311–312
Enternet Engineering Consortium, 340
Enterprise JavaBeans, 325

European Community (EC), 173, 174
European Union, 170
Evaluation process, 59
Excel, 222
Executive producer, 54
Expertise, 9
Explanatory document, 62
Extranets, 144–145, 335
E-Zines, 338–340

## F

Fair use, 191–192
FAQs. *See* Frequently asked questions.
FastTrack Scheduler Pro (AEC Software), 221
Feature set, draft/proposal, 63
Features, 72
Federal Trade Commission (FTC), 173
Fee-for-service contract, 3
File Transfer Protocol (FTP), 89, 157, 225, 315
Financial relationship, 362–365
Fireworks (Macromedia), 38
First-generation promotional site, 299
First-time site visitors, source, 77
Flames, 284
Form letters, 284
Formal proposal, 63, 64
Framing, 197–198
Free advertising, 288–289
Frequently asked questions (FAQs), 96, 142, 284, 315
FTC. *See* Federal Trade Commission.
FTP. *See* File Transfer Protocol.
Functional Specification, 135
Functionality, 72
Functions, 301
  availability, 303–315

## G

Gaming, 199
GIFs. *See* Animated GIFs.
Go Live Cyber Studio, 38
Graphic arts, 187–188
Graphic designer/ artist, 53
Gray list, 82–85
Groupware services, 324
Growth, 9–10
Guerilla marketing, 289

## H

Hands-off approach, 28
Headliner, 338
Heterogeneous environment, 320
Hidden costs, 96–97
Hosting, 74–75
  agreement. *See* World Wide Web site development.
  long-term budget implications, 145–150
  solution, choice, 150–159
Hosting engineer, 52
Hotlists, 331–332
HTML. *See* HyperText Markup Language.
HTML Writers Guild, 342
HTTP, 315
HyperText Markup Language (HTML), 33, 35, 36, 38, 46, 148, 229, 244, 279, 287, 320, 324, 326, 328, 334
  coder, 53
  coding, 243
  conversion process, 215
  documents, 137, 142
  editor, 106
  environment, 112
  pages, 137, 140, 146, 216, 319
  production, 89

## I

IMAP 4, 324
Immersion, 120–121
Incubation, 120–121
Individual privacy, 171–174
Industry analysts, 340–341
Infobeat, 339
Information
  architecture, designer, 118–120
  distribution, 309
  emphasis, 280–281
Information Technology (IT), 48, 106, 109, 356
Infrastructure components, 323
Infrastructure, review/plan, 315–319
Infrastructure specialists, 33
Integrated web functions, 318–319
Integration, 314–315
Intellectual property, 178
  rights, 165, 167, 192–196
Intelligence sources, 340–341
Interface designers, 119
International Interactive Computing Society, 342
Internet, 144, 290, 305
  agencies, 67
  books, 333
  legal issues, 168–178
  overview, 151–153
  search engines, 274
  trade shows, 100
Internet and Electronic Commerce Conference and Exposition, 340
Internet Commerce Expos, 340
Internet Explorer, 228
Internet Professional Publishers Association, 342

Internet Protocol (IP), 153
Internet Service Provider (ISP), 129–131, 136, 137, 147, 149, 150, 152, 157, 158, 290, 315, 325
choice, 154–155
hardware/software, 156
offerings, 156–158
Internet Wire, 339
Internet World, 340
Internet-related expenses, 5
InterNIc, 154
Interviews, 34–45, 47–50
Intranets, 90, 335
Invisible text trick, 292
IP. *See* Internet Protocol.
IP Next Generation (IPNG), 326
IRC, 324
ISP. *See* Internet Service Provider.
IT. *See* Information Technology.

**J**

Java, 43, 45, 46, 106, 227, 323, 324, 326
applet, 44, 50
development, 10
Java Database Connectivity (JDBC), 318, 325
Java One, 340
Java Virtual Machine, 320
JavaBeans, 323, 324. *See also* Enterprise JavaBeans.
components, 321
JavaScript, 37, 43, 46, 112, 140
JDBC. *See* Java Database Connectivity.
Junk email, 290, 291, 294–295
Jurisdiction, 176–178

**K**

Knowledge, 9
building, 78

**L**

LANs. *See* Local Area Networks.
Large web site, 23–27
Large-scale site, 49
Large-scale Web effort, 16
LDAP, 324
Lead software engineer, 51–52
Legacy systems, 316
web server interface, 317–318
Legal issues. *See* Outsourcing.
Libel law, basics, 174–176
Licenses, 189
Life cycle, 214–216
Life-cycle planning, 215
Link exchange, 288
Literary property, 185–186
Local Area Networks (LANs), 152
Local networks, 152
Long-term success, 80
Lotus Domino, 313
Lotus Notes, 314
Loyal visitors, 77

**M**

Magazines, 336–338
Mail services, 324
Mainspring, 331
Maintenance, 75
activities, management, 216–221
Malice, 174
Management, 335
Map Day, 264, 265
Market data, 73–74
Market segmentation, 75–76
Marketing, 279–285, 335. *See also* Guerilla marketing; Online marketing.
Brief, 133, 134, 136
goals, 75–77
specialist, 54
strategies. *See* One-way marketing strategies.
tips, 294
Mecklermedia, 339
Media promotional plan, 76
Media specialist, 53
Medium-size web site, 20–23
Meta-goal, 67–68
Metakeyword tags, 279
Metatags, 198–199, 279
Microsoft, 227, 246, 352
InterDev, 44
Internet Explorer, 11
Site Builder Network, 331
SQL Database, 10
Windows NT Server, 10
Middleware, 109, 116, 145
Mid-level networks, 152
Mining Company, 331
MIS, 3, 12, 14, 15, 21, 29, 32
Moral rights, 195
Motion picture clips, 188
MS-Project, 221
Multidisciplinary approach. *See* Design.
Multiple domain names, 293
Multiple subcontractors, usage, 259–261
Musical compositions, 186–187
MVS, 318

**N**

NAPs. *See* Network Access Points.
National Association of Webmasters, 342
Navigation
document, 124–125
ease, 281
Navigation flowchart, 83
NCF. *See* Networking Computing Framework.

NDAs. *See* Non-disclosure agreements.
Need, definition, 120
Netscape, 228
Netscape API (NSAPI), 227
Netscape Navigator, 10
Network Access Points (NAPs), 152
Network Computing Framework (NCF), 320–325, 326
Network connectivity, 155–156
Network Operation Centers (NOCs), 157
New York New Media Association (NYNMA), 100
New-media industry, 250
News footage, 189
Newsbot, 339
Newsgroup spamming, 291–292
Newshub, 339
NewsPage, 339
Newspapers, 336–338
NNTP, 324
NOCs. *See* Network Operation Centers.
No Request for Proposal (No-RFP), 62–63
Non-disclosure agreements (NDAs), 94
Non-proprietary information, 93
No-RFP. *See* No Request for Proposal.
NSAPI. *See* Netscape API.
NYNMA. *See* New York New Media Association.

## O

Object Request Broker (ORB), 324
Off-the-shelf technology, 49
One-way marketing strategies, 300
Online marketing, 274, 280
Online resources, directory, 274, 293–295
Operating system, choice, 262
Operational maturity, 17
Operational preparation, 77–78
ORB. *See* Object Request Broker.
Order processing, 310–311
Out-of-office expenditures, 5
Outsourcing, 47–50, 362–365
  advantages, 7–11
  choice, 6, 158–159
  definition, 4–5
  disadvantages, 11–19
  issues, 345–351
  legal issues, 365–370
  needs, prioritization, 6
  procedure, 29–30
  risks, 12–16
  scenarios, 19–27
  sharing, 30
  skepticism, 211
  track record, 28–29
  type, 13, 28
Ownership, 263
Ownership of expression, 178

## P

Paid advertising, 285–288
Para-site, 197
Partnerships, 72–73, 77, 79
Patents, 193–195
Periodicals, 336–338
Perl, 43
Phase approach. *See* Cost.
Phone calls, 60–64
Photography, 187–188
Physical objects, 189
Planning, 240–241
Politics/people, 14–15
POP, 324
Portfolio approach, 233
Preliminary design, 121
Presentation, preparedness, 83
Prioritizing, 240–241
Privacy. *See* Individual privacy.
Problems. *See* Design-related problems; Technology; Usability problems.
  analysis. *See* Development problems.
Process timeline, explanation, 81
Producer, 51
Producers, 41–43
Product catalog, 309
Product plan, 67
Production, 122–124
  artist, 36–38
  planning. *See* Design.
Programmer, 43–45, 53
Programming, 46
Project
  approach, customization, 64–66
  approval, 263
  beginning date, 84
  design, 214–216
  desireability, 79–84
  hardware, 263
  loop, 233–234
  maintenance, 263
  manager, 212–214
  movement, 269–270
  readiness checklist, 78
  scope, 82
  top ten issues, 262–264
Project components, 222
  management, 222–224
Project Cool, 331
Project management, 41, 53, 228–233
  issues, handling examples, 264–268
Project strategy, 60
  budget, 66

Promotional plan, 76–77. *See also* Media promotional plan.
Promotion/measurement results, 335–336
Proposal. *See* Formal proposal.
- contents, 93–96, 98
- cost breakdown, 94–96
- future, 98–100
- importance, 92–93
- objective, 93
- process, 82
- signs. *See* Bad proposal.

Prospects, selling, 80–81
Public domain, 190–192
Public relations, 274, 279–285
Publishing, 312–314

## Q

Qualitative details, 77
Quantitative details, 76–77
Queries, 276, 278

## R

Ranking, 277. *See also* Search engines.
- increase, 278–279
- schemes, 278

Readiness plan, creation, 77–79
Redesign scenario, 247
Regional networks, 152
Regional user groups, 342–343
Repeat visitors, 280
Repeat visits, motivation, 77
Repeated words trick, 292
Reputation, building, 280, 283–285
Request for Information (RFI), 60–61, 85
Request for Proposal (RFP), 20, 56, 57, 59, 62–64, 67, 69, 72, 74, 76, 79, 93, 132, 136, 160
- issuance, 64

Research, 120–121
Return on investment (ROI), 4, 141, 313, 353
Revenue model, 68–69
Revenue target, 68
RFI. *See* Request for Information.
RFP. *See* Request for proposal.
Right of Publicity, 195–196
Rights clearance agents, 189
Robots, 276
ROI. *See* Return on investment.
Roles, defining, 34–45

## S

Sales cycle, 307
Scalability, 134
Scenarios, 229. *See also* Redesign scenario.
Schedule estimate, 63, 64
Scope documentation, 348
Search engines, 226, 275–279, 286. *See also* Internet.
- overload, 292–293
- process, 276–277
- registries, 294
- relevance/rankings, 277–278

Second-generation sites, 297
Second-generation Web site, 10
Secure distributed network, 325–326
Secure Electronic Transaction (SET), 312
Secure Sockets Layer (SSL), 141, 157, 311
Seminars, 339–340
Semirepetitive projects, 221–222
Server foundation services, 323
Server maintenance, 45–46
Service, innovation, 80
Service plan, 67
SET. *See* Secure Electronic Transaction.
Seybold Seminars, 342
Shared servers, 154
SIGGRAPH, 100, 342
Signature, 288
Single Project Request for Proposal, 85
Single Request for Proposal, 64
Singularity, 165
Site. *See* World Wide Web site.
- Business Plan, 133
- constraints, 74
- experience, 70–72
- goals, 70–75
- traffic projections, 70
- visitors. *See* First-time site visitors.

Skills, building, 78
Small business web site, 20
SMTP, 324
Software, copyright protection, 194
Sound recordings, 186–187
Spamming, 291, 294–295. *See also* Newsgroup spamming.
Specialization, 10
Specialty services, 332–336
Specialty sites, 286
Specialty web sites, 331–332
Speed, 10
Spiders, 276
SQL, 225, 231, 325
SQL databases, 318
SQL-based data, 227
SSL. *See* Secure Sockets Layer.
Standalone server, maintenance, 317

StarBase, 231
Static web sites, 137–139, 160
Statute of Anne (1710), 181
Strategic planner, 51
Strategy Brief, 133, 134
Stub networks, 152
Subcontractors, 5
  hiring, 261–262
  usage. *See* Multiple subcontractors.
Sun Microsystems Developer Connection, 331
Sweepstakes, 199
Systems management tools, 326

## T

Tango (Everyware Development Corporation), 44
Team members, 65
Technical lead, 54
Technical Specification, 135
Technical specifications, 105–106
Technical support, 308–309
Technology
  assessment, 32
  design, clash, 112–116
  disillusionment, 302
  enlightenment, 302
  expectations, 302
  phases, 302
  Plan, definition, 133–136
  planning, 131–136
  problems, avoidance/ management, 248–251
  productivity, 302
  relief, 10–11
  selection, 319–326
  trigger, 302
Territory-ialisis, 30
Text link, 285
Tracking software, 218
Trade associations, 341–342
Trade secrets, 192–193
Trade shows, 339–340
Trademark Antidilution Act, 169
Trademarks, 168–171, 192–196
Transaction services, 324
Transaction-based web sites, 299
Transaction-enabled web site, 49
Travel, 263
Turf wars, 7

## U

UCE. *See* Unsolicited Commercial Email.
Uniform Resource Locator (URL), 129, 141, 276, 279, 288, 293
Uniqueness, 281
United States Constitution, 171, 172, 194
United States Patent and Trademark Office, 168
Unix, 43, 225, 226
Unsolicited Commercial Email (UCE), 290
URL. *See* Uniform Resource Locator.
Usability problems, avoidance/ management, 251–254
Use cases, 229
User groups, 341–342. *See also* Regional user groups.
User interface design, 267

## V

Value, adding, 280, 282–283
Value-added service, 283
Vendors, 265
  lists, 343–344
Venture launch, 61–62, 85
Version-control software, 230
Vertical expertise, 79
Virtual Promote, 332
Visitors. *See* Loyal visitors; Repeat visitors.

## W

Web. *See* World Wide Web.
Web Design & Development Conference, 340
Web Developer's Virtual Library, 332
Web Review, 332
Web Roundtable, 343, 344
Web-based business, 166, 168
Web-based content management tools, 143
Web-based form, 140
Web.Builder, 340
WebDeveloper.com, 332
Webmonkey, 332
Web-Vantage, 332
Web-X, 340
Whitepapers, 60
Windows NT, 43, 225, 226
World Wide Web (WWW / Web), 276
  browser, 116
  designs, 55
  in-house development, 8
  knowledge, 65
  pages, 279, 286
  project, 42, 101
  teams, 50–55
World Wide Web (WWW / Web) access
  definition, 286–287
  measurement process, 286
World Wide Web (WWW / Web) designer, 279
  contribution. *See* Corporate identity creation.

World Wide Web (WWW / Web) developer, 16–19, 23, 28, 50, 74, 130, 237, 246–248, 250, 254, 300, 358
finding, 100–101
World Wide Web (WWW / Web) development, 47, 91, 93, 349
agency, 98, 99
firms, 300
group, 52
needs, 3, 6
process, 351–354
project, 59
services, 1
World Wide Web (WWW / Web) development process, 18, 79, 345
concept development, 31
design, 32
editing, 32–33
functions, 31
maintenance/ management, 34
marketing, 33–34
personnel, 31–32
players, 34–45
production, 33
programming, 33
testing, 33
understanding, 30–34
World Wide Web (WWW / Web) server, 323–324
architecture, 316–319
World Wide Web (WWW / Web) site, 29, 30, 36, 40–42, 45, 56, 75, 90, 92, 94, 131, 149, 150, 155, 159, 167, 173, 212, 242, 249–252, 266, 281–283, 288, 302, 312, 355. *See also* Business-driven web sites; Dynamic web sites; Specialty web sites; Static web sites.
budget, 146
components, 93–94
hosting, 45–46, 136, 151
hosting choice, 262
linking, 196–199
look/feel, 184
maintenance/ management, 47
operation, legal issues, 196–199
options, 21
owners, specialty sites, 334–338
ownership, 178–192
planning documents, 133
project, 25, 35
World Wide Web (WWW / Web) site architecture, 32
selection, 224–228
World Wide Web (WWW / Web) site development, 20, 46, 131–136
hosting agreement, 199–207
World Wide Web (WWW / Web) site needs assessment, 136–139
determination, 140–145
WWW. *See* World Wide Web.